Transnational Advocacy in the Digital Era

Transnational Advocacy in the Digital Era

Think Global, Act Local

NINA HALL

OXFORD
UNIVERSITY PRESS

OXFORD
UNIVERSITY PRESS

Great Clarendon Street, Oxford, OX2 6DP,
United Kingdom

Oxford University Press is a department of the University of Oxford.
It furthers the University's objective of excellence in research, scholarship,
and education by publishing worldwide. Oxford is a registered trade mark of
Oxford University Press in the UK and in certain other countries

Impression: 1

Published in the United States of America by Oxford University Press
198 Madison Avenue, New York, NY 10016, United States of America

British Library Cataloguing in Publication Data
Data available

Library of Congress Control Number: 2021951443

ISBN 978–0–19–885874–4

DOI: 10.1093/oso/9780198858744.001.0001

Printed and bound in Great Britain by
Clays Ltd, Elcograf S.p.A.

Contents

Acknowledgements

In 2015, I learned for the first time about a network of digital activists, the Online Progressive Engagement Network (OPEN). I hadn't encountered MoveOn.org, Campact, or GetUp before then and was intrigued to hear of these organizations and the network that connected them. I'd spent much of the previous eight years trying to understand how bureaucrats at the United Nations (UN) influence the direction and mandate of their organization. These new digital advocacy organizations appeared to be the complete opposite to what I was most familiar with. They were small, with a tiny bureaucracy, yet could rapidly respond to new problems. As I started to read more about them and understand their reach and influence, I became more and more intrigued. Here were new kids on the block that were waiting to be studied by international relations (IR) scholars.

Two people helped me immensely in this first phase of discovery of OPEN: Ben Brandzel and David Karpf. I tracked Ben down in Berlin in the summer of 2015, as he was hosting a dinner with a group of digital activists. They were having a discussion at a restaurant, which, to an outsider, looked like a group of friends chatting about their hobbies. Ben walked several blocks with me after dinner, where I pitched to him the idea of studying the network. I was an unknown character to him, but he was curious. We continued to exchange ideas throughout 2015. Then, in December 2015, I flew to India, where he was then based, to get a concrete answer as to whether I could pursue my research on the network he had established. Since that first meeting, I have had numerous calls and meetings with Ben as he hopped around the world. He has been extremely generous with his time and frank in his reflections on the strengths and limits of digital advocacy organizations (or the 'OPEN model' as I refer to it in this book).

Dave Karpf was equally generous with his time and insights. Karpf has written the most influential books on MoveOn and the OPEN model. He had already spent years studying the network, and attending their summits, when I decided to start my research. I was a little nervous about embarking on a study which required whole new fields of expertise (political and digital communications) and getting to know an entirely new community of organizations and people, and Dave helped me navigate the major debates in the field, and understand the contribution of MoveOn and the broader OPEN network to digital organizing.

Since 2015, I have spent hours sitting with activists in the OPEN network. I've learned details about the private and public lives of activists, and shared details about my own life and work. I've shared dorm rooms with activists mentioned in the book, and hosted some to stay when they were stranded in Berlin. I have become very close to this community, which as any anthropologist knows, comes with risks to research, as one loses objectivity (if one can even claim to have this in the first place).[1] I even founded a think tank, the *New Zealand Alternative*, with the then-executive director of ActionStation, Laura O'Connell Rapira.[2] The sorts of 'data' I collected were much richer, and in many ways messier, than what I had collected in previous elite-level interviews with UN bureaucrats. These deep personal relationships have shaped this work, and I owe immense gratitude to everyone who spent time talking with me. There are dozens who are cited in this book, and many who contributed to my understanding of the OPEN model but are not cited. For all who offered your reflections and insights, and welcomed me to your offices—thank you for helping me to understand your work. Any mistakes or misrepresentations are my own.

In addition to the activists in the OPEN community, there were many others who spoke to me, including: staff of non-governmental organizations (NGOs), digital campaigning consultants, and independent experts. Thank you all for your insights. A particular thanks is due to May Miller-Dawkins and Miriam Lyons, who were there at the beginning of this project, when it was just a spark of an idea.

I was very lucky to work with several excellent research assistants over the span of the book. Lisa Schmid helped kick-start the project, while at the Hertie School in Berlin. Rebecca John, an alumna of Johns Hopkins School of Advanced International Studies (SAIS), worked for over three years on this book project. She collected the data for Chapters 4 and 6, helped analyse it, and gave extremely useful comments on various drafts. She proofed the final manuscript with eagle eyes. Charlie Lawrie, also at Johns Hopkins SAIS, helped to collect data on these organizations' campaigns and gave insightful comments on various drafts.

[1] This is often referred to as 'going native. I once recounted to a group of OPEN activists on a retreat that a classic ethnographic method was to 'soak and poke' your data; and they replied, jokingly, that they were happy to jump in the nearby swimming pool for a 'soak and poke' if that was what was needed.

[2] *New Zealand Alternative* went on to run a campaign for patent-free COVID-19 vaccines and medical equipment with ActionStation.

A massive thanks also to the many academic colleagues who read sections of this work and provided feedback. Colleagues at the Hertie School helped to support the start of this research. Thanks to Mark Dawson, Markus Jachtenfuchs, Dilek Kurban, and Daniela Stockman for providing great feedback on early versions of several chapters. Thanks to Michael Dedmon, Hans Peter Schmitz, and Tosca Bruno-van Vijfeikjen for the regular exchanges on how traditional NGOs were adapting to digital technologies; we co-authored an article on this subject. Colleagues at Johns Hopkins SAIS supported its completion—thanks to Mark Gilbert, Erik Jones, Mike Plummer, and Raffaella del Sarto. In early 2021, Jennifer Hadden, David Karpf, Mette Eilstrup-Sangiovanni, and Hans Peter Schmitz read the entire draft manuscript and provided extremely constructive feedback. In 2021, I was a senior fellow at the Weizenbaum Insittute in Berlin; thanks to Annett Heft and Michael Vaughan for the excellent conversations on how the far-right is mobilizing online.

Many others shared their insights and gave feedback. Thanks are due to: Alexandra Budabin, Azadeh Daystari, James Dennis, Dan Mercea, Hahrie Han, Stefania Milan, Gabriel Siles-Brugge, Ariadne Vromen, and Clara Weinhardt. I presented this work at various institutions, including: the Social Science Center Berlin (WZB), Frei Universitat Berlin, the Hertie School of Governance, the European University Institute, the International Studies Association, the Weizenbaum Institute (German Internet Institute), and Johns Hopkins SAIS Europe. Thanks to all the participants of these sessions for their feedback.

Thanks also to the team at Oxford University Press, especially Dominic Byatt, who supported the project at an early stage, and the two anonymous reviewers for their useful feedback, which shaped the book's trajectory.

Finally, thanks to the wide network of friends and family who helped support this work through their conversations and curiosity: Jess Auerbach, Daniel Augenstein, Max Harris, Georgio Haddad, Ralph Hall, Trish Hall, Valentina Iadarola, Steffen Lohrey, Lea Neubert, Pierluigi Musarò, Jess Panegyres, Emma Preston, and Florian Strob. A special thanks to my father, Philip Tremewan, who helped with the editing of the whole book. I hope that the book draws new connections between people and places, online and offline.

List of Figures

List of Tables

List of Abbreviations

ACF	Australian Conservation Foundation
ACTA	Anti-Counterfeiting Trade Agreement
ACTU	Australian Council of Trade Unions
AEC	Australian Electoral Commission
AFD	Alternativ für Deutschland (Alternative for Germany)
ARENA	Australian Renewable Energy Agency
ATTAC	Association for the Taxation of Financial Transactions of Citizens
AYCC	Australian Youth Climate Coalition
BBC	British Broadcasting Corporation
CAG	Climate Change Alliance Group
CAN	Climate Action Network
CANA	Climate Action Network Australia
CEL	Citizen Engagement Laboratory
CEO	chief executive officer
CETA	EU–Canada Comprehensive Economic and Trade Agreement
CSU	Christian Social Union
ECB	European Central Bank
ECI	European Citizens' Initiative
EU	European Union
EV	Environment Victoria
FOI	freedom of information
GDP	gross domestic product
GDPR	General Data Protection Regulation
GGCA	Galvanizing the Groundswell of Climate Actions
GMO	genetically modified organisms
HRW	Human Rights Watch
ICRC	International Committee of the Red Cross
ICS	investment court system
IO	international organization
IR	international relations
ISDS	investor–state dispute settlement
JEFTA	Japanese–European Free Trade Agreement
MEP	Member of the European Parliament
MMP	mixed member proportional
MP	Member of Parliament
NAZCA	Non-State Actor Zone for Climate Action
NGO	non-governmental organization
NHS	National Health Service

NRA	National Rifle Association
OPEN	Online Progressive Engagement Network
OSCE	Organization for Security and Cooperation in Europe
PAC	Political Action Committee
REDD+	Reducing Emissions from Deforestation and forest Degradation
S2B	Seattle to Brussels
SDP	Social Democrat Party
SMS	short message service
TPP	Trans-Pacific Partnership
TPPA	Trans-Pacific Partnership Agreement
TTIP	Transatlantic Trade and Intellectual Property Agreement
UK	United Kingdom
UN	United Nations
UNESCO	United Nations Educational, Scientific and Cultural Organization
UNFCCC	United Nations Framework Convention on Climate Change
UNHCR	United Nations High Commission for Refugees
US	United States
VKRF	V. Kann Rasmussen Foundation
WHO	World Health Organization
WTO	World Trade Organization
WWF	World Wide Fund for Nature

Preface

I was writing this book when the COVID-19 pandemic hit. Governments closed their borders and restricted people to their homes. The world turned to the internet to work, meet friends, go to school, and engage in political debate. While this new reality was challenging for many of us to adapt to, the activists I study in this book were already used to operating online. They all worked for digital advocacy organizations and were skilled at campaigning online, were already frequent users of Zoom, and many often worked remotely from home.[3] Shifting to an entirely online world did not cause major disruption to their work.

In addition, these organizations are wired to respond to the most salient issues of the day. They could quickly switch focus to campaign on the crisis that COVID-19 triggered. In January and February 2020 none of these advocacy organizations were campaigning on issues related to COVID-19, but by mid-March, as the pandemic was dominating headlines everywhere, their focus had shifted to the pandemic. Digital advocacy organizations encouraged their members to stay at home, help out their neighbours, and support health-care workers. On Friday 13 March 2020, for instance, Campact in Germany launched a campaign encouraging people to stay at home and 'flatten the curve', given the alarming news of the pandemic in Italy.[4] Subsequently on 6 April, Campact ran an online campaign calling for health-care workers to be paid more.[5] In the US, MoveOn launched an online petition demanding that President Donald Trump and Vice-President Mike Pence provide health-care workers with protective equipment, which gathered over 163,000 signatures.[6] GetUp in Australia rallied people around the hash-tag #viralkindness to help community members in need. Declic in Romania helped to deliver food to

[3] The first time I ever used Zoom was to interview activists working in digital advocacy organizations several years before the COVID pandemic.

[4] Campact. (2020). 'Corona Koppase Verhindern' (13 March). https://blog.campact.de/2020/03/corona-kollaps-verhindern/ (accessed 4 December 2021).

[5] Campact. (2021). 'Klink Personal: Sie verdienen mehr'. https://aktion.campact.de/klinikpersonal/appell/teilnehmen (accessed 4 December 2021).

[6] MoveOn, *Petition*. (2020). 'Healthcare Workers Need Protective Equipment Now'. https://sign.moveon.org/petitions/healthcare-workers-need-protective-equipment-now?source=mo.social (accessed 4 December 2021).

people who were at risk. Digital advocacy organizations were well placed to campaign during the COVID-19 pandemic, given their highly responsive and nimble model.

Furthermore, digital advocacy organizations had already built a strong transnational network—the Online Progressive Engagement Network (OPEN)—through which they could share strategies, messages, and tactics globally, and activists turned to each other to do this during the unfolding crisis. Senior staff in this network held regular weekly calls, and OPEN hired a 'network technology support advisor' to help OPEN groups to develop effective COVID-related campaigns.[7] Although the pandemic meant that digital advocacy organizations did not meet face-to-face, they could cooperate transnationally, thanks to these digital channels of communication and the high-degree of trust they had established over years of meeting in person, which is described in this book.

COVID-19 did not fundamentally change how digital advocacy organizations operated, domestically or transnationally. Digital advocacy organizations responded quickly, and set up new domestic campaigns. They used their transnational network to diffuse tactics, messages, and technology across the network to enhance their own national campaigns. However, they did not run a collective transnational campaign at the same time, with the same target.[8] Instead, their campaigns mobilized members online to put pressure on their national governments. National governments were central actors during the pandemic: states acted unilaterally, closing borders, and in some cases restricting the export of medical equipment. Yet even on the international aspects of COVID-19, such as debates at the World Trade Organization (WTO) over waiving intellectual property rights for COVID vaccines, digital advocacy organizations focused on national decision-makers.[9] Hence, COVID-19 reinforced a central finding of this book: digital advocacy organizations see

[7] OPEN. (2020). 'Network Support Advisor: COVID-19'. *The Idealist*. https://www.idealist.org/en/nonprofit-job/3425310e6b12450fae47c5e263701c7f-network-support-advisor-covid-19-online-progressive-engagement-network-new-york?utm_campaign=visitorshare&utm_medium=social&utm_source=email (accessed 4 December 2021).

[8] For a separate study, I collected data on MoveOn, 38 Degrees, Campact, and GetUp campaigns between 1 March and 1 June 2020, and there were no collaborative campaigns across the network (see Hall forthcoming).

[9] In early 2021, many of the digital advocacy organizations studied in this book campaigned in support of an Indian and South African proposal to waiver patents for the COVID-19 vaccine, and other COVID-related medical equipment. This proposal was initially blocked by almost all industrialized countries (including the United States, Canada, the United Kingdom, New Zealand, Australia, and all members of the European Union). In early May, the Biden administration came out in support of a narrower version of this proposal: waiving intellectual property rights for the COVID vaccine.

the state, not international institutions, as the most important locus of power, and hence the target of their campaigns. Although the global pandemic has impacted most of our lives profoundly, it did not change how digital activists campaign.

1
Introduction

On 12 August 2017, white supremacists gathered on the streets of Charlottesville, Virginia, for a 'Unite the Right' rally. Protestors on the left also turned out to protest against the far-right rally. The day turned violent when a supporter of the 'Unite the Right' demonstration drove his car into the counter-protestors, and killed one of them. In the immediate aftermath, President Trump claimed that 'both sides' were to blame, and refused to condemn the racism and violence of the far right (Merica 2017). Trump's stance was widely criticized and many chief executives who sat on two White House business advisory councils were urged to leave their positions. In the United States, MoveOn and Color of Change, both digital advocacy organizations, launched a campaign urging Indra Nooyi, chief executive officer (CEO) of PepsiCo, and other business leaders to resign. Meanwhile in Sweden, Skiftet, another progressive digital advocacy organization, also launched a rapid-response campaign demanding that Swedish-born 3M Chief Executive, Inge Thulin leave his position on a presidential business advisory council. Hundreds of Swedes, prompted by Skiftet, sent emails to Inge Thulin highlighting that Trump had 'failed to properly condemn right-wing extremists and Nazis' (Mittelman et al. 2017). These efforts added to wider public pressure in the United States and, following a number of resignations, the two councils rapidly collapsed.

Although Skiftet and MoveOn are far apart geographically, these organizations share a lot in common. They both campaign via email, online petitions, Twitter, Facebook, and viral videos. They complement online actions with offline marches, demonstrations, and vigils to push for change. They are members of a growing group of digital advocacy organizations, which are permanent institutions with professional staff. MoveOn, for instance, has been campaigning since 1998. Skiftet, a Swedish digital advocacy organization, which emulated MoveOn, has been active since 2014. Many digital advocacy organizations have large memberships: MoveOn, Campact (in Germany), and GetUp (in Australia) all have over 1 million members. Their longevity distinguishes them from important, but sporadic social movements such as

Transnational Advocacy in the Digital Era. Nina Hall, Oxford University Press.
 DOI: 10.1093/oso/9780198858744.003.0001

Indignados in Spain or Occupy Wall Street in the United States (Gerbaudo 2012; Tufekci 2017).

Digital advocacy organizations are recognized as influential actors by the media, politicians, and some academics. In 2016, GetUp, an Australian digital advocacy organization, was named by the *Australian Financial Review* as one of the top ten actors with 'covert power' in Australia.[1] Campact in Germany has powerfully mobilized public opinion against the Transatlantic Trade and Investment Partnership (TTIP) (Bauer 2016b). MoveOn was one of the 'leading advocacy organizations' mobilizing people against the Iraq War in the United States (Heaney and Rojas 2007; Busby 2010). Meanwhile, Leadnow, a digital advocacy organization in Canada, helped to unseat Prime Minister Stephen Harper in the 2015 Canadian federal election (Vromen 2017).

This new model of advocacy organization has spread around the world from the United States to Europe, Australasia, Africa, Asia, Latin America, and the Middle East. Nineteen digital advocacy organizations claim to have a total of over 20 million members.[2] In 2021 there were organizations in: Austria (#aufstehn), Australia (GetUp!), Canada (Leadnow), Germany (Campact), Hungary (aHang), Ireland (Uplift), Israel (Zazim), Italy (Progressi), France (le Mouvement), New Zealand (ActionStation), Netherlands (De Goede Zaak), Poland (Akcja Demokracja), Romania (Declic), Serbia (Kreni Promeni), South Africa (Amandla), Sweden (Skiftet), Switzerland (Campax), UK (38 Degrees) and in the United States (MoveOn). While political communications scholars have studied the emergence of these organizations in their national contexts, few have focused on the transnational dimensions of thier advocacy and what this new model of advocacy means for international relations (Chadwick and Dennis 2016; Karpf 2012; Vromen 2017).

My aim in writing this book is three-fold. First, I want to understand how the same form of advocacy organization emerged in such different contexts. What drove the global spread of digital advocacy organizations? Second, I want to contribute to international relations (IR) theories of advocacy, which have typically focused on larger international non-governmental organizations (NGOs), such as Oxfam and Greenpeace, or transnational advocacy networks focused on particular issues, such as climate change, human rights, or land mines. I ask: to what extent do digital advocacy organizations require new IR theories of advocacy?

[1] The *Australian Financial Review* defined covert power as 'indirect power that allows them to effect change and influence the overtly powerful'. The overtly powerful was a list of people who derived power from their positions or standing—and was a list of the most senior politicians in Australia, with the Prime Minister at number one' (Australian Associated Press 2017).

[2] (Online Progressive Engagement Network (OPEN), https://www.the-open.net/our-members (accessed 13 December 2021)).

Third, I explore if and how digital advocacy organizations campaign transnationally. After all, many scholars have suggested that the internet would enable more frequent transnational networking and mobilizing (Keck and Sikkink 1998). Some have even suggested that digital technology could create a 'global civil society' as 'many transborder civic activists regard themselves as world citizens in addition to (or even more than) national-state citizens (Scholte 1999: 16). The underlying logic in these arguments is that faster and cheaper international communications will lead to greater international solidarity and more frequent transnational collective action.

Digital advocacy organizations would seem an obvious case for transnational campaigning. The organizations in this book share common progressive values and operate in a highly connected, globalized world, where issues spill over borders. They can easily communicate across borders and share campaign material, thanks to email and social media. In addition, they are all part of a transnational network, the Online Progressive Engagement Network (OPEN).[3] Through this network, digital activists meet frequently in person, and exchange new technologies, skills, and tactics. They have developed deep relationships through regular summits, staff secondments, and the sharing of campaign failures and successes. In this book, I examine how, when, and why they campaign collectively on transnational issues.

The introduction is split into five parts. I first examine how the digital era has changed advocacy by lowering the costs of collective action and enabling the emergence of digitally native organizations.[4] In the second section, I explain my focus on digital advocacy organizations and their relevance for IR scholars. In the third section, I outline the book's main arguments. In the fourth section, I then explain my research methods, and finally offer an overview of each chapter.

Advocacy in the Digital Era

A Networked Public Sphere

The internet era has transformed citizens' potential to organize for action (Margetts et al. 2015; Shirky 2008; Simmons 2013). Individuals can more efficiently, cheaply, and quickly scale up collective action through distributed

[3] OPEN, https://www.the-open.net/opennetwork (accessed 13 December 2021).

[4] Karpf has argued convincingly that we should not conceive of a single digital era, but rather multiple digital eras, given the major advances in digital technology (Karpf 2020). After all, the internet of the 1990s (dial-up modems, blogs) is completely different from the internet of the 2020s (smart phones, social media). For ease of reference I refer to the digital era in the singular form, and I explore how digital advocacy organizations are adapting to various new digital technologies and platforms.

networks of weak ties (Fung et al. 2013; Shirky 2008). People can connect rapidly, self-organize, and directly influence decision-makers, without the need for traditional political institutions (unions, NGOs, or political parties) to aggregate their interests (Farrell 2012; Fung et al. 2013; Shirky 2008).[5] Think, for example, of the rapid growth and power of social movements such as #MeToo or #BlackLivesMatter.

Scholars have identified new forms of 'connective action', where people use digital platforms to build personalized, rather than collective action frames (Bennett and Segerberg 2012). Conventionally, groups coalesced around common ideologies (e.g. environmentalism) or a common identity (e.g. women). Connective action involves self-organizing networks which use digital platforms instead of conventional political organizations. In this mode, political messages travel over 'social networking sites, email lists, and online coordinating platforms' and are typified by personalized 'digitally mediated collective action frames' (Bennett and Segerberg 2013). There is little cost for the individual in engaging in action and minimal organizational coordination needed, given the affordances of technology.[6] People are less likely to be committed members of political parties or organizations, but rather affiliate to many different causes (Heimans and Timms 2018; Putnam 2000). Individuals will make transient affiliations to many causes, rather than long-term commitment to a single cause. Traditional organizations are being replaced by 'large-scale, fluid social networks' (Bennett and Segerberg 2013: 748).

According to some scholars, social media platforms are replacing traditional institutions in many areas of political life. The social media era ('Internet 2.0') has heralded a new politics, which is characterized by 'turbulence' and the ability of individuals to connect more easily than ever before (Margetts et al. 2015). Importantly, scholars have suggested that small, individual digital actions such as tweets, or Facebook posts, can scale up rapidly, and trigger significant political change (Margetts et al. 2015). Digital technology lowers the cost of communications, increases the choice of options to individuals, decentralizes information communications, and supports the growth of networks (Bimber et al. 2012). There is a growing literature which suggests that the digital era

[5] Some governments have also opened up pathways for citizens to directly communicate with citizens—the White House under Obama established a petition site, and other governments have opened up e-government to provide greater public access (Fung et al. 2013).

[6] Engaging in collective action is often a trade-off for individuals: the costs of participation time and effort may outweigh the gains, so it is often easier to freeride (Bennett and Segerberg 2013). This is not the case with connective action.

gives citizens greater voice and more sway in democratic politics (Horstink 2017).

On the other hand, there are sceptics who argue that the internet has degraded political culture by diverting attention and action into tasks that have little sustained or long-term impact (Gladwell 2010; White 2010). For these critics, the internet has led to 'slacktivism', as it creates an 'illusion of effectual political interventions' (Merkel 2017). People channel their political actions into Facebook or Twitter posts, rather than taking action on the streets. Critics argue that because the cost of organizing online is so low, tactics such as online petitions or emails have little impact on decision-makers. The relative ease of digital network formation means that networks convey a weak signal to the powerful and those in authority (Tufekci 2017).[7] Effective social change requires strong ties between activists, who are deeply committed to each other and the cause (Gladwell 2010). The civil rights movement was so effective, despite violent opposition, because people were close friends (Gladwell 2010). Digital networks are primarily based on weak ties—between people who have often never met—and thus does not result in the same level of commitment to the movement and cause. In the most sceptical view, online advocacy stifles transformative change, rather than enabling it (White 2010).

However, this debate over 'slacktivism' misses the point. Most advocacy is not conducted solely online or offline (Dennis 2019). Neither #BlackLivesMatter nor #MeToo can be reduced to a viral hash tag. These movements have galvanized millions around the world in both virtual and real-world protests. In fact, the speed and ease of forming weak-tie networks online can reinforce strong ties within a network. Hence, separating out online advocacy tactics as distinct from offline advocacy tactics is often not that useful (Han 2014), especially when most traditional NGOs use social media, websites, and email communications to help them to organize marches, disseminate reports, conduct lobbying activities, run petitions, monitor government action (or inaction), and publicize their cause (Hall et al. 2020).

New Political Actors in the Digital Era

The internet has empowered new actors who are tech savvy. These non-state actors can harness digital technologies to influence political decisions (Howard

[7] This may be the case if they have no formal organizational structure. However, many digitally enabled social movements do end up with formalized organizations (e.g. #BlackLivesMatter, #FridaysForFuture).

2015; Milan 2013; Owen 2015). Anonymous and Wikileaks, for instance, are digitally savvy and also 'decentralised, collaborative and resilient' (Owen 2015: 13).[8] New, digitally empowered actors have used their digital expertise to challenge the state and traditional political institutions.[9] Howard argues that the 'smart, stupid or surreptitious use of digital media by political actors consistently has the biggest impact on who gets what' and that 'blogging, tweeting, crowd sourcing' shape 'national policy agenda' (Howard 2015). States are also harnessing digital technologies for surveillance and repression of social movements and dissidents (Xu 2021). Here, I focus on a new generation of advocacy organizations, social movements, and political parties born in the internet era.

Digital 'native' advocacy organizations have pioneered new organizational forms, strategies, and tactics (Chadwick 2007; Chadwick and Dennis 2016; Karpf 2012; Vaughan 2020; Vromen 2017). These organizations have low levels of bureaucracy and have transformed the concept of membership. Joining these groups is often as simple as agreeing to receive an email communication or signing up to an online petition. Members do not have to commit to regular attendance at meetings, or to donate on a monthly or annual basis, as they would in many NGOs. These organizations have rapidly scaled up their influence by building large memberships, and they can draw on their members for funding, legitimacy, and power.

Although the costs of membership are low, digital advocacy organizations offer their members a high degree of power over the direction of the organization. Digital advocacy organizations regularly engage in 'analytic activism', listening to and surveying their members to identify which issues to campaign on, and how (Karpf 2016). Their model of advocacy is distinct from most NGOs, where professional staff select the campaigns based on their expertise

[8] An additional source of power is digital corporate power (Zuboff 2018). There are just five large tech platforms that control most aspects of the digital economy, and increasingly our lives: Apple, Alphabet (the parent company of Google), Microsoft, Facebook, and Amazon (Manjoo 2016). In January 2020, these companies had a combined market valuation of over US$5 trillion (Winck 2020). Their value grew significantly during the COVID-19 pandemic (while most others fell), and in August 2020 these five companies constituted 20 per cent of the US stock market's total worth (Eavis and Lohr 2020).

[9] Owen also suggests that traditional organizations could try to harness the power of digital disruptors. For instance, in 2010, the US State Department set out a new 'Civil Society 2.0' plan, whereby they sent technology experts to developing countries to train NGOs and civil society to improve their outreach and advocacy (Owen 2015: 161). In this way, traditional, hierarchical organizations may look to gain power from using digital technologies to build broad-based networks.

and their commitment to a particular issue.[10] Digital advocacy organizations rapidly start and switch campaigns, thanks to the low costs of sending an email, launching a petition, or posting on social media. They can now run campaigns that mobilize thousands of people with small staff sizes and at low costs, as will be explored in subsequent chapters (Carty 2011; Chadwick and Dennis 2016; Karpf 2012).

Since the advent of social media, we have also seen the growth of digitally enabled social movements which coalesce around hash tags such as #OccupyWallStreet, #BlackLivesMatter, #FridaysForFuture, #gezipark, and #MeToo (Tufekci 2017). These movements have galvanized thousands, and in some cases millions, of people online and offline. They have had a significant impact on issues ranging from anti-globalization to the Arab Spring (Gerbaudo 2012; Juris 2005). Many of these hash-tag-inspired social movements still rely on, or subsequently develop, bureaucratic organizations (Bimber et al. 2012; Han 2014; Karpf 2016). Organizations offer permanent, institutional structures to store information, which enables learning, and the refinement of tactics and strategies (Tufekci 2017). In fact, hierarchical organizations are more effective at digital campaigning than loosely networked groups (Schradie 2019). A division of labour allows for staff specialization in digital communications and formulation of a unified strategy (Bond and Exley 2016). In contrast, in purely grassroots, horizontal networks individual volunteers may not have the time, skills, or technological support to develop advanced digital communication skills (Schradie 2019).

Political scientists have studied the emergence of digital political parties, which are less bureaucratic than their conventional counterparts (Gerbaudo 2018).[11] These parties have lowered the cost of entry by making membership free. Rather than organizing their members in traditional party structures with

[10] Some digital advocacy organizations do focus on specific issues, e.g. 350.org, which focuses on climate change, and All Out, which focuses on Gay rights. They are not the focus of this study, although 350.org is discussed in Chapter 7.

[11] Most political parties use social media to advance their electoral campaigns (Kreiss 2016). However digital political parties are distinguished by the central role of digital technology in engaging with members and determining policy positions. Note that there is also broader literature on the use of digital platforms in electoral campaigns. Kreiss (2016), for instance, argues that Democratic Presidential campaigns for Howard Dean, and subsequently Barack Obama, invested more in digital expertise than their Republican counterparts at the time. They shifted away from 'labour-intensive' or 'capital-intensive' campaigns to 'tech-intensive' campaigns. This consisted of adapting the technology of marketing to political campaigning (Kreiss 2016). Meanwhile, Trump's 2016 Presidential campaign adeptly (and controversially) used Facebook to micro-target individuals and spread fake news about Hilary Clinton. These tactics likely helped him win the Presidency.

physical headquarters and regular in-person meetings, they engage their members online. Digital parties have also transformed the internal decision-making process of political parties, removing party cadres (or middlemen) in favour of decision-making via digital platforms. These platforms include: Loomio (developed in New Zealand during #Occupy), Rousseau (developed for the Five Star Movement in Italy), Nationbuilder (developed in the United States and used initially by France Insoumise), Consul (used by Podemos in Spain), and Liquidfeedback (used by Pirate Parties across Europe). Digital parties use these digital platforms to constantly chart 'the shifting opinion of their members, with the ultimate aim of adapting to their evolving tendencies', and thus claim to be highly responsive to their members (Gerbaudo 2018: 74). We have also seen the emergence of horizontal-movement-based organizations that are linked to traditional political parties, such as Momentum in the UK and #aufstehn in Germany (Dennis 2020).[12] These groups allow people to join easily, and exist alongside hierarchical modes of organizing in the UK Labour Party and die Linke, respectively.

Notably, new digital advocacy organizations, digital social movements, and digital political parties, have formed both on the right and left of the political spectrum, as well as a few centrist organizations, such as change.org. Far-right-wing groups have been particularly successful at using social media and messaging services such as Telegram to spread their messages transnationally (Caiani and Kroell 2015: 331; Freelon et al. 2020). Distinguishing between right-wing and left-wing groups can be useful, as these groups commonly share best practices, skills, and technology within their ideological groupings (Dennis and Hall 2020).[13] Hence, we may see the diffusion of different digital strategies and organizational forms on the left, when compared with the right.[14] In Table 1.1, I give examples of the new political actors who have emerged in the digital era. Note that digital advocacy organizations operate at international, regional, national, and local levels. These actors are important to study as they are challenging the pre-digital era organizations in their respective fields.

[12] Dennis has categorized Momentum as a 'movement faction' as it is both a movement and a faction of the UK Labour party (Dennis 2020).

[13] Traditional left and right distinctions may not always be useful, as some political movements appeal across the political spectrum (e.g. the anti-COVID-19 rallies, or Brexit).

[14] Becky Bond and Zack Exley, two senior campaigners who worked on Bernie Sanders' 2016 presidential campaign, shared their rules on how to organize digitally with progressive digital advocacy organizations in 2016 (Bond and Exley 2016). Meanwhile, former Trump advisor Steve Bannon established a new think tank, Le Mouvement, to support far-right candidates in the European Union election.

Table 1.1 Examples of new political actors in the digital era

Type of political actor	Left/progressive political orientation	Right/conservative political orientation
Digitally enabled social movements	#MeToo #BlackLivesMatter #FridaysForFuture #Kony2012 #OccupyWallStreet	America First #AllLivesMatter
'Digital' political parties (Gerbaudo 2018)	Momentum (UK) Five Star Movement (Italy) Podemos (Spain) Pirate Parties (across Europe)	Lega (Italy)*
Digital advocacy organizations	MoveOn (US) Avaaz (international) SumOfUs (international) Campact (Germany) GetUp! (Australia) Leadnow (Canada) All Out (international) 350.org (international) Meu Rio (city-based)	Right March (US) The Vanguard.org (US) Freedom Watch (US) Advance Australia (Australia) CitizenGo (international) Grassfire (US)

**Note:* Although not classified as a digital party in Gerbaudo's 2018 book, *Lega* has used digital platforms and algorithms (such as 'the Beast') to increase its appeal and support base.

Why Should IR Scholars Study Digital Advocacy Organizations?

Most IR scholars have not engaged with the growing scholarship on advocacy in the digital era. They have predicted that the global spread of communications technology—namely fax, radio, telephone, and email—will enable groups to communicate, share information, and campaign more easily (Keck and Sikkink 1998).[15] However, they have missed out the growth of new organizational forms, and in particular the emergence of digital advocacy organizations, despite IR's interest in NGOs, transnational advocacy, norm change, and contestation of the global liberal order. This book engages in detailed empirical work to examine how advocacy actors are 'utilizing new communications technologies to their advantage and/or have been changed themselves in the process' (Price 2003).

[15] Since Keck and Sikkink's seminal work, there have been major developments in technology (the invention of smartphones, 5G internet, and various social media platforms). One result is that many of us are constantly online and do not need to wait for the slow dial-up internet modem to connect with the world.

In this book, I introduce IR scholars to the political communications scholarship on digital advocacy organizations (Chadwick 2007; Dennis and Hall 2020; Karpf 2012, 2016; Trevisan et al. 2020; Vaughan 2020; Vromen 2017). These digital advocacy organizations are recognized as immensely powerful actors by politicians in their home countries, as will be detailed in Chapter 2. They have had impacts on election outcomes, legislative and policy change, and public debate.[16] For example, GetUp in Australia has influenced 'voter enrolment, mental health policy, [and] higher education funding' (Vromen 2017: 110). In Canada, Leadnow targeted conservatives in strategic constituencies, which contributed to Prime Minister Stephen Harper's defeat in 2015 (Vromen 2017). 38 Degrees helped to stop fees for general practitioners' visits in the UK (Dennis 2019). These organizations have also shaped public opinion on important international issues such as climate change, trade, and refugee rights as this book investigates.

In fact, they are part of a broader contestation of the global liberal order (Cooley and Nexon 2020; Lake et al. 2021; Simmons and Goemans 2021). Digital advocacy organizations have actively supported some elements of the rules-based multilateral order, including a strong international agreement on climate change and respect for refugee rights. However, they have contested other elements, in particular economic globalization and free trade agreements. They have mobilized their supporters in their thousands to march on the streets for climate action, to welcome refuges, and to block free trade agreements. IR needs to understand how these organizations shape and mobilize public opinion, and what influence they have on political outcomes (Bièvre and Poletti 2020).

The first generation of digital advocacy organizations have in turn created or directly inspired a second wave of new digital advocacy organizations. In the United States, MoveOn staffers directly helped to found Color of Change (an advocacy organization for Black Americans), Momsrising.org (a grassroots organization of American mothers), and Avaaz (an international digital advocacy organization) (Karpf 2012). Campact in Germany helped to launch WeMove, a European regional digital advocacy organization. Through OPEN, digital advocacy organizations have actively supported the spread and growth

[16] There are many ways of conceptualizing impact. Kolb identifies five types of substantive political outcomes for movements and campaigns: agenda impact: influencing composition of issues and concerns on the political agenda; alternatives impact: influencing issue content and resolution within policy propositions; policy impact: adoption of legislation or political decisions made based on claims or addressing grievances; implementation impact: accelerating, stopping, or slowing implementation of policy; and goods impact: influencing the provision of collective or public goods (Kolb 2005: 38). Movements and campaigns can also impact individuals' ideas, behaviour and capacities (Han 2014). Notably, Felix Kolb is also one of the founding directors of Campact, Germany, and is cited throughout this book.

of similar organizations around the world—through financing, mentoring, and training.

Digital advocacy organizations are also having an effect on political parties, social movements, and traditional NGOs. Mainstream NGOs are copying their digital campaign tactics and organizational form (Hall et al. 2020). Greenpeace, for instance, launched MobLab, a digital mobilization team inspired partly by the MoveOn model. Some national Greenpeace chapters now have member-initiated petition platforms (Silberman 2017). Traditional NGOs in Australia, aware of GetUp's influence, have partnered with GetUp and adopted some of its tactics (Vromen 2017). Former staff members of digital advocacy organizations are also establishing new organizations; ex-38 Degrees staffer, Nat Whalley, for instance, established Organize for workers who are not unionized (Sheffield 2018). Other progressive NGOs, political parties, and interest groups have sought to emulate digital advocacy organization practices.

Conservative groups, aware of the force of MoveOn and GetUp, have tried—largely unsuccessfully—to emulate digital advocacy organizations. In the United States, right-wing attempts to emulate the MoveOn model include Right March, an organization established in 2003 as a 'rapid response force against liberal onslaught', but which subsequently faded. Freedom Watch, launched in 2008, was reportedly 'plagued by gridlock and infighting', which led to the collapse of the organization (Karpf 2012: 130–131). In late 2018, a group of conservative Australians launched Advance Australia, to rival GetUp. Advance Australia claims to be 'an independent movement of mainstream Australians, who are determined to protect, advance and defend mainstream values and freedoms' (McGhee 2018). They followed the same membership model as GetUp: members only need to subscribe to their email list to join and by November 2018, claimed to have 3,500 members (McGhee 2018). Advance Australia advocated for conservative values in the 2019 Australian Federal Election, and even created a satire superhero figure, 'Captain GetUp!', to rival and undermine GetUp (Zhou 2019).[17] The right's attempt to emulate MoveOn and GetUp illustrates how powerful the organization model can be.

Digital advocacy organizations are now well established, have large memberships, and are permanent organizations. They have often been at the forefront of digital advocacy in their respective countries (Dennis and Hall 2020; Karpf 2012; Vromen 2017).They warrant study, given their impact on

[17] Some claim that this backfired and merely strengthened GetUp!'s powerful role in Australian politics (Zhou 2019).

political outcomes—from elections to legislative changes—and their second-order impact on other advocacy and political organizations (Bush and Hadden 2019; Eilstrup-Sangiovanni 2019). IR scholars need to systematically investigate and understand these new forms of digitally native advocacy organizations, and what effect they have on transnational issues and the population ecology of the advocacy sector.

The Argument

This book advances two main theoretical arguments. First, digital advocacy organizations challenge some IR theories of advocacy. These organizations gain power and authority from mobilizing members rapidly—offline and online—rather than wielding expertise over a given issue. They campaign often in rapid response mode, jumping from one issue to another, depending on their members' concerns. In contrast, most traditional NGOs are committed to a particular issue, and gain power and authority based on their knowledge of that issue.

Second, I argue that digital advocacy organizations regularly collaborate transnationally, but rarely campaign collectively at the same time, on the same issue, with the same target. Rather, these organizations share financing, tactics, technology, and messaging to enhance their own national campaigns. They focus on mobilizing national publics to put pressure on national decision-makers because they view the state as the most powerful actor on the global stage. They have developed new forms of digitally distributed transnational campaigns and campaign at the same time, on the same issue, but with different—national—targets. I outline these two arguments here in more depth.

The Power of Digital Advocacy Organizations

IR scholars have often argued that NGOs' power derives from their expertise and authority on an issue (Allan 2021; Haas 1990; Stroup and Wong, 2017). Most NGOs are focused and committed to a particular set of issues; for example, Greenpeace focuses on the environment and Amnesty International on human rights. Campaign decision-making is typically top-down, as professional staff determine which causes to focus on. NGOs regularly engage in agenda-setting and awareness-raising to educate the public and decision-makers on new issues (Keck and Sikkink 1998). They exchange their specialized knowledge to gain access to international organizations and decision-makers (Tallberg et al. 2015). NGOs often engage in lobbying: seeking meetings with decision-makers to directly influence them. There are many other strategies NGOs may engage in: monitoring government's implementation of on international agreements, 'naming and shaming' governments that do not keep their promises, litigation, or 'direct enforcement' (where they take the law into their own hands) (Eilstrup-Sangiovanni and Bondaroff 2014; Murdie and Urpelainen, 2015; Princen 1995; Setzer and Brynes 2019). NGOs can inform public opinion and mobilize 'moral movements' to put pressure on their respective governments (Busby 2010). All of these strategies involve NGOs committing to their particular causes over a sustained period, and building up a degree of expertise on this issue. IR has not examined how the digital era has changed the strategies, and power, of advocacy organizations.

In contrast, digital advocacy organizations build networked power by mobilizing people rapidly online and offline (Hall et al. 2020). They have membership lists numbering in the hundreds of thousands, even millions. They can quickly aggregate their members' preferences and rapidly set up new campaigns thanks to email, social media, and digital analytics (Fraussen and Halpin 2017). They have expertise in rapid response and digital advocacy, rather than substantive expertise on the cause for which they campaign. Hence, they can easily switch campaigns to new breaking issues because they do not assign staff to a single issue.

Digital advocacy organizations have an organizational model which is very distinct from most conventional NGOs. It involves devolving decision-making to members, who decide what issues and campaigns should be prioritized. These members then give legitimacy and force to campaigns through their actions. In the words of a digital activist, their power operates like a current: 'It is made by many. It is open, participatory, and peer-driven. It uploads, and it distributes. Like water or electricity, it's most forceful when it surges. The goal with new power is not to hoard it but to channel it' (Heimans and Timms 2018: 8). In contrast, digital campaigners argue that: 'Old power works like a currency. It is held by few. Once gained, it is jealously guarded, and the powerful have a substantial store of it to spend. It is closed, inaccessible, and leader-driven. It downloads, and it captures' (Heimans and Timms 2018). The binary distinction between new and old power is somewhat simplistic. However, it underscores a core difference between more traditional NGOs (where decision-making power is in the hands of professional staff) and digital advocacy organizations (which seek to create a participatory, member-driven form of power).

This book illustrates how digital advocacy organizations have harnessed the internet to build collective power and advance progressive policies. In doing so, it contributes to debates on the power of NGOs and advocacy actors in global governance. A wide range of scholars have examined the power of non-state actors in specific issue areas, including: climate change politics (Allan 2017; Allan 2021; Hadden 2015; Hadden and Bush 2020); trade politicization (Siles-Brügge 2017; Siles-Brügge and Strange 2020b; Bauer 2016b; Bièvre and Poletti 2017; Eliasson 2019; Kay and Evans 2018); and global migration and refugee governance (Bradely 2020; della Porta 2018; Hall 2016; Rother and Steinhilper 2019; Tennant and Wolff 2018). This book examines how digital advocacy organizations have contributed to the wider climate, anti-free trade, and refugee movements. It explores why they have been successful at mobilizing people in some cases, but not in others. IR scholars have much to learn about the impact of 'people-powered' movements in global governance.

Transnational versus National Advocacy in the Digital Era

The digital advocacy organizations I study have all the right ingredients for forging transnational campaigns. First, they share common progressive values and concerns about international issues such as climate change, refugees, trade agreements, and conflict. Second, they have created a strong transnational network, OPEN. They meet regularly in person and there is an extremely high level of trust between activists, which I observed over five years of studying them. Organizations in this network frequently share funding, staff, technology, strategies, and campaign messaging. They are highly invested in seeing their sister organizations around the world succeed.

Digital advocacy organizations also share the same *mode* of advocacy: digitally based, multi-issue, member-driven, and rapid-response. They can easily and quickly share tactics, strategies, and technologies at low cost.[18] It is easy for GetUp in Australia to share emails, online petitions, Facebook videos, or tweets with other digital advocacy organizations across the world. IR scholars may expect them to campaign transnationally, especially if they are blocked domestically (Sikkink 2005).

[18] IR scholars often treat transnational advocacy networks as the primary unit of analysis, rather than the organizations that comprise these networks (Busby 2010; Keck and Sikkink 1998). They also focus on how transnational advocacy networks form around a common *issue* (women's rights, human rights, deforestation, debt relief, the International Criminal Court, HIV–AIDS, or climate change), not around a common *mode* of advocacy.

Despite being part of a transnational network and operating in a globalized and digital era, I find that digital advocacy organizations almost always target the nation state. They frequently campaign on international issues, but rarely target international institutions. Digital advocacy organizations regularly exchange ideas with international allies, but rarely run campaigns with them. This is because digital activists see the nation state as the most important political actor. They derive their power from mobilizing citizens to put pressure on national decision-makers.

Digital advocacy organizations are part of a broader shift away from advocacy focused on international summits towards 'digitally distributed' campaigns. These campaigns occur on the same day, but with different, national or local targets. For example, Campact, GetUp, MoveOn, and other digital advocacy organizations have partnered with 350.org and #FridaysForFuture, to help mobilize millions for global days of climate action. Experienced campaigners have suggested that 'directed network campaigns', which have a centralized structure and plan and mobilize a broad network to implement campaigns, are most likely to succeed in creating change because they 'successfully marry new power with old power' (Mogus and Liacas 2016: 6). Digital activists use digital platforms to amplify their messages, broaden mobilization at the domestic level, and, most importantly, diffuse new organizational forms. IR has much to learn about the myriad ways protest can go transnational and what role digital technology plays in this (della Porta and Kriesi 1999; Tarrow 2005; Tarrow and McAdam 2005).[19]

This book also contributes to broader debates in political communications, social movement studies, and political science. Digital advocacy organizations are part of a broader trend of digitalization of advocacy and politics (Castells 2012; Farrell 2012; Fung et al. 2013). The book explains the global diffusion of a specific form of digital advocacy organization, as well as the assoicated tactics, and decision-making practices. It offers rich comparative evidence of the differences amongst digital advocacy organizations across the globe, and their evolution over time. This is needed, given that much of the existing political

[19] In parallel to the IR scholarship, social movement scholars have identified various ways national (or local) advocacy and social movements may: diffuse ideas and practices internationally; shift scale and externalize their campaigns to an international organization; or engage in 'transnational collective action', defined as 'coordinated international campaigns on the part of networks of activists against international actors, other states or international institutions' (Tarrow and della Porta 2005: 3). Tarrow and McAdam emphasize that international protest does not just emerge from 'global consciousness or economic integration' (Tarrow and McAdam 2005: 145), but must be built up through coalitions. Furthermore, a domestic movement that shifts in scale to the international level is not automatically a transnational or a global movement (Tarrow and McAdam 2005: 146). Notably, this scholarship has focused more on *social movements* than on *advocacy organizations*.

communications scholarship has focused on particular organizations within their national contexts (Karpf 2012, 2016; Vromen 2017; exceptions include Vaughan 2020; Hall 2019b).

Research Methods

This research is based on a combination of deductive theorizing (i.e. examining claims in the existing literature and identifying key hypotheses) and inductive theorizing (i.e. examining how these organizations actually operate)[20]. I employ qualitative case study research methods, and a quantitative study of campaign actions. I draw on over 100 interviews with digital activists within OPEN carried out between 2015 and 2021.[21] During this period, I built strong relationships with many of the activists I interviewed, and interviewed many multiple times over a six-year period. I visited digital advocacy organizations' offices in Australia, Austria, Germany, New Zealand, Poland, Sweden, The Netherlands, and the UK. I also interviewed NGOs, funding entities, independent experts, and decision-makers outside OPEN to understand the strengths, limits, and contributions of digital advocacy organizations.

Between 2015 and 2019, I regularly attended summits of OPEN, where I conducted interviews and participated in discussions. I used interviews and participant observation to examine the relationship between digital outputs (e.g. Twitter, Facebook, or Instagram posts) and offline campaign decision-making. On many occasions during this ethnographic fieldwork I witnessed activists making decisions about what issues to campaign on. I saw the opportunities and blockages in transnational campaigning.

In addition, I collected extensive primary documents from OPEN and its member organizations, including constitutional documents, annual reports, and budgets. This data offers a rich insight into a network which has never been studied, despite its innovative tactics and large membership base. I also draw on publicly available data from organizations' websites and social media pages. I worked with a research assistant to compile a data set of all the campaign actions that GetUp, Campact, 38 Degrees, and ActionStation conducted over a twelve-month period. Using this data set, we analysed the range of issues they campaign on and the proportion of campaign actions that: target an international institution, focus on an international issue, or involve a transnational advocacy network. These descriptive statistics allow insights

[20] The appendix covers the research methods in more depth.
[21] Many of these interviews were conducted in person, but some were conducted online.

into how often digital advocacy organizations campaign transnationally. I also analysed mainstream media coverage and academic scholarship to examine digital advocacy organizations' campaigns on climate, refugees, and trade. These three issues were highly politicized during this time period, and there were clear opportunities for transnational campaigns. This combination of in-depth qualitative research and descriptive statistics offers insights into how digital technologies are changing the nature of transnational advocacy, but not in the ways some might expect.

Overview of the Book

In Chapter 2, I illustrate how digital advocacy organizations have become powerful actors and challenge existing accounts of advocacy in IR. IR scholars tend to assume that advocacy organizations have issue expertise, long-term commitment to a cause, and professional staff who select campaigns. I suggest that digital advocacy organizations are issue generalists, who have expertise in digital campaigning, but rarely in specific issue areas. They campaign in rapid-response mode: starting, stopping, and switching campaigns frequently. Advocacy organizations' ability to mobilize people rapidly (online and offline) should be theorized as a source of power, alongside expertise and moral commitment to a cause.

Chapter 3 traces how the MoveOn model spread to Australia, Germany, Israel, Romania, South Africa, and beyond. Founders of new digital advocacy organizations were driven by a desire to push progressive politics, and emulated what they saw as an effective organizational model. Ben Brandzel, a former MoveOn staffer, actively promoted the diffusion of this model. He co-founded a transnational network—OPEN—to support new digital advocacy organizations. He also developed the 'eight-fold path', or core organizing principles of the model. OPEN has subsequently supported dozens of activists around the world to launch digital advocacy organizations in their own countries.

Digital advocacy organizations rely on their members to take action and fund their campaigns. They campaign on a broad range of issues and can launch new campaigns within hours of a breaking news story because they have less bureaucracy than most conventional NGOs. Digital advocacy organizations engage in 'analytic activism': using digital tools to listen closely to their members' interests and running tests to determine the optimal campaign messaging, formatting, tactics, and which campaigns to run (Karpf 2016).

Chapter 4 explores the strengths and weaknesses of this model, and examines whether digital advocacy organizations compete or cooperate with conventional NGOs. It draws on descriptive statistics, interviews, and participant observation data, to examine exactly how this member-driven, multi-issue, rapid-response model operates.

OPEN has enabled close cooperation across a close-knit, global network of digital activists. Chapter 5 examines the evolution of OPEN identifies the distinct modes of cooperation within the network. OPEN has organized summits, staff secondments, training, and the sharing of digital technologies. OPEN organizations have also assisted the establishment of new organizations through mentoring and financing. This chapter analyses the forms of transnational solidarity that digital activists participate in, and those they do not. I examine tensions in the network about what it should be—a platform for transnational campaigning and/or a forum for exchanging digital advocacy practices and technologies—and find that digital activists frequently share tactics, framing, and technology, but rarely develop collective campaign plans.

Many scholars have assumed that digital technology will make it easier to engage in a transnational network, campaign on an international issue, and/or target an international institution. In Chapter 6, I focus on the campaign actions of Campact, ActionStation, 38 Degrees, and GetUp over a one-year period. I find that these digital advocacy organizations often campaign on transnational issues, but do so through a national lens. They very rarely target international decision-makers or institutions, or even ally with international NGOs. Their primary strategy is to mobilize citizens to put pressure on national political representatives for change. They are member-driven organizations and see the locus of power within the state, even in a globalized, interdependent world.

Distributed campaigning is a key form of protest that has emerged in the past decade. The climate movement, in particular, has gained power and profile globally, thanks to simultaneous, mass mobilizations on a large scale, which local groups of volunteers organize online and face-to-face. Chapter 7 separates out four forms of transnational advocacy often conflated in IR scholarship. These are campaigns focused on the same issues that occur: (a) at the same time with the same target; (b) at the same time with a different target; (c) at a different time with the same target; and (d) at a different time and with a different target. This analytical distinction highlights a form of protest not well recognized by international relations scholars: actions which occur at the same time, but with different targets ('distributed campaigning'). This chapter applies this framework to examine OPEN's contribution to domestic and transnational climate campaigns.

There are limitations to the member-driven logic of digital advocacy organizations. It can be hard, for instance, to get a majority of members to support campaigns for minority rights. In addition, members can be sharply divided on some issues, such as Brexit and refugee rights. Chapter 8 outlines how some digital advocacy organizations have developed a *staff-stewardship model*. Staff in these organizations are driven by progressive values and seek to shape members' concerns. They may choose an issue which has little initial support and stick with it, despite a low number of signatories to a petition. Over time, they will seek to shape their members' interests, and even shape the membership of the digital advocacy organization to galvanize support. This contrasts with the typical *member-driven model*, which responds reactively to members' preferences. I illustrate these different models with campaigns for Māori rights, refugee rights, and against TTIP.

Conclusion

Overall, this book suggests that digital advocacy organizations are a novel, permanent, and significant addition to the international arena. These organizations challenge IR's assumption that NGOs wield power through their authority or expertise on an issue, and long-term commitment to a cause. The digital advocacy organizations studied here derive power from their ability to mobilize members rapidly, online and offline. They are shaping public opinion on many issues, including climate change, trade, and refugees. They have built a transnational network to share technology, messaging, tactics, and strategies. They rarely campaign collectively at the same time, on the same issue, with the same target. However, they have run simultaneous campaigns on the same issue, with different targets. Their campaigns to bring down President Trump's business council in 2017 followed this model. MoveOn and Skiftet mobilized their members to put pressure on business leaders from their respective countries. These organizations were powerful because they could contact thousands of people, in a matter of hours, at a crucial moment. Perhaps the clearest acknowledgement of the power of digital advocacy organizations comes from the reactions of their targets. Governments and politicians have acknowledged their impact, and even sought to limit their funding, as we will see in Chapter 2.

2

The Power of Digital Advocacy Organizations

During the European summer of 2015, the number of asylum seekers entering Europe increased dramatically.[1] On 24 August, German Chancellor Angela Merkel suspended the European Union's Dublin Regulation, which removed the need for asylum seekers to return to and register in the first European country they entered. Living in Berlin at the time, I witnessed long queues of asylum seekers outside government registration offices and saw sports halls transformed into shelters. On 2 September, the publication of a photo of Alan Kurdi, a Syrian toddler who drowned off the coast of Turkey, triggered an international outcry at the treatment of refugees. Initially, public sentiment in many European countries was welcoming towards refugees. Residents met them at train stations with food and water (Kleres 2018; Milan 2018), donated clothes, and offered accommodation to new arrivals. It was a moment of intense public interest in refugees' rights (Hall 2017a, 2019a, 2019b). Governments in Europe and beyond were faced with a hard question: how many refugees were they willing to accept?

In Ireland, the director of Uplift, Siobhán O'Donoghue, began receiving messages from Uplift members stating that they wanted the Irish government to do more to accommodate refugees in Ireland. Motivated by these members' concerns, Donoghue decided to launch an online petition in solidarity with refugees just a day before the Alan Kurdi story broke. The petition received 38,500 signatures. In the aftermath of the Kurdi story, Uplift launched a 'Pledge a Bed' campaign, which resulted in 14,000 people pledging to offer a refugee a bed. This was remarkable, given that Ireland had an opt-out from

[1] Asylum-seekers are those seeking refugee status, but who have not yet been granted it. Refugees are defined by the 1951 Refugee Convention as those 'fleeing a well-founded fear of persecution' and who must have crossed an international border. The term 'migrant' covers anyone on the move, whether voluntary or forced, internal or external migration. These distinctions are important, given that international law offers refugees 'international protection' (e.g. non-refoulement, or the right not be returned to their home country). For more on these distinctions, see Hall (2016).

Transnational Advocacy in the Digital Era. Nina Hall, Oxford University Press.
 DOI: 10.1093/oso/9780198858744.003.0002

the European resettlement plan, so was under no legal obligation to accept any refugees. Wide domestic media coverage of the campaign put further pressure on the Irish government. On 10 September 2015, the then-Taoiseach, Enda Kenny, announced that Ireland would offer a home to 4,000 refugees by the end of 2017 under the EU resettlement and relocation programme (they were previously committed to 600) (Hall 2017a). Interestingly, the Irish government enlisted the public's pledges of support to host refugees, many of which were made through Uplift, and assigned the Irish Red Cross to coordinate availability (Hall 2019b).

Digital advocacy organizations in Australia, Austria, the United States, the UK, Canada, Sweden, Poland, and New Zealand also pushed their governments to welcome more refugees (Hall 2017a).[2] These organizations employed a similar series of tactics: social media mobilizations around #refugeeswelcome, online petitions calling for central and local governments to allow more asylum seekers to enter, and vigils and rallies in the streets. In September 2015, many of these campaigns showed initial signs of success and even conservative governments agreed to increase their refugee intakes. Digital advocacy organizations were not the only organizations to advocate for refugees, and any changes in government policy should not be attributed solely to their actions. However, their organizational model enabled them to rapidly start campaigns and mobilize a range of people, many of whom would not have been affiliated with refugee advocacy organizations.

This chapter examines five attributes of digital advocacy organizations which distinguish them from traditional non-governmental organizations (NGOs). I examine each attribute in turn, drawing on the existing international relations (IR) and political communications scholarship. First, I examine how digital advocacy organizations engage in election campaigns, not only issue-based advocacy. Digital advocacy organizations have run powerful electoral campaigns and helped unseat right-wing politicians and swing marginal districts for progressive candidates in the United States, Australia, and Canada.

Second, digital advocacy organizations are member-driven rather than staff-driven. Digital advocacy organizations believe that outsider public pressure is more durable over time, compared with lobbying elites, which requires gaining access to, and influence over, these elites. They derive their power from their 'ability to attract time, effort, and other resources

[2] Note that Germany was a different case, as the government had agreed to welcome refugees, hence Campact focused on racism within Germany rather than trying to change the German government's position.

from their members' (Han 2014). They have adopted an outsider strategy, which 'primarily relies on the collective force of large-scale citizen participation to move public and private sector decision-makers towards just outcomes'.[3]

Third, digital advocacy organizations are issue generalists and campaign simultaneously across a broad range of issues. Their expertise is not in the cause they campaign for, but in a skill set of digital campaigning. Fourth, digital advocacy organizations run rapid-response campaigns rather than long-term, awareness-raising campaigns. They try to mobilize members as a decision is being taken. Finally, digital advocacy organizations use digital technologies to devolve decision-making power to their members. Unlike most NGOs, digital advocacy organizations closely monitor their members' preferences by tracking email open rates and social media views, and use this data to identify what campaigns are likely to be successful. They also enable members to start their own campaigns through online petition platforms.

These five elements work together: Online Progressive Engagement Network (OPEN) organizations gain political power because they can rapidly mobilize their large membership lists at key moments, such as the refugee crisis. They can quickly contact members and start new campaigns, thanks to their use of digital technology. They can switch campaigns because they are not experts in any one issue area. Politicians are more likely to listen to digital advocacy organizations because they can be influential during election season. Overall, digital advocacy organizations build networked people power, which is distinct from NGOs' expertise-based power.

Table 2.1 summarizes the core differences between NGOs and digital advocacy organizations examined in this chapter. Organizations are presented as ideal types and not all NGOs or digital advocacy organizations will fit perfectly within the categories, as we will see in subsequent chapters.

Importantly, all the digital advocacy organizations in this study share a set of progressive values and are part of OPEN. Their shared objectives include: 'prioritising and supporting underrepresented and historically oppressed communities to fight for liberation on their own terms, addressing the climate crisis, fighting for a robust democracy, limiting corporate and oligarchic power over workers and the state, protecting the environment and maintaining public assets for public benefit, and promoting peace inside state boundaries

[3] OPEN, https://www.the-open.net/network (accessed 4 December 2021).

Table 2.1 Comparison of attributes of digital advocacy organizations versus NGOs

	Digital Advocacy organizations	Traditional NGOs
Engage in electoral campaigning	Regularly. They campaign against conservative candidates, and/or for progressive candidates	Rarely. If NGOs run election campaigns, these are issue-focused not candidate focused
Campaign decisions driven by	Members	Professional staff
Breadth of scope	Multi-issue generalists	Issue experts
Timeframe	Rapid-response campaigns	Longer-term campaigns
Digital strategies*	Digital testing (analytics) Digitally distributed campaigning	Digital broadcasting**

Notes: *For a more detailed analysis of NGOs' digital strategies, see Hall, Schmitz, and Dedmon (2020). **Traditional NGOs have started to experiment with customization of their messages, testing and monitoring digital analytics but they have not gone as far as the digital native organizations described here.

and internationally'.[4] The progressive orientation of these digital advocacy organizations makes them distinct from other internet petition platforms, such as Change.org, which are value neutral.[5]

Election Campaigning

> When you're advocating, you're basically barking ..., why do people in any instance, react to a bark? It's because they're afraid of the bite... . If all an advocacy group can do is bark, but can't bite, they can't inflict actual consequences on politicians, and the bark loses its power to influence politicians' choices. That is why OPEN seek to bark AND bite. Often the strongest bite is electoral relevance.[6]

Digital advocacy organizations wield power not simply because of their savvy use of digital platforms, but also because they target politicians during the

[4] OPEN, https://www.the-open.net/ (accessed 18 January 2021)

[5] Change.org is the world's largest petition platform, where individuals can set up their own campaigns. It is a for-profit organization (see Karpf 2013).

[6] Ben Brandzel, interview with author, 30 January 2021.

electoral season. Digital advocacy organizations run campaigns in support of progressive candidates and to undermine right-wing politicians. Importantly, their electoral campaigns are both online and offline. These campaigns gives them 'bite', or political influence over politicians, according to Brandzel. Importantly, their engagement in electoral campaigning distinguishes them from most other NGOs, which tend to focus on issue-based advocacy.[7]

Here I examine: the resources they marshal, the strategies and tactics they use; and public acknowledgement of their political impact. I focus mostly on the established groups, MoveOn in the United States, GetUp in Australia, and Leadnow in Canada, who have a longer history of election campaigning, which has been well documented. However, OPEN-affiliated organizations in Germany, Israel, Hungary, New Zealand, Ireland, Sweden, UK, France, Austria, Switzerland, Romania, and Poland have also been active in election campaigns. There are differences among these organizations' strategies; in some cases, digital advocacy organizations sought to increase the turn-out of progressive voters, in others they endorsed specific candidates. Major differences in electoral law between these countries have shaped the strategies they can use, and their overall effectiveness.[8] In Canada, the United States, and Australia, it is possible to target politicians in marginal constituencies, and, if successful, influence the make-up of parliament. Meanwhile, the mixed-member proportional (MMP) electoral system in Germany and New Zealand means that this same tactic is not as powerful. Under the MMP system, individuals have two votes—one for a representative in their constituency, and a second for a party—and the final composition of parliament is based on the proportion of party votes a party receives. Hence, Campact and ActionStation (based in New Zealand) focus on influencing peoples' party votes rather than their constituency representative vote.[9]

[7] Many NGOs cannot engage in political campaigns, as this would jeopardize their charity status. In many countries, donations to charities are not taxed. When NGOs do engage in election campaigns, they tend to maintain their neutrality by not campaigning for any particular candidate, but rather campaigning on the issues they care about.

[8] In 2019, Zazim offered transportation to Bedouin voters who lived in remote areas and would otherwise have had to walk hours to vote in the Israeli election. They had to cancel these plans because busing voters was classified as a political activity, and hence they would need to register as an 'organization active in the election', which would curb their fundraising abilities (Lis 2019).

[9] During the German and New Zealand 2017 elections, both Campact and ActionStation respectively drew up score cards of top priority issues by asking their members what they were most concerned about. Each organization then issued a progressive scorecard which ranked parties based on their policies.

Resources, Tactics, and Strategies

GetUp, MoveOn, and Leadnow have all invested heavily in election campaigning. Their most effective strategy has been to focus on marginal constituencies and ridings where conservative candidates have slim or no leads, and then to mobilize people to vote for more progressive alternatives. They use traditional offline tactics to achieve this, sending out volunteers to canvass on the street, knock on residents' doors, and telephone voters. Their offline tactics are particularly effective because they use digital platforms to strategically mobilize and coordinate thousands of volunteers. Digital advocacy organizations often create their own election event websites, through which volunteers can coordinate amongst themselves and organize to host their own events, such as door knocking, rather than relying on paid staff members being present. Their most powerful resources are their members' time and money and they often receive more financing and volunteers during election years. They use these resources to campaign online (e.g. viral videos on social media); offline (e.g. large-scale door-knocking campaigns or telephone banking); and to hire more paid staff.

Leadnow, for instance, ran an effective campaign during the 2015 Canadian general election, which helped oust the incumbent Conservative government led by Stephen Harper. Leadnow raised $428,000 in donations from 6,800 sources to fund their election campaign (Vromen 2017: 196), and hired 14 paid election staff and 5 paid election contractors, who helped to organize 5,626 volunteers (Leadnow 2015: 5). Leadnow's campaign focused on twenty-nine marginal ridings where they believed they could beat Conservative politicians. They identified the progressive candidates and then got over 90,000 people to pledge to vote for the 'best local candidate who could defeat a Conservative' (Leadnow 2015: 5). Leadnow strategized that to help Liberal leader Justin Trudeau win, electors in sixteen ridings should cast their vote for a Liberal party candidate, and in thirteen others for the National Democratic Party candidate (Vromen 2017). Leadnow then ran targeted campaigns in those constituencies and mobilized 3,255 people to phone-bank, and 2,370 to door knock.[10] Overall, Leadnow had 1.15 million visits to their campaign page, www.votetogether.ca, and reached millions of people through hundreds of national and local newspaper, television, and radio ads.

Leadnow's recommended candidates won in twenty-five out of twenty-nine ridings. In all the ridings they targeted, the voter turnout was 5–10 per cent

[10] Leadnow mobilized its members to engage in over 20,000 voter-to-voter conversations in the final two weeks of the campaign and distributed over 74,000 flyers.

higher than the national average. In some cases, the margin of victory was smaller than the number of people who pledged their votes with Leadnow. Although it would be an overstatement to attribute Trudeau's election victory to Leadnow, one conservative commentator, Vivian Krause, has acknowledged that 'in a small number of ridings, it is conceivable that Leadnow had an impact. For example, in Elmswood-Transcona where Leadnow had paid staff and 130 volunteers, the Conservative incumbent was defeated by only sixty-one votes' (Krause 2019). Krause also noted that 'If those Conservatives hadn't been defeated, the Liberal Party of Canada would still have won the election but it would not necessarily have a majority government. As such, Leadnow's involvement in the 2015 federal election is no small matter' (Krause 2017a). Leadnow repeated these tactics in the 2019 federal election, where they focused on eight 'battleground' states and mobilized members to canvass and door knock for progressive candidates who could defeat the Conservatives (i.e. the New Democratic Party, the Green Party, and the Liberals) (Krause 2019).

MoveOn in the United States have also used similar tactics in their election campaigns. During the 2006 mid-term elections, MoveOn mobilized seven million members to make 'Calls for Change' through a web-based phonebank (Karpf 2012). This campaign was very successful according to Brandzel, who worked at the time for MoveOn: 'Talk about bite. The margin of Democratic victory in thirty-two Senate and House races was smaller than the number of turn out calls our members made. And in many cases, it was clear they would not have won without our program.'[11] MoveOn.org is comprised of two legal entities: a Political Action Committee (PAC), which fundraises and campaigns for progressive political candidates, and a Civil Action Group, which has a 501c4 tax status, and hence faces limits on its political campaigning.[12]

MoveOn has been active in many other elections, including the 2004 presidential election, the 2018 mid-terms, and the 2020 presidential election. During the 2008 presidential election, MoveOn members made calls and encouraged people to vote for Obama. In important swing states, MoveOn developed 'direct partnerships' with Obama's official field campaign (Karpf

[11] Interview with Ben Brandzel, 30 January 2021.

[12] MoveOn, 'About MoveOn Political Action', https://front.moveon.org/about-moveon-political-action/ (accessed 4 December 2021). For more on 501c(4) status see (Sullivan 2013). In 2017–2018, for instance, MoveOn PAC's total receipts were over US$31 million and its total contributions were just over US$24 million. Federal Election Commission, 'MoveOn.Org Political Action', https://www.fec.gov/data/committee/C00341396/?cycle=2018 (accessed 4 December 2021). From 1 January 2019 to 16 December 2020, MoveOn PAC generated US $48 million in total contributions and spent a total of $43 million. Federal Election Commission. 'MoveOn.Org, Political Action', https://www.fec.gov/data/committee/C00341396/?cycle=2020 (accessed 4 December 2021).

2012). Their email list 'ballooned to over 5 million' during the 2008 presidential election, thanks to viral videos and the lure of free Obama and Biden merchandise (Karpf 2012). In total, almost 100,000 MoveOn members volunteered 20,841,507 hours and donated over $88,000,000 to the Obama campaign (Karpf 2012). MoveOn was also one of the lead organizations in the political resistance to President Trump, and campaigned at the district, state, and federal level during the 2018 mid-terms (Fisher 2019b).

In Australia, GetUp has also managed large-scale election campaigns and helped to defeat right-wing politicians at the polls. GetUp typically increases its income and its staff during election years (Vromen 2017: 90). During the 2010 election campaign, GetUp mobilized 7,000 people to engage in 20,000 hours of volunteer work. They have one of the largest budgets of any third party, outside of political parties, in Australia. In 2014, GetUp had the highest political expenditure of the twenty-five organizations which made declarations to the Australian Electoral Commission (Vromen 2016: 90).[13] In the lead-up to the 2019 election, GetUp raised AUS $12.5 million in annual donations; this was a 27 per cent increase on donations in 2018 (Crowe 2019).

Like MoveOn and Leadnow, GetUp has developed digital tools and platforms to organize their volunteers effectively. In 2010, they launched a dedicated website to allow people to organize their own phone-banking events and coordinate campaign calls (Karp 2017a). Then, in 2017, two GetUp 'techies', Darren Loasby and Bridger Rossiter, built 'Koorangang', a phone-banking tool which they initially used during the marriage equality referendum in 2017, and then subsequently during election campaigning. All a volunteer needed to do was dial a specific phone number from their own phone, and then they would be immediately connected to a member of the public whom they could then engage in canvassing efforts (Rugg 2019). As GetUp campaigner Sally Rugg explained: 'After each conversation the callee is left off the hook and the volunteer is prompted to input data pertaining to the phone call, which is collected, measured and analysed before being connected to the next caller for their next chat' (Rugg 2019). Koorangang enabled volunteers to do phone banking at a much faster pace—no longer did you have to make several calls before connecting to anyone.[14]

[13] Vromen notes that GetUp claims most of expenditure on campaigning as declarable political expenditure, whereas many conservative groups give funding directly to parties.

[14] During the marriage equality campaign, GetUp had an ambitious aim to make 0.5 million phone calls and win 5.5 million votes; strategic targeting 'outside the [inner city] bubble', GetUp was one of the lead organizations coordinating the campaign to legalize gay marriage and did a lot behind the scenes developing tech and organization infrastructure to ensure that people voted (Karp 2017b).

The use of Koorangang enabled GetUp to make hundreds of thousands of calls during the 2019 federal election. Rugg claims that the tool 'transformed the energy and enthusiasm of keen supporters of marriage equality into targeted, strategic action that had a tangible, measurable impact'. This sort of technology is often used by banks and utilities to reach their users, but rarely by 'activists to organise grassroots social change' (Rugg 2019). GetUp tech staff have also custom-built online mapping tools to make door knocking more efficient. In 2017, they developed a 'turf cutter' map which thousands of volunteers have subsequently used during the marriage equality referendum, as well as the 2019 federal election. The tool provides volunteers with routes for door knocking that are optimized according to the volunteers' location and the size of their group. Users record which streets they have visited and how conversations went, giving important data to the central team managing the campaign.

In the 2019 federal election campaign, for example, GetUp targeted 'hard right' politicians including former prime minister Tony Abbott, former defence minister Kevin Andrews, home affairs minister Peter Dutton, and health minister Greg Hunt (Crowe 2019). GetUp ran a strong campaign in Abbott's Sydney constituency of Warringah and door knocked more than 20,000 households (Davies 2019). While GetUp does not officially back specific progressive candidates, it singles out conservative candidates and tells voters not to vote for them (Maley 2019). In Warringah, for instance, GetUp recommended voters who were concerned about climate change should vote for independent, Zali Steggall, or fellow independent Susan Moylan-Coombs, rather than Abbott. As GetUp campaigner Miriam Lyons stated in the Sydney Morning Herald: 'It's clear our climate can't afford another 25 years of Tony Abbott, this election Warringah will be voting for climate leadership' (Hasham 2019). GetUp also commissioned regular polls in the lead-up to the election, as their campaign momentum increased, which showed Abbott trailing (Hasham 2019).

GetUp was likely a factor in Abbott's defeat. Abbott even directly acknowledged the impact of GetUp: 'There is absolutely no doubt that GetUp, the green left, have put massive resources into this seat … and I think the message is that people have got to resist very strongly that green left ideology because it's doing enormous damage to our economy' (Maley and Hunter 2019). However, GetUp's efforts to oust the Conservative government were ultimately unsuccessful, and Conservative leader Scott Morrison became prime minister.

GetUp has even taken the Australian government to court. In 2010, they appealed the Australian Electoral Commission's decision to reject the validity of GetUp's online enrolment website. They then mounted two other cases to increase voter enrolment: the first at the high court, arguing that Howard government reforms were unconstitutional (the government reduced time for voters to enrol or update their information); and the second at the federal court, on the legality of electronic voter enrolment. They won both cases, which resulted in the enfranchisement of 98,000 voters (Vromen 2016). Importantly, GetUp obtained the consent of their membership in both cases by conducting a survey which revealed that 70 per cent of their members supported going to court (Vromen 2016: 117).

...

GetUp, MoveOn, and Leadnow have used many other tactics to help progressive candidates and progressive causes in referenda. They have run nationwide advertising campaigns, and often generated popular social media content. GetUp, for example, produced an emotionally powerful video in support of gay marriage which had sixteen million views during a referendum on the issue.[15] Leadnow ran radio advertisements and made 150,000 phone calls during the 2019 federal election (Krause 2019). MoveOn has actively engaged in the Democratic primaries and has tried to mobilize support for the more progressive candidates—campaigning, for example, for Elizabeth Warren in the 2020 Democratic primaries. In June 2020, MoveOn also hosted 'Big Ideas', the first major debate between many of the leading Democratic presidential candidates.[16]

In the UK, 38 Degrees has also engaged in election campaigns. During the 2015 election, 38 Degrees members had 'voted against' endorsing specific candidates, and 38 Degrees campaigned with a broad message of 'voting with the NHS in mind'.[17] Senior 38 Degrees staff were reluctant to criticize the 'Tories during election time when they were most vulnerable' for fear of being 'pigeonholed as a liberal organization'.[18] In 2017, they ran a 'get out to vote' campaign on Facebook, which reached four million young people (Maltby 2017). However, 38 Degrees staff have been less willing to attack the Tory government directly or to endorse progressive candidates during election campaigns.

[15] The video had been seen over 16 million times by 8 January 2018. GetUp, '"It's Time". Marriage Equality', https://www.youtube.com/watch?v=_TBd-UCwVAY (accessed 4 December 2021).

[16] Joe Biden did not participate, but many others did (Senator Cory Booker, Secretary Julián Castro, Senator Kirsten Gillibrand, Senator Kamala Harris, Senator Amy Klobuchar, Representative Beto O'Rourke, Senator Bernie Sanders, and Senator Elizabeth Warren). MoveOn, Campaigns, 'The Big Ideas Series', https://www.crowdcast.io/e/moveon-big-ideas-forum/register (accessed 17 January 2022).

[17] 38 Degrees surveyed all its members to generate its election plan and 137,105 members responded (38 Degrees 2015).

[18] Interview with Ben Brandzel, 30 January 2021.

GetUp, MoveOn, Degrees, and Leadnow have all developed important tools and online organizing infrastructure to help defeat right-wing politicians.[19] They use digital platforms to organize their members online and put pressure on politicians. They adopt an outsider strategy of public pressure rather than an insider strategy of directly influencing politicians through lobbying. In Brandzel's view: 'Being liked [by politicians] is only relevant with an insider theory of change ... our core asset is being respected, and when appropriate, feared.'[20] Digital advocacy organizations' engagement in elections has given them greater power in subsequent issue-based campaigns.

Political Power: Conservative Attacks and Progressive Recognition

Conservative and progressive politicians have recognized that digital advocacy organizations are powerful political actors who can shape election outcomes. At times, these politicians have sought to curb the influence of digital advocacy organizations by alleging that they are foreign-funded and challenging their independent, third-party status in election campaigns. Indeed, some politicians have sought to amend electoral laws to weaken digital advocacy organizations' power.[21] Conservative politicians attack these organizations because they see them as powerful.

Here, I examine allegations against two OPEN groups: GetUp in Australia and Leadnow in Canada. I also note how progressive politicians have acknowledged the influence of organizations like MoveOn due to their ability to mobilize their constituents for, or against, them. While I have chosen to focus on just three organizations, many other OPEN groups have faced attacks including in: Poland, Sweden, Israel, and Germany.[22]

GetUp is considered a powerful force in Australian national elections and the Conservative government have repeatedly tried to restrict GetUp's activities. Tasmanian senator Eric Abetz has been particularly vocal in his criticism

[19] Many political parties have also developed similar tools; however, it is rare for NGOs or advocacy organizations to invest in these.

[20] A 'theory of change' is a term (and method) activists use to describe how their actions will achieve their desired change in the world. The eight-fold path encapsulates the OPEN theory of change. Interview with Ben Brandzel, 30 January 2021.

[21] In 2013 and 2014, the UK parliament debated and eventually passed the Transparency of Lobbying, Non-Party Campaigning and Trade Union Administration Act. 38 Degrees campaigned against what they called the 'gag' act, which they argued would limit their ability to fundraise and campaign in the UK (Blue and Green Tomorrow 2013). See also: Chloe Smith, 'Don't Gag Campaigners', 38 Degrees, https://web.archive.org/web/20140725190351/https://secure.38degrees.org.uk/page/speakout/chloe-smith-lobbying-bill (accessed 4 December 2021).

[22] Campact, for instance, lost its charity status in 2019 (Civic Space Watch 2019).

of GetUp, and stated that: 'GetUp's grubby tactics in the 2016 election are rightly deserving of examination and I have confidence that the joint standing committee will consider these matters in detail' (Murphy 2016). He continued: '[GetUp] aren't subject to the same regimes political parties are, yet it is clear they can have a political impact.' (Murphy 2016). Abetz has further argued in the Australian Senate that GetUp is part of a global network of left-wing organizations supported by the businessman George Soros, and has criticized GetUp for accepting foreign funding.[23]

Liberal and National party candidates and the Murdoch press have regularly alleged that GetUp acted more like a partisan political party with foreign funding than a politically independent NGO with charitable objectives. In 2018, the Conservative government targeted GetUp when they passed the foreign donations bill. As a result, from January 2019 GetUp could not receive any foreign donations (from individuals or foundations) above AUS $1,000, as it was classified as a 'political campaigner' under the electoral act (Coggan 2019). Conservative attacks against GetUp continued during the 2019 Australian federal election campaign. The Conservative and Liberal coalition spokesperson and Senator Simon Birmingham, for instance, claimed that GetUp are 'nothing more than a front for Labor and the Greens' (Crowe 2019). Andrew Bragg, a Liberal candidate running then for the Senate, also attacked GetUp's independence: 'Pretending to be independent when they are not and seeking to exempt themselves from a ban on foreign donations is outrageous behaviour' (Crowe 2019).

Other conservative critics of GetUp have initiated several reviews of GetUp's independent status with the Australian Electoral Commission (AEC). However, the AEC has always ruled that GetUp is not an 'associated entity' of any political party, but rather an independent organization (*SBS News* 2019).[24] Interestingly, 38 Degrees has also been attacked by conservative British politician David Davies for claiming to be independent, but really being a 'left-wing organization' steered by 'wealthy metropolitan socialists' (Davies 2014).

Meanwhile, in Canada a minister in the former Harper government, Kerry-Lynne D. Findlay, has raised concerns about Leadnow's international links.

[23] Senator Eric Abetz, The Senate Proof, Governor-General's speech, address in reply, 12 September 2016.

[24] See also the Electoral Commission announcement, https://web.archive.org/web/20180202150231/http://www.aec.gov.au/Parties_and_Representatives/compliance/AEC_Advice/2010-nov-get-up.htm (accessed 4 December 2021). Note that subsequent to these attacks, GetUp released a statement detailing their independence from political parties, and outlining the importance of engaging in elections, https://www.getup.org.au/about/getup-statement-of-independence (accessed 4 December 2021).

In 2018, Findlay made a detailed written submission to a parliamentary committee investigating third-party status under Canadian electoral law.[25] Findlay noted that:

> Leadnow is based in Vancouver, BC and created in 2010/2011. One of Leadnow's original founders was Ben Brandzel. At the time, Brandzel was the Director of Strategic Incubation at the Citizen Engagement Laboratory ('CEL'), based in Oakland, California. With funding via The Tides Foundation, the CEL began in 2008. Leadnow qualifies as carrying on business in Canada, but it is an American brainchild, working in concert and funded by many American interests.[26]

However, a seventeen month investigation found that Leadnow had not broken Canadian electoral laws (Krause 2019).

Findlay's concerns were likely informed by Vivian Krause, a concerned conservative citizen, who has extensively researched Leadnow and their links to OPEN. Krause raised concerns to the Office of the Commissioner of Canada Elections 'about Leadnow's use of U.S. funds and in-kind support from outside Canada in both the 2011 and 2015 federal elections'(Krause 2017). Krause alleged that they had received funding from OPEN, the Tides Foundation, and Engaging Networks to power their election campaign. In 2017, Krause wrote and submitted a report, 'Who is Leadnow?', to the Office of the Commissioner, in which she noted that '[in] January of 2016, Leadnow's Amara Possian attended an OPEN summit in Australia where Leadnow won an award for its 2015 campaign to help defeat the Conservatives. Logan McIntosh, Leadnow's executive director, went to Australia during its 2016 election and worked with Get-Up, another member of OPEN'(Krause 2017b: 3). Krause has dedicated significant time and energy to researching and publicizing LeadNow's foreign links precisely because she sees them having a significant impact on Canadian election results.

[25] A third party means a person or a group, other than a registered [political] party, registered association, candidate or nomination contestant' that wants to influence political elections in Canada. See Canada, Elections Act, S.C. 2000 c. 9, https://laws-lois.justice.gc.ca/PDF/E-2.01.pdf (accessed 4 December 2021). Note that Third Parties are prohibited from using Foreign Funds. Krause also presented to the committee reviewing Canada's electoral legislation on third parties on 6 June 2018. See https://www.ourcommons.ca/DocumentViewer/en/42-1/PROC/meeting-112/minutes (accessed 4 December 2021).

[26] This characterization was slightly incorrect as Brandzel was a founding advisor, not a founder of the organization. Hon. Kerry-Lynne D. Findlay, PC, QC, Senior Legal Counsel, Mediator (British Columbia), Consideration of Bill C-76, An Act to Amend the Canada Elections Act and Other Acts to Make Certain Consequential Amendments, Committee Hearing Date: Wednesday 6 June 2018.

Progressive politicians have also on occasion recognized the power of digital advocacy organizations. Felix Kolb, an Executive Director of Campact, recalled that a senior Social Democratic (SPD) politician from Baden-Württemburg complained that his own rank-and-file party members were following Campact messaging more than the SPD party leadership on trade policy. Campact was able to communicate directly to the SPD rank and file through their regular email newsletters.[27] Meanwhile, Ben Brandzel, recounted that during his time at MoveOn, he met the Chief of Staff for Congresswoman Jan Schakowsky, a Democrat who represented Illinois 9th District. He asked the Chief of Staff why they considered MoveOn a serious political force. Schakowsky responded that: 'you have so many members in our district we have to take you very seriously' as those members would closely follow MoveOn's evaluation of the Congresswoman's performance.[28]

However, many politicians do not understand the OPEN model. They are not aware of how digital advocacy organizations aggregate and represent their members' preferences. Brandzel noted that often US politicians thought MoveOn was a conventional lobby group and did not understand they were a member-driven movement. Brandzel visited Congress soon after the 2006 mid-term elections and recalled meeting Henry Reid, Nancy Pelosi, and 'and a young up-and-coming senator from Illinois, Barack Obama'.[29] Brandzel claims that Obama 'was the only one to really understand the movement building dynamics'. As he elaborated: 'For a lot of people in DC—it [MoveOn] was this crazy, internet bomb that had gone off in their orderly lives.'[30] Obama, who had a background in community organizing in Chicago, understood that MoveOn's power and legitimacy came from channelling their members' desires, not gaining direct access to 'wheel and deal' with decision-makers.[31]

Let us now examine the four other elements of the eight-fold path which makes them distinct from lobby groups and NGOs.

[27] Interview with Felix Kolb, 15 March 2021.
[28] Note Brandzel was recalling this quote in 2021. Interview with Ben Brandzel, 30 January 2021.
[29] ibid.
[30] ibid.
[31] ibid.

Staff vs Member-Driven Campaigning

Professional Staff Select Campaigns in NGOs

Most international NGOs have professional staff that select campaign issues. They do this based on their expertise and organizational mission (Stroup and Wong 2017). Human Rights Watch (HRW), for example, campaigns consistently on human rights, since this is their mandated cause. Within the broad arena of human rights, HRW's professional staff will decide to campaign on a particular issue, such as killer robots, based on their knowledge of the most pressing new issues and their relationships with other human rights NGOs (Carpenter 2007b). Human Rights Watch does not typically survey its members to ask them what it should campaign on. Greenpeace, Transparency International, Amnesty International, Oxfam, and smaller NGOs like the Sea Shepherd Conservation Society are similar in this regard. They hire professional staff with expertise in particular issue areas, and these professional campaigners identify issues to campaign on.

In recent years, there has been an increasing professionalization of NGOs, which hire and place value on staff with specific technical and subject area expertise (Simmons 2014; Chalmers and Shotton 2015). This has increased staff control over campaign selection and weakened members' influence in many NGOs founded before the digital era (Hestres 2015). NGOs are reluctant to take on new issues that are outside their policy expertise because they will not have the contacts or relevant information to run a successful campaign (Halpin et al. 2018: 4–5). NGOs that use insider strategies and directly lobby politicians are unlikely to take on new issues because they derive their influence from their expertise and authority on core issues (Stroup and Wong 2017). Simmons has noted that some human rights organizations are now 'too professionalised and bureaucratised to respond nimbly to emerging human rights violations' (Simmons 2014).

There is some variation across NGOs in how centralized the decision-making process is, and the ratio of professionals to volunteers (Wong 2012). NGOs may delegate or distribute power to their members to: (a) propose new campaigns; (b) veto or influence campaign selection; or (c) implement the campaign. Yet even in NGOs with strong, active memberships such as Amnesty International, staff ultimately make the decision about what issues to campaign on (Wong 2012). Amnesty International, for example, describes itself as 'a global movement of more than seven million people who take injustice personally ...'. However, it hires staff with expertise in human rights campaigning, and these staff will choose which campaigns to pursue.[32] Amnesty staff sitting in London select the prisoners of conscience for their rapid-response, letter-writing campaigns, and members simply write the letters (Lake and Wong 2009). Membership-based NGOs rarely, if ever, give their members power to decide what issues they should campaign on.

Member-Driven Campaigning

Digital advocacy organizations derive their power from their members and must be member-driven to be part of OPEN.[33] Many of the larger, more established organizations claim to have over one million members. GetUp, for instance, had one million members in December 2015 and has one of the largest memberships of any political organization in Australia (Vromen 2017). These organizations have amassed such large memberships because they have redefined what membership means (Karpf 2012: 32). In most digital advocacy organizations, membership is equated with anyone who signs up to receive an email, and regularly engages in their campaigns (e.g. by signing an online petition). Members do not have to donate to the organization or attend meetings. Precisely because these organizations have decoupled fee-paying from membership, it is hard to compare their size directly with other political organizations.[34] They mobilize people through loose, digitally based affiliations, and members may not even be aware that they are members (Chadwick and Dennis 2016; Karpf 2012).

Digital advocacy organizations see their members as a source of power and legitimacy. GetUp has 'heralded proudly' its total membership on its homepage (over 1 million in early 2021) and refers to it frequently when campaigning (Vromen 2017: 87). In 2010, GetUp's then Executive Director, Simon Sheikh, noted that the offices of Julia Gillard, Kevin Rudd, Tony Abbott, and Malcolm Turnbull actively engage with GetUp—and have little choice but to do so because they 'understand the size and the power of the movement' (Snow 2010).

[32] In 2017, Amnesty International advertised a position for a legal/policy adviser and stipulated that the person applying '[would] be expected to bring or to develop specific areas of expertise, including on human rights and environment and on children's rights'. The person taking this role 'would be required to draft policy documents recommending a position for the organization on new or emerging human rights issues'.

[33] OPEN, 'About Us', https://www.the-open.net/ (accessed 18 January 2022).

[34] The Green party of Australia have around 10,000 financial members and 80,000 signed up for digital communications from the party. Hence, if we were to consider anyone that received an email as a member, they would be eight times larger (Vromen 2017: 88).

Digital advocacy organizations are aware that a large list of email addresses, or a large following on social media, does not deliver political outcomes on its own. To turn this into political power, they need to mobilize their members to take action, whether it be online or offline. As a result, most groups send between one and two emails a week to any given member outlining an action they can take, such as a petition to sign or a march to attend. Many groups differentiate between active and passive members, and some only count as members those who regularly take an action, excluding those that never open an email or take an action. As one GetUp staff member explained in 2015: 'it's great that we're a million people, a million email addresses now, but what we care about is active people' (Vromen 2017). Hence, a measure of 'Members returning for Action' (i.e. those that engage more than once, for instance, by signing more than one petition) is often a more useful measure of their political power.

So, who are the typical members? There is little publicly available data on membership in digital advocacy organizations. The groups I spoke with often referred to their typical member as a middle-aged, well-educated, left-wing woman.[35] Vromen's comprehensive survey of GetUp's members confirmed this, finding that they were 59 per cent women compared with 36 per cent men (with the remaining 5 per cent as non-responders) (Vromen 2017). GetUp members were, on average, older than the average Australian; and over 75 per cent had a diploma, bachelors degree, or a post-graduate degree, compared with 29 per cent of the Australian population. Research on the US resistance to President Trump, which was partly mobilized by MoveOn, found that the largest group of the participants were well-educated, left-wing, middle-aged women (Fisher 2019b).

During my visits to OPEN organizations, I frequently met volunteering members, who fitted this profile of being middle-class, educated, and mostly female baby boomers (Heimans and Timms 2018: 59). Some OPEN organizations report that it is difficult to attract a younger, digital-native generation. This may be because many OPEN organizations were not as active on newer platforms such as TikTok, Snapchat, and Instagram, but prefered email, Facebook, and Twitter during the period I studied them. Amandla.Mobi in South Africa is the only OPEN organization that has made an explicit decision to serve one sector of their society: black women living in low-income

[35] Note that I have no access to demographic data of members of digital advocacy organizations, so cannot verify whether their description of their members is accurate.

communities, and communicates with their members predominantly via Whatsapp and SMS.[36]

Digital advocacy organizations listen closely to their members' preferences and select campaigns that their members will support. They will not proceed with a campaign without the 'explicit endorsement from a substantial sub-section' of their list because they rely on members to take action and power campaigns (Fraussen and Halpin 2017: 7). To identify member preferences, they conduct 'rigorous testing, response benchmarks, polling, voting, and well-interpreted anecdotal inputs'.[37] They regularly survey their members to ask them what issues they should campaign on. In 2018, GetUp, for example, sent a survey to its members to identify how Australia could become more 'fair, flourishing and just' (GetUp 2018). Many groups also equip members to start and run their own campaigns and then assign organizational resources, such as online petition platforms, to promote those campaigns.

OPEN organizations are financially beholden to their members, who give small individual contributions to specific campaigns or to the organization as a whole (Karpf 2012; Vaughan 2020: 116). They do not accept government funding and are 'fiercely independent from any political party'.[38] The size and depth of commitment of their membership is their critical source of power and influence (Gulbrandsen and Andresen 2004). Digital advocacy organizations must campaign on issues that are salient to their members, and often are more focused on scoring immediate victories rather than promoting or implementing long-term solutions.

Digital advocacy organizations draw heavily on the theories of community organizing of Saul Alinsky, an American community activist.[39] Alinsky believed that social change was realized by mobilizing communities and holding political decision-makers–local or national–accountable. As he saw it, 'people power is the real objective' (Alinsky 1989). He emphasized the importance of grassroots, multi-issue organizations, which constantly switched tactics and issues to keep people engaged. As he explained: 'a wide-based membership can only be built on many issues' and a single-issue organization is a 'fatal straight-jacket that will stifle the life of your organization', as it 'won't last and will be

[36] Amandla.Mobi focuses on sending SMS and Whatsapp messages, rather than emails, as this is the best way to reach its audience, and it also regularly runs campaigns in four languages.

[37] The Commons, 'The Eight Fold Path: 8 operating principles for building a progressive people's movement' https://commonslibrary.org/the-eight-fold-path/ (accessed 18 January 2022)

[38] ibid.

[39] There are many others influential community organizers such as Marshall Ganz and Cesar Chavez. For a useful summary of community organizing, see Chapter 1 in Price 2017.

small' (Alinsky 1989). Multiple issues mean 'constant action and life' for an organization, crucial for keeping a community engaged (Alinsky 1989).

Alinsky argued that community organizations had to keep taking action to prevent any one campaign or tactic losing its impact. As he explained, 'this means constantly cutting new issues, as the action continues by the time the enthusiasm and emotions for one issue have started to de-escalate, a new issue has come onto the scene with a consequent revival' (Alinsky 1989). If a campaign continues for too long, people will lose interest and the organization will lose power, as their power is based on peoples' willingness and commitment to take action. The principal aim of community organizing for Alinsky was not about winning a particular issue, but 'creating broad coalitions, and training community members to conduct hardball campaigns that let them win on lots of issues … Professional organizers focus on building community and power', and 'Issues are simply tools for the building process' (Miller 2010).

Alinsky's ideas have been profoundly influential in the United States. Barack Obama taught the Alinsky method as a community organizer in Chicago, which is probably why he understood the MoveOn model as a young senator. Hillary Clinton knew Alinsky personally, and wrote her senior thesis on Alinsky's mode of organizing. Some groups on the right, such as the Tea Party, have also employed his methods (Vogel 2010). Digital advocacy organizations have drawn on Alinsky's theories to build powerful campaigns offline and online (Price 2017). For these organizations, power is the 'quantity and depth of relationships aligned around a mission and the collective resources that those relationships bring to bear'; as one leading digital campaign advisor has argued, 'having the best information isn't going to lead to a win' (Price 2017). Notably, most practitioners and scholars see digital tools and face-to-face campaigning as complementary. They should not be seen as distinct analytically—or in practice—as the most powerful campaigns are those which marry 'digital tools and in person organizing' (Price 2017).

Listening has historically played a key role in people-powered organizing. In Alinsky's time, this meant spending time in communities to understand their grievances. Since the advent of the internet era, digital technologies have enabled advocacy organizations to generate thousands—if not millions—of online followers (sometimes referred to as 'members'). They can then efficiently, and effectively, aggregate these members' preferences (Hestres 2015: 196). NGOs were not previously able to aggregate members' interests as quickly or as efficiently as digital advocacy organizations can today (Jordan and Maloney 1998).

Digital advocacy organizations use digital analytical tools to listen to their members and develop campaigns based on their preferences. Karpf has called this 'analytic' activism, and has identified three main features which distinguish it from other forms of activism (Karpf 2016). The first is analytic activism prioritizes *listening* through digital channels such as Facebook, Twitter, email, and website traffic. Second, analytic activism embraces a *culture of testing*, where organizations test their email communications to see which campaigns members are endorsing and taking action on. This information then guides organizational learning and organizational practices and helps these groups to innovate. Finally, analytical activism *demands scale*, as organizations can only conduct robust tests if they have large enough mailing lists. Without such digital analytics expertise and technologies, NGOs cannot campaign as responsively to member preferences.[40] In this sense, digital advocacy organizations have a tremendous advantage in identifying issues which will gain rapid popular support, as will be discussed in Chapter 4.

Issue Experts vs Issue Generalists

Traditional NGOs as Issue Experts

Most major NGOs, such as Greenpeace or World Wide Fund for Nature (WWF), and transnational advocacy networks have subject *expertise* on the causes they campaign for (Keck and Sikkink 1998; Tarrow and della Porta 2005). As advocacy organizations campaign over sustained periods of time, they develop specialized knowledge and hire subject area experts. Expertise gives advocacy organizations significant power, legitimacy, and access to decision-makers (Tallberg et al. 2015; Haas 1992; Haas 1990; Allan 2021).[41]

Traditional NGOs may focus on broad issue areas (human rights, climate change, humanitarian relief), or more specific issues (anti-whaling, anti-child labour, banning landmines). Greenpeace and the Climate Action Network, for instance, have expertise on climate change, and a strong moral commitment to reducing greenhouse gas emissions (Allan 2021; Hadden 2015) Human Rights

[40] Analytical activism demands scale as you can only conduct robust tests if you have a large enough email list (Karpf 2016).

[41] Epistemic communities are defined by their knowledge of a particular issue (e.g. climate scientists or fisheries experts). Their influence and power is derived from this expertise, which states and international organizations may value. Some IR scholars separate out those with shared *causal ideas* (i.e. scientific experts) from those with shared *moral principles and values* (i.e. NGOs and advocacy organizations) (Keck and Sikkink 1998).

Watch and Amnesty International are seen as experts on human rights causes (Stroup and Wong 2017). Their reports on human rights abuses have a high degree of legitimacy, given their staff expertise (Hopgood 2006; Lake and Wong 2009). Transparency International's annual Corruption Perception Index is influential because the organization is an expert on corruption. The WWF and Sea Shepherd Conservation Society have expertise on the protection of endangered species; the International Committee of the Red Cross (ICRC) on international humanitarian law (Cali 2009; Ratner 2011; Eilstrup-Sangiovanni 2019).

Expertise is crucial for NGOs that engage in *insider* lobbying (Tallberg et al. 2015). Advocacy organizations and NGOs will use their expertise to access decision-makers and shift states' positions. NGOs also use *outsider* strategies: mobilizing public support or opposition through boycotts, protests, or direct action (Princen 1995). These NGOs also need a degree of expertise to convince the public the issue is worth caring about and to convince decision-makers to change course. Some NGOs use both insider and outsider strategies. Greenpeace has sought to be an 'intellectual leader' on climate change and engaged in 'knowledge construction, using scientists and analysts to acquire further understanding on complex issues', and also to mobilize people to protest against government inaction (Gulbrandsen and Andresen 2004).[42]

IR scholars have identified and investigated the use of *information politics* to influence decision-makers. Information politics involve advocacy organizations using their expertise to provide credible and useful information to influence states' positions (Keck and Sikkink 1998). For example, Berliner has illustrated how an NGO, Article 19, influenced freedom-of-information (FOI) laws by publishing detailed legal analyses of draft FOI legislation and persuading policymakers to pass stronger laws (Berliner 2016). Decision-makers listened to Article 19 because of their credibility and status as legal experts (Berliner 2016: 127). Meanwhile, Gulbrandsen and Andresen (2004) have

[42] Scholars have sought to explain why advocacy actors may choose one strategy over another and highlighted the role of NGO goals, access to decision-makers, group networks (Hadden 2015) and funding sources (Dellmuth and Tallberg 2017). Hadden (2015) argues that more contentious outsider tactics were used by newer environmental groups, while older groups (such as Greenpeace and the Climate Action Network), used more insider tactics in the climate change regime. She suggests that the selection of protest tactics depends on the networks NGOs are part of: NGOs in networks which use more contentious strategies will adopt these. Others have suggested that NGOs will be driven to outsider strategies when they rely heavily on members contributions and thus need to maintain high-profile public campaigns, whereas NGOs which have government (or other large donors) are more likely to follow an insider strategy (Dellmuth and Tallberg 2017). IR scholars tend to focus more on insider advocacy and social movement scholars on outsider advocacy (such as protests, boycotts) (Tarrow 2005: 45).

demonstrated how NGOs influenced international negotiations on the Kyoto Protocol's compliance mechanisms. NGOs with expertise are more likely to gain access to international negotiations and be influential (Dellmuth and Tallberg 2017).

Meanwhile, Stroup and Wong argue that leading international NGOs have a 'deep well of expertise', which is a key source of their authority (2017: 6).[43] They explore how authority varies across different NGOs and suggest that because some NGOs are more successful at developing expertise, they are more widely recognized and wield greater authority (Stroup and Wong 2017). In some of the IR scholarship, the role of expertise is not as explicit as in Stroup and Wong's work. However, it is often implied that advocates are committed to an issue, and over time build up a degree of expertise on this cause. They are unlikely to start campaigns on new issues where they lack policy expertise, as they will not command the same authority (Halpin et al. 2018).

Beyond the IR literature, other scholars have highlighted the rise of issue specialists in advocacy and social movements in the 1990s. Tarrow and della Porta explain that the 'world of the 1990s saw a focus on single issues, and hope that epistemic communities would build a new cooperative world' but they suggest that this has now changed (Tarrow and della Porta 2005: 232). Tony Judt noted that human rights advocacy offered a seductive 'anti-politics' which 'misled a generation of young activists into believing that ... they should forsake political organization for single-issue, non-governmental groups unsullied by compromise' (cited in Mishra 2018). These scholars collectively argue that advocacy in the 1980s and 1990s was based on issue-focused organizing, and this may now be changing, perhaps due in part to the rise of digital advocacy organizations.

Multi-Issue Generalists

> There is no such thing as a single-issue struggle because we do not live single-issue lives.
>
> (Lorde 1984)

OPEN organizations do not adopt a single focus, but campaign across many issues simultaneously. They justify this approach according to the same logic as Lorde because 'people, unlike most organizations, focus on and care about

[43] Stoup and Wong (2017) note that NGO authority may also come from their experience, and/or virtue, but they focus predominantly on expertise in their book.

many different issues based on their set of values'.[44] They contend that the daily news presents people with a range of topics that 'will inflame their support or ire' and OPEN organizations try to channel that energy to grow and create change, 'wherever change is most urgent and possible' and bring a 'surge of power to single-issue campaigns when it matters most'.[45] Their power comes from their ability to mobilize their members, not from their expertise on an issue. They pursue outsider strategies of change, not insider lobbying strategies.

Being member-driven and multi-issue go hand-in-hand for OPEN organizations. They campaign simultaneously on climate change, gay rights, economic inequality, environmental issues, and refugee protection. They use email, online petitions, and social media, to rapidly and frequently establish, switch, and drop campaigns, depending on what issues gain most attention and support (Price 2017: 38). Thanks to the low costs of organizing online, they have few sunk costs in any particular campaign. They attract a broader range of people than issue-specific NGOs such as Human Rights Watch or Greenpeace. They campaign 'full-spectrum', meaning that they offer members multiple ways to engage in issue-based advocacy and election campaigning. Members may contribute their skills, opinions, social networks, knowledge, votes, material resources, and money in advancing a campaign. These organizations do more than offer online petitions.

Staff in digital advocacy organizations have expertise in a skill set: digital campaigning. They hire staff specifically for their tech expertise and have permanent positions for software developers who can build and maintain websites, content management systems, and digital analytics tools to track members' engagement. New staff learn how to write engaging emails to their members and make concise, catchy Facebook content. Their use of a wide range of digital tools enables them to rapidly and efficiently mobilize hundreds—if not thousands—of people.

In contrast with most traditional NGOs, digital advocacy organizations do not have subject area expertise. Rather, they call on external experts to provide input and check that their campaigns are factually correct (Horstink 2017: 116). Avaaz, for example, which runs campaigns on issues ranging from lesbian, gay, bisexual, and transgender (LGBT) rights to anti-whaling, does not have in-house experts on all the issues it campaigns on. In 2016, Avaaz ran a campaign against whaling in Norway, and had to check with a marine biologist

[44] OPEN, https://www.the-open.net/network (accessed 4 December 2021).
[45] ibid.

expert whether the whales of concer were in fact officially endangered before sending an email to its members.[46]

Sustained Commitment vs Rapid Response

The Infantry: Sustained Commitment to a Cause

IR scholars often focus on advocacy organizations who have a sustained commitment to a cause, regardless of the level of public support (Busby 2010; Finnemore and Sikkink 1998; Jurkovich 2020; Medie 2020). Activists such as the suffragettes and abolitionists lobbied to get their respective causes into the mainstream precisely when the elite and most of the public did not care about the issue (Keck and Sikkink 1998). Both of these campaigns sought to reframe the public debate and convince decision-makers to change their policies through long-term, sustained action. These activists will continue to campaign in the face of strong opposition (Bob 2012).

IR scholars have examined how NGOs can exercise influence through agenda-setting (Keck and Sikkink 1998). Their power derives from framing and defining a new problem and offering a policy solution. Groups may advocate for new international legal agreements, as in the campaign to ban landmines (Price 2003); campaign for a fair and ambitious climate change agreement (Dellmuth and Tallberg 2017; Hadden 2015); or argue for freedom of information laws (Berliner 2016). They may also monitor compliance with existing international laws and hold businesses to account for abuses of human rights (Wong 2012) or monitor illegal fishing activity (Eilstrup-Sangiovanni 2019). Advocacy actors may change their strategies and tactics according to political opportunities, but remain committed to a particular cause for principled, moral reasons.[47]

NGOs do not typically start a campaign and then immediately drop it. Campaigns are fought on contested issues, where strong vested interests block changes to the status quo (Bob 2012). Advocacy organizations need a strong, principled commitment to their cause to sustain pressure over a long period of time. They often have to navigate intransigent, or reluctant governments, and face public backlash and critique (Bob 2012).

[46] Discussion with digital campaigner, April 2017, Berlin.

[47] Note that more recent scholarship has problematized whether transnational NGOs are principled or 'instrumental' actors, maximizing their funding to survive. Research on over 150 transnational NGOs finds that they are 'principled instrumentalists' and stay committed to their cause, while navigating funding constraints (Mitchell and Schmitz 2014).

Most NGOs have a relatively stable list of issues they campaign on, given that it can take years—if not decades—to make significant progress. Rogers (2018) has studied Greenpeace International's issue commitment and found that it is 'remarkably consistent' in the main issues it campaigns on. Between 2006 and 2012, it ran campaigns every year on: nuclear energy, oceans, forests, climate, and peace and disarmament (Rogers 2018). Although a few other issues—genetic engineering and sustainable trade—appeared during this time, there was continuity in its core campaigns. Greenpeace continues to campaign in the face of public and elite issue fatigue because it is morally committed to environmental issues. Many other NGOs derive their power and authority from their expertise and commitment to an issue, and typically sustain their campaigns over several years.

The Cavalry: Rapid-Response Campaigning

> It is sometimes said that traditional issue campaigning groups function like an infantry unit. They do the hard, critical work of slogging away in the trenches day after day on whatever issue is most important to them—regardless of the odds of success or attention being paid at any given time. This type of advocacy is essential for pushing issues out of obscurity towards key decision points and building a core base of committed support. But on its own, it is incomplete. The new model, on the other hand, functions more like a cavalry unit—a highly mobile fighting force that can be rushed into battle whenever there is a critical tipping point moment and an influx of new troops can bring victory within reach.
>
> (Brandzel 2010)

Digital advocacy organizations are 'highly reactive' to the issues that grab political and public attention (Vaughan 2020). As Brandzel describes, they operate like 'cavalry', swooping in to provide the final force to win a campaign. A sense of urgency is also important to mobilize members to sign or donate. OPEN groups will look out for a 'crisitunity', a term coined by Brandzel to describe moments which are both a crisis and an opportunity, and mobilize public pressure to sway a decision (Dominus 2010).

In their email communications, digital advocacy organizations will set a deadline—often a few days later—and a description of the crisitunity situation to spur members to take action (Horstink 2017). They will offer 'their members a means to take immediate action' and encourage them to be 'decisive and act quickly'. As Brandzel has explained: 'Because we are member driven, we "Chase the Energy"' and 'Energy flows with news cycles, and the opportunity to make a difference'.[48]

Precisely because they are constantly scanning for new politically salient issues, digital advocacy groups can claim a comparative advantage in identifying tipping-point moments and mobilizing people rapidly to pressurize decision-makers. Tipping-point moments could include a decision-making deadline such as an international summit, an election or referendum (e.g. Brexit), or a new urgent issue which has gained public attention (e.g. refugees entering Europe in the summer of 2015). By comparison with most traditional NGOs, digital advocacy organizations are less likely to campaign for an issue that is not already on the public agenda (Halpin et al. 2018; Hall 2019b; Vaughan 2020). For this reason, some decision-makers and other civil society organizations perceive digital-based organizations as opportunists, as will be explored further in Chapter 4.

Digital-based advocacy groups can rapidly launch new campaigns, thanks to their low levels of internal bureaucracy. They can set up a new campaign webpage, contact their members, send out an online petition, and put pressure on decision-makers within hours of breaking-news stories. They have chosen to prioritize nimble organizational processes over formalized bureaucratic processes so they can start and switch campaigns within hours (Hall and Ireland 2016). There are typically few sign-off processes to initiate a petition or email members, although staff may require a sign-off to send an email to their full list.

Thanks to the lower costs of campaigning and communicating via the internet, these advocacy organizations can also jump from one issue to another. Failure is not costly (Shirky 2008) because it takes little time and cost to send an email or post on social media (Carty 2011; Chadwick and Dennis, 2016; Karpf 2012). Organizations can start a campaign and then drop it a day or two later if members are not interested, or if another, more pressing issue emerges (Karpf 2016). In contrast, most traditional NGOs spend significant time and staff resources researching, strategizing, planning, and executing campaigns. They then pay to post letters to members, purchase advertisements in mainstream media, and hire people to spend hours collecting signatures or donations on the street. These invested costs made it difficult to abandon a campaign from one day to the next (Fraussen and Halpin 2017).

[48] Brandzel cited in Hayes (2008).

NGOs occasionally engaged in urgent actions even before the advent of the internet. Humanitarian organizations, for example, made mass appeals for funding after a natural disaster. Amnesty International's original letter-writing campaigns were a form of rapid response at the time.[49] However, these NGOs relied on the postal system, newspaper and radio advertising, and subsequently television, to communicate directly to members, which, of course, took time. Staff had to write a letter, place hundreds of letters into envelopes, and then post them.[50] It then took several days, at a minimum, for post to reach members and so it was virtually impossible to respond rapidly to breaking news (even if the news cycle was also much slower in the pre-internet era) (Karpf 2012). Amnesty's urgent letter-writing actions were *fast* responses but were often part of sustained, long-term campaigns for prisoners of conscience.

Digital Campaigning

Digital Broadcasting

Most NGOs use email, social media, and other digital platforms to broadcast their messages.[51] For example, a 2019 survey of 5,721 NGOs from around the world found that 80 per cent have a website, 71 per cent regularly send email updates to donors and supporters, and 90 per cent habitually use social media to engage their members and donors (Nonprofit Tech for Good 2019). Of the NGOs surveyed, 78 per cent agreed that social media is effective for creating social change. However, the survey did not investigate if or how social media is effective in campaigning. NGOs frequently use their websites, social media, and email communications to release reports and share news stories. They use digital platforms to broadcast their messages to their members and the broader public.

Some NGOs have also begun to test and customize their messaging to different audiences and to devolve power to their members to launch their own campaigns (Hall et al. 2020). Greenpeace, for example, has experimented

[49] Thanks to Hans Peter Schmitz for this point. Amnesty International researchers in London identified prisoners of conscience and asked their membership to write letters on their behalf to political leaders (Lake and Wong 2009).

[50] The author speaks from personal experience. She was hired as a university student to do mail-outs for Oxfam New Zealand and it often took days to stuff and send a few hundred letters.

[51] There are at least two other digital strategies NGOs can employ: conversing and testing. I focus here on digital broadcasting, as it is most frequently used by NGOs, and testing is most commonly used by digital advocacy organizations and will be discussed later. See Hall et al. 2020 for a longer discussion of NGOs' digital strategies.

with decentralized, distributed campaigning (Silberman 2017). Some national Greenpeace chapters have experimented with e-petition platforms, where members can start their own online petitions. Greenpeace International in 2018 also outlined a new 'disruption theory of change', which emulated the rapid-response mentality of OPEN organizations. As it explained, 'We can and should continue working on issues in a long-term way, but we must also be able to react quickly when something shifts in the world. We must be both agile and tenacious' (Greenpeace 2018). It also emphasized that it wanted to put 'people power at the heart of what we do and how we do it' (Greenpeace 2018). However, Greenpeace also wants to ensure it has effective and coordinated national and international campaigns and would not delegate power completely to its members to choose all campaigns.

Most NGOs are risk-averse and reluctant to devolve decision-making power to their members. Amnesty International, for example, has a centralized process whereby staff propose new campaigns (Wong 2012). Amnesty's members are generally not human rights experts, and have jobs, families, and other commitments. Members pay Amnesty staff to do human rights monitoring on their behalf and inform them of important issues to campaign on.

Even Greenpeace did not fully delegate decision-making power to members to choose core campaigns. A former Greenpeace staffer who worked on digitally distributed campaigns explained that: 'larger organizations have trouble breaking out of the command and control model, and letting people take control of the organization and the mission'.[52] This is because their power is most commonly derived from their expertise and moral authority over an issue; as Wong states, 'information is the value added by NGOs' (Wong 2012: 77). While many NGOs are experimenting with digital strategies, they rarely build 'digitally' networked power amongst their members, unlike digital advocacy organizations (Hall et al. 2020).

Digitally Networked Power

Digitally networked power involves distributing tools and resources to members, and enabling them to coordinate actions and lead campaigns in their own districts (Hall et al. 2020). Staff build a 'movement story' about how a particular campaign or action will contribute to political change.[53] Digital organizers focus on members' experience within the organization (often referred to as

[52] Interview with Michael Silberman, 4 March 2021.

[53] Ben Brandzel, email training Powerpoint. On file with the author.

the 'member journey') and look to deepen and broaden their commitment (Han 2014). Digital advocacy organizations will facilitate their members to act collectively and put pressure on decision-makers.

Seasoned digital campaigners frequently refer to this new model of networked power as their source of influence. Jeremy Heimans, one of the founders of GetUp, has noted that 'new' power 'is made by many. It is open, participatory, and peer-driven' (Heimans and Timms 2018: 8). Digital advocacy organizations are willing to hand over a significant degree of power to their members to select campaign issues, tactics, and actions; and use digital platforms to facilitate this. Thanks to email, social media, and other digital tools, these advocacy organizations can listen to, and aggregate their members' preferences and mobilise them to take action. As Becky Jarvis, former 38 Degrees and OPEN staffer explained, 'you don't have to go around a pub collecting signatures one-by-one', but can put up an online petition and overnight have thousands of signatures without hiring any extra staff.[54] Other NGOs and social movements also use outsider strategies—mobilizing people to demonstrate dissatisfaction with the status quo—and many are now setting up digital petitions. However, most traditional NGOs do not delegate power to their members to select the issues they campaign on, or the tactics they should use.

One way to build digitally networked power is through distributed campaigning. Distributed campaigning involves a loose affiliation of individuals who are not part of a federated organization with formal membership obligations (e.g. membership fees) (Gibson 2015; Fisher 2019b). Activists have no defined geographic location, but are connected online through a digital advocacy organization such as MoveOn (Karpf 2012). This form of bottom-up campaigning uses technology to connect people (Fisher 2019b: 15). Importantly, individuals are given the freedom to decide how to engage with any campaign. This approach means using tactics that allow for a 'locus of leadership in the hands of many individuals'.[55] This can entail asking individuals to chair their own local group, host events, or run their own petitions. As I have argued elsewhere, 'the power generated in this scenario is not derived from controlling a specific material or ideational resource, but from establishing a non-hierarchical form of collective action with abilities to adapt and scale up' (Hall et al. 2020: 163).

[54] Interview with Becky Jarvis, 20 June 2019.
[55] Interview with Ben Brandzel, 30 January 2021.

Although IR scholars have not studied digital advocacy organizations, they have explored how power can be derived from the ability of actors to organize collectively, scale up rapidly, and adapt to changing circumstances (Slaughter 2016; Slaughter 2004; Hafner-Burton et al. 2009). This type of power involves working closely with others to accomplish goals that no one actor could achieve alone (Sikkink 2020).[56] Scholars have also contrasted traditional conceptions of hierarchical power—where outcomes are imposed by one actor over another—with the power of networks. As Slaughter explains, 'Networks are not directed and controlled as much as they are managed and orchestrated. Multiple players are integrated into a whole that is greater than the sum of its parts' (Slaughter 2009). Obama's 2009 election campaign, for example, was successful in part because of its relatively flat structure and emphasis on devolving power to individual organizers (Slaughter 2009). Obama's campaign could mobilize and coordinate thousands of volunteers' time and funding, thanks to digital technologies.

Digital advocacy organizations regularly experiment with devolving power to their members, and distributed campaigning tactics. For example, in 2012, MoveOn decided to make a radical shift in its campaigning and put its members in charge of all its campaigns.[57] Justin Ruben, the Executive Director of MoveOn's political action group explained that: 'we're turning over the keys of our technological toolset to our more than 7 million members, asking them to step up and lead their own campaigns, and putting them squarely in the MoveOn driver's seat' (Ruben 2012). MoveOn built 'DIY [do it yourself] organizing tools' such as SignOn.org, which members use to start their own petitions and invite other members to take part.[58] Most other OPEN organizations emulated MoveOn, and later launched their own member-initiated petition platform. What was remarkable in MoveOn's case was that for a period *all* of its campaigns were member-initiated, and it ran no national, staff-driven campaigns.

Ruben (2012) saw great power and potential in handing over control to MoveOn's members. As he described:

[56] Sikkink, for instance, has also argued that we need a theory of 'networked responsibilities' to tackle complex global issues, such as climate change and digital privacy, for which 'decisions are decentralized and are especially in need of networked obligations' (Sikkink 2020: 12–13).

[57] According to Ben Brandzel, they had considered launching a member petition platform in 2006/2007 but had decided against it as it was seen as too expensive, and there was a concern that MoveOn would decentralize their efforts and dilute the influence of their members. Interview with Ben Brandzel, 30 January 2021.

[58] MoveOn also supported over 175 volunteer-led local councils that then ran their own local campaigns (Ruben 2012).

> The old model was: MoveOn members set our direction, and then MoveOn staff decided which tactics to employ, and when. Our reach was necessarily limited by the small size of our staff. We're turning that model inside out. Now our reach will be limited by the number of leaders we can empower. Imagine thousands of grassroots leaders, engaging over 7 million MoveOn members far more deeply than we ever have before, popping out victories from coast to coast.
>
> (Ruben 2012)

The result was that MoveOn ran many reactive and more local campaigns, but no national campaigns. A former MoveOn staffer, Ben Brandzel, claimed, MoveOn made this shift because of the competition from Change.org (a for-profit campaigning company that had become popular in the United States and enabled people to start their own petitions with almost no organizational moderation). In addition, 'they had reached their limit with what they could do with Obama' and national campaigning was stuck because the Republicans controlled Congress.[59] MoveOn later returned to hosting both staff and member-initiated campaigns because it realized that staff-driven campaigns were still important. This trade-off between staff and member-led campaigning is explored in Chapter 8.

Distributed campaigning, in its purest form, is not a *coordinated* national campaign. Power is distributed to a loose affiliation of individuals who initiate their own campaigns. However, digital advocacy organizations and political parties often employ 'directed network' strategies. In this situation, an organization will offer a centralized structure and plan *and* mobilize a broad network to implement campaigns online and offline. Political parties often adopt this strategy, as their core goal is to get a particular political leader elected, and they want to mobilize as many as possible. Gibson emphasizes that the 'innovative aspect lies in the extent of the ordinary citizen input that occurs in their initiation and execution via digital media. So while not becoming equal partners in the election enterprise, grassroots supporters are given a stronger "co-producing role" in the campaign than has hitherto been the case' (Gibson 2015: 187).[60] Indeed, some digital activist experts have argued that groups have greater impact when they combine distributed campaigning with a centralized campaign plan (Mogus and Liacas 2016: 6; Bond and Exley 2016).

[59] Interview with Ben Brandzel, 30 January 2021. Brandzel, who was then no longer at MoveOn, was 'critical of the move—not of the tactic, but [rather the] complete abrogation of MoveOn's national campaigns'.

[60] Gibson uses the term 'citizen-initiated campaigning' rather than distributed campaigning, but the concept is very similar. She defines it as when 'digitally registered supporters who are not necessarily members make use of online tools crated by the party of the candidate team to campaign both online and offline on its behalf' (2015: 187).

Chapter 7 will explore further the power of digitally distributed campaigning in the climate movement.

US presidential candidates have frequently used directed distributed campaigns to mobilize supporters. The Democrats began hiring digital campaigning experts and gave them high-level decision-making power in election campaigns well before the Republicans (Kreiss 2016). Howard Dean's campaign in 2004 used MeetUp to enable volunteers to connect. Obama's campaign crowdsourced micro-donations and organized event pages where people could sign up and volunteer to host their own events. Becky Bond and Zack Exley, two senior campaigners for Bernie Sanders's 2016 presidential campaign, outlined the importance of a 'big organizing' strategy in *Rules for Revolutionaries.*[61] Big organizing involves maximizing the number of people involved in a movement by using digital platforms such as Facebook, Twitter, and email. Bond and Exley suggested that a centralized campaign plan is critical to ensure that volunteer actions work towards a common goal (Bond and Exley 2016). However, they also suggested that campaigns should devolve decision-making to volunteers to take leadership. After all, relying on paid professional staff limits the human resources and reach of a campaign. Bond and Exley shared their 'rules' for campaigning with OPEN start-ups at a summit in Berlin in August 2016 (Dennis and Hall 2020).[62] Many OPEN groups find that there is a delicate balance between devolving power to volunteers and keeping control of campaign decisions within professional staff. This is often expressed as a tension between stewardship campaigning and purely member-driven campaigning; this will be examined further in Chapters 4 and 8.

IR scholars have noted the power of networks in international politics (Kahler 2009; Slaughter 2016). However, to date IR scholars have not examined this new generation of digital advocacy organizations and how they are harnessing digitally networked power.

Conclusion

Thanks to the internet, a new generation of powerful digital advocacy organizations has emerged. They have helped to defeat conservative candidates in Canada, the United States, and Australia, and are recognized by politicians and the media as exercising considerable influence in national politics. In fact, in several countries conservative politicians have sought to change electoral rules

[61] The title *Rules for Revolutionaries* emulates Saul Alinsky's *Rules for Radicals.*

[62] The author was present at this summit.

to curb their influence. These organizations' power comes from their ability to mobilize people rapidly at tipping-point moments. They rarely have expertise on the issues they campaign on, but rather foster skills in digital campaigning. They hire tech staff to develop specific tools and technologies—such as Koorangang (GetUp's phonebanking tool) and Sign.on (MoveOn's distributed petition platform). These tools enable members to self-organize actions and invite other members to engage.

Digital advocacy organizations have power because they listen closely to members' preferences, and campaign on the issues members are most concerned about. They have a different model from most NGOs. Digital advocacy organizations regularly run surveys, test their email messages, and use digital analytics to efficiently aggregate members preferences and decide on tactics and campaign issues. Staff constantly monitor what is most salient to members and can quickly react to breaking news. When the model works successfully, they can mobilize thousands of their members at tipping-point moments and facilitate digitally networked people power.

How did this model emerge and spread internationally? Chapter 3 will examine how and why activists in South Africa, Poland, New Zealand, Romania, and beyond emulated this organizational model. It explores why activists decided to form nationally based digital advocacy organizations, despite living in a globalized world.

3

The Global Growth of Digital Advocacy Organizations

At age twenty-four, Jamie Biggar was on the leadership team of the Canadian Youth Climate Coalition. Like many other climate activists, he hoped that the 2009 United Nations Framework Convention on Climate Change (UNFCCC) summit would deliver a strong and binding international agreement. It did not. The two-week-long negotiations in copenhagen culminated in an all-night session in which states failed to reach an agreement. Rather, states were invited to 'take note' of the final accord (Werksman 2009). Disillusioned with the lack of a precise, strong, and legally binding international agreement, climate activists such as Biggar looked for other models of organizing (Moor 2020; Fisher 2010).

In the aftermath of the 2009 summit, traditional environmental non-governmental organizations (NGOs), such as Greenpeace, realized that the tactics and strategies they had been using for decades were no longer working as effectively as in the past. Kumi Naidoo, the international executive director of Greenpeace, described the Copenhagen summit as a 'Burning platform moment—a time to embrace a new model for impact or risk becoming irrelevant' (*MobLab* 2017). Greenpeace had seen the success of Avaaz and 350.org, which had mobilized millions worldwide for climate action with just a handful of staff, thanks to their savvy use of the internet. In contrast, Greenpeace, a large climate NGO with decades of experience and significant funding, had struggled to mobilize on the same scale. Staff realized that the organization relied on an older organizing model that did not take advantage of digitally networked people power, and would be 'eaten-up by the start-ups'.[1] These 'small-scrappy organizations' had 'out-performed' traditional NGOs, thanks to their ability to facilitate digitally networked power.[2] In response, in 2010,

[1] Online interview with Tom Liacas, 13 April 2017.
[2] ibid.

Transnational Advocacy in the Digital Era. Nina Hall, Oxford University Press.
 DOI: 10.1093/oso/9780198858744.003.0003

Greenpeace launched a new initiative, *MobLab*, to emulate 350.org's successful digitally distributed campaigning.

Meanwhile, for other activists there was an increasing realization that single-issue climate organizing had been taken 'as far as it could go', and that activists needed a 'broader, faster-acting, but also more deeply engaged constituency than what climate organizing alone could ever deliver'.[3] Jamie Biggar was one of these activists. After many conversations with Ben Brandzel, a former MoveOn staffer, about the power of multi-issue digital advocacy organizations, Biggar decided to launch Leadnow in Canada. In his resignation letter to Leadnow many years later, he explained that:

> The seed [for Leadnow] began to grow as people from the Canadian youth climate movement emerged after the wreckage of the Copenhagen Climate Conference. We came out of Copenhagen ready to do everything we could to bring people together across party lines to defeat Harper, strengthen our democracy and take on major challenges facing our generation.[4]

This chapter charts the emergence and spread of digital advocacy organization worldwide. It identifies two distinct phases which are illustrated in Figure 3.1[5]

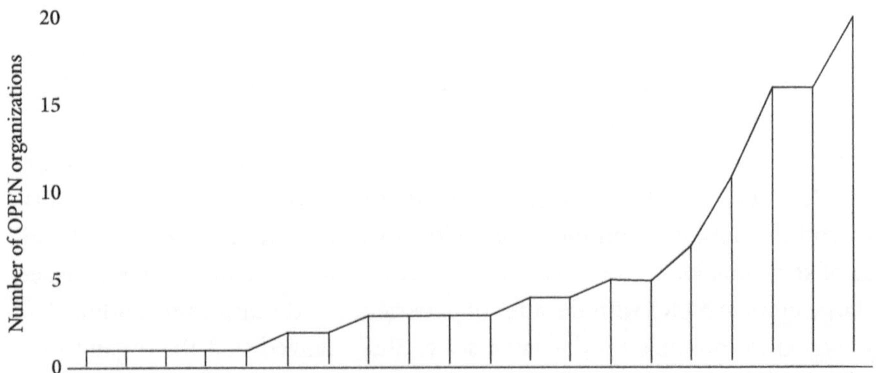

Fig. 3.1 The growth of OPEN organizations
Source: OPEN. (2018). 'Growth of OPEN Organizations'. (On file with author)

[3] Email communication with Ben Brandzel, 29 June 2021.

[4] He stated that the 'seed for Leadnow was planted by a tiny crew that set up Canadians for a Progressive Coalition after the 2008 election', https://www.leadnow.ca/dear-leadnow-community-thank-you/(accessed 5 December 2021).

[5] There are several other newer initiatives which are not included in this graph: De Goede Zaak in the Netherlands, Serbia on the Move in Serbia, and Nossas, a Brazilian organization. Nossas grew

During the first phase (1998–2013), new digital advocacy organizations were established in the United States (MoveOn), Germany (Campact), Australia (GetUp), the UK (38 Degrees), and Canada (Leadnow). Then, in 2013, these five organizations met and decided to form a transnational network: the Online Progressive Engagement Network (OPEN). Subsequently, OPEN hired secretariat staff, and actively supported the spread of digital advocacy organizations. In the second phase (2013–2020), OPEN supported the propagation and/or emulation of digital advocacy organizations in over fifteen countries, albeit with some failures. Importantly, all those involved in OPEN established *nationally based* digital advocacy organizations which tackled global issues. The chapter examines why this particular form was promoted by OPEN.

The MoveOn Model Goes Global (1998–2013)

United States and MoveOn (1998)

In 1998, Bill Clinton was impeached after being caught lying about his relationship with Monica Lewinsky. Two software developers—Wes Boyd and Joan Blades—developed an online petition to encourage the US Congress to censure Bill Clinton and 'move on' to other pressing issues facing the country. The concept was simple: they set up a website and asked people to fill in their name and contact information as a means of expressing their discontent with the impeachment process. They then sent an email to 100 friends with a link to moveon.org. Shortly afterwards, the local San Francisco Chronicle mentioned their petition and noted that the site had attracted 500 signatures in its first day online (Hayes 2008). By the end of that week, the petition had received 100,000 signatures and eventually received 500,000 signatures.

While the petition did not have a significant impact on the impeachment process in Congress, Boyd and Blades realized that they had found a powerful way to mobilize citizens at rapid pace (Karpf 2012).[6] They had a hit upon a new model that enabled large numbers of people to take action, who otherwise

out of a Rio-based organization, Meu Rio, which focused on mobilizing people at the city level. They attended an OPEN summit for the first time in 2019 as prospective members. OPEN tends to classify organizations as: 'prospective members'; 'start-up', or 'full members'.

[6] Notably, Facebook and other social media platforms did not exist when MoveOn was launched in 1998, so campaigns were primarily based on email.

would not. As Blades recalls: 'I still remember one of our early e-mails: a woman wrote in and said, You know, I've never done anything political. I'm a single mom. I get home and feed my son. This [signing a petition, forwarding an e-mail] is something I can do' (Hayes 2008). Boyd and Blades hired staff, and launched a series of other email petition campaigns. In its early years, during the Clinton presidency, MoveOn was not seen as an influential or 'game-changing powerhouse' but more an 'odd-anecdote' illustrating the ease of internet mobilizing (Karpf 2012).

However, MoveOn grew rapidly during George W. Bush's presidency, as progressives looked for new ways to organize and campaign (Karpf 2012). MoveOn positioned itself as an independent, progressive organization and was a leader of the anti-Iraq war movement (Heaney and Rojas 2007). In the aftermath of 9/11, Boyd and Blades hired Eli Pariser, a young activist who had launched an extremely successful independent online petition to encourage international leaders to use 'moderation and restraint' in their response to the attacks (Hayes 2008). Pariser's petition received 515,000 signatures within the first two weeks and Pariser agreed to merge his email list with MoveOn's. From the beginning of Bush's war on terror, MoveOn had a large, and engaged membership who wanted to restrain the United States' response.

MoveOn was powerful because it kept email addresses for all those who signed a petition, enabling them to recontact signatories for future campaigns.[7] Ruben, later an executive director of MoveOn, explained that the model works because 'every action taken ends up in our database. It's all in one place and the data set is enormous, which if you're a geek is awesome' (Hayes 2008). Brandzel has described the power MoveOn derived by storing emails from one campaign to another as 'potential energy' which can then be used later as 'kinetic energy' when there is a critical moment of resistance.[8] MoveOn also relied on these members to fund the organization. This different from the approach of many traditional NGOs, which often rely on grant funding, in addition to membership dues. MoveOn's campaigns against the Iraq war gained attention worldwide, including in Germany.

[7] Note that political campaigns have always sought to create large contact lists of potential supporters, even in the pre-internet era (Perlstein 2012). However, MoveOn did this in an innovative way through use of online petitions and email.

[8] Interview with Ben Brandzel, 30 January 2021.

Germany and Campact (2004)

In 2004, Felix Kolb, a PhD student in Bremen, Germany, walked past a colleague's office and noticed on the wall a MoveOn poster saying, 'Regime change begins at home'.[9] Kolb, whose academic work focused on the impact of social movements, had worked with petitions before. However, MoveOn presented a novel way of mobilizing people by capturing their email addresses for future campaigns. Kolb explained to me that: '[it] never occurred to me to use this as an organizational model'.[10]

Kolb was already well connected within the German and broader European activist community. In 2000, he and his friend, Christoph Bautz, had helped set up the German branch of the Association for the Taxation of Financial Transactions of Citizens (ATTAC),[11] a French-based organization that advocated for a Tobin tax on currency transactions.[12] Using what Kolb described as a savvy media strategy, in 2001, Kolb and Bautz helped ATTAC Germany to become the 'de-facto umbrella organization of the German global justice movement' (Kolb 2005). Kolb and Bautz, through ATTAC, became well networked within the broader European global justice movement.

In 2003, Kolb convinced Bautz to go to New York with him to meet Eli Pariser, then the executive director of MoveOn. They wanted to pitch starting the 'German MoveOn', similar to how they had replicated ATTAC in Germany.[13] Their idea was to take the name, model, and most importantly, MoveOn's German email list (which had grown significantly during the Iraq war) to set up an autonomous organization. They saw potential in the model for the 'empowerment of people in Germany'.[14] Pariser met with them, but in the end did not give them a green light to take MoveOn's name, or their German followers. Pariser knew neither Bautz nor Kolb, and MoveOn wanted to focus on advocacy in the United States (Kanter 2015).

Kolb and Bautz were undeterred. In 2004, they established their own German version of MoveOn, Campact, to 'fill a gap' in Germany advocacy.[15]

[9] Interview with Felix Kolb, 9 February 2018. The poster was part of MoveOn's anti-Iraq war campaign.

[10] ibid.

[11] ATTAC was founded in 1998 in France; Kolb and Bautz were involved in setting up a German chapter.

[12] For an excellent summary of ATTAC's development from Kolb's perspective, see Kolb (2005). The Tobin tax was a proposal by economist James Tobin in the 1970s. He suggested levying a small tax—for instance, 0.1 per cent—whenever money was exchanged from one currency to another. See https://www.ft.com/content/6210e49c-9307-11de-b146-00144feabdc0 (accessed 5 December 2021).

[13] Interview with Felix Kolb, 9 February 2018.

[14] Interview with Campact co-founder, 9 February 2018.

[15] Interview with Günter Metzges, 9 December 2016.

They worked with Günter Metzges, the third co-founder, and established an office in Verden, near Bremen, where ATTAC was also headquartered. One of Campact's first campaigns was successful: Campact called for the income of German parliamentarians to be publicly disclosed, won the campaign, and, most importantly, added its first 10,000 email subscribers to its list.[16] As Campact grew, it campaigned on a broad range of environmental, economic, and social issues. These included campaigns against genetically modified organisms (GMOs), nuclear power, tax evasion, climate change, and free trade agreements.

Bautz, Kolb, and Metzges emulated and adapted the MoveOn model to the German context. They used their large email lists to organize mass demonstrations, which attracted thousands of people. They coordinated closely with other German civil society organizations to organize large anti-Transatlantic Trade and Intellectual Property Agreement (TTIP) protests across Germany, including one of the largest demonstrations in Germany since the Iraq war protests.[17] They were the first and only group to date to have replicated the MoveOn model from afar with no strong personal ties to MoveOn or other digital activists.

Australia and GetUp (2005)

Meanwhile, in Australia, two seasoned activists, Jeremy Heimans and David Madden, decided to establish GetUp in 2005 (Vromen 2017: 83). They had both worked at MoveOn and were inspired by how powerful it was in the United States. They wanted to use the same underlying principles (rapid-response, digitally based, multi-issue, membership-driven advocacy) to build a digital mass movement of progressive Australians (Vromen 2017: 84).[18] Heimans and Madden worked closely with a union organizer, Amanda Tattersall, who provided an initial start-up grant of $50,000 Australian dollars (Vromen 2017: 84).[19] GetUp benefitted from having well-established personal networks with former MoveOn staffers.

[16] ibid.

[17] There were reports of between 150,000 protesters (police estimate) and 250,000 protesters (organizers' estimate) who marched to the Brandenburg Gate in Berlin. See https://www.tagesschau.de/wirtschaft/ttip-proteste-103.html (accessed 5 December 2021).

[18] GetUp, 'Jeremy Heimans on New Power', Facebook interview, https://www.facebook.com/GetUpAustralia/videos/10155239945361455/ (accessed 5 December 2021).

[19] GetUp is now funded by small donations from individuals, and does not accept funding from political parties or government agencies (Vromen 2017).

Heimans, Madden, and Tattersall were particularly concerned by the re-election of a conservative prime minister, John Howard. Howard's party had also taken control of the Senate and supported Bush's war in Iraq (Heimans and Timms 2018: 57; Vromen 2016). One of GetUp's first major campaigns was to bring home David Hicks, an Australian detainee in Guantanamo. This campaign was not merely about one individual, but about Howard's close alliance with the United States in the war on terror. Hicks was eventually returned to Australia in 2007 (GetUp 2017), and it became a defining campaign for GetUp, representing what the organization was willing to take on. The organization grew rapidly during the Howard years. By late 2015, GetUp had launched over 150 campaigns on issues as diverse as funding the mental health sector, helping asylum-seekers in detention, and advocating for social welfare and economic equality. GetUp developed quickly into a powerful organization because its founders had direct contact and experience with MoveOn, and so were easily able to replicate the model.

International and Avaaz (2007)

In 2005, Ricken Patel approached MoveOn with the vision of taking their model global. Patel was then working at Res Publica, but had previously volunteered with MoveOn, and had a sense of the model's power. MoveOn directly assisted the establishment of Avaaz. They 'seeded' Avaaz by giving Patel their international list of 700,000 people who had previously signed MoveOn Petitions.[20] MoveOn had no use for these international email addresses, as the voice of non-US citizens was unlikely to be as effective as US citizens at pressurizing the US Government. MoveOn even ran a campaign, led by Brandzel, to encourage people to join Avaaz (the campaign called for a ceasefire in the 2006 Israel–Lebanon war).[21] Although MoveOn never actively promoted the diffusion of its model, it was instrumental in launching Avaaz.

Avaaz's co-founders were part of a close-knit digital activist community, which enabled Avaaz to inherit critical resources.[22] Other co-founders included Jeremy Heimans, David Madden, Eli Pariser, Tom Perriello, Tom Pravada, and Andrea Woodhouse. Ben Brandzel, MoveOn's advocacy director

[20] Email correspondence with Ben Brandzel, 28 June 2021.

[21] Email communication with Ben Brandzel, 22 June 2018.

[22] Avaaz, AboutUs, https://web.archive.org/web/20080110084550/http://www.avaaz.org/en/about.php (accessed 5 December 2021).

Table 3.1 Transnational vs domestic organizing

	National	**Transnational**
Single-issue	National Rifle Association (NRA)	Greenpeace Amnesty International
Multi-issue	MoveOn.org Church groups Community groups	Avaaz

Note: This table is sourced directly from Avaaz (2006: 11).

(2004–2006) was particularly supportive of Avaaz. He subsequently became a founding member of the Board of Directors (2007–2016) as a MoveOn representative. He was also an early campaign director at Avaaz in 2007 and led training at the first staff meeting in Spain in 2007.

However, Avaaz differs fundamentally from all the other organizations described in this book because it an *international*, rather than a *national,* digital advocacy organization. In fact, Avaaz's 2007–2008 business plan identified a major gap in transnational, digital, multi-issue organizing (see Table 3.1). Avaaz argued that there were few effective digital organizations outside of the United States and saw an important global niche that MoveOn was not filling:

> existing civil society is overwhelmingly organised along national lines. Globalization has bought increasingly strong transnational networks, but they remain inter-national networks of national groups. Due to the constraints of travel, communication and cost, very few grassroots efforts involve building community that genuinely transcend borders. Citizens in different countries rarely connect directly with each other except through the leadership of civil society organizations they belong to. However, the internet offers the potential to build a truly transnational community for the first time …
>
> (Avaaz 2006: 11)

Avaaz sought to build a 'multi-lingual, online community of citizens across the world committed to global civil engagement' (Avaas 2006: 12).

In early 2021, Avaaz claimed to have 65 million members in 194 countries from India to Lebanon, Brazil, to Nauru.[23] Avaaz also has roughly 100 international staff scattered around the world. Staff do not work from any central offices, but rather from home, cafés, or start-up hubs. Avaaz campaigns can

[23] Avaaz, 'Community', https://secure.avaaz.org/page/en/community/ (accessed 5 December 2021).

be nationally or globally targeted. For instance, Avaaz played a significant role in Brazil's anti-corruption campaigns against leading politicians.[24] It also ran an international petition against Donald Trump when he was elected, stating, 'As citizens of the world, we stand united against your brand of division.'[25] However, Avaaz has a more centralized decision-making process than most organizations described here.[26] Even though Avaaz is primarily member-funded, and members are regularly consulted on campaigns, senior staff influence what campaigns are run. Avaaz is not part of OPEN, because it draws an international membership, rather than a national membership, and at times competes with the organizations described in this book for members' attention and funding.

The UK and 38 Degrees (2009)

By 2007, former MoveOn-staffer Ben Brandzel realized that the MoveOn model was taking off around the world. He had visited GetUp in Australia in 2007 and saw how quickly the organization had grown into a powerful force, and wondered whether he could replicate the model elsewhere. He then wrote an email to MoveOn's then executive director, Eli Pariser, and outlined his idea to: 'take the best of MoveOn to where it can help similar independent progressive groups around the world, and simultaneously bring the best of those groups to where it can help MoveOn' (Karpf 2013). Although Pariser thought that the idea had potential, he cautioned that 'You'll probably have to devote five years of your life to this.' Subsequently, Brandzel wrote in an email to a friend at Avaaz, Ben Wikler: 'I feel Project Appleseed beginning.' The underlying concept of OPEN was born and Brandzel started to proactively seed this new model of advocacy (Karpf 2013).

In 2008, Ben Brandzel travelled to the UK with the intention of starting a British version of MoveOn. Brandzel noticed that although both the United States and the UK had large anti-Iraq war demonstrations, groups in the

[24] Honorary Brazilian Consulate in Seattle, 'Avaaz's campaign in Brazil won a victory against corruption', email received from Ricken Patel, 28 July 2010, http://www.brazilianconsulateinseattle.com/2010/07/28/a-massive-online-campaign-by-the-avaaz-community-in-brazil-has-just-won-a-stunning-victory-against-corruption/ (accessed 5 December 2021). Avaaz has a very large membership in Brazil (over 18 million in 2021, according to their website, https://secure.avaaz.org/page/en/community/ (accessed 5 December 2021).

[25] Avaaz, 'Dear Mr.Trump', Avaaz online petition, https://secure.avaaz.org/campaign/en/president_trump_letter_loc/ (accessed 5 December 2021).

[26] Avaaz also has a very strong organizational culture—it has an internal document listing eight core cultural principles, and puts particular emphasis on giving and receiving feedback and cultivating a collaborative culture. It hosts regular (at least twice a year) summits where all Avaaz staff members meet in person to discuss campaigns and organizational development.

United States such as MoveOn had been able to 'capture' and 'store' the energy for future protests, whereas no groups had managed this in the UK.[27] This disparity between digital organizing in the United States and the UK motivated him to try and start a new digital advocacy organization from scratch.

Brandzel spent much of 2008 in the UK scouting for, assembling, and then working with the founding team. Brandzel worked with UK-based activists Nina Kowalska, Warren Puckett, and David Babbs to launch 38 Degrees. Babbs, like Leadnow's Jamie Biggar, was an environmental activist, who had previously been the head of activism at Friends of the Earth, and later became the first 38 Degrees executive director. They secured initial financing from Gordon Roddick (the husband of late Anita Roddick), Henry Tinsley, Pete Myers, and Paul Hilder. 38 Degrees states on its website that it was founded in 'memory of Anita Roddick [also the founder of the Body Shop], a lifetime champion of the power of ordinary people to make a difference'.[28]

As the 'chief founding advisor', Brandzel helped 38 Degrees founders to understand the MoveOn model (Karpf 2013).[29] Previous efforts to set up a UK-based digital advocacy organization had not worked, partly because people had tried to replicate the digital tactics of MoveOn without understanding the underlying model. Brandzel sought to 'demystify the wiring' of MoveOn by documenting its 'model of decision-making' and 'the practices of the staff that allowed them to successfully be member-driven'.[30] While in the UK, he developed the 'The 8-fold Path of New Organizing' or 'operating principles', which he often used to explain the organizing model to activists, and potential funders.[31] These eight operating principles are: multi-issue, nimble, member-led, digital, progressive, people-powered change, independent, and full-spectrum campaigning.

38 Degrees was established under a Labour government and grew considerably after the Conservative government was elected in 2010. By 2013, it had 1.7 million members (Karpf 2013), and in early 2021 it claimed to have two million members.[32] 38 Degrees established a permanent office in London, and

[27] Interview with Ben Brandzel, 30 January 2021.

[28] 38 Degrees, FAQs, https://home.38degrees.org.uk/faqs/faqs/ (accessed 5 December 2021).

[29] Online interview with Ben Brandzel, 30 January 2021.

[30] ibid. See also 38 Degrees (2008: 4).

[31] Online interview with Ben Brandzel, 30 January 2021. The eight elements are: multi-issue, nimble, member-led, digital, progressive, people-powered change, independent, and full-spectrum campaigning. The Commons (2016). "The Eight-Fold Path" https://commonslibrary.org/the-eight-fold-path/ (accessed 20 January 2022)

[32] 38 Degrees, 'About', https://home.38degrees.org.uk/about/ (accessed 5 December 2021). 38 Degrees has changed its definition of membership over time. Initially, membership was generally equated with email subscribers, but later it only counted members as those who had opened an email in the past three months. Email correspondence with Ben Brandzel, 28 June 2021.

now has twenty-five staff and an additional office in Edinburgh.[33] They campaign on a broad range of issues, including the National Health Service (NHS), the BBC, protecting national and woodlands parks, and tax credits for low-income families in work. 38 Degrees was the first digital advocacy organization Brandzel instigated, and there were others to come.[34]

Canada and Leadnow (2010)

In Canada, Jamie Biggar had also taken note of MoveOn's success. Alongside his work in climate activism, Biggar had helped to create Canadians for a Progressive Coalition, a petition which asked Canada's opposition parties to work together to defeat the Stephen Harper conservative government (Price 2017). He later met Ben Brandzel, who was then working at Citizen Engagement Laboratory (CEL), a US-based NGO which supported social entrepreneurs and start-ups to leverage the internet for social change. Brandzel was CEL's director of incubation and international programmes, and in this position could experiment, support, and incubate new digital advocacy organizations (Karpf 2013). Brandzel explained the eight-fold path to Biggar and helped Leadnow to emulate 38 Degrees, GetUp, and MoveOn.

Biggar became LeadNow's first executive director, and inherited an email list of 5,000 from the Canadians for a Progressive Coalition. After it launched, Leadnow ran a series of rapid-response campaigns and its membership grew to hundreds of thousands and is now over 600,000 (Price 2017).[35] Leadnow has staff members across Canada and a headquarters in Vancouver. It focuses 'on building a broad base of political power that can mobilize across issue sectors and engage large groups of people at critical moments in order to put issues on the map, or keep them in the public eye'.[36] It uses digital platforms to 'aggregate our supporters' voices, time and money into a powerful, democratic force'.[37] It relies overwhelmingly on member funding: in 2019, more than 93 per cent of its funding came from members' donations.[38] Biggar argues that there is value in asking people to take action: 'it's amazing how a not very political person will go from signing a petition to hosting a rally. It's because we

[33] 38 Degrees presentation at OPEN summit, Kangeroo Valley, Australia, January 2016.

[34] Interview with Ben Brandzel, 30 January 2021. Brandzel describes 38 Degrees as his first 'heavy proactive' engagement.

[35] Leadnow, http://www.leadnow.ca/faq/ (accessed 5 December 2021).

[36] ibid.

[37] ibid.

[38] ibid.

ask' (Price 2017). Former campaign's director, Logan McIntosh, has explained Leadnow's source of power: 'we win by engaging lots of people. For us we're finding we build better campaigns if we're informed by what people want to do' (Price 2017). Leadnow is an example of successful emulation of MoveOn, with 'heavy' support from Ben Brandzel.

The Formation of a Transnational Network

These five new digital advocacy organizations all saw MoveOn as an effective advocacy organization and sought to emulate it.[39] There were strong links between Anglo-sphere digital activists. Campact was the only organization that developed with no support from current or ex-MoveOn staffers. In fact, Brandzel has described Campact as a 'Galapagos' case, where 'all the Anglo-sphere [digital activists] were very connected to each other and knew each other but Campact was the only group of the entire 19 members of OPEN to begin fully on their own'.[40]

Interestingly, MoveOn as an organization never actively promoted its organizational model globally. 'Project Appleseed' was Brandzel's personal initiative. After working with Avaaz and MoveOn, Brandzel had initially tried to graft this new model onto international NGOs, such as Amnesty and Greenpeace, in the UK, the United States, and Australia.[41] However, he found it difficult to incorporate MoveOn tactics into established NGOs, which were often reluctant to devolve power to their members to determine campaigning issues and tactics.[42] Professional NGOs had high levels of bureaucracy, and tasked professional staff with selecting and running campaigns, not their members. Brandzel determined that the OPEN model could not be grafted onto existing organizations, but rather new organizations needed to start from scratch. After helping 38 Degrees, GetUp, and LeadNow in their formative years, Brandzel then decided to try and launch other new digital advocacy organizations around the world.[43]

In 2013, Brandzel, Michelle Dixon, Simon Sheikh (executive director of GetUp), and David Babbs (executive director of 38 Degrees) co-convened a

[39] This has also been described as a 'hybrid' model, which combines elements of political parties, interest groups and social movements and can switch rapidly between online and offline tactics in their campaigns. See Chadwick (2007).

[40] Email correspondence with Ben Brandzel, 29 June 2021. Brandzel recounts meeting the Campact founders for the first time at the Campact ten-year anniversary, Gala-Abend, 20 November 2014, https://www.youtube.com/watch?v=I-kWQyxa1e0&t=4722s (accessed 5 December 2021).

[41] Email communication with Ben Brandzel, 22 June 2018.

[42] Interview with Ben Brandzel, 17 October 2016.

[43] ibid.

summit of thirty-two activists in Holmes, a small town in upstate New York. The summit bought together the executive directors and founders of MoveOn, Leadnow, GetUp, 38 Degrees, and Campact, as well as several other activists from around the world (Karpf 2013). The summit was the first time all these activists, and organizations, had met. The attendees recognized the 'enormous potential for further collaboration' and decided to establish an international network: the Online Progressive Engagement Network (OPEN).[44]

OPEN was established on the belief that 'despite the vast differences of geography, governance, and language, their [members] shared values and unique approach to organizing—making engagement simple and accessible for every citizen became a multiplying force for other activists and groups around the world looking to create change at home.'[45] The attendees at the first summit asked Brandzel to serve as the executive director of what they called the 'OPEN alliance'. They also empowered the executive directors of each organization to be a secretariat that Brandzel could report to.[46] Several organizations committed funding to the new network, and Campact volunteered to host the 2014 summit in Germany.[47]

OPEN was born out of a desire to develop and strengthen digital advocacy organizations around the world. It is distinct from most other transnational advocacy networks in that it is united by a common *mode* of advocacy rather than a common *issue* such as women's rights, or climate change (Khagram et al. 2002). Typically transnational advocacy networks wield a degree of expertise on their cause so that they can intelligently address questions from the press and public about what policies, or laws are needed to redress the issue they campaign on. In contrast, the purpose of OPEN is to enhance, and diffuse a particular model of digital-advocacy organizations globally. As Brandzel stated, OPEN should: 'Help new sister organizations move from conception, to launch, to sustainable success, strengthening people-powered progressive change in more key countries around the world.'[48] The common model of advocacy is captured in the eight-fold path, summarized in Table 3.2.

The eight-fold path encapsulates what makes digital advocacy organizations distinct from most traditional non-governmental organizations (NGOs). Many NGOs may describe themselves as progressive, independent, and may even be member-based or engage in rapid-response campaigns; however, no

[44] OPEN, https://www.the-open.net/ (accessed 20 January 2022).
[45] ibid.
[46] David Karpf, OPEN summit summary, 2013.
[47] Interview with Felix Kolb, 9 February 2018.
[48] OPEN, grant request to Arca Foundation, February 2014 (on file with the author).

Table 3.2 The 8-fold-path
(also referred to in this book as the OPEN model)

(1) Progressive
(2) People-powered change
(3) Member-led
(4) Multi-issue
(5) Nimble
(6) Full-spectrum campaigning
(7) Independent
(8) Digital

The Commons (2016). "The Eight-Fold Path" https://commonslibrary.org/the-eight-fold-path/ (accessed 20 January 2022).

other NGO combines all eight elements of this model. These eight attributes work collectively to create the 'OPEN' model described in this book.

Nationally Focused and Transnationally Networked

> *We face:* Global problems requiring many national solutions.
> *We need:* Power optimized for domestic influence, yet networked for global scale.
>
> — Ben Brandzel[49]

OPEN was based on an explicit theory of change: many of today's pressing problems are transnational, but nation states wield the most power.[50] Brandzel and his OPEN co-founder Michelle Dixon, saw power in domestically based organizations that were transnationally networked. This analysis of power was the underlying and core motivation for creating national organizations rather than transnational groups. He frequently outlined the importance of nationally based organizations that were transnationally networked in grant applications he wrote on behalf of OPEN. As he elaborated in one grant application:

> More than ever before, the most pressing problems we face in each of our countries—including xenophobic populism, democratic erosion, widening

[49] OPEN, Powerpoint presentation, December 2017 (on file with author). Variations on this quote were used in several OPEN grant applications.
[50] Interview with Ben Brandzel, 30 January 2021.

> inequality, and ecological devastation—are actually national manifestations of tightly interlocked global phenomena. The challenges themselves physically cross borders as inevitably as refugee flows and extreme weather patterns ... .
>
> At the same time, however, the actual decisions required to overcome these global challenges are still predominantly rooted at the national level. National governments hold the hard levers of policy change regarding both domestic laws and international agreements. And the distinct national electorates of each country respectively shape their own politics, culture and economy within an information environment and popular narrative that is still fundamentally national.[51]

Brandzel and Dixon established OPEN because they saw a real gap in transnational organizing. Domestic NGOs were often cut off from global best practices and resources, and hence spent a significant amount of their time reinventing the wheel. Meanwhile, internationally federated NGOs, such as Oxfam or Greenpeace, could share best practices transnationally, but had limited 'licence to authentically take on politically difficult issues domestically'.[52] Their tax status as charities meant that they could not engage in election campaigns, as Dixon explained, 'no-one ever heard of Oxfam running a dangerous election campaign'.[53]

Brandzel and Dixon saw the power of transnational digital advocacy organizations like Avaaz or SumOfUs as 'optimised' for 'transnational coordination' because they can quickly set up campaigns without the bureaucratic hurdles of getting approval from national chapters.[54] However, these transnational organizations have a major disadvantage precisely because they are transnational: they cannot easily engage in election campaigning. Avaaz, for example, is legally a US organization, which can 'advocate, stamp their feet and yell, but there's not much they can do in other countries' elections to punish politicians'.[55] Meanwhile for OPEN groups, election campaigning is a core part of the model (see Chapter 2).

[51] OPEN, Multi-Year omnibus grant request 2018—2020 to the Open Society Foundations (on file with author).

[52] Online interview with Michelle Dixon, 30 January 2021.

[53] ibid.

[54] ibid.

[55] Brandzel saw several other limitations with the Avaaz model: Avaaz staff are global and work on domestic campaigns for countries other than those where they live, whereas in OPEN organizations' staff come from, and are based in, the country in which they campaign. As a result, OPEN staff have a better understanding of domestic politics than Avaaz staff. Interview with Ben Brandzel, 30 January 2021.

OPEN organizations can engage in domestic elections because they draw their membership from an exclusively national membership base.[56] They are not answerable to an international secretariat, such as Oxfam or Greenpeace, or an international membership, such as Avaaz. OPEN organizations' power is derived from the actions and donations of citizens of the country they belong to. Although, as we saw in the previous chapter, this domestic legitimacy has been challenged by conservative politicians. OPEN's aim was to spread this model to other countries, and influence national politics legitimately, through bottom-up progressive organizing. This not an unusual pattern: other international NGOs, such as Amnesty International and Transparency, have also supported the establishment of national affiliates to enhance their own national influence (Brown et al. 2012). A common logic for OPEN and international NGOs is that the most powerful way to influence politics in another country is to create a *national* advocacy organization, which can then legitimately put pressure on national decision-makers.

Brandzel dedicated over ten years of his life to promoting the OPEN model internationally. Many OPEN organizations shared Brandzel's dream of expanding the network worldwide. 38 Degrees and Campact, for instance, were both eager to see someone set up a digital advocacy organization in France, given the country's importance in European affairs and its proximity to both countries; as one 38 Degrees staffer explained, it is 'our closest neighbour'.[57] In 2016, Brandzel spent time in Paris identifying and interviewing potential candidates for the role of executive director of a potential French organization, and 38 Degrees staff helped in the selection process.

Campact was particularly generous and offered financing and support to many European start-up organizations. Campact's executive director, Felix Kolb, identified several benefits for Campact: they get 'lots of innovation out of it' and new OPEN groups also 'increases return for them, more than hiring one more person in Germany'.[58] Campact also saw instrumental value in establishing values-aligned organizations in Europe to influence European Union (EU) politics. It gave them 'partner groups to engage in 'strategic campaigning at EU level'.[59] For instance, in 2014, Campact supported the launch of Skiftet in Sweden during the height of the anti-TTIP protests with a grant of €250,000 to campaign against the TTIP. They wanted to see a strong, progressive Swedish digital advocacy organization. They also wanted to put domestic

[56] ibid.
[57] Online interview Robin Priestley, 6 December 2018.
[58] Interview with Felix Kolb, 9 February 2018.
[59] ibid.

pressure on Swedish EU trade commissioner, Cecilia Malstrom as part of a broader anti-TTIP campaign. Campact's funding enabled Skiftet to launch its first campaign: an online petition outlining the dangers of TTIP to European food safety standards, which urged people to 'stand with us and sign to stop TTIP'.[60]

Campact also helped to establish a European-wide digital advocacy organization, WeMove. A senior member of Campact sits on their board, alongside a member of 38 Degrees. WeMove has a small physical office in Berlin, and staff spread across Europe.[61] WeMove often collaborates with other OPEN organizations on European-wide campaigns, such as the European parliament election in 2019. However, it is not part of OPEN because it is regional, and not a national organization.

OPEN groups believe intrinsically in the power of digital advocacy organizations, and hence see value in spreading it elsewhere.

OPEN Membership: Zero Competition

Despite its name, OPEN is not an open, all-inclusive network, but a close-knit community whose membership is tightly controlled. The network only includes organizations that are nationally based and follow the eight-fold path. Brandzel believed that a high bar of 'methodological commonality' was important to ensure that the network was useful to its members.[62] He wanted to guarantee that 'as an OPEN member, your questions would find relevant answers, and your answers would find relevant questions'.[63] As OPEN's website explains, 'all OPEN groups share eight common ways of working: a common DNA that allows them to work as a coherent and productive network'.[64] The website elaborates: 'OPEN seeks a high degree of ideological and methodological alignment across the network, to ensure each group recognizes every other as being on the same team, even if they work on different issues at different times. This fuels the engine of collaboration.'[65] OPEN members needed to see

[60] Interview with Robin Zachari, 24 November 2017.

[61] WeMove's founding executive director, Oliver Moldenhauer, had previously worked for Attac Germany. We Move Team, https://www.wemove.eu/team (accessed 5 December 2021)

[62] Interview with Ben Brandzel, 30 January 2021.

[63] Email correspondence with Ben Brandzel, 28 June 2021.

[64] Although the website also notes that OPEN organizations are 'completely autonomous' and may adapt these organizing principals to match their own context. OPEN, https://www.the-open.net/ (accessed 20 January 2022).

[65] ibid.

an inherent value in 'teaching, learning, and exchanging resources with other members', otherwise the network would not function.[66]

OPEN works closely with new start-up organizations to ensure that the eight-fold path is integral to its organization model but gives organizations flexibility in interpreting it. As one start-up member explained, 'OPEN offers some guidelines and pillars, but it is up to each group to let its own spirit out in each particular context.'[67] OPEN has described its role as supporting new initiatives to help them past 'capacity choke points', which block their development.[68] Although all member organizations are expected to follow the eight-fold path, OPEN rarely enforces this. Brandzel describes OPEN as having a policy of 'heavy doors and high walls'; that is, it's hard to push the doors open to get in, but once you do, it's very hard to be pushed out.[69] OPEN organizations have adapted the eight fold path, as we will see in Chapter 4.

OPEN has a strict rule of only one organization per country to avoid competition for funding and members. It excludes several large and important digital advocacy organizations, including: Avaaz (international), WeMove (European), SumOfUs (international), and 350.org (international, climate-specific). OPEN's founders believe that allowing digital advocacy organizations with overlapping membership which competed for financing and credit could block full transparency and generosity between coalition partners. They wanted a network of 'zero competition' to enable 'high-trust' and deep collaboration.[70] As Michelle Dixon, one of OPEN's founders explained, the network had to be 'very low ego.'[71] Groups needed to be generous with each other and honest about their deficiencies and mistakes, and not judge each other's campaigning or issue positioning. This would only work if organizations were not competing with each other in their national context.

Although OPEN does not include international or regional digital advocacy organizations, the network maintains strong personal relationships with many. They run climate campaigns with 350.org, and Avaaz. Staff from SumOfUs, WeMove, and 350.org are also invited to present and attend parts of OPEN summits. The founding executive director of SumOfUs, Taren Stinebrickner-Kauffman, attended the very first summit in 2013 and was later on the OPEN

[66] OPEN, Organizational Charter, 2017 (on file with the author). The Charter was revised in 2019, but also affirms the importance of members sharing a core methodology. OPEN, Organizational Charter, Version 3.0, adopted 7 December 2019 (on file with author).

[67] Interview with Laura Rico Gutiérrez de Piñeres, 23 November 2017.

[68] OPEN, grant report, February 2014.

[69] Correspondence with Ben Brandzel, 29 June 2021.

[70] Online interview with Ben Brandzel, 30 January 2021.

[71] Online interview with Michelle Dixon, 30 January 2021.

Core Group (OPEN's governing council). However, OPEN does not work with Change.org as it is not aligned politically. According to Brandzel, Change.org does not try to 'create a values cohesive community' and members use their online petition platform for whatever causes they want.[72]

Institutionalizing and Staffing OPEN

After the first OPEN summit, Campact, 38 Degrees, and GetUp established a core group comprised of senior staff from each organization. The core group became the de facto Board of Directors that Brandzel reported to and they developed a charter for the network.[73] The charter outlined core criteria for full and start-up membership, as well as the zero-competition principle. The OPEN core group would use these criteria to evaluate when a start-up organization was ready to progress to full membership status. Full member organizations of OPEN were expected to pay membership fees of 1–1.4 per cent of their previous (non-election) year's revenue to support the growth and development of the network. Interestingly, MoveOn is the only group that regularly violated the charter it co-wrote by not paying its full membership dues. This mirrors a culture of US exceptionalism in US foreign policy: the United States often does not see the need to follow the rules it has put in place, or pay dues to international organizations.[74]

In 2014, OPEN established a foreign minister structure whereby one staff member in each organization became responsible for coordinating engagement with the rest of the network. The core group also approved OPEN's first budget and OPEN could then hire staff explicitly to support the network. These staff are referred to here as OPEN staff. Between 2014 and 2020 the OPEN secretariat hired: a managing director, a tech director, a development and growth advisor, and a director of development and storytelling.[75] Phil Ireland, for example, was working for Purpose in the UK, when Brandzel 'pitched compellingly to get involved' with OPEN and he became OPEN's

[72] Online interview with Ben Brandzel, 30 January 2021.

[73] Core group had the power to approve the annual budget, strategic plan, and support and evaluate the Executive Director. This is an arrangement that is not legally binding, as OPEN was legally incorporated through the US-based CEL Education Fund and thus their official board of directors was the Board of CEL Education Fund.

[74] Interview with Ben Brandzel, 30 January 2021.

[75] There were also shorter-term, campaign-specific positions (e.g. OPEN trade campaigner, and later OPEN COVID response campaigners). There is a full list of current OPEN staff at https://www.the-open.net/the-open-team (accessed 22 January 2022).

managing director.[76] Ireland saw that many traditional organizations, such as churches and NGOs, 'felt increasingly powerless in the public sphere and had declining members, but OPEN groups were all growing quite quickly, and could impact on democratic debates', hence his desire to work with OPEN.[77]

The OPEN secretariat staff work remotely, from the UK, the United States, Australia, France, Spain, Germany and India, although they travel frequently to visit OPEN organizations and run OPEN summits. They closely monitor OPEN organizations through email, social media, and Slack, and facilitate exchanges across the network. These staff are accountable to and supervised by the core group, a board of representatives of the member organizations. Importantly, OPEN does not centralize power in the secretariat, nor did it attempt to establish a federated international structure like many other international NGOs (Brown et al. 2012). The implications of this are explored in Chapter 5 and 6.

Growing the Global 'Sisterhood' (2013–2017)

Since the network's first meeting in 2013, OPEN has grown from five organizations to nineteen organizations operating in nineteen different countries, as illustrated earlier in Figure 3.1. There are two ways that new members joined the network. First, activists approached OPEN, looking for support and assistance to *emulate* the organization in their own context (e.g. in New Zealand, Sweden, Romania, and Poland). OPEN staff also *proactively* sought to establish or 'propagate' new organizations (e.g. in Israel, Ireland, and France). In some cases, OPEN provided 'heavy' support throughout the start-up phase.[78] In other cases, OPEN gave 'light' support, which may have consisted of coaching and connecting activists to others in the OPEN community. These differences are captured in Table 3.3.

The vast majority of my interviewees described the role of Brandzel as pivotal in supporting their organization in the start-up phase. However, Brandzel was not equally involved in establishing all organizations. In some cases, Brandzel convinced an individual to set up a digital advocacy organization, and without his presence it is unlikely that these organizations (e.g. Uplift and Zazim) would have been established. In other cases, local activists had already

[76] Interview with Phil Ireland, 7 September 2019.
[77] ibid.
[78] Online interview with Ben Brandzel 30 January 2021. Brandzel has coded all OPEN organizations as either 'heavy' or 'light'; 'reactive' or 'proactive' from OPEN's perspective.

Table 3.3 Examples of emulation and propagation of the OPEN model

	Propagation	Emulation
Light	Aufstehn (Austria) De Goede Zaak (Netherlands)	Campax (Switzerland) Akcja Demokracja (Poland) Declic (Romania) Kreni Promeni (Serbia)
Heavy	38 Degrees (UK) Uplift (Ireland) Le Mouvement (France) aHang (Hungary) Zazim (Israel)	ActionStation (New Zealand) Leadnow (Canada) Skiftet (Sweden)

Note: Three organizations were established without any direct input from Ben Brandzel or OPEN: GetUp, MoveOn, and Campact. This table is adapted from one produced by Ben Brandzel for OPEN.

decided to establish a digital advocacy organization before meeting Brandzel (e.g. Skiftet, #aufstehn, and ActionStation). This section compares emulation and propagation of the OPEN model.

Emulation

Activists from Sweden to South Africa have sought to emulate the OPEN model. Some of them had worked within OPEN organizations, saw the power of the model, and sought to emulate it in their own country. Paul Mason, for instance, co-founded Amandla.Mobi with Koketso Moeti, a leading South African activist, after working with GetUp in Australia.[79] In 2013, Mason reached out to GetUp's director, Simon Sheikh, who then contacted Brandzel for advice on how to 'set-up a version of GetUp in South Africa'.[80] Brandzel encouraged several GetUp and MoveOn activists to meet with Mason in Cape Town. Amandla.mobi's founders had strong networks with OPEN, and a good grasp of how the model operated before they launched the organization.

Activists who had no direct experience working in an OPEN organization also sought to replicate the model. For example, Polish activist Weronika Paszewska first heard about the OPEN model when she was talking with an

[79] AmandlaMobi, http://www.amandla.mobi/about (accessed 5 December 2021).
[80] Original email correspondence with Ben Brandzel (on file with author).

Ultimate Frisbee friend, Piotr Trzaskowski, who was then working for the European Climate Foundation.[81] Trzaskowski and Paszewska were both keen to set up a Polish digital advocacy organization and so invited Felix Kolb, Campact's executive director to Poland to learn more. After meeting Kolb, they then talked Brandzel and the OPEN team, who supported their initiative. In 2015, Trzaskowski and Paszewska launched Akcja Demokracja, and it became an important force mobilizing Poles against the right-wing Law and Democracy's party justice reforms in 2017.

In Sweden, Robin Zachari had heard about MoveOn in the United States but was not sure if the model would work in Sweden, given differences in political culture and population size. Zachari travelled to the UK to meet with staff from SumOfUs and 38 Degrees. 38 Degrees put Zachari in contact with Brandzel, who explained how start-up groups were emerging in smaller countries, such as New Zealand and Ireland. After learning more about the campaign model, Zachari reasoned that if the model worked in these smaller countries, it might also work in Sweden, and co-founded Skiftet.[82]

During his time with OPEN, Brandzel received dozens of emails from activists curious to hear more about the model. Activists were often referred via other members of the OPEN community, and he typically responded with great encouragement, enthusiasm, and a detailed document outlining the eight-fold path. Brandzel would subsequently engage in a longer conversation about the activist's aims and explain the organization model, and often visited the activists in country. These conversations did not always result in the creation of a new organization and some activists chose different models. Here, I describe in detail two successful cases of emulation, in New Zealand and Romania.

New Zealand and ActionStation (2014)

In New Zealand, a group of social entrepreneurs championed by Joe Cederwall from the Enspiral Network, were inspired by the growth and impact of GetUp in Australia.[83] After contacting GetUp to find out how they could emulate their advocacy model, they wrote terms of reference to establish a New Zealand equivalent. The Enspiral collective then reached out to Megan Salole, a former Green Party campaign manager, to see whether she would set up the new organization. Salole was unsure about taking the role, but said that if there

[81] Interview with Weronika Paszewska, co-founder and former Executive Director of Akcja Demokracja, 23 November 2017.

[82] Interview with Robin Zachari, 24 November 2017.

[83] Enspiral, 'What's Your "Meaningful Work" to Do in the World?', https://www.enspiral.com/ (accessed 5 December 2021).

was enough community support for the project, she would take it on. Over five frenzied days, they raised over NZ$14,000 (approximately US$10,000) from sixty-three donors by using a newly launched local crowdfunding platform called PledgeMe.[84] Following this fundraising success, Salole took on the role, and worked closely with GetUp, spending time at its office in Australia to learn about the model.

GetUp offered 'immense generosity' to the New Zealand start-up, in Salole's words.[85] Simon Sheik, then director of GetUp, offered ActionStation use of technology platforms and also helped with branding. Ben Brandzel spent three weeks in New Zealand to help Salole find start-up funding. Brandzel worked with Salole to refine her fundraising pitches, and they successfully convinced a few wealthy individuals to give them NZ $200,000 (approximately US$160,000) to recruit a full-time staff member and fund the start-up costs for the first year. Brandzel was integral to ActionStation winning financial backing because he was able to convince donors who were unfamiliar with OPEN that the model was viable and impactful. He was, according to Salole, 'a cheerleader, a sounding board, a confidante, he was so intimately, emotionally involved' in the creation of ActionStation.[86] Salole claimed that 'without Ben, saying to funders this is what she is going to build, and gesturing wildly in a Ben-like way, I would never have been able to bring it together'.[87]

Salole worked for two years, mostly on a voluntary basis, and led the ActionStation team into collaborations with domestic NGOs—to increase paid parental leave and to stop the sale of state-owned assets. Once the start-up funds were finally secured, Salole recruited Marianne Elliott to become the first executive director. Elliott officially launched ActionStation in July 2014. As of 2021, ActionStation has more than 150,000 members and has run over fifty campaigns on a wide range of issues, including the Trans-Pacific Partnership (TPP), climate change, child poverty, decolonization, and Māori rights.[88] ActionStation greatly benefitted in its early years from Brandzel, GetUp, and the larger network.

Romania and Declic (2015)

Declic in Romania was founded by a couple: Roxana Pencea and Tudor Brădățan. For over a decade, Pencea and Brădățan had been actively involved in a campaign to protect Roșia Montană, a picturesque village, from

[84] Interview with Megan Salole, Founder of ActionStation, 18 October 2017.
[85] ibid.
[86] ibid.
[87] ibid.
[88] ActionStation, 'About Us', https://actionstation.org.nz/about (accessed 5 December 2021).

mining.[89] They created Mining Watch, a network of NGOs, to stop the proposed mine by highlighting its environmental, social, and cultural costs. In 2013, the Romanian parliament rejected a bill that would have enabled mining to go ahead (*The Ecologist* 2013). Following this victory, Pencea and Brădăţan looked for other ways they could continue campaigning for social change. Brădăţan worked briefly with WeMove, a European-wide, OPEN-style organization, as the Central Eastern European campaigner. Through their activist networks, they became aware of Campact and grew excited about the idea of setting up a Romanian equivalent.[90] One Romanian scholar who knew them both explained that they 'saw scope to harness the energy' and go beyond the environmental movement to push for social change in Romania.[91]

Declic's founders approached Brandzel and his colleagues in OPEN about setting up an organization in Romania. Brandzel visited them in Cluj, Romania and OPEN gave them materials and invited them to the 2015 start-up summit in Berlin, where they met other activists emulating the MoveOn model in their own contexts. From this point onwards, they had regular mentoring from OPEN to help them develop a Romanian digital advocacy organization. As Brădăţan explained, the 'First moment we heard of them [OPEN] we wanted to be part because [we had] an instinct to follow campaigns from other countries. We looked a lot at US, Canada, Western Europe' and 'No other Romanian groups [were] doing this sort of activism, and we needed to speed up the game and let the best inspire us.'[92]

Brădăţan and Pencea teamed up with several other activists from the anti-mining campaign to found Declic. Stephanie Roth, a Berlin-based environmental activist who had worked in Roşia Montană for eight years, and connected them to funders. Between 2015 and 2018, they received significant grants from OPEN, Campact, 38 Degreees and over a dozen other organizations.[93] This initial funding enabled them to hire two staff members and purchase digital technology. In May 2015, Declic launched its first campaign, inviting members from the Roşia Montană email list to sign a petition to

[89] In 2013, the Roşia Montană protests peaked when the Romanian Prime Minister declared the mine a national project of 'overriding interest'. Interview with Tudor Brădăţan, co-founder and executive director of Declic, 22 November 2017.

[90] Interview with Stephanie Roth, 22 November 2017 and interview with Tudor Brădăţan, co-founder and executive director of Declic, 22 November 2017.

[91] Interview with Dr Dan Mercea, Reader in Media and Communication City University of London, 20 November 2017.

[92] Interview with Tudor Brădăţan, co-founder and executive director of Declic, 22 November 2017.

[93] In 2015, 38 Degrees donated £20,000 and in 2016, Campact donated approximately €2,000 Euros and OPEN €13,000. Declic, https://www.declic.ro/transparenta/ (accessed 5 December 2021).

end illegal logging in Romania.[94] Although the organization was still being set up, it gathered 25,000 signatures and was successful, as parliament passed the bill it had supported.[95] Like other OPEN groups, Declic campaigns through online petitions, emails, and social networks, as well as public meetings, street demonstrations, and creative protests.

Given that Romania does not have a strong culture of philanthropy or individual donations, the Declic team was initially concerned that a member-funded organization would not work.[96] In its early years, the organization relied on external grants, but by 2017 it was 50 per cent member-funded.[97] An additional challenge was that Declic could not be branded as 'progressive' because many Romanians eyed leftist movements with suspicion, given the country's communist history.[98] Instead, Declic publicizes its commitment to a fair, equal, and democratic society, and to environmental sustainability.[99]

Declic is very public about the support it has received from OPEN:

> Declic draws inspiration and shares the values of sister organizations such as MoveOn in the United States, GetUp in Australia, 38 degrees in the UK, Campus in Germany, or Akcja Demokracja in Poland. We use a similar organizational model, technologies and similar mobilization techniques to involve over 9 million people around the world.[100]

Declic now has 880,000 members, has launched 250 petitions, and was actively involved in the large Romanian anti-corruption protests in 2016.[101] In the words of Brădățan, OPEN 'gives us everything we need to be great' and 'we wouldn't be in this place without OPEN'.[102] Brădățan and Pencea were not

[94] Interview with Tudor Brădățan, co-founder and executive director of Declic, 22 November 2017.
[95] ibid.
[96] ibid.
[97] ibid.
[98] ibid.
[99] Declic outlines its values on its website in full:

> We want people to live and evolve into a fair society, driven primarily by courage and compassion; We want equal rights and chances for all citizens of this country, regardless of their ethnicity, the color of their skin, who they worship or who they love; We want a democratic state with responsible officials to respect ordinary people and the laws of the country; We want active citizens who are involved in the good course of society, protecting nature and the health of the planet, assuming responsibility for future generations.
>
> Declic website https://www.declic.ro/despre-noi (accessed 5 December 2021).

[100] Declic, https://www.declic.ro/ (accessed 5 December 2021).
[101] ibid.
[102] Interview with Tudor Brădățan, co-founder and executive director of Declic, 22 November 2017.

novices: they already had years of activism experience in Romania, but OPEN helped them to establish a member-driven, digital advocacy organization.

Propagation

While outsiders have had success emulating the OPEN model, the network itself has also actively tried to launch new organizations. Brandzel secured external grants and/or support from the OPEN community to launch organizations in France, Israel, and Ireland. In many cases of propagation, Brandzel first conducted a feasibility and desirability study. These studies examined: internet access and use, democratic traditions, the existing progressive movement, and philanthropic culture. Brandzel often travelled to target countries to identify and recruit a leadership team. Here, I describe how this approach worked in Israel.

Israel and Zazim (2015)

In November 2013, Brandzel flew to Israel to investigate launching an Israeli OPEN-style organization. He was supported financially by the New Israel Fund, a progressive Jewish American organization. Brandzel met with over sixty progressive Israeli activists, writers, politicians, funders, and thinkers, in Tel Aviv and Jerusalem.[103] Brandzel and the New Israel Fund were eager to establish an Israeli group if they could find someone with the appropriate skills and values to lead it.

While in Israel, Brandzel met with Raluca Ganea, who was then working for Avaaz. Ganea had built up Avaaz's Israeli email list from zero to 60,000 followers, with local campaigns on environmental, social, economic issues, and on the Israeli occupation of Palestine.[104] Over time, Avaaz had become less focused on Israeli issues and Ganea had become more of a global campaigner. Ganea began to look for ways to 'focus on the future of [her] own country and do everything possible to end occupation of Palestine and [ensure] Israel is a democracy'.[105] She was curious about setting up an Israeli version of Avaaz, and was a good match for Brandzel.

[103] Ben Brandzel, Israel Feasibility Study memo, 25 January 2018.

[104] Ganea had previous experience organizing online, and in 2004 had held one of the world's first interactive online rallies while working at the Geneva Initiative. The Geneva Initiative is an accord to end the Israeli–Palestinian conflict, based on previous international agreements. See http://www.geneva-accord.org/ (accessed 5 December 2021). Ganea organized a rally through phone and internet and also held an offline street event. It was her first experience with online organizing. Interview with Raluca Ganea, founder of Zazim, 23 November 2017.

[105] Interview with Raluca Ganea, founder of Zazim, 23 November 2017.

Ganea agreed to what she thought would be a short meeting at a café, and talked with Brandzel for over three hours. As she described, it was 'amazing because Ben has a unique talent of understanding the full picture from small details' and it was 'very easy to find common friends'.[106] After the meeting, Brandzel submitted a report to the New Israel Fund outlining the feasibility and desirability of setting up a digital advocacy organization in Israel. He highlighted Israel's democratic tradition, the financial viability of crowdsourcing an NGO, and the appetite amongst progressives for a new organization.[107] The New Israel Fund provided seed funding for the organization and published a call for a founding executive director. They ran a competitive selection process and hired Ganea for the job in October 2014. Ganea launched Zazim in December 2015, and ran its first campaigns in 2016.

Since then, Zazim has grown considerably. In mid-2021, it had a team of nine—Jews and Palestinians—and campaigns in both Hebrew and Arabic. They describe their common values as 'human rights, combatting the occupation and racism, and social and environmental justice'.[108] Like all the OPEN groups, Zazim run campaigns online and offline. Campaigns include ending the occupation of Gaza; democracy and civil rights in Israel; stopping the development of beachfront areas; and stopping deportation of refugees. In 2019, over 80 per cent of its expenses were covered by member contributions, and the rest came from foundations, including the New Israel Fund and the Rockefeller Foundation.[109]

Brandzel and the New Israel Fund enabled the creation of Zazim. Zazim openly acknowledges the influence of OPEN and explains on their website that: 'Zazim is based on the OPEN work model, which has proven itself over and over to be effective in gaining influential victories of people power all over the world'.[110] Zazim's website site clarifies that 'Each of the OPEN organizations acts independently in their respective countries for a better present and future. We make use of the professional knowledge and experience of other organizations in order to produce winning, impactful campaigns, and in order to best serve our community.'[111]

[106] ibid.
[107] Ben Brandzel, Israel Feasibility Study memo, 25 January 2018.
[108] Zazim, https://www.zazim.org.il/en/home-en (accessed 5 December 2021).
[109] Zazim, https://www.zazim.org.il/en/about#whoFunds (accessed 5 December 2021).
[110] Zazim, https://www.zazim.org.il/en/about (accessed 5 December 2021).
[111] ibid.

'Failed' Cases

Since the early 2000s, activists in over a dozen other countries, including Nigeria, Indonesia, and Nepal, have reached out to Brandzel and OPEN, curious to learn more about the model and the network. In some cases, the conversation did not get very far and activists decided not to pursue the model or join the network. In other cases, activists attended the OPEN summit and started to set up organizations, but failed to launch. In some cases, activists ended up choosing a different organizational model which had greater financial return. In two cases, new digital advocacy organizations were launched as part of OPEN, but then left the network. Here, I discuss a few illustrative examples of 'failed' cases and Table 3.4 provides an overview of other attempts to propagate or emulate the OPEN model.

A Spanish activist, Francisco Polo, created an online advocacy organization, Actuable in 2010 (Cano 2010). He contacted Brandzel who at the time had 'nothing to offer him' except an explanation of the eight-fold path because the OPEN community did not yet exist.[112] Actuable amassed a large membership, but Polo decided to sell the organization and its email list to Change.org. Thanks to the merger, Change.org in Spain grew significantly, and Polo subsequently became a Minister for Digital Development in the Spanish government

Table 3.4 Examples of failed attempts to propagate or emulate the OPEN model

	Propagation	Emulation
Light	Costa Rica	Columbia (Bulla) France (Powerfoule) Switzerland (Operation Libero) Guatemala Mexico Croatia Moldova Spain (Actuable)
Heavy	Indonesia	Nepal (Garjan) Italy (Progressi)

Note: There are also several cases of attempts to launch digital advocacy organizations without OPEN or Brandzel's involvement: Nossas (Brazil), ActNow (Papua New Guinea), Enough is Enough (Nigeria), and Kõigi Eesti (Estonia). This table is adapted from a table authored by Ben Brandzel.

[112] Interview with Ben Brandzel, 30 January 2021.

from 2018–2020. Brandzel claims that Polo missed an important chance to set up a Spanish OPEN-style organization.[113]

There were also cases where activists were quite close to launching an organization, but ultimately did not. Colombian Laura Rico, an activist who had also worked at Avaaz, attended OPEN start-up summits multiple times. She was very engaged in OPEN and wanted to establish Bulla in Colombia, but faced many set-backs. She explained to me that 'activists are more at risk' than in most other OPEN contexts.[114] She took a year to decide that "I'll do this, put my name, and my time, and people under me to set-up an organization. Because everything is a risk. Friends have had bombs in their office, every week they get a message of harassment.'[115] Laura reports that she was urged by her board of advisors to 'launch now' but held them off, and told 'everyone to be more cautious, when [we] have the money and when [we] have basic procedures in place to make sure we don't fall apart and ensure security conditions'. Brandzel was clear that OPEN does not have 'that experience or know-how [on security] and do not have the infrastructure to make you feel secure'.[116] Laura was the only activist from Latin America in the network at the time and ultimately decided not to launch Bulla, given the personal risks and challenges she faced. However, she also noted that being part of OPEN meant that she was 'much stronger than other groups in Colombia to see innovation in tech, campaigns, how to build a team, management, infrastructure etc.'.[117]

There have been two instances where OPEN organizations were launched but subsequently left the network. Operation Libero, launched in Switzerland in 2014, left the network in 2017, following its work supporting European pro-free trade groups, which went against the ideology of other OPEN groups. Operation Libero came under attack in the network for sharing the OPEN model with liberal groups, including in Austria, without prior support of #aufstehn, the Austrian organization. It went against the OPEN principle of zero competition: not having more than one organization active in any one country. Operation Libero continues to exist, but is not affiliated with OPEN. OPEN now has a new affiliate member in Switzerland: Campax.[118]

113 ibid.
114 Interview with Laura Rico Gutiérrez de Piñeres, 23 November 2017.
115 ibid.
116 ibid.
117 ibid.
118 Campax describes itself as 'a Swiss campaigning and mobilizing organization. Campax leads campaigns of its own about selected subjects, and supports individuals as well as other organizations in the accomplishment of their goals. Campax is a member of the OPEN network—a growing sisterhood of national grassroots campaigning organisations.' See Campax, https://www.campax.org/en (accessed 5 December 2021).

Meanwhile, Progressi launched in Italy in 2015 and campaigned against trade liberalization, against labour exploitation in agriculture, and for greater refugee rights. Progressi was led by a journalist of Eritrean descent, Vittorio Longhi.[119] However, it did not remain in OPEN. Longhi explained that it was challenging to get members and funding at the beginning, given competition from Change.org (which already had 5 million members in Italy) and the Five Star Movement, a political party which used digital methods to organize.[120] In 2019, Longhi left the organization and a group of Italian and US digital activists took over. A year later, the organization stopped campaigning. A group, Powerfoule, was also started in France, but never properly got off the ground and has since been replaced by a new French start-up, Le Mouvement.

It would require a separate study to understand the factors that enabled some groups to succeed where others did not. Factors such as internet penetration, philanthropic culture, the existing population of progressive advocacy organizations, and leadership, are all likely to influence success. The OPEN model has been particularly successful at spreading in Europe, as neighbouring countries have assisted each other. There are OPEN organizations now in Hungary, Serbia, and Poland, as well as Romania, and they have had impressive membership growth. These groups meet frequently as a cohort of Eastern Europeans, and support each other.

In 2018, Brandzel resigned from his position as executive director, in part to enable the network to grow independently from him. In 2019, the OPEN core group then hired Giovanna Negretti, a Puerto Rican activist, to be the next executive director. Negretti had co-founded and led ¿Oiste?, which campainged for greater representation of Latinos in US politics. She sought to diversify the network's membership, in particular to include activists from the Global South. Since Brandzel left his position as executive director, OPEN has not propagated the model in any additional countries. This may be because Brandzel's support was often crucial in launching a new organization or because OPEN now has other priorities, as will be discussed in Chapter 5. The COVID pandemic may have also made it more difficult to establish new groups.

[119] Vittorio Longhi has written for *The Guardian*, see https://www.theguardian.com/profile/vittorio-longhi (accessed 5 December 2021).
[120] Online interview with Vittorio Longhi, 21 March 2018.

Conclusion

MoveOn's impact on US political organizations is well documented (Karpf 2012); however, scholars have not looked at its international impact. This chapter suggests that activists around the world sought to emulate this model of digital advocacy organization. In some cases, they reached out to other digital advocacy organizations learn about the model; in other cases, Brandzel and his team proactively sought to set up new organizations. Regardless of who initiated contact, Brandzel helped new executive directors to find funding, coached them in the model, and mentored organizations in the start-up phase. He created a network of organizations, OPEN, and elaborated core organizational principles, espoused in the eight-fold path. Brandzel travelled the world at a relentless pace, and many activists interviewed for this study described his charisma and ability to convince them—and potential donors—of the power of digital advocacy organizations.

Senior staff members from other OPEN organizations—such as Campact, 38 Degrees, and GetUp—have also actively supported new start-up organizations. Campact was important in the development of Skiftet and Akcja Demokracja; GetUp's support was critical for ActionStation's development. These more established groups supported the launch of new organizations with finances, technology, campaign tactics, and strategies, and often mentored and hosted new Executive Directors.

OPEN is distinctive because all the members of the network share a similar organizational model, but operate in vastly different contexts. The network is united by a common organizational form and values rather than a commitment to a common issue. Subsequent chapters in this book will examine how this network operates and how the activists involved in this network are 'rooted cosmopolitans' (Tarrow 2005), concerned with global issues but focused on tackling them domestically. Chapter 4 dives deeper into how these organizations campaign. It explores how OPEN organizations interpret and apply the eight-fold path in countries as diverse as Poland and New Zealand. It focuses on four elements of the eight-fold path (multi-issue, member-driven, rapid response, and digitally enabled), which make them distinctive from other NGOs and advocacy organizations.

4
Campaigning

In mid-December 2016, I visited the campaign offices of #aufstehn in Vienna. A small team of three, they were in the midst of moving to a new office and writing up end-of-year reports. When I arrived there were no new campaigns on the horizon. By the following day, however, news emerged that Bashar al-Assad's troops were taking over the city of Aleppo in Syria, with media reports of civilians being killed (*Al Jazeera* 2016). Citizens in Aleppo were trying to leave and humanitarian agencies were trying to set up a safe humanitarian corridor to evacuate them. For #aufstehn, this was a 'crisitunity'. When I arrived in the office at midday, one staff member was busy looking for an image to reflect the dire humanitarian situation, the other was already drafting an email to #aufstehn's members. There was a clear sense of urgency—civilians were already dying.

Within 30 minutes, #aufstehn had launched a petition page urging the Foreign Minister, Sebastian Kurz, to 'actively campaign for the evacuation of the civilian population!'. The page would enable users to directly email Kurz's press spokesperson, as well as Kurz's personal email address. The petition was shared on #aufstehn's Facebook and Twitter feeds and a direct tweet was sent to Kurz.

#aufstehn also wrote an email to all its members outlining why they should contact Kurz. It pointed out that Austria was chair of the Organization for Security and Cooperation in Europe (OSCE) and could use this role constructively.[1] One staff member explained that it was a 'good thing to do to give members a sense of being able to do something, as everyone feels so helpless right now'.[2]

[1] This was one of the rare occasions that I influenced the framing of a campaign. I mentioned to #aufstehn that Austria was now the chair of the OSCE while they were brainstorming their campaign. Austria had only just taken over the Chair of the OSCE the previous Friday, 9 December 2016 (*Die Presse* 2016).

[2] Author's field notes from visit to #aufstehn offices, Vienna, 13 December 2016.

Transnational Advocacy in the Digital Era. Nina Hall, Oxford University Press.
 DOI: 10.1093/oso/9780198858744.003.0004

By 12.48 p.m., #aufstehn had received an email from Austria's Foreign Ministry. Irritated with the large number of emails coming into its inbox, the ministry wanted #aufstehn to call them urgently. The #aufstehn team discussed its options and decided it would have a conversation with the press office of the Ministry, but would only stop its campaign if it was given assurances from the Foreign Minister that the government was doing everything it could on the issue. By 2 p.m., 1,000 people had emailed the Minister; by 6.10 p.m., there were 3,629 emails. The Ministry had not responded to their phone calls by 6.25 p.m. that day so the campaign continued. By midday on Friday 16 December, #aufstehn members had sent almost 10,000 emails.

It is difficult to ascertain the impact of this particular rapid-response campaign. Kurz was in fact already publicly commenting on the situation in Aleppo. On 13 December, before the #aufstehn campaign began, he tweeted: '#Aleppo: all those responsible for the horrendous crimes must be brought to justice!'[3] Aleppo was also discussed on the sidelines of the OSCE ministerial meeting on 8 December 2016, which Kurz attended (Delegation of the EU to the Central African Republic 2016). What is notable is the speed with which #aufstehn launched a new campaign, and the rapid growth of emails to the Foreign Ministry expressing support for an evacuation of civilians.[4] #aufstehn's campaign is not unique. Many other digital advocacy organizations ran rapid-response campaigns on Aleppo in the same week (e.g. Campact[5] and ActionStation[6]).

This chapter examines the inner workings of digital advocacy organizations and how they engage in rapid-response, multi-issue, member-driven, digital campaigning. Although these dimensions can be separated out analytically, in practice they work in unison. OPEN organizations can rapidly launch new campaigns and switch to breaking-news thanks to the speed of communication online. They can aggregate member preferences efficiently at a large

[3] Sebastian Kurz, Twitter, https://twitter.com/sebastiankurz/status/808694557818896384(accessed 6 December 2021).

[4] Not all members were supportive of this petition. #aufstehn received sceptical messages from a few individuals who thought that the ceasefire would help the Islamic State. When I discussed this campaign with #aufstehn staff three years later, one acknowledged that they did not have a very clear theory of change and explained that they would do it very differently now.

[5] On 14 December 2016, Campact posted on Facebook a call for financial support for Syrian Refugee Sponsors, an organization which brings Syrian refugees to Berlin, https://www.facebook.com/campact/posts/10154212302841365/(accessed 6 December 2021).

[6] Rhiannon Evans initiated a petition on the 'our' ActionStation site. It targeted the New Zealand Minister of Foreign Affairs and Minister of Immigration and called for the safe evacuation for people trapped in Aleppo. ActionStation. (2016), 'Petition for New Zealand Government Support for Aleppo' (15 December), https://our.actionstation.org.nz/petitions/petition-for-new-zealand-government-support-for-aleppo(accessed 6 December 2021).

scale thanks to digital analytics. These organizations are a product of the internet era, but cannot only be defined solely by their use of digital technologies (Chadwick and Dennis 2016; Karpf 2012, 2016; Vromen 2017).

The chapter draws on extensive field work and interviews, as well as publicly available data from organizational websites and social media pages, to examine the regular routines of OPEN organizations and the limitations of their model of activism. It is divided into five sections. I examine what it means to be: (a) member-driven; (b) multi-issue; (c) rapid-response; and (d) to use digital analytics.[7] A fifth section reflects on whether digital advocacy organizations collaborate or compete with traditional NGOs. This chapter illustrates how digital advocacy organizations campaign in a starkly different way to most NGOs, and this has strengths and weaknesses.

Member-Driven Campaigning

A defining feature of OPEN organizations is that they are member-driven. This means that members directly or indirectly choose what organizations to campaign on and take action to advance these campaigns. Organizations are also largely member-funded. Older NGOs, such as the Sierra Club and Amnesty International, are also membership-based and, similar to the OPEN organizations, also use outsider strategies mobilizing people through demonstrations, letter-writing campaigns, boycotts, and petitions to put pressure on decision-makers.[8] However, OPEN organizations are distinct because they use digital technology to determine which campaigns are likely to be the most successful.

'People Power' — Members Take the Actions

OPEN organizations describe themselves as 'people powered'. They rely on their members to take action and drive their campaigns. They run mass mobilization campaigns—whether it be mobilizing thousands to sign a petition or to take to the streets. Their power comes from the number of followers they have and their ability to mobilize them.

[7] I focus on these elements of the eight-fold path as many other NGOs are also independent, people-powered, and progressive. Digital advocacy organizations are also distinctive from most NGOs because they engage in election campaigns, pushing for progressive candidates or against conservative candidates, as elaborated in Chapter 2.

[8] OPEN organizations rarely, if ever, run insider campaigns—campaigns which are based on gaining access to influential decision-makers—and cannot trade in their expertise for access to international negotiations and international organizations, unlike many other NGOs (Tallberg et al. 2015).

Membership in digital advocacy organizations is different to that of most traditional NGOs. Traditional NGOs expect members to actively sign up and offer regular donations (they may also receive some identifying card or merchandise as members). By contrast, digital advocacy organizations view their members as anyone receiving and regularly reading the organization's email, short message service (SMS), or Whatsapp communications. In many digital advocacy organizations, membership is equated with those who have taken at least one campaign action in the past few months.[9] Digital advocacy organizations tend to distinguish followers (those who just receive emails or social media messages) from those who have a deeper level of engagement with the organization. Every email subscriber or social media follower is a resource, a person waiting to be mobilized, regardless of whether the individual sees themselves as a 'member' or not.

To become part of OPEN, digital advocacy organizations must have a large list of subscribers. The 2017 OPEN charter stipulated that full members of OPEN must have a 'Directly re-contactable individual membership, which has taken at least 2 actions with the organisation, that constitutes at least 0.25% of internet users in that nation OR 50,000 individuals, whichever number is least'.[10] For countries with large populations, such as the United States (327 million) or Germany (82.7 million), the 50,000 members threshold is easier than gaining 0.25 per cent of internet users. Meanwhile, organizations operating in smaller countries such as New Zealand, Ireland, and Austria find it is easier to reach 0.25 per cent of the population. Once established, many of these organizations attract large memberships (Gründinger 2017a: 129).

While staff of digital advocacy organizations have expertise in digital campaigning, it is the members who decide which issues to campaign on. Members are highly valued because they provide legitimacy for the organizations' demands. Organizations are therefore not only conscious of maintaining members' trust, but are also keen to bring in new members and incentivize them to engage across multiple campaigns. At 38 Degrees, for example, staff will initially seek low-cost actions from members, such as 'liking' a Facebook post, signing a petition, or retweeting a post, and then attempt to attract higher commitment actions (Dennis 2019: 102). Digital advocacy organizations often

[9] Groups such as 38 Degrees have changed their definition of membership over time. Initially, membership was equated with email subscribers, but later they only counted members as those who had opened an email in the past three months. Email correspondence with Ben Brandzel, 28 June 2021.

[10] OPEN Charter, last updated January 2017 (on file with author). The charter has since been revised and the 2019 version does not include this criteria.

address their emails directly to an individual member (e.g. 'Dear Rebecca'). Some write to them as a member ('Dear MoveOn member') to create a sense of community and to indicate that they are in fact members. The size of an organization's membership, and the depth of their members' commitment is the organization's 'currency' (Heimans and Timms 2018).

Members Fund the Organization

OPEN requires full member organizations to be primarily member-funded.[11] It does, however, allow for new start-up organizations to accept a higher proportion of funding from foundations or philanthropic individuals, and from other OPEN organizations, in their early years. OPEN organizations do not accept funding from governments because they want to be independent and to be able to critique government policy.

As demonstrated in Figure 4.1, the majority of funding in these OPEN organizations comes from members (over 55 per cent in all seven cases). Member funding is important because it ensures the organizations are not only independent, but primarily responsive to members' concerns. In the larger, more established organizations such as 38 Degrees, MoveOn, and GetUp, which have multi-million-dollar budgets, funding from members is over 90 per cent, as illustrated in Figures 4.1 and 4.2. The smaller, newer organizations such as ActionStation, Declic, Uplift, and Zazim, have a larger proportion of grant funding.

Staff of digital advocacy organizations regularly ask their members to donate both to specific campaigns and to the organization as a whole. Recurring monthly donors are prized because they provide more financial stability for the organization than one-off donations. OPEN organizations are constantly testing and refining the most effective way to raise funds. In 2020, Campact, for example, sent an email to its members urging them to donate 'even 2 euros', stressing that 'Campact is only as strong as our supporters make us'.[12] They informed their members that almost three million people had supported their campaigns in the first nine months of 2020, but only 0.24 per cent of people who joined in the past six months had donated. The organization emphasized

[11] In cases where it is harder to get member funding, digital advocacy organizations need to demonstrate progress towards being majority member-funded.

[12] From the German: 'Campact ist nur so stark, wie unsere Unterstützer*innen uns machen.' Felix Kolb, 'DAS ist eine schlechte Zahl'. Email to members, 14 September 2020.

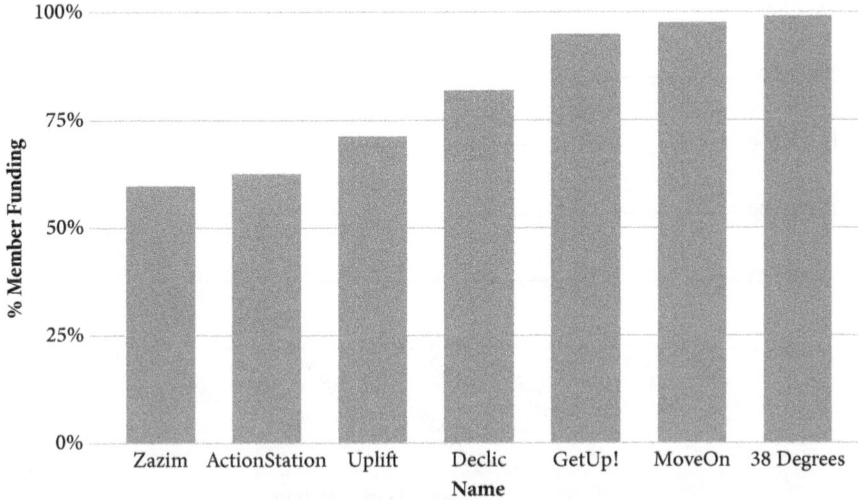

Fig. 4.1 Percentage of member funding for select OPEN organizations in 2018
Note: To generate this figure we examined OPEN organizations' annual reports and other publicly available data on their finances. However, not all OPEN organizations publicly declare the percentage of member funding. Hence, only a select number of OPEN organizations is presented here. MoveOn comprises two entities - MoveOn Civic Action and MoveOn Political Action - both receive contributions. However, the data above only includes MoveOn Civic Action, as we did not have data on the proportion of member funding for MoveOn Political Action.

that this lack of funding was 'not enough to take action at short notice or to react quickly to current politics with new campaigns'.[13] Campact is one of the most successful organizations at securing regular monthly donations in OPEN.

There are significant differences in annual revenue across digital advocacy organizations, as Figures 4.2 and 4.3 illustrate. MoveOn in 2018 had the highest single revenue, partly because it was an election year (when it is easier to fundraise). However, if MoveOn's Political Action Committee (PAC) is not included (as in Figure 4.3) their annual 2018 revenue is less than Campact's although still more than the other organizations. Importantly, all of the OPEN organizations for which we had financial data saw an increase in their revenue between 2015 and 2018.

Large differences in GDP, population size, access to the internet, and philanthropic culture, influence each organization's revenue and viability of a purely member-driven model. Uplift in Ireland and ActionStation in New Zealand operate in countries with a population of just over 5 million, far smaller

[13] Felix Kolb, 'DAS ist eine schlechte Zahl'. Email to members, 14 September 2020.

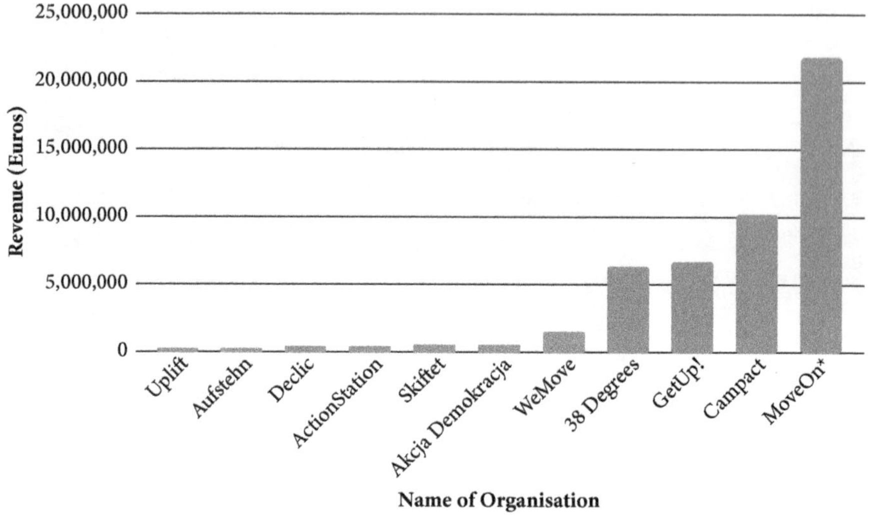

Fig. 4.2 Revenue of some Digital Advocacy Organizations (2018)

Note: * MoveOn financial revenue includes both MoveOn PAC and MoveOn Civic Action. Data on revenue was primarily taken from annual reports and/or financial statements on the organizations' websites. Some organizations (e.g. Declic) did not have financial statements, but did have revenue data on their website. Data for MoveOn Civic Action has been taken from Form 990 on Guidestar (USD 10,017,366) and data for Political Action through the Federal Electoral Commissions PAC filings for MoveOn (Total Contributions line 11b: USD 15,932,560) to give a total of $25,949,926 or EUR 21,992,562. Some organizations, such as Leadnow and Amandla.Mobi, did not have sufficient publicly available financial data to be included in this figure (see here Amandla.Mobi, 'Funding', https://amandla.mobi/funding/). The currency is listed in Euros, as this is the most common currency used across the network. For all foreign exchange rates, we have used historical rates on https://exchangerates.org.uk and given different year-ends. We have used the average exchange rate over 2018.

than the United States or Germany. In wealthy countries with a strong philanthropic culture, such as the United States, it is relatively easy to be fully member-funded.[14] In others, such as South Africa, it is much more difficult. Amandla.Mobi's membership is predominantly working-class black women who have little disposable income to donate. As a result, Amandla relies more on philanthropic grants, which has led them to evaluate and report on their impact more regularly than most other digital advocacy organizations.

Some other OPEN organizations supplement donations from members with funding from foundations. However, they will rarely accept funding if it does not align with their members' preferences. For example, one foundation I spoke with offered MoveOn money to work on a particular issue. MoveOn had previously worked on this issue, but was no longer actively campaigning on it.

[14] Skype interview with OPEN staffer, 26 May 2016.

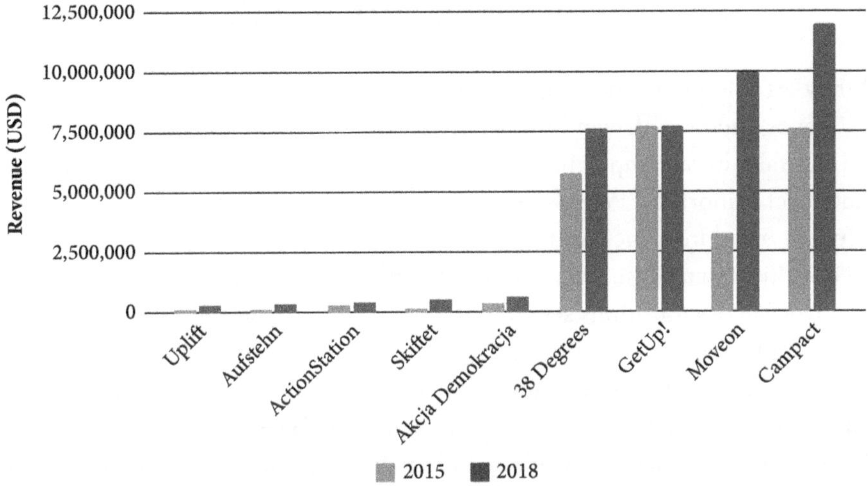

Fig. 4.3 Revenue comparison in 2015 and 2018 (USD)
Note: Figure 4.3 does not include MoveOn PAC funding for 2015 or for 2018.

MoveOn staff considered the funder's proposal, but decided it was premature, and rejected the funding on the basis that they needed to have 'a better sense of where membership will be on the issue' before engaging, in the words of the funder.[15] Although the funder recounted being initially frustrated with this response, they subsequently realized that this was a strength of MoveOn: it can mobilize a large group of people where other more issue-specific organizations cannot.[16]

Notably, all the digital advocacy organizations in OPEN share strong progressive values and seek to attract progressive members. The first campaigns digital advocacy organizations launch are particularly important because the members they acquire will shape future campaigns. Brandzel often gives the analogy of flamingos, which eat pink shrimp and thus have pink feathers. He explains to new OPEN organizations that they need progressive members to stay progressive. If organizations draw too much support from members who are on the centre or right of the political spectrum, then it will be harder for them to run strong, progressive campaigns. There are strong path-dependent mechanisms at play in campaign selection, unless organizations remove members, or members unsubscribe, both of which can occur. Ultimately, these organizations are only as progressive as their members.

[15] Interview with funder to MoveOn, 17 June 2019.
[16] ibid.

The Limitations of Member-Driven Campaigns

Purely 'people-powered' campaigns are subject to the tyranny of the majority. Hence, member-driven campaigns can fall into the same trap that populist politics falls into: campaigns cater to the majority and so may ignore issues that affect minorities. When OPEN organizations run campaigns to welcome refugees or address racism, they often receive criticism from members who do not think that these issues should be prioritized. In response, some digital advocacy organizations segment their lists. ActionStation in New Zealand, for example, received a high number of negative responses to an email about increasing the refugee quota and, as a result, created a section of their email list that would not be sent anything to do with refugees (Stephens 2018: 77). An additional limitation of this member-driven model is that issues which are a priority for members one month may be deprioritized the next. In 2015, for example, staff at 38 Degrees campaigned to welcome refugees, but subsequently dropped the campaign when it became a low priority for members, as will be explored in Chapter 8 (Hall 2019a and b).

Given that the staff and supporters of OPEN organizations largely hail from the educated middle class, organizations do not directly represent the views of the most marginalized in society. According to Brandzel, membership of OPEN organizations 'skews towards the professional fields, information workers, retired people, and folks with disposable time and money on their hands' and those with 'enough civic entitlement' to believe that their voice could at least make a difference.[17] Digital advocacy organizations do campaign for disadvantaged and minority groups, but these campaigns rely on the empathy and strong progressive values of supporters and staff.

Staff of digital advocacy organizations are increasingly aware of the dangers of purely member-driven campaigning, and as a result, some are adopting a stewardship logic (where campaigning is staff- and values-led). This will be explored in Chapter 8.

'Multi-Issue' Campaigning

The OPEN model is based on the belief that most members do not just care about one thing but about multiple issues. In fact, one of the most 'exciting things' about the model, according to one OPEN staffer, is that 'we can

[17] Email correspondence with Ben Brandzel, 28 June 2021.

'cross pollinate'.[18] Members might get engaged in one campaign (e.g. to save a national park), and then be encouraged to join another (e.g. to stop a trade agreement). The same OPEN staffer described meeting a member of 38 Degrees who first signed a petition on bees, then became really interested in a campaign for the National Health Service (NHS), and went on to organize a public meeting with their Member of Parliament (MP).[19] This ability to get members engaged in multiple issues is 'one of the key ways that we grow' as an organization.[20] ActionStation, for instance, notes that, 'While many other organizations think in "issue-sectors", people think in "crises, opportunities and values".[21] Digital advocacy organizations thus 'act where there is passion and the potential for change'.[22]

Political communications scholars have described OPEN organizations as 'issue-generalists' because they do not stick to one issue area (Karpf 2012; Dennis 2019; Vromen 2017: 116).[23] Brandzel believes that there is power in channelling peoples' concerns across a range of issues. As he explains:

> While people choose some issues abstractly as the most important, when they read the paper every day, they see decisions and provocations on a range of topics that will inflame their support or ire, depending on their values. The energy produced in response to that range of topics is what OPEN organizations need to engage in order to grow to scale and to create change wherever change is most urgent and possible. So, while the OPEN model is values-coherent, it is also inherently and deeply multi-issue. Being multi-issue, in turn, offers significant movement-building advantages.[24]

Being multi-issue works hand-in hand with being member-driven because organizations can rapidly react to members' changing interests and priorities.

To illustrate the multi-issue nature of these organizations' campaigns, I worked with a research assistant to collect and code campaign actions taken by 38 Degrees, Campact, GetUp, and ActionStation between 1 September 2018 and 31 August 2019.[25] I chose these groups because they include some of the

[18] Interview with Becky Jarvis, OPEN staff member, 20 June 2019.
[19] ibid.
[20] ibid.
[21] ActionStation, 'ActionStation Evolution of the 8-Fold Path 2019' (on file with author).
[22] ibid.
[23] In her work, Vromen collected GetUp emails to members over a three-month period and found that they campaigned on an extremely wide range of areas. These include internet censorship, carbon emissions, mental health, refugees, native forests, and the national election (Vromen 2017: 116).
[24] OPEN. "8-Fold Path" (on file with author).
[25] Thanks to Rebecca John for her contributions to this section.

largest (Campact, GetUp!) and one of the smallest organizations (ActionStation). It also reflects a geographic spread (New Zealand, Australia, the UK, and Germany). Looking at Figures 4.4, 4.5, 4.6, and 4.7 collectively, we can see that these organizations all campaign across a wide range of issues: from hate speech to saving the bees. It would be hard to find many other advocacy organizations that have such a wide variety of issues on which they campaign.

There is some national variation in what issues they concentrate most on, as detailed in Figures 4.4–4.7. 38 Degrees, unsurprisingly, focused on Brexit, Campact on climate change (36 per cent of campaign actions), and ActionStation on Māori rights (28.6 per cent of campaign actions). However, no single issue captured more than 40 per cent of any organization's campaign attention over the year. There were some common issues across all the organizations, reflecting the issues that were salient at the time, as well as the progressive focus of these organizations (e.g. all campaigned on climate change).[26] Overall, these pie charts illustrate the breadth and multi-issue nature of these organizations.

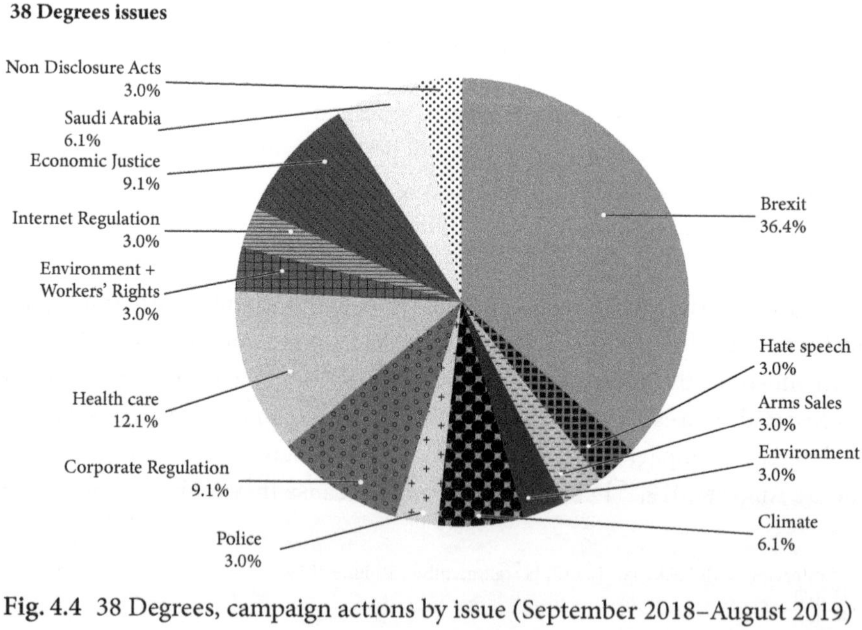

Fig. 4.4 38 Degrees, campaign actions by issue (September 2018–August 2019)

[26] Note that we did distinguish between climate change and environmental issues to illustrate the predominance of climate change over other environmental issues (e.g. plastic pollution, biodiversity, conservation).

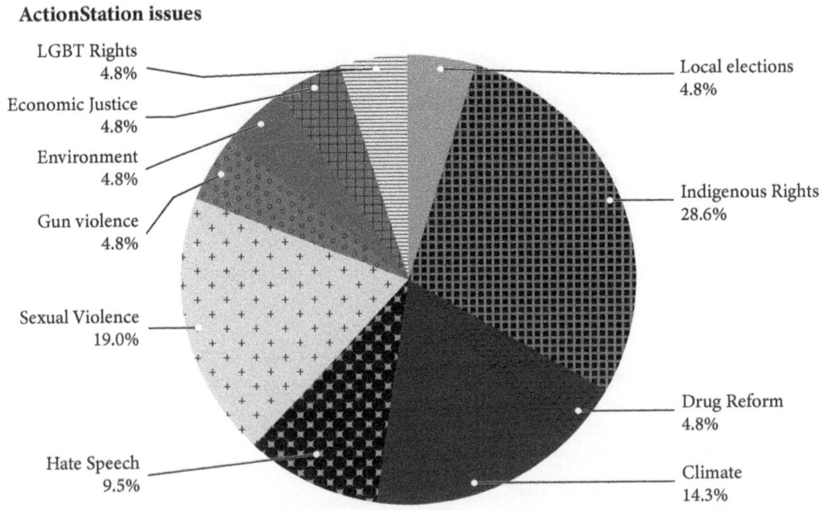

Fig. 4.5 ActionStation, campaign actions by issue (September 2018–August 2019)

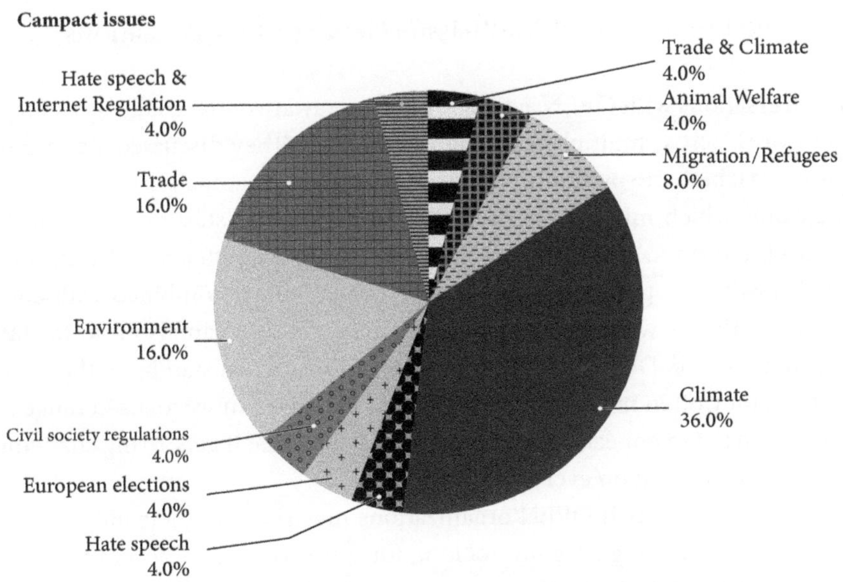

Fig. 4.6 Campact, campaign actions by issue (September 2018–August 2019)

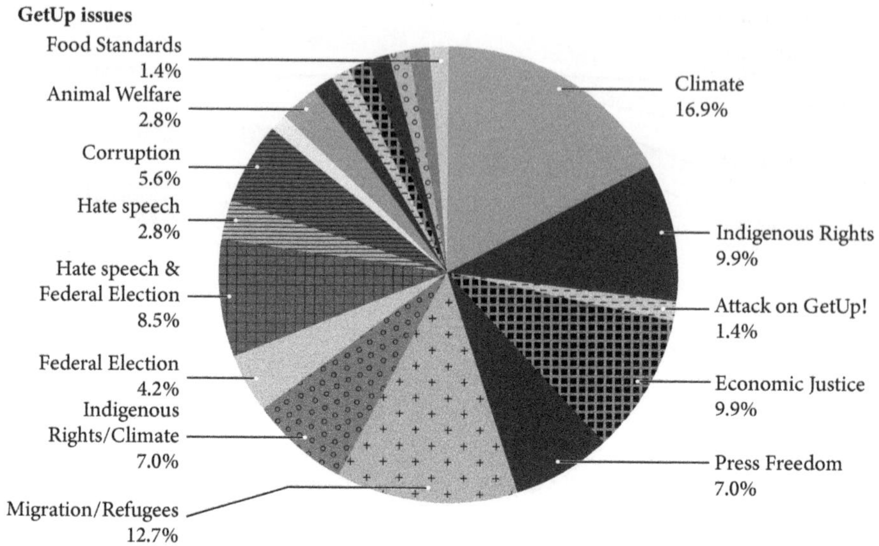

Fig. 4.7 GetUp, campaign actions by issue (September 2018–August 2019)

The Limitations of Multi-Issue Generalist Organizations

In conversations with OPEN activists, many are aware of the challenges of trying to work across multiple issues simultaneously. They discussed a constant tension: is it better to put more energy into an existing campaign, or try to start a new one, which might do better? There is pressure to start new campaigns and drop old ones. According to the OPEN logic it's better to fail fast, than to fail slowly. The pace of rapid-response campaigning, combined with constantly starting new campaigns across a range of issues can also lead to staff burn-out. One 38 Degrees staff member noted that when staff leave the organization, they often move to an NGO with a narrower, more focused range of issues, such as Greenpeace or Oxfam. He explained that it gets 'tiring changing issues you campaign on every week'.[27]

Another issue is that OPEN organizations may simplify their message because they are moving speedily, looking for quick wins, and do not typically have expertise on the issues they campaign on (although there are some exceptions, as we will see). As a result, digital advocacy may also choose the wrong target, message, or strategy for a campaign, or even intervene in a way that

[27] Interview with James Rees, former 38 Degrees staffer, 9 June 2017.

undermines the cause. Their desire to be as popular, accessible, and participatory as possible means that their messaging may be overly simplified. As a result, they may: 'dumb down the complex realities into simple narratives of good and bad to be remedied by simple solutions. Such narratives squeeze out the more nuanced views … and the deeper underlying causes of conflict and end up promoting superficial victories rather than real change' (Green 2016: 223).[28] Some digital advocacy organizations incorporate more nuanced evidence into their campaign communications (e.g. footnotes and links to news stories at the end of their emails). Yet there is often a tension in the model between mass-participatory, accessible campaign messaging and more nuanced, complex messaging.

Some issue-expert NGOs have criticized digital advocacy organizations for ignoring their expertise, running campaigns without the relevant background knowledge, mobilizing people based on problematic messaging, and/or claiming that their work alone led to a campaign victory. Avaaz, for example, has been criticized for stealing the limelight in the climate movement after claiming that its members' actions led to the Paris Climate Agreement. In reality, Avaaz was part of a much broader climate movement and there were many other contributing factors. Brandzel warns against digital advocacy organizations getting 'bogged down' in NGO coordination or coalition meetings where 'in-group politics takes precedence over member service.'[29] However, he argues that OPEN groups need to develop and foster relationships with issue-expert organizations to get the 'information and analysis they need to give the best possible content and most impactful asks to their members.'[30]

Many OPEN organizations do actively forge partnerships and collaborations with other NGOs, expert organizations, and/or academics to mitigate their own lack of issue expertise. MoveOn notes that they: 'leverage close partnerships to scale our operation where needed, and avoid building internal staff [sic] wherever possible.'[31] GetUp, for instance, has partnered with academics at the Sydney University of Technology. It commissioned an academic report on tax avoidance, which was paid for with over 1,700 members' donations and

[28] Note that Green was not referring explicitly to campaigns run by OPEN organizations. He gave as an example Kony 2012, a campaign video about Joseph Kony, the founder of the Ugandan Lord's Resistance Army, that went viral.

[29] Email correspondence with Ben Brandzel, 28 June 2021.

[30] Ibid. He elaborated that:

> the more time you spend developing and nurturing those relationships, the less they interfere with acting quickly when a real crisitunity hits.
>
> (Email correspondence with Ben Brandzel, 28 June 2021)

[31] MoveOn, 'How We Staff—Small and Nimble,' https://front.moveon.org/moveon-way-how-we-staff/ (accessed 6 December 2021).

then followed up with a year-long research programme focused on fair taxation (Vaughan 2020: 125). As Vaughan notes, 'Partly due to professional focus on mobilization and partly due to the breadth of issues they deal with, GetUp relies on technical and policy expertise for much of the substance of their policy asks' (Vaughan 2020: 125). ActionStation has also forged collaborations with academics to write reports (e.g. on criminal justice reform) and has collaborated with specialist NGOs to work on child poverty.[32] The relationship between NGOs and digital advocacy organizations is explored further at the end of this chapter.

Staff and Structure

Despite being multi-issue, some OPEN organizations have hired staff with issue expertise and even set up campaign teams dedicated to particular issues. GetUp, for example, at the time of writing, had three campaign teams: one focused on the environment and climate change; a second working on human rights and refugees; and a third team focused on the economy and democracy. MoveOn has also become more committed to sustained campaigns for migrant and refugee rights during the Trump presidency, and in 2019 had a dedicated migrants' rights campaigner.[33] In short, some OPEN organizations have developed expertise and conduct longer-term, sustained campaigns, in partnership with other specialized civil society organizations.

In 2019, Campact also had three main campaign teams. One campaign team focused on democracy, fair trade, and finance and was focused on 'launching short-term rapid actions'.[34] This team has been involved in campaigns to combat hate speech and right-wing populism, the EU election in 2019, and trade agreements. Campaign team two focused on the environment and sustainable agriculture. Campaign team three (the newest of the teams) was created in response to the success of #FridaysForFuture and is focused on backing the broader climate movement and mobilizing people throughout Germany.[35] Climate change and other environmental issues are a core priority for many

[32] ActionStation has developed at least eight models of collaboration, which it shared with OPEN organizations in January 2017. It routinely emphasizes the role of these partners in leading campaigns and argues that these collaborations lead to 'better and more informed campaigns', as well as building 'brand credibility', and can increase their membership. In ActionStation's 2019, 'Evolution of the 8-Fold Path', it commits to being 'movement generous' and note that they 'depend on partners and we love to collaborate'.

[33] Interview with MoveOn Staffer, June 2019.

[34] Campact, 'Uber Campact Team', https://www.campact.de/campact/ueber-campact/team/ (accessed 6 December 2021). (Quote is translated from the German.)

[35] ibid. These campaign teams changed again in 2021.

Campact members. GetUp and Campact are examples of stewardship-led campaigning, whereas Skiftet and 38 Degrees reflect a more member-driven, multi-issue model, where staff have expertise in digital campaigning, but rarely develop expertise on a particular issue.[36]

Other OPEN organizations dedicate a person to work on a cluster of issues, and some even receive grant funding for a specific position. Skiftet and ActionStation, for example, received funding from the Omidyar Network to work on internet regulation.[37] Akcja Demokracja has received funding to work on climate change and has a staff member with previous expertise in the environmental movement. In smaller organizations with less than ten staff, staff have to cover many issues simultaneously and it is harder for them to become specialized unless they have specific funding to support this.

Rapid-Response Campaigning

OPEN activists prize the speed with which they can launch new campaigns. Their mode of campaigning is trial and error, fast failure. They are deeply wedded to being nimble and responsive, and their organizational structure and daily practices enable this. As ActionStation in New Zealand, explains, drawing on the original 8-fold path:

> We 'chase the energy' for maximum impact. The sweet spot is when 'high information' and 'high actionability' combine. This often happens unexpectedly and when they come, the energy flow demands we pounce. This means we work in a low bureaucracy environment and we know that done is better than perfect. We have the courage to listen, learn, try—and fail or succeed—try again. We lead from curiosity and openness, rather than having all the answers.[38]

These digital advocacy organizations do not expect every campaign they start to successfully mobilize their members, let alone win. Experienced campaigners encourage new groups to 'prospect' (i.e. to scan for) and trial new

[36] Although member-driven organizations can also become more focused on certain issues over time because of their membership. 38 Degrees members, for instance, strongly support the organization campaigning on the National Health Service, and over time associate the organization with this issue. 38 Degrees then attracts new members who support campaigns for the NHS.

[37] See ActionStation, 'About Our Funding', https://www.actionstation.org.nz/about/our-funding (accessed 6 December 2021), and Zachari (2018).

[38] ActionStation New Zealand. (2019). 'Evolution of the 8-Fold Path' (on file with author).

campaigns on a weekly basis.[39] Prospecting is quick: it simply involves putting together an online petition and sending it out to a small proportion of an email list to test. If it is received well, the organization would then invest more time producing content, such as graphics or social media content, to accompany the petition. OPEN core staff actively encourage organizations in the network to prospect and launch new campaigns regularly. Michael Snook, OPEN's tech director for several years, explained that 'we encourage smaller organizations to trial at least one campaign every week' and larger organizations at least two or three per week. Prospecting helps them to identify what will go viral.[40]

OPEN organizations' ability to launch new campaigns is enabled by low levels of bureaucracy. Staff generally do not need sign-off from senior managers to start a campaign, so can trial them directly with a proportion of members. For groups with an email list of more than one million members, staff may send a trial email to between 10,000 and 50,000 of them. If a large enough proportion of members open this trial email and take action, the organization will run with the campaign. If not, they drop, or deprioritize it. Most organizations have set thresholds for selecting campaigns. One important metric is 'clicks over opens', which corresponds to how many people click the petition link embedded in the email as a proportion of the total population that opens and reads the email.[41] In a successful trial, with an easy action such as a petition, over 30 per cent of people would click through.

There are different thresholds across OPEN needed for a campaign to go ahead. Organizations may also look at the open rates (i.e. how many people open an email); or conversion rate (the percentage of people who actually complete the action once they've clicked through to the relevant website page).[42] Digital advocacy organizations may prospect multiple campaigns over the course of a week, and based on member response rates (i.e. how many opened

[39] Online interview with Michael Snook, 19 October 2018 and email correspondence with Michael Snook, 30 June 2021. Becky Bond and Zack Exley, two senior campaigners who worked on Bernie Sanders's primary campaign, outlined the importance of trial and error in a speech at an OPEN start-up summit in August 2016. They summarized this as Rule 80/20: 20 per cent could be bad; 80 per cent could be good. As they said: 'Do we want to be perfect, or do we want to be big?'. The answer they gave is: big (meaning a big movement).

[40] Online interview with Michael Snook, 19 October 2018 and email correspondence with Michael Snook, 30 June 2021.

[41] Correspondence with Ben Brandzel, 28 June 2021.

[42] However, Brandzel argues that these rates are less useful for identifying a potentially popular campaign. Open rates depend more on the overall 'health' of the email list. This is 'typically between 5%–25%' for an email to the full membership. Conversion rates tend to reveal more about how effectively the website page is set up rather than whether the audience is interested in the campaign. These rates should be quite high (e.g. around 80 per cent) because 'by the time people get to the landing page, they should want to complete the action'. ibid.

an email, signed a petition, or took a particular action), they will determine where to put their energy.

OPEN organizations are always on the hunt for new campaigns and have daily routines and decision-making processes which facilitate this. Activists frequently scan the news and social media to identify issues which are getting attention. Some organizations even have specific teams dedicated to identifying new campaigns. 38 Degrees in the UK, for example, has 'Team Opportunities Crew', which is a revolving group of staff that meet at 9.30 a.m. most mornings to brainstorm new campaign ideas. Uplift in Ireland looks for rapid-response campaigns on Facebook and also through its networks with grassroots community groups, to try and spot campaigns that may not feature in mainstream media.

Meanwhile in Sweden, Skiftet uses its morning meeting to talk through an angle for a new campaign. Staff will write the campaign material before lunch, at lunch send it to a small proportion of its members, and then follow how much attention the campaign attracts.[43] If it is popular it will be sent to the full list. As a result, its staff are always 'scrolling the news cycle', looking at internal dashboards which collate data analytics on its campaigns, and keeping track of its most popular campaigns on its Slack channel.[44] Skiftet also monitors the number of signatures on its petitions, and has daily updates at 9 a.m. and 3 p.m. on how petitions are progressing. During the week, it has a couple of meetings where staff discuss which campaigns they should focus on, and which to drop.

Email has been the primary means of communication between OPEN organizations and their members (Vromen 2017: 4). The aim of an email is to get readers to take a first action (Karpf 2012). OPEN emails often follow a set script: they begin by highlighting the urgency of an issue: the '*crisitunity*'. The crisitunity—a term coined by Homer Simpson and popularized by Brandzel[45]—is a real-world situation that is either a crisis about to unfold, or a potential opportunity to be achieved.[46] It could be an important vote in Congress or parliament, a major international summit (e.g. Paris climate summit), or an unfolding crisis overseas. This is the critical hook to get members to act urgently (i.e. in the next few days). Emails then outline a reader-focused 'theory of change', which begins with something the reader can do, and ends with the resolution of the crisitunity.[47] Staff will then include a specific ask

[43] Author's visit to Skiftet and interview with Robin Zachari, 13 June 2018.
[44] ibid.
[45] Worldwide Words, 'Crisitunity', https://www.worldwidewords.org/turnsofphrase/tp-cri2.htm (accessed 6 December 2021).
[46] Brandzel has summarized his guidelines for email writing in a slide deck: Brandzel (2019).
[47] ibid.

(e.g. write to your member of Congress/parliament, sign the petition, contact the phone number below) and a deadline for completing this.

New OPEN staffers are coached in writing these emails at workshops at OPEN summits. They also receive one-to-one mentoring from Becky Jarvis, OPEN's former start-up mentor and chief email writing coach, as well as from Ben Brandzel. The emails aim to emotionally connect with the recipient. They are written colloquially, directly addressing the receiver by name, and in a way that is easy to scan.[48] The most important element of communicating with members, however, is conveying urgency. As one OPEN executive director explained, 'If you ever have Becky edit one of your emails, [she'll ask] 'where's the emergency'? I have a Becky bot which is basically just—"urgency"'.[49] For a rapid-response campaign to succeed, it is crucial to communicate a clear narrative of why getting involved in this campaign matters *now*.

Being nimble means that digital advocacy organizations can quickly shift their resources to new important issues, which traditional NGOs find harder to do. Importantly, rapid-response campaigning is not limited to the digital world. Digital advocacy organizations use social media, and email, to rapidly mobilize the public on the streets or take part in vigils. In the aftermath of the violent attacks on two mosques in New Zealand in March 2019, where 51 people were killed, ActionStation quickly redirected its energy and helped to organize some of the mass vigils. Meanwhile, Amnesty in New Zealand was not able to shift staff resources as quickly because it was already committed to existing campaigns. During the Trump years, MoveOn pre-organized and 'banked' major offline demonstrations, which could be triggered if needed. MoveOn ran a 'predictable emergencies' project, which identified escalating military conflict with North Korea or Iran as possible actions Trump might take. MoveOn then asked local organizers to identify locations and register online to host emergency rallies, which could be launched and populated with attendees, if and when the situation got to a 'red alarm' status.[50]

'Pivoting', or switching campaign focus, is an integral part of the OPEN model. Digital advocacy organizations regularly give up campaigns that are not gaining member support. Robin Zachari, the executive director of Skiftet, noted that: 'we've abandoned hundreds of campaigns', we 'abandon [campaigns] on a weekly basis'.[51] As he explained: 'we burn for many issues, [but are] quicker to abandon when [a campaign] doesn't work because there's often a

[48] Becky Jarvis, online presentation on email writing, February 2016. Brandzel (2019).
[49] Interview with Siobhán O'Donoghue, 20 June 2019.
[50] Email correspondence with Ben Brandzel, 28 June 2021.
[51] Interview with Robin Zachari, 13 June 2018.

new campaign to launch. We try to strike balance.'[52] Another Skiftet colleague confirmed this in a separate conversation, stating: 'we fail campaigns all the time, because we are trying campaigns all the time'. She explained, 'Our goal is just to try so much as we can.'[53] MoveOn also emphasizes this culture of fast failure on its website:

> We believe that MoveOn, first and foremost, is playing the role of an innovator in the world of politics. We're breaking convention and aggressively trying new things. We're not afraid to fail, but only because we have to try a lot of stuff to find those things that succeed, and break open new ways of doing business.[54]

38 Degrees, in particular, has cultivated a culture of rapid-response campaigning. When inducting new staff, it shares a document outlining key elements of this culture, which include: 'Be prepared to get things wrong', and 'Never let the perfect stand in the way of the good' and 'Be nimble'. The organization encourages staff to 'be trusting and trustworthy' and so if you get something wrong, admit it. Finally, it instructs staff not to be siloed, 'bunker', or 'huddle too closely in a small team', but rather to keep an eye on the latest news and keep fresh. 38 Degrees makes decisions quickly, and will speedily 'go from reading the news to taking action'.[55] 38 Degrees has recommended that other organizations wanting to follow its model should aim to 'pivot quickly and surge on one moment' and 'get as many hands on deck to get [campaigning] as quickly and ambitiously as possible'.[56]

I visited the 38 Degrees offices in London in October 2016 and witnessed how it put this into practice. The Brexit referendum had been held just four months prior to my visit, and staff were in the midst of a busy campaigning period. People were working away on their own laptops in an open plan office. Staff had no fixed seats or desks. They would shift their working space, depending on who they were working with, and that could change daily, and even over the course of the day. David Babbs, then the executive head of 38 Degrees, sat in the middle of the office on a bean bag and people passed by to have quick meetings.

The fast-changing seating plan is an explicit policy of 38 Degrees to facilitate rapid-response campaigning. Teams can form, make collective decisions,

[52] ibid.
[53] Interview with Skiftet staff member, 19 June 2019.
[54] MoveOn, 'How We Staff—Small and Nimble', https://front.moveon.org/moveon-way-how-we-staff/ (accessed 6 December 2021).
[55] 38 Degrees, 'Running Rapid Response Campaigns' shared at OPEN summit, 22 November 2017.
[56] ibid.

and dissolve rapidly, without having to relocate all of their belongings. In fact, their operations manager at the time explained to me that her job was to support 'fluid decision-making' because they 'didn't want to have too much bureaucratic structure' and this style of decision-making is 'the essence of 38 Degrees'.[57] 38 Degrees stands out amongst the older, larger OPEN organizations in this respect. None of the other OPEN organizations that I visited had such open-plan, fluid seating arrangements in their offices.[58]

The Limitations of Rapid-Response Campaigns

There are, of course, downsides to rapid-response campaigning; organizations may be caught up in 'presentism' and always focus on the most recent events. A regular topic of concern amongst OPEN activists is whether they are winning the battles but losing the war, given their fleeting engagement with many causes. Most of these organizations want to see seismic, progressive shifts in their national politics. Sometimes concentrating on short-term reactive campaigns can blind the organizations from deeper political problems and changes. For instance, many environmental campaigners in North America thought they had won a major victory when Obama came out against the Keystone pipeline. But then Trump was elected to power, overturned Obama's decision, and pulled the United States out of the Paris Climate Agreement. However, these same environmental groups would likely claim a victory with the election of Joe Biden in 2020. Biden made strong commitments in his first year in office to address climate change, with one of his first acts as president being to re-enter the Paris Climate Agreement.

Rapid-response campaigning also assumes that other organizations are doing the longer-term, sustained agenda-setting campaigns to get issues on to the public agenda. Many OPEN staffers are aware that they rely on other NGOs and civil society organizations' hard work. These staffers see their role as complementary to the traditional, sustained campaigning mode. OPEN organizations' distinct advantage, in this view, is that they can quickly mobilize a much broader movement than issue-specific NGOs. However, digital advocacy organizations may also move too fast, and undermine the work of committed, expert NGOs. They may also fail to follow through and ensure that a campaign win is not just a political pledge, but is actually implemented.

[57] Interview with Operations Manager, 38 Degrees, 27 October 2016.
[58] MoveOn is distinct, as all staff work remotely and there is no organizational headquarters.

OPEN organizations differ in how much emphasis they place on rapid-response campaigning. Some, such as 38 Degrees and Skiftet, prioritize prospecting, while others put more emphasis on longer-term, planned campaigns. Campact has typically concentrated on one major campaign over several years, such as ending Germany's use of nuclear energy, and stopping the Transatlantic Trade and Investment Partnership (TTIP).[59] However, at the time of writing, this trend was changing. In 2018, one of Campact's senior staff members explained to me that, for 'more than one year we've had no big topic, [we] have to adapt to this'.[60]

Although most OPEN organizations take pride in rapid-response campaigning, they may be part of sustained, longer-term campaigns. Experienced OPEN staffers such as Becky Jarvis have run sessions at OPEN summits on 'how to build a long-term strategic campaign out of a series of rapid response moments'.[61] GetUp's refugee campaigns in Australia are a good example of this. In 2015, GetUp employed human rights campaigner, Shen Narayanasamy, and set a goal of getting all asylum seekers out of detention in Manus and Nauru. For the next five years, GetUp's staff worked consistently on this issue, running a number of different campaigns, such as #Letthemstay and #No Business in Abuse, which had various rapid-response moments (Hall 2017a, 2019a and b).

Digital Analytics

> We often say every email is a survey.
>
> – Benjy Cook, Zazim[62]

Digital technology enables this rapid-response, multi-issue, and member-driven model. OPEN organizations use digital technologies to rapidly aggregate their members' preferences and determine which campaigns to run. They engage in sophisticated digital analytics to identify the most effective framing and tactics for campaigns (Karpf 2016). As Zazim staffer Benjy Cook noted above, every email to members operates like a survey as organizations can test what issues and messaging will capture their members. To my knowledge, no other major international NGO has regularly used digital analytics to test campaigns and determine which issues to focus on, or which tactics to use.[63]

[59] Campact may still use rapid-response tactics within a longer-term, issue-focused campaign.
[60] Interview with Campact staff member, February 2018.
[61] Becky Jarvis, presentation at OPEN start-up summit, Berlin, 2015.
[62] Benjy Cook, Zazim Staff member at OPEN summit, Langenselbold, 20 June 2019.
[63] ibid. See also Karpf (2016); Hall et al. 2020.

A/B Testing

Many of the OPEN groups embrace 'analytic activism': a culture of testing their communications with members to trial campaigns and identify those with the most support (see also Karpf 2016). A/B testing is the simplest and perhaps most commonly used form of testing. Two versions of an email are developed, which are similar, except for the subject line heading, or some other content or feature (e.g. 'Demonstrate on Friday for the Climate' vs 'Get out on the streets to save the climate'). Staff will send several thousand people email A, and several thousand email B. After seeing which version has the best opening rates, staff then send that email to their full list. Using an A/B test can increase the likelihood that members subsequently open emails, read them, and take action. OPEN organizations will test what issues to campaign on, what tactics to use, and what arguments to use to mobilize supporters. They also test communications on Facebook, Whatsapp, and other platforms.

Some OPEN organizations also segment their list according to members' interests; for example, some members will be more interested in human rights than the environment, so the majority of emails these members receive will be human rights-related. One member may receive an email alerting them to the environmental impacts of a trade agreement, while another may receive an email focused on the human rights impact of that same agreement. In this way, OPEN organizations can campaign across multiple issues simultaneously, while appealing to their members' primary concerns. As an example, in 2015, Campact experimented with different emails for its TTIP campaign. It had three different versions of an email: one emphasized economic justice, another the environment, and the third democracy. Each was then mailed to different sections of Campact's list.

The process of testing starts with campaign staff. Staff choose a campaign issue, and/or email subject line to test. They then choose the sample size of those who will receive the email, and how long the testing will last for (e.g. three hours or one day). 38 Degrees, for instance, tests around three to four new issues per week.[64] Staff coordinate tests to ensure that different sections of their email list receive them. Campaigners will monitor how many emails the organization is sending collectively to their members. 38 Degrees does not send more than one email per day to its members.[65]

[64] Online communication with Robin Priestely, 38 Degrees Staff member, 30 June 2021.
[65] ibid.

OPEN organizations look for campaigns that will immediately take off. They seek out emails with the highest open and action rates, petitions that are growing fast, and campaigns that are generating high levels of donations and/or recruiting new members. Skiftet, for example, used to trial its campaigns on Facebook (before Facebook changed its algorithm), and if a campaign received 500 signatures in the first 24 hours, staff would then email the campaign to Skiftet's full list.[66] Organizations following this model are driven by campaign growth and member engagement (i.e. the number of subscribers who open an email, who watch a Facebook video, or share a Tweet about a campaign). Many OPEN organizations have internal dashboards, which collate data on membership growth, petition growth, donation rates, and action rates. Staff will refer to this data when making decisions about which campaigns to run.

OPEN organizations test a wide range of features of their communications and engagement with members. Organizations have tested what colour donate button gets the most donations (orange is better than blue) or monitored the popularity of their social media posts. They may also test door-knocking strategies and scripts. MoveOn, as Karpf has documented in detail, has particularly sophisticated analytics capabilities (Karpf 2016). The organization can calculate how much money an email is likely to raise if it sends to everyone at once, versus sending to a smaller component of the list over time.[67]

Larger OPEN organizations have enough members to generate statistically significant results. However, some of the smaller organizations do not have such large membership lists, and so rely on results from a small number of users (e.g. this may be in the hundreds rather than thousands). These organizations are below the 'analytics' floor whereby test results are not that informative for predicting the future success of a campaign (Karpf 2016). Nonetheless, OPEN staffers will often encourage new OPEN start-ups to use A/B test campaigns, and/or monitor other analytics (e.g. growth rates of petitions, donation rates, membership growth) to embed these practices, which they see as integral to organizational success.

[66] Author's visit to Skiftet, Stockholm, 13 June 2018.

[67] Some OPEN organizations retain information about a members' preferences from one campaign to the next. This data can help advocacy organizations to customize and reach members more effectively.

Member Surveys on Campaign Preferences

OPEN organizations also regularly consult their members using weekly, monthly, and/or yearly surveys. These surveys enable staff to rapidly identify what issues their members want them to campaign on. OPEN organizations vary in how regularly they use surveys.[68] 38 Degrees typically surveys members once a week, whereas Skiftet does so only every other month or so. 38 Degrees' weekly survey asks members to list the top issues they want the organization to campaign on that week. Staff then meet every Monday morning to select campaigns based on the results of this member survey (Karpf 2016). In its biannual survey, Skiftet asks members: What topics are urgent to you? What campaigns do you like the most? And what skills can you share? And do you want to donate money to Skiftet?[69] Skiftet also does issue specific surveys on bigger campaigns.

In 2018, Akcja Demokracja in Poland gave its members over twenty different campaign topics and, for each one, asked them which category it fitted into:[70]

- Yes, very important to me. I want Ackja to deal with it.
- Rather Yes. The action should be taken care of.
- I have no opinion.
- No. This is not what you do.

The issues members were asked to comment on included independence of the judiciary, health care for all, election manipulation, renewable energy resources, health care and housing conditions for the elderly, discrimination against lesbian, gay, bisexual, and transgender+ (LGBT+) peoples, refugees, rights of tenants, disability, environmental protection, junk contracts, smog, hate speech, the right to a roof over your head, TTIP, the EU–Canada Comprehensive Economic and Trade Agreement (CETA), the right to abortion, public space, protection of trees against felling, independence of institutions approving the election, and climate protection. Members were also asked at the end of the survey: 'Do you have other ideas on themes?', which Akcja Demokracja could work on.

OPEN organizations differ in how they use surveys. Some will first identify campaigns, brainstorm viable campaign strategies, and only go to members

[68] I do not have information on what percentage of the membership on average responds to surveys, and thus what proportion of the membership determines the direction of the organization.

[69] Skiftet fieldwork notes, Stockholm, 13 June 2018.

[70] Ackja Demokrajca, weekly survey to members (15 June 2018), https://dzialaj.akcjademokracja.pl/surveys/50?utm_source=weeklypoll (accessed 6 December 2021).

if they identify a viable strategy. Campact, for instance, typically brainstorms campaigns based on 'scanning and scouting of issues' across a full range of media and from conversations with other civil society organizations. If it sees potential for a campaign, then a campaigner will develop a campaign concept, and in parallel start a survey of members. As a former Campact founding director explained: 'If the survey shows interest and [the] assessment demonstrates relevance then they will launch a campaign.'[71] Members still play a pivotal role in determining campaign selection, but staff do initial work to scope out viable campaigns. They will only run a campaign if there is a clear theory of change and it has member support.

Surveys offer a snap shot of members' preferences at a particular time, and these preferences evolve as new controversies and crises unfold. Digital advocacy organizations do not always follow members' preferences as revealed in annual surveys (Vromen 2017). There are at least two reasons for this: organizations ignore members' preferences and pursued whatever issues staff wanted; or they rapidly adapted their campaigning priorities during the year as new issues arose (Vromen 2017: 116). Organizations which try to closely mirror their members' changing preferences are more likely to switch priorities in response to new crises.

Member-Initiated Petitions

OPEN organizations have also delegated power to their members to launch their own campaigns.[72] OPEN organizations have developed separate petition websites, based on ControlShift software, which enables anyone to write their own online petitions by simply filling in an online form.[73] It is extremely quick to do, taking only minutes to detail the petition's aim, the targeted decision-maker (person or institution), and why other members should get involved. Members can start campaigns on any issue that affects them at local, regional, or international level. Staff often moderate these member-initiated petitions to remove campaigns that do not align with their values or guidelines (e.g. a campaign to open more coal mines would not be accepted on most platforms). Both the individual and the digital advocacy organization benefit from member-initiated petitions. The individual gets an easy and free platform

[71] Interview with Günter Metzges, 9 December 2016.

[72] See Table A1 in the appendix for a full list of the member-initiated online petition sites.

[73] ControlShift Labs, https://www.controlshiftlabs.com/ (accessed 6 December 2021) and see also 38 Degrees, 'Campaigns By You', https://you.38degrees.org.uk/petition/new?source=homepage (accessed 6 December 2021).

to run a petition, and can re-engage petition signatories on further related issues. Meanwhile, OPEN groups can attract new members to their organization. The software behind these petitions, produced by Nathan Woodhull, was commissioned by GetUp in 2011 and now serves a wide range of progressive organizations.

OPEN organizations differ in how much staff time and organizational resources are dedicated to monitoring and promoting member-initiated petitions.[74] ActionStation relies on ten to fifteen volunteer *kaitiaki* (guardians) of ActionStation's community values, who review every campaign submitted to OurActionStation.[75] 38 Degrees has involved the 'biggest users of member-initiated petition platforms' across OPEN and there is 'tonnes of action through ControlShift', according to one OPEN team staffer who oversees the network.[76] 38 Degrees have a team that moderates petitions and actively coaches members who start campaigns. 38 Degrees will even 'pick up the phone and call them and say "hey I think this campaign would be stronger if we presented it like this or worded it like that … do you have a good photo you could upload? … do you know anybody who works for the local paper? Could you give them a call?"'.[77]

Staff may invest significant time to support a member-initiated petition. For example, in 2018, 38 Degrees staff promoted a petition started by Geraint Ashcroft, which asked Walkers Crisps to 'ditch plastic packaging'. After seeing how fast the petition was gaining support, 38 Degrees staff publicized this petition to its wider membership, asking members to send an empty packet of Walkers Crisps back to Walkers (Belam 2018). Following this public pressure, Walkers eventually announced it would launch a scheme to recycle crisp packets.[78] 38 Degrees sees power in giving members a platform to run their own campaigns.

The Limitations of Digital Analytics

Campaigners looking to optimize member growth and engagement may select campaigns which are most likely to get member support, and ignore important causes. As Karpf has pointed out, 'you are what you measure' (Karpf 2016: 133). Activists can use digital analytics to avoid making difficult decisions. They may

[74] Online interview with Michael Snook, 19 October 2018.

[75] OurActionStation, 'About Us', https://our.actionstation.org.nz/about_us(accessed 6 December 2021).

[76] Online interview with Michael Snook, 19 October 2018.

[77] Email correspondence with Michael Snook, 30 June 2021.

[78] Geraint Ashcroft (2018). 'Walkers Crisps: Ditch Plastic Packaging'. 38 Degrees campaign (5 October), https://you.38degrees.org.uk/petitions/recyclable-crisp-packets (acessed 6 December 2021).

focus on campaigns that generate good action rates, but have no theory of change. Organizations may concentrate so much on optimizing their subject lines that they neglect other issues which are harder to address. In fact, some OPEN organizations don't run A/B tests for campaigns they think are unlikely to gain majority support, regardless of how they are framed (e.g. racism or campaigns related to Palestine). Digital advocacy organizations which chase membership growth may prioritize easy, popular, campaigns, such as saving the bees rather than running on more difficult issues, such as criminal justice reform. Simply chasing membership growth does not result in long-term impactful organizations which advance progressive change.

Sometimes members and staff prioritize issues differently. For example, in 2017 GetUp asked its 1+ million members whether they should campaign to legalize gay marriage. Members had little interest in the campaign and overall ranked gay marriage between tenth and thirteenth on a list of priority issues.[79] GetUp may sometimes 'drop' a campaign, 'if it doesn't perform well' when it is put to members, but in this case it did not.[80] Rather, staff 'Made an institutional call—that members would be proud of the work [if they continued with the gay marriage campaign]'.[81] GetUp became a lead coordinator of the equal marriage campaign, working alongside corporations including Qantas and Monsanto, and many civil society organizations (Karp 2017a; 2017b; Bettles 2017) . The campaign was ultimately successful; over 60 per cent of Australians voted in favour of legalizing same-sex marriage in a national poll.

There are other instances where staff in digital advocacy organizations have run campaigns which initially had little member support, but have subsequently convinced members it was a worthwhile cause.[82] Notably, one of Akcja Demokracja's largest and most important recent campaigns started with low interest from members.[83] The Law and Justice Party, which took power in 2015, sought to control the Polish judiciary by setting term limits for judges in the Supreme Court. The initial proposed legislation would have removed independent judges, given parliament powers to appoint the judiciary, and forced current judges to retire early (Davies 2018). However, according to Weronika Paszewska, Akcja Demokracja's executive director, their membership had 'little sympathy' for judges and low interest in defending them.

[79] Interview with Michael Poland, 22 November 2017.
[80] ibid.
[81] ibid.
[82] Staff in one major OPEN organization described running a campaign on racism even though they had only received a 1 per cent action rate when it was tested.
[83] Interview with Weronika Paszewska, co-founder and former executive director of Akcja Demokracja, 22 November 2017.

Paszewska thought that the campaign would bring them 'no members, no money, and no media' and should therefore be dropped.[84] However, in 2017, Ackjca Demokrajca made a 'long-term commitment' to the campaign because its 'core values triumphed over [member] growth'.

Over time, members grew increasingly supportive of this campaign.[85] In July, people called on the Polish president, Andrzej Duda, to intervene and stop the forced retirement of the judiciary (Davies 2018). Ackja Demokrajca worked with other civil society organizations and co-organized large demonstrations, which attracted thousands of people. The protests in July 2017 were somewhat successful: President Duda vetoed part of the government's legislation (Davies 2017). However, the Polish government has continued to try and pass legislation to control the judiciary, leading to an EU court ruling against it in June 2019. Ackja continued to mobilize its members on the streets to protest for an independent judiciary (Rankin 2019). Digital advocacy organizations not only respond to their members' immediate revealed preferences, but can shift these preferences over time.

In sum OPEN organizations exist on a spectrum between a staff-driven logic and a purely member-driven logic. Chapter 8 examines in depth the differences between these two logics.

NGOs and Digital Advocacy Organizations: Cooperation or Competition?

So how do digital advocacy organizations fit into an already crowded advocacy sector? Do they cooperate or compete with traditional NGOs? A growing field of IR scholars are turning to population ecology to unpack the relationships between NGOs within particular sectors (Abbott et al. 2016; Eilstrup-Sangiovanni 2019; Bush and Hadden 2019). These scholars would not be surprised by the emergence of digital advocacy organizations, as they have predicted that new forms of advocacy organizations will emerge in densely populated advocacy sectors (Bush and Hadden 2019).

At its most general level, population ecology scholarship predicts cooperation in less densely populated sectors, but competition in densely populated sectors (Bush and Hadden 2019: 1134). We might expect digital advocacy

[84] Interview with Weronika Paszewska, co-founder and former Executive Director of Akcja Demokracja, 23 November 2017.

[85] ibid.

organizations to find niches where they can satisfy demand for their advocacy, without having to directly compete with traditional NGOs. Scholars have noted that older NGOs are more likely to use conventional tactics, while newer organizations are more likely to employ radical tactics (Eilstrup-Sangiovanni 2019). While existing studies offer insights into specific advocacy sectors (e.g. environmental advocacy in the United States), their predictions are harder to apply for these multi-issue digital advocacy organizations precisely because they campaign across many issues simultaneously. Here, I take a look at the evidence for cooperation and competition between NGOs and digital advocacy organizations.

Competition

A recurring theme for some NGOs is that digital advocacy organizations steal the limelight and claim victory for themselves. Staff in digital advocacy organizations are also aware of their reputation of being 'pesky kids'. As one former 38 Degrees staffer explained, they were initially known for 'being brash, big boots and trampling on everything'.[86] While other groups might spend years developing relationships to lobby decision-makers, 38 Degrees could quickly mobilize thousands, then claim credit for any win. However, this former 38 Degrees staff member also noted that the organization's reputation had changed over time, particularly as it had become more engaged in the NGO sector. As she noted: 'Most of the [38 Degrees] staff spend 8 hours a day on the computer, and need to get out more, get fresh new ideas, and connect with people.'[87] Whether staff at a digital advocacy organization attend meetings with other NGOs is a good sign of their relationship to the sector as a whole. Some, such as Skiftet, report that they very rarely attend meetings because they do not have time to do so. Other organizations, such as GetUp, Campact, and ActionStation, have made efforts to coordinate other NGOs on particular issues.

NGOs have also flagged concerns about losing staff to digital advocacy organizations. In November 2017, I attended a meeting of Oxfam advocacy directors from around the world, and one senior staffer noted that they were losing all their top staff to digital advocacy organizations. Some NGOs feel threatened by new digital advocacy organizations. A trade expert I spoke with

[86] Interview with 38 Degrees former staff member, 27 October 2016.
[87] ibid.

noted that 38 Degrees, with its 'amazing email list, could reach a lot of people' during its anti-TTIP campaign, whereas other specialized NGOs could not and found this 'difficult'.[88] A staff member of a UK-based NGO explained that the 'problem is for people who think they have a monopoly over an issue'.[89] This follows the predictions of population ecology: newcomers to a sector threaten established organizations' turf.

Collaboration

Yet there are also dozens of examples of digital advocacy organizations collaborating with established NGOs and civil society organizations. This is particularly the case in stewardship-led organizations. Campact, for instance, regularly works with other advocacy actors in Germany, and even across Europe. They work in coalitions to mobilize supporters to attend large marches against free trade agreements, for example, or for climate action. As founder Günter Metzges explained to me in 2016, Campact are 'different from MoveOn as they have a deep collaboration perspective' and regularly work with other organizations such as Greenpeace, Friends of the Earth, and social justice organizations.[90] Jurjen Van den Bergh launched De Goede Zaak in the Netherlands with the aim of running campaigns in partnership with other Dutch advocacy groups.

ActionStation also prioritizes collaborative campaigns with issue-expert NGOs. This is partly because it is such a small organization, where you can count the number of full-time staff on two hands. Furthermore, because it operates in a small country, where everyone knows each other, ActionStation staff are conscious that if you annoy a fellow NGO, it will come back to bite you. Murdoch Stephens (2018), who partnered with ActionStation for the 'Double the [Refugee] Quota' campaign, noted that:

> it might have looked like ActionStation starting and leading dozens of campaigns but while they initiated some, at the centre of each of these early campaigns was often an individual or a group who had been working in the area for years. They were a perfect match for our campaign—we'd developed

[88] Discussion with UK-based trade expert, 19 June 2020.
[89] Online interview with Alex Randall, UK Climate and Migration Coalition, 29 November 2016.
[90] Interview with Günter Metzges, 9 December 2016.

> the specific ask and they had an audience likely to be sympathetic to that.
> (Stephens 2018: 70)

But why would other NGOs collaborate with OPEN organizations? Issue-based NGOs typically have smaller membership bases than digital advocacy organizations. They benefit from having (indirect) access to larger membership lists, which can be mobilized rapidly to build broad movements. For example, Stephen's campaign to double the [refugee] quota in New Zealand, received access to 100,000 emails of New Zealanders by partnering with ActionStation.[91] He explained that he explicitly chose to partner with ActionStation because 'Rather than being the hub of expertise and passion for just one issue, ActionStation became something akin to the cavalry who would arrive to support a pressure campaigner just as their efforts were starting to receive mainstream attention' (Stephens 2018: 69–70). He elaborated that ActionStation 'functioned like a floating resource for pressure campaigns that suddenly find their time in the spotlight' (Stephens 2018: 70).

Meanwhile, digital advocacy organizations benefit from others' issue expertise. ActionStation benefitted from Stephen's knowledge of New Zealand's refugee policies. GetUp and 38 Degrees, in their tax justice campaigns, for instance, formed 'collaborative relationships with other groups around mutual benefit, offering their mobilization capacity and broad supporter lists, and usually acknowledging their lack of policy expertise' (Vaughan 2020: 125). Vaughan found that 'multiple UK organizations similarly talked about the value 38 Degrees brought to joint campaigns by mobilizing a wider pool of public supporters at critical campaign moments, as opposed to long-term organizing or policy development' (Vaughan 2020: 125).

In this view, digital advocacy organizations are filling a distinctive niche in the advocacy ecosystem. Alex Randall, who works at the UK Climate and Migration Coalition, explained that:

> The existence of 38 degrees, Avaaz, 350.org have shaped how we work. When I'm getting to a point in my advocacy where I think I need an on-line petition then I stop, because I'm not geared up for this. Instead I reach out to these organizations and ask them if they would do an on-line petition? Could it work?'.[92]

[91] Stephens had tried their first online petition with Avaaz, but it was a 'miserable failure', collecting less than 380 signatures in the first six months of the campaign (2018).

[92] Online interview with Alex Randall, UK Climate and Migration Coalition, 29 November 2016.

He elaborated that many other advocacy organizations would be 'happy' they were 'part of the ecosystem'.[93] OPEN organizations can be constructive allies to traditional NGOs.

Emulation

Some larger traditional NGOs are now looking to emulate elements of the OPEN model (Hall et al. 2020). Oxfam has hired OPEN campaigners as consultants to advise on digital campaigning. In 2010, Greenpeace set up *MobLab* after witnessing how effective 350.org and other digital advocacy organizations were at mobilizing people with much fewer staff and less financial resources. *MobLab* aimed to introduce rapid-response, member-driven digital campaigning into Greenpeace, and several national chapters launched their own member petition websites using the same ControlShift software, as noted in Chapter 2. Some NGOs have also started using digital analytics to identify the most effective campaign messaging (e.g. subject line or formatting). As far as I am aware, none have used digital analytics to select the issues they campaign on.

We are likely to see NGOs experiment with various digital tactics, but not to fully embrace the OPEN organizational model. This is because many large NGOs are risk averse and do not want to delegate power to their members (or the broader public) to determine campaigns. In addition, many NGOs are reluctant to switch campaigns regularly because this would not endear them to the philanthropic foundations and government donors which fund them. Moreover, NGOs are emmeshed in specific areas of global governance, such as anti-corruption and human rights, where their subject expertise is a real source of power and legitimacy. Digital advocacy organizations are unlikely to replace traditional NGOs, as they rely on them for their issue expertise and agenda-setting powers.

Conclusion

Digital advocacy organizations rapidly launch campaigns and switch between issues, thanks to email, social media, and the ease of launching petitions online.

[93] ibid.

They use digital analytics to aggregate members' preferences, and identify what issues to campaign on, what tactics to use, and how to frame their messaging. These characteristics make them distinct from the traditional NGOs most frequently studied by IR scholars.

There are serious limitations to this model. Digital advocacy organizations may run campaigns which have support from an immediate majority of members, but ignore minority rights issues, such as racism or refugees' rights. Their rapid-response model means that they may not follow through and ensure that campaign wins are implemented. They may simply drop a campaign if it is not gaining traction, even if it is a worthy cause. Meanwhile, these organizations rely on other NGOs to provide issue expertise and to do the long-term battle of capturing the public's hearts and minds. Many digital advocacy organizations are aware of the limitations of running purely member-driven, rapid-response campaigns. Campact, GetUp, and ActionStation, for example, often run longer-term campaigns and build up expertise in areas such as refugees' rights and climate change.

The following chapters now turn to the transnational level. We know that the *organizational forms* of advocacy have changed in the digital era, but how does this affect transnational campaigning and collaboration?

5

The Purposes of a Transnational Network

Activists from around the world gathered in a conference room for the first session of an Online Progressive Engagement Network (OPEN) summit. As a warm-up exercise, the facilitator asked us to find others in the room who had the same shoe size. What had seemed like a simple task quickly became complicated as we realized that shoe sizes were not universal. Some tried to translate their shoe sizes into British, Australasian, North American, and European measures. Others lined up their feet and tried to compare them by sight. Once we had found our shoe size match, the facilitator asked us to find people who had worked in an OPEN organization for the same amount of time. There was quite a bit of variance: one person had just started one month before, while another had been with an organization for fourteen years. We then stood in groups with people who shared the same job function. Categories included operations, campaigners, tech, and executive directors. A cluster of participants were 'hybrid' and covered multiple roles. These exercises demonstrated that there were many similarities amongst people across OPEN: some of these were useful (e.g. years of experience or position); others perhaps less so (shoe size). However, the shoe size exercise proved the most powerful because it demonstrated the importance of understanding different contexts: a size 7 shoe size in the United States meant something different in the UK. And one size does not fit all.

OPEN facilitates knowledge transfer by building trust and solidarity between activists so that they can share their successes and failures in activism. To make this knowledge transfer work, OPEN activists have developed a common language to describe what they do. If a campaign message, tactic, or strategy works in one country, it may work in another.

A GetUp email which successfully mobilized the Australian public to support refugees may also have similar success in the United States. Many OPEN summit sessions are built on this assumption: groups share the lessons they have learnt campaigning on issues such as trade, refugees, and climate issues; or share common tactics or strategies used in fundraising, contacting members, and organizing events. OPEN organizations also share a culture

Transnational Advocacy in the Digital Era. Nina Hall, Oxford University Press.
 DOI: 10.1093/oso/9780198858744.003.0005

of 'fast failure' experimentalism, which drives these organizations to try out different messages, tactics, or strategies. This culture of testing, described in Chapter 4, facilitates global lesson-learning, as digital advocacy organizations are more likely to be risk takers than many other non-governmental organizations (NGOs).

OPEN is an unusual network in that all of its constituent organizations share the same model of advocacy rather than a commitment to a common issue such as debt relief, women's rights, or climate change (Busby 2010; Keck and Sikkink 1998; Krook and True 2010; Hadden 2015).[1] Full members of OPEN pay membership fees to a central secretariat, and have created a common charter and governance structure. However, each organization retains complete autonomy to determine what it campaigns on, when, and how. Scholars have explored how the structure of advocacy networks influences the tactics they employ and the collaborations they form (Hadden 2015; Brown et al. 2012).

This chapter examines the forms of trust, solidarity, and cooperation across OPEN. It asks: how does the structure of OPEN influence the forms of transnational cooperation that occur? It argues that the activists in this network share a deep commitment to common progressive values and a similar mode of campaigning. They regularly exchange information over email, Slack, Facebook, Zoom, Whatsapp, and most importantly, via deep personal connections forged through in-person summits and staff secondments. The first section describes these channels of transnational cooperation and emphasizes the importance of face-to-face meetings, even in the digital era.

The second half of this chapter examines three different forms of collaboration within OPEN: growing, *enhancing* and *cooperating*. Although member organizations are strongly committed to the network, they have differing views of its purpose. Some want OPEN to support the diffusion of digital advocacy organizations worldwide, to *grow* the network. Some see OPEN as a community of practice, where new staff can learn about the OPEN model and more experienced staff can refine and *enhance* their digital advocacy. In this mode, OPEN should focus primarily on connecting staff and enhancing the work of national organizations. Others, meanwhile, see OPEN as a platform for *cooperation* on transnational campaigns. In this view, OPEN should actively foster common and collaborative campaigns. There are tensions and trade-offs between these visions of OPEN.

[1] International relations (IR) scholars often treat transnational advocacy networks as the primary unit of analysis rather than the organizations that comprise these networks (Busby 2010; Keck and Sikkink 1998). They see a primary purpose of these networks as information-sharing as well as establishing and reinforcing a common identity to reinforce collective action (Hadden 2015: 53).

The lessons of this chapter extend beyond the community of OPEN. First, online collaborations are important, but survive and thrive only with regular, face-to-face meetings. IR scholars should be cautious in over-emphasizing the role of internet communications in transnational advocacy (Warkentin 2001; Lavelle 2020: 224; Scholte 1999). Second, the governance structure of OPEN has resulted in few collaborative transnational campaigns. OPEN has an intentionally weak secretariat with no centralized power to set international campaigns (Brown et al. 2012). Each digital advocacy organization owes primary accountability to its individual, national members, not to the international secretariat. In addition, the member-driven model of each organization means that campaigns are targeted at national priorities, not global ones. IR scholars should further examine how the structure of a transnational network shapes the development of common advocacy campaigns.

Connecting: Channels of Communication

Many IR scholars have claimed that the internet would enable greater connections among activists around the world (Warkentin 2001; Narlikar 2020). There is an obvious logic here: the internet has become central to many of us, especially during the COVID-19 pandemic, when many relied on it to work, shop, and keep in touch with friends and family. So how central is the internet in enabling this scattered network of activists to connect and collaborate? OPEN organizations do interact regularly through email, social media, Skype/Zoom conversations, and Slack. However, the most important interactions, which stimulate cooperation, are carried out face-to-face at summits and staff secondments, where a member of one organization is embedded and works in another organization. Most staff will engage in multiple channels of communication across OPEN over the course of a year. However, some staff will be more engaged than others. The 'foreign minister' and executive director of each OPEN organization are likely to have more contact with other OPEN staffers than a new, junior member, who may have no regular, direct contact with OPEN.[2] Table 5.1 summarizes the different channels of communication which were most often initiated and supported by the OPEN secretariat. The OPEN secretariat staff closely monitored all of these communication channels, and looked for ways to increase the quantity and quality of exchanges

[2] The foreign minister is responsible for representing their digital advocacy organization to OPEN and for liaising between OPEN and their organization. Their role is to make sure that their colleagues were aware of opportunities to learn from, or contribute to, other organizations.

Table 5.1 Examples of channels of communication

Channel	Examples of communication exchange	Audience	Online/face-to-face
Slack	Clustered into specific areas of expertise, e.g. trade	Interested or relevant people participate, not directed at all OPEN members (and private—i.e. only accessible with a password)	Online workspace
Email	Sharing successes/failures; and specific inquiries	Can be bilateral conversations between organizations or emails through OPEN's listserve (e.g. 'OPEN-Friends' group)*	Online
Facebook	Share campaigns; personal stories/support	Available to all OPEN members, but within a closed Facebook group	Online
Whatsapp/SMS/Signal**	Organize logistics during a summit, share photos, news items	Available to OPEN members	Online
Skype/Zoom	Coaching sessions, webinars, campaign development and coordination, including 'OPEN live' webinars	Available to all who join a meeting	Online
The Commons	A library of resources for campaigns	Available to all members of OPEN	Online
Summits	In-depth discussion on the OPEN mode, campaigns, technology, common challenges	Select representatives of OPEN	Face-to-face
Secondments	Staff member hosted in another organization	Bilateral exchange between organizations (one sends an employee, and the other hosts)	Face-to-face

Note: *In 2015 OPEN's listserv and social media connected more than 200 staff from OPEN's member groups. Eighty-four per cent of all member staff took part in OPEN's email groups (listserve), and 83 per cent were part of the OPEN Collaborator's Facebook group. OPEN. (2015). OPEN 2015 Annual Report (on file with author). ** OPEN shifted to Signal due to security and privacy concerns regarding Whatsapp.

across the network. For example, they regularly surveyed OPEN members to ascertain which of the network activities they found most useful for their work.

As Table 5.1 demonstrates, activists working in digital advocacy organizations often cooperate online. Slack, for example, is a particularly important space, as it enables groups to share ideas in one centralized space, organized around a topic, and avoids cluttering email inboxes with messages. Slack groups are managed by OPEN and are not for public viewing. However, all of these online channels work because of close relationships built face-to-face at summits or through secondments. As one OPEN staffer explained, Slack is 'where the real work and conversations happen, after the summit'.[3] as the example below illustrates Slack is used for sharing best and worst practices across the network. It allows people to follow particular topics.

An example of a Slack notice, 28 May 2018[4]

Julia Olszewska_Akcja_Demokracja [2:51 p.m.]

Friends!: Recently we have recorded a short video, encouraging our members to stay with us after the introduction of GDPR [General Data Protection Regulation]: https://www.youtube.com/watch?v=iEXoa9oAw84

I suggest a quick round of exchange of any recent videos your organizations have produced recently. Let's the inspirations, good (and bad) practices spread around the network! 3, 2, 1 … go! :clapper.

Summits are vital to OPEN. They are a space to meet offline and to build connections, develop trust, and innovate collectively. Even though OPEN is a network of digital activists, the summits are crucial to enable further online collaboration. As one staff member explained, this is 'where you can feel the magic that you don't get in a Zoom [call] or other off-line exchange', and 'where everything starts'.[5] Others have emphasized how much they value the summits, and how important and powerful an experience it is to connect with people

[3] Interview with OPEN staffer, 5 August 2019.

[4] The EU's GDPR rules meant that many digital advocacy organizations had to explicitly ask their members to opt in to receive their emails. In the past, some groups had simply kept and used email addresses for subsequent campaigns. Many OPEN groups were concerned they would lose members if they had to explicitly ask them to opt in.

[5] Interview with Stephanie Roth, OPEN staff member, 5 August 2019.

who have common values and face similar challenges. One activist explained that at the summit she would meet people that became close friends 'like you never know they existed', she elaborated: 'it's my crowd'.[6] Another noted the importance of meeting in person as it 'can sustain digital connections'.[7] I will now examine these summits and, in particular, what forms of collaboration they precipitate.

In an average year, OPEN hosts four summits, each focused on different aspects of the network: technology, the core group, start-ups, and executive directors. By the end of 2017, the network had hosted 18 summits, with a cumulative total of 400 participants.[8] As the membership of OPEN has grown, the network has modified the summit format and schedule: as of June 2019, the start-up and core group summit had merged into a single summit for the entire OPEN community. There have been: several regional summits, issue-specific summits on refugees and climate change, as well bilateral meetings between organizations.

Typically, summits last an entire work week, with people arriving on a Monday morning and leaving on Friday afternoon. Everyone stays in the same hotel, or camp dormitory, and there is an intense schedule of back-to-back meetings. Summits occur around the world. I have attended summits in Australia, Canada, Germany, and India. Each organization has a strict quota of attendees relative to their size. Smaller organizations may receive some financial support from OPEN to attend. The summits are typically closed to outsiders, with the exception of a small handful of trusted people.[9]

The summits begin with 'ice-breakers'—exercises that enable attendees to get to know each other and build trust. Facilitators typically encourage all to be mentally and emotionally present throughout, to switch off from the internet, and get out of fast-paced, reactive campaigning mentality. Few have computers in the plenary sessions and instead focus on listening and engaging deeply with each other. On the first day of the summit, all attendees will discuss and agree on community norms to ensure that it is a safe space for all. A common refrain is the importance of speaking slowly, so all can follow. English is the working language of the OPEN community, but most participants speak it as a

[6] Interview with Laura Rico Gutiérrez de Piñeres, 23 November 2017.
[7] Discussion with Zazim Staff member, 17 November 2017.
[8] OPEN, data on summits (on file with author).
[9] The author is one of the regular outsiders that attends these summits. Other regular outside participants include a technology developer, Nathan Woodhull, and Associate Professor David Karpf, who has also studied OPEN. In addition, OPEN regularly invites external guest speakers such as several former Bernie Sanders campaigners. Potential donors and/or other NGOs, such as 350.org and SumOfUs, may attend specific sessions.

second language. Language and cultural differences can limit comprehension and collaboration between groups.

Before the summit, OPEN organizes a loose agenda with a few set plenary sessions. The vast majority of time is dedicated to 'open space'. Open space allows for maximum flexibility and spontaneity. People propose sessions they would like to run, or topics they would like to learn more about. The agenda is then built on the spot during the summit. People are free to move between sessions that run in parallel and there is a strong focus on conversation and learning between groups rather than presenting pre-prepared speeches. The summits enable activists to connect on whatever issues they think are important, instead of what a conference committee might want them to discuss. Generally, the OPEN summits are extremely well facilitated and create a strong sense of community and appreciation for the network. The summits are not important decision-making fora.[10] Their primary purpose is to connect activists, socialize them in the OPEN model, and offer new insights to even the most experienced digital campaigners.[11]

Participants can add new sessions on the same day or host a popular session twice to enable others to attend. For example, at the 2019 summit, a session on gender and power was held several times, due to its popularity. In these sessions, OPEN organizations regularly share new tactics, technology, or campaign successes, with the aim of learning from each other. The assumption is that learning will flow from older to younger organizations, and from younger to older organizations. If an older, larger OPEN group instructs other newer organizations on the best way to do something, the latter often push back. The OPEN summits also build in time for reflection. People are assigned to 'summit crew' (a mix of people from different OPEN organizations), who they meet with daily to share what they have learned. Individual OPEN organizations make sure to spread their staff across sessions and then regularly debrief, in their mother tongue, on what they have learned. In short, OPEN summits are a fertile place for brainstorming, sharing ideas, building new collaborations, and setting concrete goals. The summits spark new collaborations, which may continue through the online channels mentioned.

Summits are also high-energy, social, and fun. In between sessions, some participants may leap up to have a quick dance to raise the energy in the room if people are getting tired. Most days, there are social activities such as a scavenger hunt or karaoke. The last night of the annual summit is the biggest

[10] There are no binding decisions taken at the OPEN summit. Decisions are more likely to be taken by OPEN's Executive Council (created in 2019) and before that by OPEN's Core Group.

[11] They are also used to gather input before the OPEN core group meeting (now Executive Council).

night of all: the 'Opies' (OPEN's spin on the Oscar awards). OPEN organizations compete to win awards, such as: the best cooperation, best reactive campaign, best proactive campaign, biggest institutional shift, biggest innovation, most generous movement-giving, and biggest failure. People dress up, enter on a red carpet, and with much merriment listen to the master of ceremonies, who reads out the nominees for each prize. Participants vote by pen and paper and there are stellar talent show performances (Brandzel sings every year). These awards enable groups to learn about others' campaigns and, importantly, have a good time, while creating a norm of celebrating generosity and cooperation within the network. After the awards, there is dancing, and a party atmosphere, regardless of whether the summit is in a small German town or a school camp on the edge of the Canadian Rockies. Although they may not all share the same shoe size, they can and do dance to the same tune!

People tend to leave the summits with deep friendships and a strong awareness of what other organizations are doing. As Karpf explained in his 2013 report after the first summit, 'There is deep theory behind the laughter here ...Maintaining that conversation across hectic schedules and global time zones depends on cementing the network ties among individuals. If this first OPEN Summit indeed becomes the first of many, its participants will remember it best for the sledding and song.'[12] One attendee described the experience of spending extensive time with similar organizations as 'mind-blowing' and 'transformative'.[13] The participants saw value in meeting regularly in person with their counterparts in other countries to share technology, tactics, and strategies. As Karpf noted in 2014, 'Groups like Campact, GetUp, and 38 Degrees do not have within-country peers that they can compare notes with. They are unique within their own nations but can harvest lessons from their global peers.'[14] OPEN was created to connect these 'sister' organizations and enable them to learn from and support one another in a high-trust and high-solidarity network.

Staff exchanges, or secondments, are another innovative way OPEN organizations learn from each other. Staff from one organization will often be sent to another for several weeks, or even months, to help with particularly important campaigns, such as an election. Once there, they immerse themselves in the work of the partner organization. The logic is that both the guest and host organizations learn from each other. In its first year (2013–2014), OPEN organized exchanges to and from all five founding groups. No such staff exchanges had

[12] David Karpf, OPEN summit report 2013 (on file with author).
[13] Interview with Felix Kolb, 9 February 2018.
[14] David Karpf, OPEN summit report 2014 (on file with author).

occurred prior to the establishment of OPEN.[15] By late 2018, there had been 135 physical visits between OPEN organizations, including short visits of less than one week. In addition, OPEN secretariat staff had conducted eighty-one physical visits to OPEN organizations or potential start-ups.[16]

The OPEN secretariat actively cultivated exchanges between OPEN organizations. It regularly surveys the network's staff and asks them: where they would most like to work; what skills they could share; and what skills would most benefit them. The OPEN secretariat then plays a match-maker role, identifying who could be sent where. It also identifies when an OPEN organization might need extra support (e.g. for an upcoming election). The OPEN secretariat also tracks secondments and keeps a list of which organizations are sending and receiving the most. OPEN sees secondments as a vital way to enable the network to share tactics, strategies, and technologies. In fact, sending and receiving secondments is a requirement for full membership of OPEN.

Brandzel has highlighted that these relationships of inspiration, support, and solidarity across the network have enabled OPEN to stick together against the odds. As he explained in one of his last emails to OPEN as executive director in 2018:

> OPEN is like the bumble bee that, according to physics, shouldn't be able to fly. We are 19 fully independent domestic groups fighting for unique member-generated priorities, each rapidly responding to 19 different media cycles, in 13 different working languages, stretching across 20 time zones—with no common branding, very little common funding and zero central authority. By all normal laws of social physics, this community shouldn't be able to come together, stay together, or lift off the ground. But somehow, the relationships we've forged—along with the inspiration, support and solidarity that flow through them—allow us to defy gravity. It's been the greatest privilege of all to be part of that little miracle.[17]

The OPEN secretariat is faced with a daunting task: it has no centralized power, but must continually show its relevance and utility to its member organizations. So what do OPEN members and secretariat staff want from the network?

[15] OPEN, Secondment data, 2019 (on file with author).
[16] ibid.
[17] Ben Brandzel, Email to OPEN, 2018 (on file with author).

The Purpose of OPEN

OPEN publicly advertises four principal purposes of the network: to *connect* digital advocacy organizations, *enhance* the work of existing members, *grow* by supporting the creation of new OPEN organizations, and *collaborate* on common campaigns.[18] These purposes can be mutually reinforcing, but can also pull the network in different directions and place strain on limited funding and human resources. Connecting, which is achieved through summits, secondments, and the various digital channels of communication described above, is critical for all the other three functions to work. OPEN secretariat staff put significant energy into facilitating and monitoring these connections.

Grow

OPEN secretariat staff provide ongoing support to help new organizations fundraise, campaign, and learn from each other. They help with organizational development (e.g. staffing plans, board composition, fundraising); leadership (e.g. managing the personal costs and stresses of start-up life); and the 'specific craft' of online campaigning and building a movement. OPEN offers regular coaching to activists who are new to the model. They help start-up organizations choose, customize, and launch their websites, petition platforms, and campaigns. Becky Jarvis, a former OPEN staffer offered: 'Coaching support, mentoring, helping them launch, and network [with] people who are doing the same things'.[19] Perhaps most importantly, OPEN staff introduce prospective members to the broader OPEN community.

For most, the OPEN summits are the first real introduction into OPEN. Many of the founding executive directors of OPEN organizations report that they had little awareness of the network, or how the model worked, before attending a summit. Maria Mayrhofer, #aufstehn's first executive director, travelled to Berlin to attend the OPEN start-up summit when she was just two weeks into her new job. The summit was a pivotal introduction to digital, rapid-response advocacy, and connected her to other activists setting up organizations in their own countries. The founders of Akcja Demokracja in

[18] OPEN, 'What We Do at the OPEN', https://www.the-open.net/what-we-do (accessed 6 December 2021). The OPEN secretariat closely monitored its success in each of the four categories, and surveyed member organizations for their feedback.

[19] Online interview with Becky Jarvis, 26 May 2016.

Poland were also invited to attend the 2014 start-up summit, which was 'the tipping point when we decided it would work' according to Paszewska.[20]

At summits, senior OPEN staff run regular sessions explaining the eight-fold path, offer advice on digital analytics, and guide staff of new and prospective organizations on how to write rapid-response emails. Jarvis sees emails communication as one of 'the most important skills that a campaigner has'.[21] While email was initially the principal way that OPEN organizations communicated and built trust with their members, social media and Whatsapp have become increasingly important tools. Jarvis runs workshops on the key principles for writing emails to mobilize members to take action. She encourages them to present an urgent crisis in the subject line and in the first line of the body of the email, and then to offer an opportunity to sign a petition or donate.[22] There is a real craft to writing an email to communicate to members why their action can make the difference.

Many start-up groups emphasize how important OPEN is, not just for these practical and technical skills, but for emotional support and solidarity. As one activist explained, 'Trying to do this [set up an OPEN organization] on my own—it's too risky, too demanding, too solitary.' Raluca Ganea emphasized that OPEN 'gives me so much strength' as the organizations face 'similar challenges' across the network and it is 'reassuring to know we're not alone, and will never be behind on tech or strategy [as we] have the best knowledge resources available and will always be at front of everything'.[23] One of Declic's co-directors explained that the 'confidence I have in my work comes from you guys [at OPEN]. When I'm at home, I have this energy, as if we are all here together, thinking together.'[24] Weronika Paszewska, Akcja Demokracja's first executive director also saw a great 'advantage of OPEN'.[25]

Many activists said they relied on OPEN for training and support because there were no other domestic organizations or networks they could turn to. This was especially important at the beginning, when many would otherwise

[20] Interview with Weronika Paszewska, co-founder and former executive director of Akcja Demokracja, 23 November. See also list of founders here: Akcja Demokracja, https://www.akcjademokracja.pl/zespol-i-rada/ (accessed 5 December 2021).

[21] Online interview with Becky Jarvis, 26 May 2016.

[22] Ben Brandzel, Slide Deck: 'From Moment to Movement and Beyond, A guide to Email writing for Action', available at https://www.digital-advocacy.com/advocacy/what-is-a-crisitunityhttps://www.digital-advocacy.com/advocacy/what-is-a-crisitunity (accessed 5 December 2021).

[23] Interview with Raluca Ganea, founder of Zazim, 23 November 2017.

[24] Interview with Declic co-founder, OPEN start-up summit, 24 November 2017.

[25] Interview with Weronika Paszewska, co-founder and former executive director of Akcja Demokracja, 23 November 2017.

feel quite alone.[26] They turned to OPEN to answer a range of questions on technology, financing, management, and campaigns. In Poland, for instance, 'it was not easy to transfer the concept, the model' and many Poles said 'it wouldn't work'.[27] Poland lacked a history of crowd-fundraising, as the Polish NGO sector was largely created in 1989, after the Cold War, and with foreign financing. Hence, civil society organizations in Poland were largely project-driven and grant-driven, 'with no connection to the people'.[28] The founders of Akcja Demokracja researched peoples' willingness to donate to prove that the OPEN model could work in Poland. Akcja Demokracja also received initial grants from Campact, 38 Degrees, and the European Climate Foundation, and was attacked for doing so.

OPEN has helped start-up organizations to fundraise in-country and internationally and has also supported them through OPEN's start-up grants, or through bilateral grants from other OPEN organizations, such as Campact or 38 Degrees. These funds are often critical in the early years, when organizations are not yet well known enough to gain sufficient crowdfunding (or even philanthropic funding). The OPEN grant is a competitive grant which all OPEN registered start-ups can apply to.[29] In 2015, Skiftet received 64 per cent of its annual total revenue from OPEN and sister organizations.[30] This financial support covered many of its operational costs during its early years. Akcja Demokracja in Poland also received significant funding from OPEN organizations in its early phase. In 2015, Campact, for example, donated approximately €20,000 and 38 Degrees €27,000.[31] Akcja Demokracja was also funded by donors outside the network, including the European Climate Foundation, the Global Greengrants Fund, and Purpose Climate Lab. ActionStation[32] and Amandla.Mobi[33] also benefitted from Campact grants,

[26] ibid.

[27] ibid.

[28] ibid.

[29] Grant decisions were based on four broad criteria: (a) the organization's sustainability and need for resources; (b) the likely impact of that organization in their country; (c) the potential impact of their country internationally on key OPEN issues (e.g. climate change, progressive taxation, trade, refugees/immigration); and (d) how much the organization would contribute back to OPEN. OPEN, Guidelines for ROI ratings for the OPEN fund (on file with author).

[30] Skiftet received 1 million Swedish Kronor, which is equivalent to almost €100,000. Skiftet, 'Donantionstransparens', https://skiftet.org/donera/donatinspolicy/ (accessed 5 December 2021).

[31] Akcja Demokracja, 'Report for 2015', https://dzialaj.akcjademokracja.pl/campaigns/raport-01-#pieniadze (accessed 5 December 2021). The figures are estimates as they are converted from Polish Zloty using the average currency conversion for 2015 available here: European Central Bank, Euro Exchanges Rates, https://www.ecb.europa.eu/stats/policy_and_exchange_rates/euro_reference_exchange_rates/html/eurofxref-graph-pln.en.html (accessed 5 December 2021).

[32] ActionStation, 'Who Funds Us?', https://www.actionstation.org.nz/about/our-funding (accessed 5 December 2021).

[33] Amandla.Mobi, 'Funding', https://www.amandla.mobi/funding (accessed 5 December 2021).

although neither organization has publicly disclosed the total value. Most often, OPEN grants have been provided for general organizational development, not earmarked for a particular campaign.[34] This is important, as other funders tend to restrict their grants to specific issues.[35]

Many of the digital advocacy organizations established after 2013, express a strong commitment to OPEN and their fellow organizations. They are aware of how much they owe the network for their own growth, and see significant benefits in cooperating internationally. They also want to give back generously to the network, which helped them in their early, critical years. In contrast, the older established groups do not see OPEN as so central to their organizational development. After all they existed before the network was established. Instead, they look to OPEN to help them enhance their existing campaigns.

Enhance

From the outset, OPEN sought to connect digital activist organizations and enable them to exchange information and learn from each other to improve their own campaigns. OPEN was created because there were no other similar organizations from which MoveOn, Campact, 38 Degrees, or GetUp could learn in their own country. If these organizations wanted to discuss how to improve their rapid-response, multi-issue, digital advocacy model, they had to look beyond their own national borders. In this sense, OPEN constitutes a community of practice for established digital advocacy organizations.

Technology ('tech') development and exchange is one of the most important aims of OPEN. A former OPEN tech director noted that OPEN groups will collaborate on tech exchange even when there are political tensions which prevent them from cooperating in other areas. A key motivation for creating OPEN was to invest in mutual tech development. At the first summit, there was a 'general agreement that the OPEN groups have common technological needs and ought to collaborate around shared platforms'.[36]

Parallel to the creation of OPEN, Brandzel secured a three-month pro-bon contract with ThoughtWorks, a global software development firm, to support Nathan Woodhull's efforts to develop technology specifically for OPEN

[34] OPEN groups have occasionally offered funding for specific campaigns. 38 Degrees, for example, donated £98,042 to other OPEN groups across Europe to help it campaign against the TTIP (Whalley 2016). Campact also financed OPEN organizations' anti-TTIP campaigns (Bauer 2016b).

[35] For example, Omidyar funded Skiftet and ActionStation's work on digital governance and democracy.

[36] David Karpf, OPEN summit report 2013 (on file with author).

organizations. Woodhull is committed to providing progressives with technology, and is by far the most engaged non-OPEN staffer in the network. He was a co-host of the first OPEN tech summit in April 2013, attends most of the OPEN summits, and is in regular contact with OPEN organizations throughout the year. He developed ControlShift software which enables OPEN organizations to set up distributed campaign events, local groups, and member-generated petitions. ControlShift Labs is described as '[your] distributed organizing toolbox [...] the best software for putting people at the center of your campaigns'.[37] Many of the organizations expressed interest in distributed campaigning at the first summit in 2013, and again in 2014, and subsequently adopted ControlShift software.[38] Woodhull operates as an OPEN technology consultant, developing new platforms and features that work specifically for OPEN's organizational needs. He consults OPEN groups on what technology they would like him to develop, and has offered large discounts to new, start-up OPEN groups.

OPEN organizations have regularly discussed and shared new software and technology. A common refrain amongst OPEN organizations is that they need to innovate and diversify away from email as a primary form of communication. Email faces the 'diminishing returns of a once-novel communications medium'.[39] In the past few years, many have trialled short message service (SMS) and Whatsapp campaigning, peer-to-peer messaging, and videos on Facebook. During the summits, OPEN groups share their reflections on what works and what doesn't in sessions such as: 'Beyond Email: Mobile, Social and Video Techniques and Tactics'. At a summit in 2017, for example, GetUp shared how they used Facebook advertising in the 2016 Australian Federal election.[40] Meanwhile, MoveOn shared the successes of its new Video Lab, which received millions of views by taking advantage of the then new features of Facebook Live.[41]

Meanwhile, at the start-up summit in 2017, the Israeli member organization Zazim presented how it used Facebook tools to customize and target its campaigns effectively.[42] Using information publicly available on Facebook, Zazim demonstrated how it could determine how many of its members are women, how many are parents, and what other Facebook groups or pages people follow

[37] ControlShift Labs, https://www.controlshiftlabs.com/ (accessed 6 December 2021).
[38] David Karpf, OPEN summit report 2014 (on file with author).
[39] David Karpf, OPEN summit report 2013 (on file with author).
[40] David Karpf and Nina Hall, OPEN summit report 2017 (on file with author).
[41] ibid.
[42] Note that this information is only available at the aggregate level, and does not display individual-level data.

(e.g. environmental groups or human rights groups). This has helped Zazim to understand who supports which campaigns. It found that some campaigns reach women more successfully than men. OPEN organizations are also experimenting with Instagram to reach younger generations who do not use email or Facebook as regularly. An underlying concern is that their membership is ageing and so they need to reach new audiences to stay strong. OPEN activists have discussed the potential of using Facebook bots to engage members and respond to their concerns through automated dialogue.

At the OPEN core group summit in 2017, 38 Degrees presented Identity, a new tech tool which made many developers and campaigners visibly excited. Identity enabled 38 Degrees to develop multi-channel, customized messaging across email, Facebook, and SMS using a single platform. 38 Degrees had previously used separate platforms for interactions with its members on petition pages, email, and phone. Identity made it possible to target people via the platform where they would be most likely to respond: if someone did not open, or respond to an email, 38 Degrees could then follow up with a targeted SMS. Although 38 Degrees tech had put significant resources and time into developing Identity, it was willing to share this with other OPEN groups because the staff 'feel very integrated' with other tech teams in OPEN.[43] As the 38 Degrees tech lead at the time explained, 'we are giving quite a lot away [for free], [and] at first glance might seem we don't get much back. It does give you a lot of work now that everyone wants to use Identity'.[44] However, he also saw the advantage of sharing tech among OPEN groups, as 'other people find problems with tech before you do; they find and fix bugs, they tidy code up or add whole new features'.[45] OPEN organizations collaborate to experiment with, and advance, new forms of analytic activism.[46]

Technological requirements and development capabilities vary significantly across the network. 38 Degrees has invested in tech development and is well known for being generous within the network. MoveOn has the most access to new tech because of its large size and access to the US tech market. However, it often uses US market-specific platforms (e.g. Twilio). Meanwhile, OPEN organizations such as Campax in Switzerland need to operate in multiple languages (Swiss German, French, and Italian), and the platforms that Anglophone groups use are not always easily adaptable.

[43] Denny de la Haye, 38 Degrees tech lead, 1 March 2017, OPEN summit.
[44] ibid.
[45] ibid.
[46] GetUp has shared its phone banking tool, which it used during elections to contact voters, as described in Chapter 2.

Yet overall, common technology is one of the major benefits of OPEN membership. As Giovanna Negretti, the current executive director of OPEN explained on the OPEN friends email list in January 2020: '*At the start of 2020, almost every organisation in the Network is using some core tech that was built by some organisation in the Network*, and these pluggable, shareable tools now cover so much of the overall organising tech landscape that together they're being referred to as the OPEN stack' [Negretti's emphasis in italics].[47] This tech infrastructure is critical for smaller OPEN organizations, who generally do not have the financial resources to develop their own. They rely on larger OPEN organizations to share tech innovations with them.

In addition to tech collaborations, OPEN organizations regularly share fundraising, outreach, and campaigning tactics, as well as organizational and management practices. Campact and MoveOn, for instance, have shared fundraising strategies through which they have gained regular donors. Regular monthly donors are sought after, as they provide financial stability and security. OPEN groups often share which campaigns, messages and emails brought-in high donations, and other groups will copy directly text, images, and formatting.

Member engagement is another central element of OPEN organizations' discussions. Staff regularly discuss their 'members' journeys', or how members experience their interactions with their organization. At summits, staff share ways to deepen and broaden member engagement. A common theme is whether groups should follow a 'ladder of engagement', whereby you start with an easy ask (such as signing an online petition), and then ask members to do more difficult or time-consuming tasks (e.g. turning out for a demonstration, and organizing their own event). An alternative strategy is to directly ask members to take a 'high-bar' action rather than a lower-cost action. Becky Bond and Zack Exley, two campaigners who had previously worked for Bernie Sanders, promoted the latter strategy at the OPEN start-up summit in 2016. They pointed out that some people want to 'do big things', such as getting arrested to stop the Keystone pipeline, even if they have never signed a petition (Bond and Exley 2016). Similarly, Akcja Demokracja asked its members to take 'high-bar' actions, such as holding strikes in support of women's rights in Poland in 2017.

Groups often discuss how to best support their members to run their own campaigns. OPEN organizations' staff left their first summit with plans to experiment with Woodhull's distributed campaign tools. Subsequently, many OPEN organizations established member-initiated campaign websites and

[47] Giovanna Negretti, email to OPEN friends (on file with author).

processes to moderate these campaigns (e.g. removing petitions which were against their values and helping those that aligned). At subsequent summits, OPEN organizations have regularly reflected on how to support their members to develop their own campaigns. Campact, for example, has encouraged petition starters to engage in offline actions. MoveOn has a basic tool kit for members who start campaigns, which outlines how to do press outreach and how to report back to petition signatories. OPEN organizations also educate and share information with their members on tactics and campaign planning. There are regular discussions about the right balance between distributing campaigning power to members and centralizing it within staff hands.[48]

OPEN organizations also share specific tactics for offline campaigns. Campact regularly hosts a session at summits on how to organize large-scale demonstrations. Campact is well known in Germany and in the network for its role in coordinating large marches in Germany. These have included: the Hamburg G20 summit, the United Nations Framework Convention on Climate Change (UNFCCC) in Bonn 2018, and various anti-TTIP marches in 2015 and 2016.[49] MoveOn began to organize more large-scale demonstrations in the Trump presidential era. In January 2017, for example, it mobilized people to protest against Trump's immigration ban. MoveOn became a leader of the resistance movement, and helped to organize many other large marches, such as the Women's March and March for Our Lives (Fisher 2019b).

OPEN groups also regularly share election campaigning tactics. For the 2018 mid-term elections, MoveOn developed 'Real Voter Voices'. It asked members to record a short video explaining why they would vote for the Democrats. MoveOn then shared videos on social media, and targeted them at swing voters who lived in the same district as the member who made the video. In 2019, Campact adopted a similar model for state elections in Brandenburg and Thuringia. Meanwhile, GetUp adopted Campact's tactic of producing and distributing door hangers, which focused on free trade agreements, to their members.

While OPEN organizations engage in both online and offline tactics, they rarely discuss or use more radical forms of protest, such as direct action (Graeber 2014).[50] Instead, they opt for tactics that are likely to get mass scale support, such as petitions, demonstrations, and letters or phone calls

[48] David, Karpf, OPEN summit report 2013 (on file with author).

[49] OPEN groups have targeted international organizations or negotiations when the summit is hosted on their home territory. This is discussed in Chapter 6.

[50] According to Graeber, 'Direct action means insisting on acting as if one is already free.' (2014: 207), by which he means free from state structures (of violence). Direct actions could involve occupying a public or private space (e.g. OccupyWallStreet or Greenpeace's occupation of oilrigs), blockades, sabotage, squatting, or taking other actions deemed illegal by the state, or on the fringes of legality.

to MPs (Han 2014).[51] Only on one occasion did I witness a discussion on direct action, which was chaired by someone from outside the OPEN community. OPEN groups likely believe that the majority of their members would not take more radical, direct action tactics. OPEN influences what tactics digital advocacy organizations use by promoting some tactics (e.g. online petitions, social media campaigns, or large demonstrations) over others. This finding resonates with other IR scholarship: who NGOs regularly interact with in a network influences how radical the tactics are that they will take. (Hadden 2015).

Underlying the OPEN summits is a puzzle, familiar to any comparative political scientist: if a tactic, or messaging works in one country (e.g. Germany), under what conditions will it work in another (e.g. Australia)? The political culture of a country, its demographic make-up, and its electoral system can influence what can be successfully shared and implemented across OPEN. Not everything shared at OPEN summits will inherently 'enhance' another organizations' campaigns. Every activist and organization engaged in OPEN has to identify what may work in their country. The differences between national contexts also poses challenges for cooperating on the same campaign, at the same time, which I turn to now.

Collaborate

OPEN has created a high-trust network built on common progressive values and shared digital advocacy methods. However, it is rare for these organizations to establish common transnational collaborations on specific campaigns. Some IR scholars may be surprised that organizations in such a dense network, which regularly meet face-to face and operate in a highly globalized world, rarely campaign collectively on transnational issues (Lavelle 2020; Warkentin 2001).

OPEN summits have held sessions on specific transnational issues such as trade, climate change, and the far right. Activists will meet in these sessions to share the lessons they learned campaigning in their own context. It is remarkably rare for these conversations to develop into a plan to campaign

[51] Han (2014) distinguishes between *mobilizing* (which is mostly about scale or quantity of actions/supporters), and *organizing* (which is more focused on the quality or *depth* of commitment to a cause, and occurs when organizations develop their members' capacity to run campaigns themselves). OPEN organizations tend to engage more frequently in mobilizing than organizing.

collectively.[52] Rather, these conversations tend to focus on identifying what worked in one context and reflecting on what lessons can be transferred and tried in another. Digital advocacy organizations may also share their most embarrassing failures, and worst worries, but these discussions rarely translate into transnational campaigns which focus on the same issue, the same target, at the same time. To demonstrate this pattern, I examine conversations at summits between 2017 and 2020 on tackling the far right. In Chapter 6, I expand this analysis by looking at the frequency of transnational campaigns across four OPEN organizations over a one-year period.

The far right was a common concern across many OPEN countries, triggered by the 2016 Brexit referendum in the UK and the election of President Donald Trump in the United States. There was also increased popular support for far-right political parties in many other OPEN countries, including Australia, Austria, Germany, Hungary, Poland, and Sweden. The February 2017 OPEN summit was the first time most OPEN organizations had met since Brexit and Trump's election and featured a 'deep discussion of how we *unite* to build the power to counter the appeal of demagogues' [italics as in the report].[53] Groups reflected 'intensely on the role of the OPEN organisations in combating populism and addressing the rise of the far-right'.[54] These conversations happened as a whole group, in smaller break-out open sessions, and over breakfast, lunch, and dinner.

On the first day of the Vancouver summit in 2017, OPEN held a two-hour plenary session to discuss the following questions: 'What are the global trends in populism? And what can be learned—regarding political developments, and campaign strategies—across countries?'.[55] Attendees broke into groups, uniting with their colleagues from the same organization, to map out what was happening in their national political contexts. Pens and flip-chart paper were distributed and groups drew or wrote their perspectives to present back to the plenary. Groups were then mixed to discuss a series of guided questions about global trends in populism and the far right. Finally, there was a discussion about what could be learned across all the OPEN organizations. Participants reflected on whether there were key ways of framing conversations to combat the far right and avoid adding fuel to their fire. I was a participant observer at this summit and assisted the one representative of

[52] One exception is the EU summit in Berlin in February 2019, where European OPEN teams developed a common election tactic for the 2019 European elections. However, even this was challenging to execute, as groups faced very different national contexts.

[53] Nina Hall and David Karpf, OPEN summit report 2017 (on file with author).

[54] ibid.

[55] ibid.

ActionStation in summarizing the situation in New Zealand. Although all activists in the room felt that the issue was important, it was hard to find collective campaign strategies, given that the phenomena of the far right and populism were so different across countries in OPEN.

Thanks to the flexible format of the OPEN summit, activists and groups created other sessions at the 2017 summit to continue the conversation. There was a session hosted by Campact on 'How to campaign against the populist far-right on social media.' One concern a Campact member voiced was: if Campact campaigns on Alternativ für Deutschland (AfD), does this play into AfD's hands?[56] ActionStation, whose staff had been on the receiving end of social media attacks, presented on how it was training its members to conduct anti-trolling work online. Meanwhile, GetUp described how it was using paid advertising on Facebook to talk to 'middle-Australia' (an ambiguous term, commonly used to refer to people who are not aligned to a particular political party) rather than trying to convert the far right.[57] GetUp shared its campaign messaging—which focused on negative campaigns against conservative candidates—rather than promoting a particular progressive candidate. GetUp representatives also noted that they were trying to find messaging that might work against One Nation (Australia's most xenophobic party) by explicitly 'Not focusing on race ... as we can't convince racists not to be racist, but can convince them not to vote for a party that's against their interests.'[58] Many expressed concern about Cambridge Analytica and the potential impact of bots in other election campaigns.

At 5 p.m. on the last full day of the summit, there was a subsequent conversation around the rise of the right, which twelve people attended from Canada, the United States, Germany, Ireland, and New Zealand. One participant mentioned that the first-day plenary session was a 'problem-based discussion' rather than a 'solution-based' one. This session started by taking a 'temperature in the room' on how bad the situation was for them and their members on a scale of one to ten, with ten being the worst. Most groups reported a seven, eight, or nine. Participants then discussed specific examples of what OPEN organizations were doing to stop the right and/or advance a progressive message. MoveOn, for example, reported that member energy was 'really high' as people 'are creating their own actions' and 'organizations are trying to tap into grassroots energy'.[59] It explained that the airport demonstrations

[56] Nina Hall, OPEN summit notes 2017 (on file with author).
[57] ibid.
[58] ibid.
[59] ibid.

against Trump's immigration ban in January 2017 were spontaneously organized, but that MoveOn had created a weekly call to coordinate people. Finally, the groups discussed if and how their own organizations were changing to adapt to the far right. Brandzel made a final intervention stating that OPEN was ready to 'support in any way possible'. It would in particular continue to spot trends, and make sure 'our victories are shared, and our challenges are shared'.[60]

In short, while there was a deep commitment in many OPEN organizations to tackling the rise of the far right, there was no obvious collective, transnational campaign to be forged. Although populism and nationalism continued to be a dominant theme of many future discussions and summits, OPEN organizations have not identified a common campaign to combat this issue. This is partly because the phenomenon of the far right is different in each country, but also because one effective way to counter the far right is to campaign against them at regional, national, and local elections. Given the vastly different electoral systems in OPEN countries, it makes little sense to collaborate on a common campaign beyond sharing the lessons each group has learned.

In fact, this pattern of conversation was quite typical of many OPEN summit sessions. Activists would present their campaigns on refugees, trade, climate change, or online hate speech. They would have robust discussions to identify the key lessons learned from a particular campaign, which would often be followed up with bilateral exchanges after the summit through email, Slack, Facebook, and other forms of social media. However, as one activist from the Global South noted, 'not everything is applicable across all contexts'.[61] Thus, it was rare for OPEN organizations to forge common campaigns, with the same target and issue, at the same time.

Staff of the OPEN secretariat did their best to highlight potential areas for cooperation through newsletters, email, or social media. However, they did not have the power to start or set campaigns. As Brandzel explained to me, he had 'no transnational binding authority' to set campaign priorities.[62] This had to be done by a member organization, and OPEN organizations often found it hard to identify a common 'crisitunity' across the entire network.

OPEN's decision-making is decentralized and driven by national priorities. Even if one OPEN member organization wanted to run a coordinated global campaign, it still had to convince other OPEN organizations to collaborate.

[60] ibid.
[61] Interview with global south activist, 6 February 2018.
[62] Interview with Ben Brandzel, 30 January 2021.

MoveOn for instance, wanted to run an international campaign to prevent President Trump going to war in 2017. MoveOn was concerned that Trump would trigger a war with North Korea due to his aggressive rhetoric, unpredictable behaviour, and dismissal of foreign policy expertise. MoveOn, which had played an active part in the anti-Iraq war protests, hired a new staffer, Jessica Shearer, and tasked her with coordinating global actions to push for peace. It was one of the rare occasions where MoveOn sought international assistance to help a domestic campaign and it looked to OPEN for help.

Shearer worked closely with Brandzel and put this campaign on the agenda for the 2017 start-up summit in Berlin. Brandzel and other OPEN secretariat staff encouraged all participants to attend a session on stopping Trump's war. (Although there was no enforcement of this, many organizations sent at least one representative.) Shearer led the discussion and spelled out the urgency of taking action. As she saw it, there was a '50 percent chance of [the US] going to war this year'.[63] Brandzel spoke strongly for all OPEN groups to work with MoveOn on the campaign. He emphasized the importance of international pressure, as he claimed that the decision to go to war is one of the 'very few times that the US cares about what the rest of the world thinks'.[64]

However, the other activists in attendance were not so convinced that there was a clear theory of change for their members to influence Trump's decision.[65] One pointed out that Trump did not act rationally, and was more likely to accidentally end up going to war. Others suggested that to influence Trump, you needed to appeal to his supporters, and OPEN groups had no leverage over them. A Romanian activist noted that it would be difficult for them to run a campaign because many Romanians were strongly pro-United States (and anti-Russia), and would see it as 'treason' not to support the United States. The discussion ran for over two hours and in the end there was just a small group of active participants because other attendees had left for other sessions.

By the end of the 2017 start-up summit, Brandzel and Shearer had managed to convince a small cohort to consider action. They proposed a global online meeting for peace. Every OPEN organization would encourage its members to join and listen to a series of speeches about the need to stop a war (translated into their own language). MoveOn would manage the logistics of the call with OPEN support and make it as easy as possible for OPEN groups to participate. Brandzel and Shearer saw the online call as a tactic to cultivate global support for future action against President Trump. However, not all groups were

[63] Jessica Shearer, OPEN summit, Berlin, November 2017.
[64] Ben Brandzel, OPEN summit, Berlin, November 2017.
[65] Discussions at OPEN summit, Berlin, November 2017.

convinced of the tactic. One senior campaigner argued that it made little sense because there was no way a common call would gain media attention, let alone influence Trump. Nevertheless, Shearer was impressed with how 'open' and 'willing [the OPEN groups] were to try and experiment with a campaign, even if it doesn't seem to make sense [to them all]'.[66]

In the following months, OPEN and MoveOn worked together to organize the logistics and the speakers for the call, which included Bernie Sanders. OPEN encouraged all groups to advertise it to their members and to send the details to their full list. Given that MoveOn was much less engaged in the network than other groups, Brandzel wanted to demonstrate the value of the OPEN community to them. However, as executive director of OPEN, he had no control over whether or how OPEN groups advertised the global call. It was up to each organization to decide whether and how to get involved. Not all were convinced of the action, nor actively involved, given other competing national priorities.[67]

In summary, the structure of OPEN limits its ability to coordinate campaigns across multiple countries. OPEN has a weak central secretariat and each organization has complete autonomy from the others. All groups engage voluntarily in the network. The secretariat staff can facilitate the sharing of information and tech across the network, but can't determine campaign priorities.[68] OPEN is made up of autonomous national 'movement building organizations' (Brown et al. 2012). Each digital advocacy organization responds to its national context when campaigning, and derive its accountability from its individual members (Vaughan 2020).

OPEN is starkly different from other international NGOs, which have centralized secretariats that coordinate campaigns across multiple countries. Greenpeace International, for example, is a federation of national chapters with a powerful international secretariat, which can determine campaign priorities (Brown et al. 2012). Greenpeace opted for this centralized, hierarchical structure because it wanted to campaign more effectively, coordinate resources, and create a global environmental movement (Zelko 2013: 314). 'Mission-driven' organizations such as Oxfam and Greenpeace, which have long-term commitment to a cause, tend to opt for hierarchical and centralized

[66] Jessica Shearer, OPEN summit, Berlin, November 2017.

[67] Most OPEN groups did publicly support the call and many OPEN organizations featured in a short video introduction to it.

[68] OPEN does occasionally receive grant funding for common transnational campaigns (e.g. on trade or climate); however, even in these cases, it cannot override national priorities.

governance structures because it allows them to run coordinated campaigns (Brown et al. 2012).[69]

In contrast to Greenpeace, Oxfam is a confederation and power resides largely in the national organizations rather than the international secretariat. However, Oxfam International can still set campaign agendas. In fact, Oxfam created the confederate structure to coordinate its advocacy activities internationally. According to two former staff members, the Oxfam affiliates 'felt that they too needed to be international in the way they organized their advocacy' because many of the institutions they wanted to influence were also 'international in nature' (Atkinson and Scurrah 2009: 53). They created a confederation to have 'all the Oxfam affiliates around the world saying the same thing at the same time, via the media, popular campaigning, lobbying, etc to the same targets' (Atkinson and Scurrah 2009: 58). Oxfam's theory of change was that 'the same story with the same message would hopefully appear in many media outlets around the world at the same time, each reinforcing the other' (Atkinson and Scurrah 2009: 58). OPEN has an intentionally weak secretariat that cannot set global campaign priorities or override national concerns.

In January 2021, I asked Brandzel whether he had ever considered creating a more centralized OPEN secretariat. He responded that:

> I had gone around for years, saying we owe power to members ... you need to respect them, you have to have unimpeachable domestic legitimacy, all that adds up. How can I believe that they have accountability to their members and then they sacrifice this to empower Ben to make them work together? So it's antithetical to the theory of change. I had to create a network that was co-created... The network is the exchange between the groups. I could observe and cross-pollinate'.[70]

Brandzel wanted OPEN to be 'co-created' by digital advocacy organizations who actively sought to exchange with each other. Brandzel argued that such a network could not be built with coercion, but had to come from the groups' desire to engage. He never proposed to be a voting member of the board because he wanted the groups to feel 'they owned and governed' the network and the executive director served it.[71] OPEN is accountable to its member

[69] Greenpeace also opted for direct action tactics, which required 'planning, discipline, and secrecy' and hence created a more professional, centralized, and hierarchical structure (Zelko 2013).

[70] Online interview with Ben Brandzel, 31 January 2021.

[71] ibid.

organizations, who in turn are accountable to their individual members. A networked governance structure is common amongst member-driven organizations (Brown et al. 2012). In contrast, mission-driven organizations, such as Greenpeace, opt for more centralized governance structures, with more powerful secretariats that can coordinate campaigns (Brown et al. 2012: 2207). Importantly, OPEN's decentralised structure gives each member organization greater legitimacy in election campaigning. Unlike NGOs they are not accountable to any international secretariat, only beholden to their members.

Different Visions for OPEN

Activists affiliated with OPEN have different visions of the network's core purpose. Here, I illustrate these views and how they pull the network in different directions to: grow, enhance, and collaborate.

Grow

Some activists are eager to see the network expand into new countries. New organizations, regardless of where they are, can bring innovative ideas and tactics to OPEN. In addition, there are strategic benefits of having OPEN groups in neighbouring countries. This is particularly the case in Europe. 38 Degrees and Campact, for instance, were both strong supporters of establishing an OPEN organization in France, given how strong France is in the European Union. At the same time, some OPEN organizations are concerned about too much focus on growth, as it takes up significant OPEN staff time and comes with a risk of failure. These organizations want the network to focus on supporting existing members and deepening cooperation between them. These differing views of OPEN echo debates within the European Union: should cooperation be broader or deeper?

Another view is that OPEN should be a global progressive movement, which tackles global injustices, and not simply a 'professional network' to enhance campaigns.[72] According to this stance, OPEN should focus on establishing new groups in the Global South and enabling them to thrive. Under Brandzel, OPEN made efforts to support new potential groups in Nigeria, Nepal, Colombia, Indonesia, and Papua New Guinea. However, he found it

[72] Interview with digital advocacy organization staff member, OPEN summit, Kangaroo Valley, January 2016.

hard to find funding to support these initiatives and none were ultimately successful. OPEN's second executive director, Giovanna Negretti, made it a priority to establish more groups in the Global South, starting with Latin America. OPEN summits have also discussed: 'What does it mean for the global north to help global south groups?' Some have raised the question of whether a percentage of OPEN's budget could go from Global North to new Global South groups.

Coinciding with this concern, there are also regular, intense conversations about diversity in OPEN. At the 2017 Vancouver summit, several sessions focused on how to address structural racism within OPEN, which affects everything from hiring practices (OPEN organizations are predominantly staffed by white people, even in multicultural societies such as Australia and the United States) to who their members are. Some OPEN organizations have sought to employ ethnic minorities and hired diversity trainers to change organizational cultures, which in some cases are dominated by white, middle-class professionals.

Enhance

Some network members see OPEN as a 'community of practice' whose core aim is to connect and enhance digital advocacy organizations globally.[73] OPEN should focus on enabling existing members to share tactics and technologies. After all, 'innovation anywhere in the network, can help everywhere' as most problems are international.[74] As a staff member of MoveOn explained: 'For us [OPEN is] more about nuts and bolts of how we organise [as digital-first, rapid-response, multi-issue organizations]' rather than collaborating on common campaigns.[75] According to this view, starting new groups, or running transnational campaigns, is time-intensive, risky, and less likely to bring direct benefits to existing organizations.

Not all members expect much from the network. Milan de Vries at MoveOn suggested that there is 'no clear theory in MoveOn what OPEN should be' but that it's 'good to be in solidarity with other organizations'.[76] De Vries explained that MoveOn 'do not expect to get concrete deliverables from the network',[77]

[73] Interview with Mark Hanis, Core Group member, 2016.
[74] Interview with Phil Ireland, 22 November 2017.
[75] Interview with MoveOn Foreign Minister to OPEN, 20 June 2019.
[76] Interview with Milan de Vries, MoveOn, former data analytics head, 19 June 2019.
[77] ibid.

but explained it is appreciative when it benefits from new tech or tactics. Unlike many of the other organizations, MoveOn can draw on a rich and robust nationwide pool of digital advocacy organizations, including Color of Change, which it helped create. MoveOn sees its involvement with OPEN as a donation to the broader global movement.

However, Trump's presidency has forced MoveOn to reconsider its role, and who it can learn from in the network. According to de Vries, the United States now has more in common with eastern European organizations, such as aHang in Hungary or Akcja Demokracja in Poland, than '38 Degrees or Campact, which are much more grounded in a functioning democracy'.[78] Another MoveOn staffer noted that they were 'always compelled to work with OPEN, and in [the] Trump administration it seems more urgent'.[79] They elaborated that 'as we watch the global rise of the right, Americans need to reckon with what that means for the world, and how that informs policy elsewhere'.[80] MoveOn's efforts to set up a transnational campaign to prevent a US war with North Korea is one example of its active engagement with OPEN during the Trump presidency.

Collaborate on Transnational Campaigns

Some organizations want OPEN to become a platform for transnational campaigns. Recall that Brandzel's vision for OPEN was 'Power optimized for domestic influence, yet networked for global scale', as noted in Chapter 3. OPEN's former managing director, Phil Ireland, explained that 'many of OPEN's staff and stakeholders would like it [OPEN] to get to a point where we can do transnational campaigns and all groups campaign openly and collectively'.[81] At the 2015 start-up summit, for example, OPEN dedicated an entire day to 'the power of joint campaigning'. Sessions were held on the People's Climate March, the Great Barrier Reef campaign, trade campaigning, and climate campaigning in the lead up to the global climate summit in Paris.[82] OPEN staff often nudge groups into forging common campaigns. In February 2018, Becky Jarvis

[78] ibid.

[79] Interview with MoveOn Foreign Minister to OPEN, 20 June 2019.

[80] ibid.

[81] Interview with Phil Ireland, 22 November 2017.

[82] For more details on the People's Climate March and the Great Barrier Reef Campaign, see the OPEN website case studies: OPEN, Case Studies, https://www.the-open.net/case-studies(accessed 22 January 2022).

organized a summit to help prepare a common strategy for the EU elections. This summit did result in common messaging and a common action, as will be seen in Chapter 6. Jarvis has also written rapid-response emails for OPEN groups, where she sees international opportunities for them to campaign. For example, she helped to draft an email to Skiftet members urging them to help shut down Trump's business council (mentioned in the introduction to this book).

However, most OPEN activists I talked with did not see OPEN's primary purpose—whether now or in future—to be creating a platform for transnational campaigns. Several noted that the OPEN model, mobilizing national citizens about issues that concern them, makes it difficult to campaign on international issues. As Milan de Vries from MoveOn explained: 'domestic politics are often more salient than foreign policy' for Americans.[83] The view that members are more interested in domestic issues than international ones was echoed by many others who I spoke with between 2015 and 2020.[84]

Conclusion

OPEN organizations are united by a common mode of advocacyand a common set of progressive values, rather than a common issue. There is a high level of trust and commitment within this digital advocacy network as activists meet regularly in person at summits and on secondments, as well as communicating through email, Slack, and social media. This chapter has emphasized the importance of face-to-face meetings for building a strong network of digital advocacy organizations. OPEN organizations frequently share campaign tactics, tech, strategies, and even staff. Through these exchanges, OPEN organizations enhance their national campaigns.

Despite their common model and progressive values, OPEN groups rarely develop collective transnational campaigns. This is partly because the network has an intentionally weak secretariat, with little power to set common campaign priorities. It is also because each member organization derives power from mobilizing citizens at the national level. There are also differences within OPEN about what the network's priorities should be: growing the network,

[83] One exception is MoveOn's support for the Iran nuclear deal when Obama was in office. Interview with Milan de Vries, MoveOn, former data analytics head, 19 June 2019.

[84] One illustrative example is ActionStation's attempts to create a progressive people's agenda in the lead-up to the 2017 general election. When it solicited members' views on New Zealand's foreign policy, very few members commented, although they had strong views on other domestic issues.

enhancing existing organizations, or collaborating transnationally on campaigns? The governance structure of this network, and the member-driven model of advocacy, have shaped how digital advocacy organizations engage in transnational campaigns. Chapter 6 explores in detail how often these groups focus on an international issue, target an international institution, or work with international allies.

6

Trends in Transnational Campaigning: Issues, Targets and Partners

In September 2016, the United Nations held a high-level meeting on refugees and migration. World leaders met in New York and outlined their commitment to 'protecting the safety, dignity, and human rights and fundamental freedoms of all migrants, regardless of their migratory status, at all times'.[1] They agreed to launch inter-governmental negotiations on a Global Compact for 'safe, orderly and regular migration' (Tennant and Wolff 2018).[2] The Compact became extremely politicized. In December 2017, the Trump administration pulled the United States out of the agreement, declaring that the 'global approach in the New York declaration' was 'not compatible with US sovereignty' (Wintour 2017). This assertion was wrong: the Compact explicitly acknowledged governments' sovereignty and created a set of non-legally binding standards (Goodwin-Gill and McAdam 2018). However, the Trump administration's concerns gained global attention and vocal protests against the Compact took off around the world, from New Zealand to Sweden, Germany to Canada.

Far-right critiques shaped the public debate. Critics argued that the Compact was a globalist plot to undermine states' sovereignty and enable the United Nations to determine immigration policies. Between July and December 2018, Australia, Hungary, Switzerland, Israel, Austria, the Czech Republic, Slovakia, Italy, the Dominican Republic, and Chile pulled out of the final summit in Marrakesh. In the end, five countries voted against the agreement, (the Czech Republic, Poland, Hungary, Israel, and the United States), four of which had active Online Progressive Engagement Network (OPEN) groups. A further twelve countries abstained, including three countries with active OPEN groups—Australia, Austria, and Romania (*UN News* 2018).

[1] UN General Assembly, A/Res/71/1/, New York Declaration for Refugees and Immigrants, 19 September 2016, Section III (41), http://undocs.org/a/res/71/1(accessed 6 December 2021).

[2] In parallel, states were also involved in a lower profile Global Compact on Refugees, which was shepherded by the United Nations High Commission for Refugees (UNHCR). It was not as controversial as the Global Compat on Migration, partly because the UNHCR sought to keep discussions to more technical issues.

Transnational Advocacy in the Digital Era. Nina Hall, Oxford University Press.
 DOI: 10.1093/oso/9780198858744.003.0006

There was also strong opposition to the Compact in many other countries which eventually signed it. In Germany, the Alternative für Deutschland campaigned to pull Germany out of the Compact, but was ultimately unsuccessful. When the German parliament voted in favour of signing the Compact, 1,000 people protested the decision next to Berlin's Brandenburg Gate.[3] In New Zealand, the centre-right opposition, the National Party, adopted similar rhetoric to Trump, stating that it would not support the Compact if it was in government (Hall 2018). Opposition to the Compact followed a general trend of scepticism towards global institutions and a desire to close borders to migrants—ideas that were associated with the spread and electoral popularity of populist, nationalist political parties around the world.[4]

Most OPEN organizations were actively campaigning against the far-right during this time. Yet the network did not run a transnational campaign to support the Global Compact on Migration. Many OPEN organizations had run active welcome refugee campaigns in 2015, but they did not try to mobilize these same supporters in 2018 to counter the far-right protests against the Global Compact. Only #aufstehn in Austria ran a symbolic, last-minute, rapid-response campaign to demonstrate support for the agreement. It came too late because the Austrian government had already decided to abstain.[5]

Given OPEN progressive values, and support towards migrants and refugees, why didn't the network campaign for the Compact? OPEN organizations are staffed by issue generalists, and they did not have expertise on global migration governance and were not closely following the international negotiations. The Global Compact on Migration was not a high-profile, progressive issue until it was politicized by the far right, and OPEN groups do not typically campaign on issues with low salience. The non-governmental organizations (NGOs) that actively campaigned for the Global Compact on Migration were those with the skills, capacity, and funding to attend negotiations in New York and engage in insider lobbying (Rother and Steinhilper 2019; Tennant and Wolff 2018). OPEN organizations were not part of this transnational advocacy network for migrants' rights given their preference for outsider advocacy.

[3] *RBB24* (2018). The author observed the protest.

[4] In the words of the Foreign Minister of Slovakia, and the then Chair of the United Nations General Assembly: the GCM [Global Compact on Migration] became the 'scapegoat of a wider problem'. In Eastern Europe, there was a particular fear of the EU imposing set quotas of refugees that countries had to accept (Lajčák 2018).

[5] #aufstehn asked its members to individually sign the Global Compact as an act of defiance to the government and a vote of support for the Compact. The campaign, however, was too late to change the government's decision. Interview with Maria Mayrhofer, #aufstehn, 19 June 2019.

The Global Compact on Migration is a single, and perhaps unusual, case. It may not be a typical case of whether and how digital advocacy organizations engage with international institutions and transnational issues. This chapter looks at broader trends in how frequently OPEN organizations engage transnationally. I separate out three dimensions of transnational advocacy often conflated by international relations (IR) scholars, but distinguished by social movement scholars (Caiani and Graziani 2018; Rucht 1999).[6] First, I examine whether campaigns focus on *transnational issues* rather than national or local concerns. Second, I examine when and why NGOs target *international institutions* rather than domestic institutions. Third, I explore how frequently digital advocacy organizations work with *international allies* or NGOs. I separate out these three dimensions to illustrate how advocacy may be transnational in one dimension, but not in another (see also Froio and Ganesh 2019: 516).

The chapter focuses on four digital advocacy organizations: 38 Degrees in the UK, Campact in Germany, GetUp in Australia, and ActionStation in New Zealand. These four organizations are all at least five years old, are full members of OPEN, and represent a range of geographic areas. Campact, 38 Degrees, and GetUp are among the largest of the OPEN organizations in terms of membership size and annual revenue, while ActionStation is one of the smaller full members of OPEN. Working with a research assistant, I compiled a complete list of all these organizations' campaign actions between 1 September 2018 and 31 August 2019. To identify campaigns, we combed through the organizations' Twitter and Facebook pages and triangulated these results with information from their websites and blogs. We then cross-checked our list with academics who had previously conducted research on the organizations, and with lists of campaigns from the organizations themselves.[7] Campaign actions included online petitions, reports, demonstrations, emails to politicians, mass phone calls to politicians, submissions, and posts on social media.[8]

The chapter is divided into three sections. I examine how frequently these digital advocacy organizations: (a) focused on a transnational issue; (b) targeted an international institution; and (c) partnered with international allies. Each section draws on IR scholarship and interviews with OPEN activists to explain the patterns that emerge. I find that OPEN organizations frequently

[6] Caiani and Graziani identify three ways a social movement can become *transnational*: (a) transnational actors connect on campaign (i.e. a transnational network or alliance); (b) the target is transnational; or (c) actors mobilize and take action on an issue which is transnational (2018: 1033).

[7] A more complete description of our methods can be found in the appendix.

[8] Petitions were the most common form of action across the organizations.

campaign on transnational issues, but very rarely target an international institution, or work with transnational partners to campaign. As we saw in Chapter 5, OPEN enabled organizations to connect, listen, and learn from each other. However, their campaigns almost always target national decision-makers, even when addressing a transnational issue. Their organizational model (member-driven, issue-generalist, and rapid-response) shapes how digital advocacy campaign transnationally.

Focusing on a Transnational Issue

Digital advocacy organizations regularly campaign on transnational issues. Transnational issues spill across borders and cannot be addressed by any single state alone. Given how interconnected our world is, examples of transnational issues abound: climate change, international migration, regulation of the internet, warfare, and international trade. Here, I separate out *domestic* from *transnational* issues.[9] Domestic issues tend to be contained within national borders and regulated by national governments, for example, the provision of health care, public parks, and libraries. I have also included a 'Brexit' category for 38 Degrees in the UK. Issues included in the Brexit category might be categorized as domestic in other countries (e.g. food standards or public health) but were inherently tied up in the UK's decision to leave the European Union (EU). Hence, they are treated as transnational issues here.

Almost 40 per cent of the total campaign actions conducted by Campact, GetUp, 38 Degrees, and ActionStation between 1 September 2018 and 31 August 2019 related to a transnational issue (see Figure 6.1). If we include the special case of Brexit, then 47.3 per cent of all campaign actions related to a transnational issue. Just over half (52.7 per cent) were purely domestic. Figure 6.2 illustrates variation across the four organizations: Campact campaigns most frequently on transnational issues (80 per cent), while Action-Station focuses the least on transnational issues (19 percent). Meanwhile, 66.6 per cent of 38 Degrees' campaigns related to a transnational issue (including the Brexit category), and 36 percent of GetUp's campaigns.

Notably, most of the campaign issues which we coded as 'transnational' related to domestic policymaking on an international issue. For example, all

[9] Note that these distinctions are not always straightforward. IR scholars have argued that the categorization of issues as 'local' or 'global' is often a political decision (Hall and Persson 2018; McKeon 2017; Scholte 2019). For the sake of simplicity, I use transnational and domestic here, and the appendix clarifies how I apply these terms in the coding scheme.

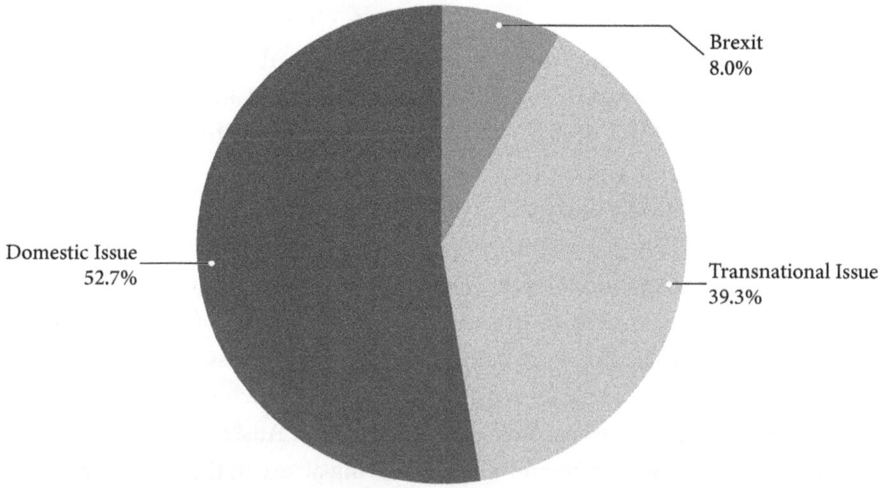

Fig. 6.1 Total percentage of campaign actions relating to a transnational issue in 38 Degrees, ActionStation, Campact, and GetUp

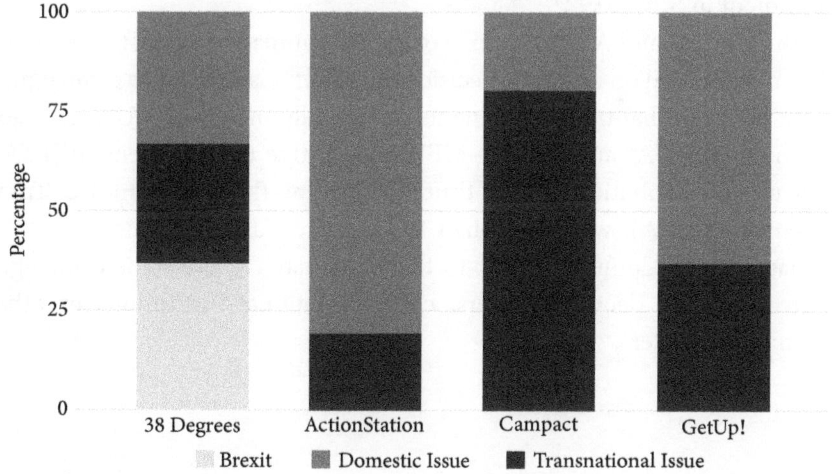

Fig. 6.2 Comparison of campaign actions focused on a transnational issue in 38 Degrees, ActionStation, Campact, and GetUp

four organizations conducted climate change campaigns. GetUp campaigned to save the Great Barrier Reef, to stop the Adani mine, to join a climate strike, and to invest in renewable energy. Campact campaigned against the German automobile industry, promoted the school climate strikes, demanded that Germany stop coal mining, and rallied people to protect the Hambacher Forest from mining. 38 Degrees urged the UK government to 'take urgent action to stop the climate crisis', and pushed the Museum of Science and Industry to 'drop Shell' as a sponsor.[10] ActionStation urged its members to make submissions to the Zero Carbon bill, which would see New Zealand become carbon neutral by 2050, and to write to the government to impose a moratorium on new oil or gas exploration. All of these actions targeted national decision-makers to take domestic action on climate change.

These four OPEN organizations targeted domestic decision-makers in other campaigns on transnational issues. GetUp, for instance, regularly petitioned the Australian government to get 'the kids off Nauru' an offshore detention centre where asylum seekers are held.[11] They also put pressure on the government to pass legislation known as the Medevac bill, which would give asylum seekers adequate access to medical care in mainland Australia. Campact petitioned the German government to 'end the dying at sea' in the Mediterranean, where thousands of asylum seekers had drowned while attempting to enter Europe. Campact also demanded the release from prison of Carola Rackete, the German captain of a humanitarian ship who was arrested by the Italian government in July 2019.[12]

Both Campact and ActionStation conducted campaigns against hate speech online and focused on domestic decision-makers.[13] Campact also campaigned against international trade agreements, specifically the Japan–EU Free Trade Agreement (JEFTA) and the EU–MERCOSUR free trade agreement (FTA), (both under negotiation at that time), as well as the Canadian–EU Trade Agreement (CETA), which still had to be approved by the Bundesrat (the German Federal Council, similar to the US Senate). These trade campaigns targeted national decision-makers, not international institutions or other government's leaders.

[10] 38 Degrees, 'Museum of Science and Industry: drop Shell', https://speakout.38degrees.org.uk/campaigns/4250(accessed 6 December 2021).

[11] Note that GetUp's transnational campaigns related either to climate change or to refugee issues. For example, GetUp, 'Let's inundate the Morrison Government', https://www.getup.org.au/campaigns/refugees/email-coalition-politicians-and-tell-them-kidsoffnauru/let-s-inundate-the-morrison-government(accessed 6 December 2021).

[12] Campact, Beendet das Sterben auf See! Freiheit für Carola Rackete!, https://aktion.campact.de/seenotrettung/appell/teilnehmen(accessed 6 December 2021).

[13] We coded hate speech as a transnational issue, as it is not easily stopped by geographical borders. ActionStation wrote a major report, 'The People's Report on Online Hate, Harrassment and Abuse', which was released in 2019, soon after the Christchurch attacks, where a far-right white supremacist live-streamed his massacre of fifty-one Muslims. ActionStation also set up a ten-week programme, and trained and supported a team of volunteers to counter hate speech online (particularly hate speech which targeted Maori and migrant communities) (ActionStation 2019).

38 Degrees is a somewhat special case, given that Brexit dominated the political debate for much of 2018 and 2019.[14] The debates about whether, and how, to withdraw the UK from the EU revolved around issues which might typically be considered domestic. These included immigration, the National Health Service (NHS), animal welfare standards, food and environmental standards, and Northern Ireland. Yet all of these issues were tied up with the UK's departure from the EU, and hence we consider them transnational. 38 Degrees campaigns on Brexit were almost always domestically focused. They campaigned to 'keep the good Friday agreement off the negotiating table' and campaigned not to 'shut down parliament' when Prime Minister Boris Johnson prorogued parliament in August 2019.[15] The high proportion of 38 Degrees campaigns (36.4 per cent) relating to Brexit is no surprise, given its dominance in UK politics at the time (see Figure 6.2).

38 Degrees conducted other transnational campaign actions which were not Brexit-related. They urged then British Chancellor, Sajid Javid, to 'make Amazon pay their fair share [of taxes]'.[16] They demanded then-Foreign Minister, Jeremy Hunt, and, in a separate action, the Secretary of State for International Trade, Liam Fox, to stop British arms sales to Saudi Arabia. 38 Degrees also called on Boris Johnson and Jeremy Hunt to 'Call Trump's Comments What They Are: Racist'.[17] This campaign was in reference to President Trump's tweets asserting that Ilhan Omar, a US congresswoman who had arrived almost thirty years previously as a child refugee in the United States should 'go back' to where she was from. 38 Degrees also urged Theresa Villiers, the then Secretary of State for Environment, Food and Rural Affairs, and Michael Gove, who had previously occupied that ministerial post, not to 'backtrack on bottle deposits', out of concern about plastic pollution in the ocean.[18]

OPEN organizations campaigned on a range of transnational issues in the 2018–2019 period. In a globalized world, many issues spill over borders, and cannot be addressed by a single state (Johnson 2020). Furthermore, many of these issues had high public salience and media attention during the period we studied (e.g. climate change, online hate speech, free trade agreements,

[14] Note that 38 Degrees ran a neutral campaign during the referendum, as its membership was split on whether to leave or remain in the EU.

[15] 38 Degrees, Petition, 'Tell Your MP Matthew Hancock: Push for Stronger FOI Laws', https://speakout.38degrees.org.uk/campaigns/626 (accessed 6 December 2021).

[16] 38 Degrees, Petition, 'Make Amazon Pay Their Fair Share', https://speakout.38degrees.org.uk/campaigns/4178(accessed 6 December 2021).

[17] 38 Degrees, Petition, 'Call Trump's Comments What They Are: Racist', https://speakout.38degrees.org.uk/campaigns/6300 (accessed 6 December 2021).

[18] 38 Degrees, Petition, 'Don't Backtrack on Bottle Deposits', https://speakout.38degrees.org.uk/campaigns/5335 (accessed 6 December 2021).

and migration policy). Hence, it is not surprising that OPEN organization campaigned frequently on transnational issues. What is more interesting is *how* they campaigned on these issues.

International Targets

Campaign actions, whether online petitions or offline demonstrations, typically target an institution or decision-maker (Han et al. 2021). Digital advocacy organizations seek to mobilize members of the public to apply outsider pressure on these decision-makers. Campaigns target individuals as well as institutions. For example, 38 Degrees wrote an open letter to then Foreign Minister Jeremy Hunt demanding that 'Those responsible for the assassination of Jamal Khashoggi must be held to account and Britain could help get to the truth by halting arms sales to Saudi Arabia until they are'.[19] GetUp, meanwhile, targeted the Australian government and asked its members to 'stand in solidarity' with those still imprisoned in Australia's '[cruel] offshore processing regime' in reference to Australia's detention centres for asylum seekers.[20]

Some campaigns target multiple institutions or decision-makers. Campact's campaign to 'Stop MERCOSUR, Save the Amazon' targeted three senior federal politicians: the German Federal Chancellor, Angela Merkel, the Federal Minister for Economic Affairs, Peter Altmaier, and the Environment Minister, Svenja Schulze.[21] GetUp's petition, 'Don't Give Billions to Adani', targeted both the Prime Minister, Scott Morrison, and the Premier of Queensland, Annastacia Palaszczuk.[22]

This section examines whether the campaign target was domestic or international.[23] As Figure 6.3 shows, the vast majority of campaign actions between September 2018 and September 2019 targeted domestic decision-makers. It was rare for any of the four organizations to target an international

[19] 38 Degrees, Open Letter, 'Halt Arms Sales to the Saudi Arabian Government', https://speakout.38degrees.org.uk/campaigns/4557 (accessed 6 December 2021).

[20] GetUp, '#SixYearsTooLong Nationwide Rallies', https://www.getup.org.au/campaigns/refugees/six-years-too-long/sixyearstoolong-nationwide-rallies (accessed 6 December 2021).

[21] Campact, 'MERCOSUR Stopped, Amazonas retten!', https://aktion.campact.de/mercosur/amazonas/teilnehmen(accessed 6 December 2021).

[22] The campaign was to stop a coal mine in Queensland, which was funded by Gautam Adani, an Indian businessman. It asked: 'Can you sign the petition and tell the Morrison and Queensland Governments to rule out any public subsidies to Adani's coal mine?'. GetUp, 'Don't Give Billions to Adani', https://www.getup.org.au/campaigns/adani/no-public-money-for-adani/don-t-give-billions-to-adani (accessed 6 December 2021).

[23] Digital advocacy organizations may also pioneer new tactics for influencing international negotiations, such as Twitter storms, Facebook video campaigns, or online petitioning. However, their tactics are not the focus here but whether or not they even target these institutions.

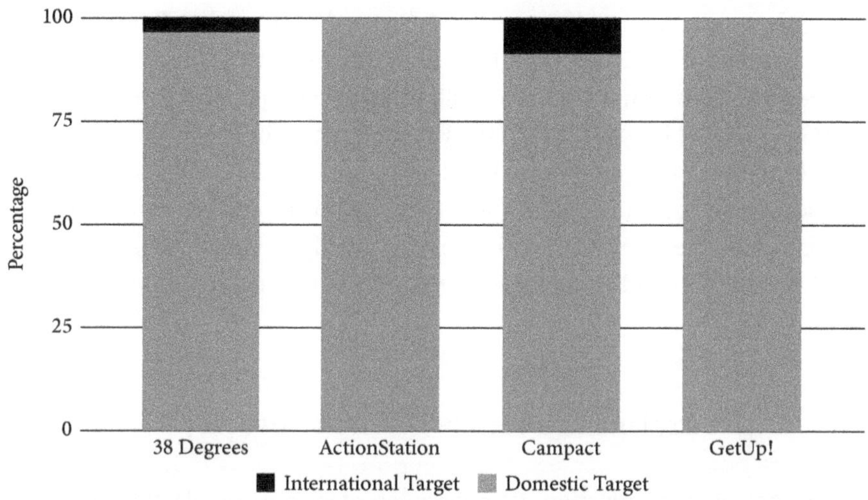

Fig. 6.3 Percentage of campaigns with an international target by organization

corporation, institution, or politician. Only 2 per cent (or three campaigns out of 150) targeted an international institution or actor. Moreover, two organizations, ActionStation and GetUp, did not conduct a single campaign action targeting an international actor. 38 Degrees and Campact had a very small proportion of campaigns directed at an international institution or actor (3 per cent and 8 per cent, respectively). This represents just two campaigns for Campact and one campaign for 38 Degrees.

The two occasions where Campact targeted an international actor were related to the EU. Campact asked the President of the European Commission, the President of the Council of the EU, representatives of the EU Member States and Members of the European Parliament, to cancel the 'special rights' for corporations provided by new trade agreements.[24] The second case was when Campact urged people to demonstrate in over fifty European cities and vote against nationalism in the EU elections. Here, the target was the EU Parliament.[25] The only 38 Degrees campaign targeting an international institution was a petition directed at Susan Wojcicki, the chief executive officer (CEO) of Youtube. It asked her to '[please] protect children who use your website from paedophiles. In particular please introduce: robust age verification rules

[24] Campact, 'Konzernklagen stoppen!', https://aktion.campact.de/konzernklagen/appell/teilnehmen?pk_vid=40a24983adee25b515655970781d2128 (accessed 6 December 2021).
[25] Campact, 'Ein Europa fuer alle', https://www.ein-europa-fuer-alle.de/ (accessed 6 December 2021).

and better moderation of live-streamed content.'[26] Given that Germany is an active member of the EU, it is perhaps unsurprising that Campact's campaign actions targeted international actors slightly more frequently than ActionStation, GetUp, or 38 Degrees. While the UK was part of the EU during this study, it was in the midst of negotiating the Brexit withdrawal agreement.

In summary, these four digital advocacy organizations very rarely targeted international actors, even though they frequently campaigned on transnational issues. Why did these OPEN organizations rarely target international institutions?

Explanation: Member-Driven Advocacy

Digital advocacy organizations do not see international organizations as worth targeting. Rather, their theory of change assumes that states are the most important actors in international politics. They seek to mobilize citizens domestically to put pressure on elected decision-makers. In fact, when I presented my findings to digital advocacy organizations, none were surprised that they mostly targeted domestic actors.[27] One activist explained that 'there are no strong reliable actors that we can target [at the international level]' and that international institutions they 'usually perceive as toothless'.[28] Another digital activist explained that targeting international institutions is not a 'strong theory of change' because there are no real decision-makers within international organizations; instead, they are facilitators for states to discuss common issues.[29] The weakness of international organizations, compared with the state, was a common refrain.

Another seasoned 38 Degrees staff member explained that 38 Degrees targeted national decision-makers because this is their 'theory of where our power comes from'.[30] 38 Degrees has a 'direct relationship with MPs and Ministers' and can mobilize constituents and put pressure on these elected politicians.[31] It cannot do this with international institutions or actors. This same staffer explained, 'our power is weaker' if they put pressure on international actors. 38 Degrees, for instance, has no leverage over the US Senate. If it

[26] 38 Degrees, https://speakout.38degrees.org.uk/campaigns/youtube-childsafety (accessed 6 December 2021).

[27] I held three focus groups with OPEN activists in early 2021 where I resented the figures in this chapter and dicussed explanations for these trends. See the appendix for further details.

[28] Akcja Demokracja Activist, OPEN focus group, 16 February 2021.

[29] Holly Dawson, OPEN focus group, 16 February 2021.

[30] Robin Priestley, 38 Degrees online focus group, 16 February 2021.

[31] ibid.

tried to mobilize a group of 38 Degrees members and say to the Senate, 'please don't do X ... you can just imagine them in the Senate thinking, well who really cares?'.[32] Its power comes from mobilizing citizens *nationally* to put pressure on *domestic* decision-makers.

Digital advocacy organizations rarely target international institutions, even though their staff and many members have cosmopolitan views. OPEN activists believe in solidarity with Black Lives Matter, assistance for refugees, and assisting those worst affected by climate change and the COVID-19 pandemic (Hall forthcoming). However, staff look for targets that are much closer and visible to their members. As Siobhán O'Donoghue from Uplift in Ireland explained, when a 'target or an issue is very far-removed from a domestic, urgent issue, it's very hard to make a case' that their members should get involved in the campaign.[33]

OPEN organizations rarely try to campaign in other countries. If they want to run a campaign targeting an actor or institution in another country, they simply ask their sister OPEN organization to do it for them. A 38 Degrees staffer, who previously worked at Greenpeace, explained:

> when I used to work at Greenpeace ... if you wanted to campaign on a transnational issue, then your director would need to write to the other Greenpeace offices in that region to get permission to campaign on that issue—for example, if you wanted to target a foreign owned company that was drilling for oil in the country we were campaigning in. Then all these politics would come into play .... But it's nothing like that with OPEN organizations. Generally if your target is in Germany, you would write to Campact and be like 'hey, are you aware of this thing? Maybe you could run a campaign for us on it?[34]

She suggested that it would be unlikely for 38 Degrees to try run a campaign with a German target, as 'it wouldn't feel quite right—it'd feel like we were stepping on their [Campact's] toes'.[35] 38 Degrees can pass campaigns to other OPEN organizations because there is no competition in the network for members and staff see power in domestically based groups. Another 38 Degrees staffer explained: 'we're not trying to build a US or a German list'.[36]

[32] ibid.
[33] She noted that it was difficult even in Ireland, where Irish are proud members of the EU. Siobhán O'Donoghue, Focus group with OPEN activists, 16 February 2021.
[34] 38 Degrees staff member, 38 Degrees focus group, 22 February 2021.
[35] ibid.
[36] Robin Priestley, 38 Degrees focus group, 22 February 2021.

Interestingly, even Campact, which is based in the EU, targeted the German government more than the EU. Campact executive director, Felix Kolb, explained that the 'European Commission is a powerful actor .... But we are quite sceptical about the leverage we can have with the European commission .... It's much easier to influence European decision-makers or national governments than the commission.'[37] Rather, Campact often passes on European-wide campaigns to WeMove, a pan-European digital advocacy organization that Campact helped to establish.[38]

When I discussed these results with OPEN activists, some raised the point that digital advocacy organizations working in less democratic countries may target international institutions more frequently than their counterparts. A Polish activist who works for Akcja Demokracja, for instance, explained: the organization 'didn't see any hope' in targeting the Polish government because it no longer respected basic democratic norms. Akcja Demokracja has focused more campaigns at the EU as it is 'one body that can do something for us now'.[39] Although he also noted that it is quite difficult for it to mobilize its members for EU-related campaigns, even though Poland is one 'of the countries with the highest support for a presence in the EU' because the 'knowledge about the institutions is very low, and people don't recognise its powers'.[40] IR scholarship offers other explanations for why advocacy groups may target domestic institutions more frequently than international actors. Let us turn to these now.

Alternative Explanations: Political Opportunity Structures

The IR advocacy literature has sought to explain when, and why, NGOs target international institutions (Hadden 2015; Hanegraaff et al. 2016; Tallberg et al. 2015). NGOs typically identify where the locus of authority lies with respect to the changes they want to see, and forum shop to identify the institution where they are likely to have most influence (Young 2017a: 530). When they are blocked at the national level, NGOs turn to the international level to seek out other forums through which they can advance their cause—the so-called

[37] Felix Kolb, Campact focus group, 15 March 2021.
[38] Campact focus group, 15 March 2021.
[39] Akcja Demokracja activist, OPEN focus group, 16 February 2021.
[40] ibid.

'boomerang' model (Keck and Sikkink 1998).[41] Social movement scholars have noted that such upward scale shifts are often advantageous because they increase the group of potential participants in a movement (Tarrow 2010; Vaughan 2019).

Political opportunity structures both 'enable and constrain' the influence of advocacy groups (Dellmuth and Bloodgood 2019). Democratic states, for example, tend to offer NGOs more domestic opportunities for advocacy than authoritarian states (Dellmuth and Bloodgood 2019: 260). GetUp, Campact, ActionStation, and 38 Degrees all operate in democratic states and are rarely completely blocked domestically. This could partially explain why these organizations targeted domestic actors more frequently than international institutions, although during this time period both GetUp and Campact lost their charity tax status and GetUp was under regular attack from the Australian government.

It is worth recalling that IR scholars writing in the early days of the internet believed that new technologies would mean that NGOs had a larger presence in international organizations (Gordenker and Weiss 1995). Technology would open up new political opportunity structures for NGOs and civil society. National borders would become less important, and technology would enable activists to shape global norms and influence international institutions (Price 2003: 627; Wapner 1995). Many of these scholars were writing in the aftermath of the Cold War—an era of optimism about democracy, globalization, liberal values, and technology ('techno-optimism'). A 1990s 'techno-optimism' perspective would suggest that OPEN organizations might engage more frequently with international institutions and summits than they did.

More recent scholarship has tempered these claims. NGOs also operate within national borders and cultures and will only 'go international' when it is to their advantage (Stroup and Wong 2018). The 'boomerang model' is never the optimum form of political activism, but rather 'a complement and compensatory option' to domestic activism (Sikkink 2005). Most advocacy efforts target national decision-makers rather than international institutions (Tallberg et al. 2015). This is because domestic political change is 'closer to home and more directly addressed' and activists will 'concentrate actions there' (Sikkink 2005). Caiani and Graziani, for instance, find that the majority of

[41] Although some international institutions offer more generous access to NGOs than others (Tallberg et al. 2015).

anti-Transatlantic Trade and Intellectual Property Agreement (TTIP) protests in Europe focused on domestic actors (especially nation states), even though TTIP was being negotiated by the EU (Caiani and Graziani 2018: 1034). There is also a shift away from 'global summitry' towards national-level advocacy, which uses locally generated strategies and tactics (Green 2016). Transnational climate activists, for example, are shifting away from targeting the United Nations Framework Convention on Climate Change (UNFCCC) (Moor 2020). This may in part be because of disillusionment with international summits and a rise in nationalism in many major countries.

OPEN organizations could be following these broader trends: targeting domestic actors in their transnational campaigns. However, unlike most NGOs, they do *not* venue shop for international institutions where they might have more luck at pushing their cause. Traditional NGOs have specialist expertise, and use this to monitor, access, and influence global negotiations. As Tallberg et al. explain, the 'more NGOs engage in information provision, the greater their access to IO [international organization] bodies, increasing the likelihood of NGO influence on policy making in IOs' (2015: 218).[42] OPEN organizations rarely have issue-specific expertise and do not pursue insider advocacy at the international level.

Some OPEN activists see lobbying at international institutions as 'important', but simply not what digital advocacy organizations do.[43] Several OPEN activists noted that other NGOs are better placed to engage in lobbying at the international level. As one explained, 'The people who trawl the halls of international institutions are people who use different kind of tactics, they're writing lobby papers, it can be very academic, it's very much influence from the inside',[44] while others maintained that it was 'not politically strategic' as it is not a 'strong theory of change'.[45] OPEN organizations view outsider tactics, or what they call 'people power', at the domestic level as more powerful than expert-based advocacy at international institutions (such as the United Nations (UN), the World Health Organization (WHO), the World Bank, or G7). Digital advocacy organizations member-driven model means they rarely directly target international institutions.

[42] NGOs with larger financial resources tend to have a greater impact on global governance outcomes (Dellmuth and Bloodgood 2019). NGOs and advocacy organizations may also build, and use, coalitions to have greater impact. How complex and salient an issue can influence whether policy makers need specialist information, and thus how willing they are to accept advocacy organizations' advice (Dellmuth and Bloodgood 2019). NGO influence may also depend on how they frame an issue, and whether it resonates with 'gatekeepers' preferences (Busby 2010).

[43] Discussion with Nicola Browne, Uplift Campaigner, OPEN focus group, 16 February 2021.

[44] ibid.

[45] Discussion with Holly Dawson, OPEN staffer, OPEN focus group, 16 February 2021.

Transnational Partners

Digital advocacy organizations may choose to work alone on a campaign or team up with other NGOs and civil society organizations. Who they ally with will depend on the nature of the campaign and the issue at hand.[46] In August 2019, GetUp, for example, encouraged its members to join a 'Climate Strike Mass Online Call'.[47] This was a call in preparation for the 20 September 2019 global #climatestrike, led by #FridaysForFuture, a youth organization initiated by Greta Thunberg. While GetUp hosted the call, it noted in the advertisement that: 'this event is a collaborative effort hosted by the Australian Conservation Foundation, GetUp, Tipping Point, 350 Australia, Amnesty International and ActionAid'.[48]

In 2019, Campact launched an online petition to stop hate speech online ('Hate Speech im Netz stoppen!').[49] It did this with a number of other German NGOs, including NetzTeufel, Lovestorm, Das Nettz, Fearless Democracy, No Hate, Liberal Islamischer Bund (the Liberal Islamic Association), and ichbinhier ('I am here'). ActionStation worked with the Child Poverty Action Group to put pressure on the New Zealand Parliament to '[put] children and whanau [family] wellbeing at the heart of welfare'.[50] In Figure 6.4, I examine the percentage of these four OPEN organizations' campaigns where they collaborated with an *international* NGO or civil society group.

GetUp, ActionStation, Campact, and 38 Degrees rarely collaborated with international NGOs on a common campaign.[51] In fact, neither GetUp nor ActionStation worked with an international NGO, or transnational advocacy network between 1 September 2018 and 31 August 2019. GetUp and

[46] Future research could examine trends, and variation, in how frequently digital advocacy organizations campaign with other domestic NGOs. The research I have conducted here suggests some organizations (e.g. Campact and ActionStation) do so frequently, while others do so much less frequently (e.g. 38 Degrees).

[47] GetUp, 'Climate Strike Mass Online Call', https://www.crowdcast.io/e/climate-strike-call/register (accessed 6 December 2021). Note this was the only instance of GetUp working with domestic allies but leading a campaign action in our sample. There were numerous other instances of GetUp reposting on social media to other NGOs campaign actions (e.g. #FridaysForFuture).

[48] GetUp, 'Climate Strike Mass Online Call', https://www.crowdcast.io/e/climate-strike-call/register (accessed 6 December 2021).

[49] Campact, 'Hate Speech im Netz stoppen!', https://aktion.campact.de/hate-speech/appell-bundesweit/teilnehmen?pk_vid=40a24983adee25b515655965511d2128(accessed 6 December 2021).

[50] ActionStation, 'Put Children and Whanau [Family] Wellbeing at the Heart of Welfare', https://our.actionstation.org.nz/petitions/make-our-welfare-system-great-again(accessed 6 December 2021).

[51] There were instances where domestic NGOs used GetUp, 38 Degrees, ActionStation, or Campact's member petition platforms to start their own campaigns. There were also occasions where these digital advocacy organizations reposted other NGOs' campaigns on social media (e.g. #FridaysForFuture climate strikes were often retweeted or shared on Facebook). Campaign actions were only included if the digital advocacy organization actively partnered with another organization. See the appendix for further details on the coding approach.

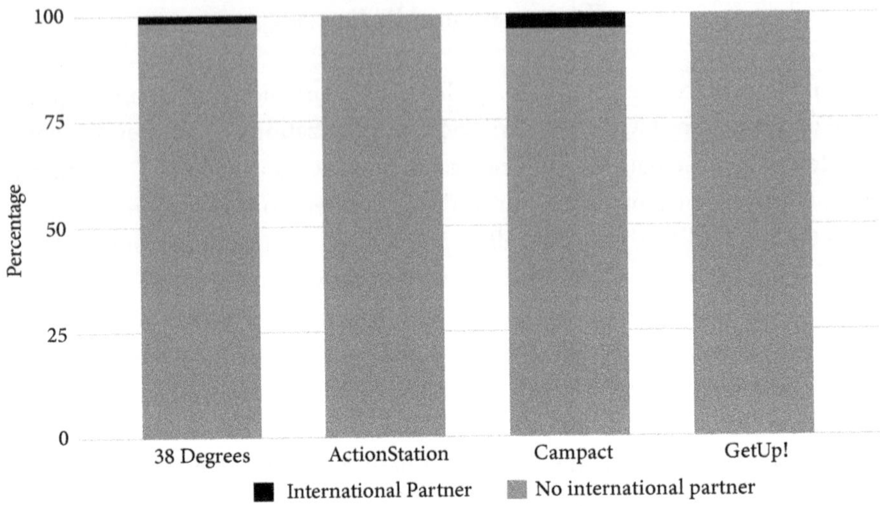

Fig. 6.4 Percentage of campaign actions with an international partner by organization

ActionStation were also the two organizations that did not target international institutions in any of their campaign actions. These two findings are likely related: if a campaign only targets national decision-makers, it is unlikely to have international allies. According to the 'boomerang model', advocacy organizations are unlikely to look for outsider assistance to apply pressure to their senior politicians unless they are blocked domestically, which is more commonly associated with repressive states (Keck and Sikkink 1998).

38 Degrees had one campaign action (equivalent to 3 per cent of its total campaigns) where it worked with a transnational ally. It partnered with Uplift, its Irish counterpart in OPEN. In March 2019, 38 Degrees and Uplift published a full-page advertisement in then Prime Minister Theresa May's local newspaper, the *Maidenhead Advertiser.* The letter stated that 'no matter which way people voted on Brexit, no one wants to put peace in Northern Ireland at risk. Please don't let divisions in your party risk the fragile peace in Northern Ireland. It's too important to sacrifice.'[52] The letter was signed by 72,833 members of 38 Degrees and Uplift. Meanwhile, a 38 Degrees campaign targeting the CEO of YouTube did not include other international NGOs or

[52] 38 Degrees also shared this letter via tweet, which is how it was identified and included in this study. See also 'Full-page ad in Theresa May's local paper calls on Tory Leader to 'protect the peace' (*The Irish Times* 2019).

allies. It could have considered working with SumOfUs, an international digital advocacy organization which specializes in 'stopping big corporations from behaving badly', but did not.[53]

Campact had only one campaign where it worked with an international NGO, although it had numerous campaigns with other German NGOs.[54] This campaign was 'One Europe for All' ('Ein Europa für alle'), a campaign to encourage all voters in the European parliamentary elections to vote for pro-European candidates rather than nationalists. The One Europe for All campaign was a collaborative campaign involving a number of OPEN organizations: Skiftet in Sweden, Akcja Demokracja in Poland, Declic in Romania, A-Hang in Hungary, #aufstehn in Austria, and le Mouvement in France, as well as several non-OPEN organizations.[55] Campact's previously mentioned campaign to prevent the inclusion of investor–state dispute settlement (ISDS) clauses in free trade agreements targeted senior EU politicians and the EU Parliament, but did not include either WeMove or other OPEN organizations.[56]

In summary, OPEN organizations very rarely campaigned collectively with transnational allies. In the two cases where they did, it was because they were focusing on a transnational issue (Brexit and/or the EU elections). In both cases, they partnered with a member of OPEN: 38 Degrees and Uplift; Campact and other European OPEN organizations. Collaboration on the same issue, at the same time, with the same target rarely occurs in OPEN. I now examine why this is.

Explanation: Member-Driven, Rapid-Response, and Multi-Issue Advocacy

Member-driven advocacy organizations frame their campaigns around national concerns, and hence look for national, rather than international, allies. Domestic partners often provide the issue expertise that digital advocacy organizations lack (Vaughan 2020). International allies in OPEN cannot provide this expertise because they are also issue generalists, although they may offer suggestions on digital tactics or strategies. For these reasons, Vaughan finds in

[53] SumOfUs, https://www.sumofus.org/ (accessed 6 December 2021).

[54] Campact has fewer campaign actions overall during the period studied than 38 Degrees.

[55] One Europe for all, https://www.ein-europa-fuer-alle.de/(accessed 6 December 2021). See the Youtube video for a full list of the organizations involved in the campaign, https://www.youtube.com/watch?v=tIYwhBVxrIo(accessed 6 December 2021).

[56] Although some of Campact's other campaigns on ISDS clauses did include international partners. Campact, Focus group, 15 March 2021.

his study of 38 Degree and GetUp's tax justice campaigns that the 'collaborative relationships most useful to digital advocacy organizations' are 'largely local rather than transnational' (Vaughan 2020).

In the focus groups I ran with OPEN activists to discuss these results, none were surprised that there were few common transnational campaigns within OPEN. However, some suggested that in previous years, there may have been periods with slightly more OPEN coordinated collaborations, particularly during the height of anti-free trade campaigns. Several activists noted that OPEN is not set up to rapidly launch international campaigns. OPEN is better suited to sharing best practices and enhancing national campaigns. One 38 Degrees staffer explained that there is 'not an obvious model or template for how to campaign collaboratively cross-borders within the OPEN network'.[57] As he elaborated:

> Everyone on this call in about five minutes could come up with a campaign strategy based on what 38 degrees normally does, but we don't have that immediate sort of institutional awareness of how to do an international partnership with partner organizations. We don't, I think, have really established processes for either working with other OPEN partners across borders or working with other transnational organizations.[58]

The interim executive director of 38 Degrees, Zoe Whyatt, agreed. She also highlighted that the fast-paced mode of campaigning did not easily lend itself to international collaborations. She explained that:

> Because it takes some more longer-term planning to work with partners around the world, and a lot of what we do is reacting to the news day to day—so, just practically, joined up efforts which take some coordination are not always going to be compatible with a quick and reactive approach to campaigning.[59]

She did, however, see potential for OPEN to develop the ability of the network to campaign collectively. There are examples of OPEN enabling transnational campaigns; however, these campaigns rarely targeted the *same institution* at

[57] Stewart Kirkpatrick, former 38 Degrees staffer, 38 Degrees focus group, 16 February 2021.
[58] Stewart Kirkpatrick, former 38 Degrees staffer, 38 Degrees focus group, 16 February 2021.
[59] Zoe Whyatt, 38 Degrees focus group, 16 February 2021.

the *same time*. In sum, OPEN supports digital advocacy organizations to connect and learn from each other, but rarely to plan and coordinate common campaigns. These oganizations want to connect with their domestic members, and because they are issue generalists tend to look for domestic allies with expertise on a particular issue.

Alternative Explanation: The Benefits and Costs of Engaging in Transnational Networks

NGOs engage in transnational networks because they offer great benefits. By participating, NGOs gain ideational support, normative frames for persuasion, material resources, political responsibility, and information (Murdie 2014). Coalition building may also 'increase advocacy group effects on policymaking and implementation by combining forces to compensate for individual weaknesses' (Dellmuth and Bloodgood 2019). International allies can assist in making a domestic case stronger, particularly when decisions-makers are vulnerable to outside pressure (Green 2016). Hale argues that 'operating transnationally allows these [advocacy] networks to gain additional power by sharing resources of information or by leveraging political relationships across borders' (2020).

By being part of a transnational network, NGOs gain greater leverage to set the global agenda, while also generating media and public attention. In addition, transnational advocacy networks are thought to be more successful when they have a large membership base which spans many different countries, allowing them to tap into greater financial resources and reach a wider international audience (Eilstrup-Sangiovanni and Bondaroff 2014). While activists may focus on local or national issues, many are also ideologically in favour of promoting global justice as they are 'rooted cosmopolitans' (Tarrow 2005; Yeo 2011).[60] Transnational networking may lead to transnational mobilizations when there is a common motive and an opportunity to mobilize and cooperate on a common issue (Young 2017a).

However, advocacy organizations' involvement in transnational networks, coalitions, and social movements also comes with costs (Bloodgood and

[60] They are cosmopolitan, but their ideological disposition is not their defining characteristic (Tarrow 2005: 20). They have a 'cache of experience and social connections one derives from being within proximate activist networks which in their turn link into worldviews and concerns held beyond a single locality' (Mercea and Bastos 2016: 141). They are highly invested in collective deliberations and decision-making.

Clough 2016). It takes time to form international coalitions and follow international negotiations, which can distract from nationally focused campaigns. Organizations need resources to coordinate and cooperate, and 'any form of political mobilization beyond the state requires even more [resources]' than domestic-level coordination (Tarrow 2005; Young 2017a).

Writing in 1998, Keck and Sikkink argued that international networking was costly, owing to 'geographical distance, nationalism, the multiplicity of languages and cultures, and the costs of fax, telephone, mail or air travel' (1998). The internet era has reduced these costs significantly: it is almost free to communicate over Skype, Whatsapp, email, Twitter, or Facebook.[61] Thus, we might expect digital advocacy organizations to cooperate more frequently, and more intensely, given their high use of these digital technologies.

In fact, much of the transnational civil society literature in the 1990s suggested precisely this. Price for instance, argued that 'the internet has not replaced the need for activists to travel and make personal contacts. But these technological developments do lower the transaction costs of engaging in transnational political activism compared to previous eras, and they facilitate denser political engagement across borders' (1998). Gordenker and Weiss suggested that new digital technologies 'have literally made it possible to ignore borders and to create the kinds of communities based on common values and objectives that were once almost the exclusive prerogative of nationalism' (1995: 365). Meanwhile, Spiro claimed that 'modern communication is much less dependent on location, increased travel, the fax' and 'perhaps most important the Internet has created the possibility of a cohesion that is not tied to a territory' (Spiro 1995: 47).

Some IR scholars writing in the 1990s argued that the internet would create a global civil society (Gordenker and Weiss 1995; Germain and Kenny 1998). People could communicate much more quickly, and for less cost using the internet, and hence 'establish and maintain [transnational] social relationships that are [the] basis of global civil society' (Warkentin 2001). Scholte suggested that much 'civic activism has become global through the internet' and has led to new forms of global identity and 'supraterritorial solidarity' as 'many trans-border civic activists regard themselves as world citizens in addition to (or even

[61] It is worth noting that there are some costs involved in digital communication for the advocacy organization and the individual. Both have to purchase a phone and internet contract to have access to digital platforms and there are clear 'digital divides' globally and within countries. Schradie, for instance, demonstrates how difficult it is for working-class Americans to be regularly online (Schradie 2018). In addition, organizations also have to spend staff time managing their social media and website, and their email lists. They may need to pay for their website, a server, and/or other information technology expertise.

more than) national-state citizens' (Scholte 1999).[62] Many other IR scholars pointed to the emergence of a global civil society in the 1990s, where activists campaigned transnationally but without 'directly pressuring states' (Wapner 1995), although not all of them referenced the internet as the prime cause of this—Wapner, for instance, did not.

Some recent scholarship has continued this line of argument. IR scholars have argued that digital communications, and especially social media, have 'levelled power differentials' and enabled groups to 'get messages across networks at low cost' (Narlikar 2020: 16). The internet has facilitated the spread of ideas, and new norms, and the depth and breadth of ties between people. Social movement scholars, writing in the aftermath of the Arab Spring (2011) and the Occupy Movement (2011), suggested that digital technologies were enabling new forms of digital social movements. They suggested that these 'movements spread by contagion in a world networked by wireless internet and marked by fast, viral diffusion of images and ideas' (Castells 2012). The internet was a 'free public space' and enabled the formation of a 'network society' organized around autonomous 'networks in each domain of human activity connected to interests and values of actors' (Castells 2012). The digital era led to a 'new species' of social movement, which was 'multi-modal, digital networks of horizontal communities' and was the 'fastest, most autonomous, interactive, reprogrammable and self-expanding means of communication in history' (Castells 2012: 15).

However, not all agree with these predictions that the internet would create a transnational civil society. Keck and Sikkink were sceptics even in 1998, arguing that: 'we lack convincing studies of the sustained and specific processes though which individuals and organizations create (or resist the creation of) something resembling a global civil society' (1998).[63] Murphy and Pfaff found that even the large anti-World Trade Organization (WTO) protests in Seattle, which are often depicted as a high point of transnational mobilization, were driven by local organizations. They argue that 'much of the literature overestimates the influence of new communications technology and overlooks the importance of local and domestic contexts of collection action' (Murphy and

[62] Scholte suggested that a global civil society would address 'transworld issues', involve transnational communications, have a global organization, and operate on the basis of 'supraterritorial solidarity' (Scholte 1999). While these four attributes often accompany one another, civic associations can also have a global character in only one or several of these four respects.

[63] Keck and Sikkink had a conception of transnational civil society as 'an arena of struggle, a fragmented and contested area'. This echoes much of the more recent norm contestation literature (Stimmer 2019; Wiener 2018).

Pfaff 2005). Busby, writing in 2010, reflects on this earlier scholarship: 'the internet was relatively new and the mobilization of attention and people across borders through new media and communication was fresh and novel' (Busby 2010: 5).

Yet, in an era of growing nationalism and populism, where civil society actors face increasing restrictions, it may be risky for NGOs to form strong transnational networks (Sriskandarajah 2017). The world is currently witnessing 'increasing nationalist and authoritarian tendencies in domestic politics [which] will limit the ability of sub- and non-state actors to link across borders' (Hale 2020). NGOs that share progressive values and campaign collectively may undermine their chances of success by banding together (Tallberg et al. 2015).

Transnational campaigns can provoke a backlash due to their *transnational* nature. NGOs may open themselves up to domestic criticism and/or repression by collaborating with, and receiving funding from, international progressive allies (Bob 2012). The Indian government, for example, has made it very difficult for NGOs operating in India to receive foreign funds. As a result, Amnesty International had to shut its offices in India in September 2020 (Ellis-Petersen and Doherty 2020).

Domestic NGOs may appear to be less 'authentic' if they work with foreign groups, and critics may claim that they are puppets for other actors. In fact, Keck and Sikkink, writing in 1998, noted that transnational alliances between the Global North and Global South can be problematic for those in the Global South due to 'ingrained nationalism common to main political groups in the developing world' (1998).[64] The rise of nationalism in the United States and Europe increases the risks of forming transnational alliances. In some cases, transnational allies can even jeopardize the very existence of an NGO. In Hungary, for instance, it became increasingly problematic for NGOs to receive foreign funding if they worked on migration issues (Amnesty International 2018).

Working with international allies involves reputational costs and even potential repression. In fact, one OPEN staffer mentioned that 'new foreign interference laws' which restricted the abilities of NGOs to receive support and funding from overseas actors may have prevented more collaborations

[64] However, they did not expect alliances between groups in the Global North to be problematic, as they argued that they were from the same 'cultural milieu of internationalism that is generally optimistic about the promise and possibilities of international networking' (Keck and Sikkink 1998: 16). Yet today, this is no longer the case.

within OPEN.[65] In Canada, LeadNow, as noted in Chapter 2, was embroiled in a scandal regarding the influence of foreign funding in Canadian elections (Globe Editorial 2017)

However, most OPEN organizations are transparent about their membership of OPEN, and even publicly advertise it on their websites and in their communications with members. In my interviews, most groups emphasized that they wanted to be open about their participation in OPEN, even in the face of attacks. Hence, the fear of being associated with an international partner cannot fully explain why digital advocacy organizations rarely campaign together on the same issue.

Conclusion

Campact, 38 Degrees, ActionStation, and GetUp frequently campaigned on transnational issues, whether for a ban on arms sales to Saudi Arabia, the closure of coal mines, refugee rights, or demonstrating against ISDS courts in free trade agreements. They have played a significant role domestically on transnational issues and mobilized large crowds for anti-Iraq war marches, climate action protests, and anti-trade demonstrations. This chapter found that almost half of their collective campaigns focused on a transnational issue (if we include 38 Degrees' Brexit-related campaigns). However, these four digital advocacy organizations rarely targeted international institutions, or worked with international allies. In fact, over 97 per cent of their campaign actions between mid-2018 and mid-2019 targeted a national decision-maker and had no transnational partner. These four digital advocacy organizations frequently campaigned on transnational issues, but did so through a national lens.

IR scholarship may partially help explain these patterns. There were greater political opportunity structures at the domestic level, hence these four organizations sought to influence national decision-makers rather than international institutions. There were also significant costs and risks of forming alliances with international NGOs. OPEN organizations hence opted for domestic NGOs partners instead of running campaigns with international allies.

In addition, the distinctive model of OPEN organizations helps to explain these patterns. These organizations seek to mobilize citizens *nationally* to put pressure on domestic and democratically elected decision-makers. These activists have cosmopolitan views: they believe in international solidarity and

[65] Discussion with Holly Dawson, OPEN staff member, OPEN focus group, 16 February 2021.

assistance for refugees, and in helping those worst affected by climate change. However, they still see the nation state as the most important locus of power, even for those countries within the EU. They often focus on the domestic ramifications of international problems: offshore detention of asylum seekers in Australia, coal mines in Australia or Germany, or oil and gas exploration in New Zealand. They have most power when mobilizing outsider pressure on national governments rather than using insider tactics at international summits.

In summary, their organizational form influences their patterns of engagement with international institutions and transnational allies.[66] Precisely because they are member-driven, and because their members are drawn from national constituencies, they frame their campaigns in national terms. To mobilize their members, digital advocacy organizations try to relate their transnational campaigns to members. This explains why it was hard to target international institutions such as the Global Compact on Migration, which to many members are far away and irrelevant to their everyday lives. OPEN organizations are issue generalists, aiming to influence domestic debates, and as a result rarely campaign collectively with international allies. Rather OPEN groups looks for domestic partners who have issue-expertise. OPEN has enabled digital advocacy organizations to share tactics, tech, and strategy on campaigns related to climate change, refugees, trade, and the far right. Digital Advocacy Organizations have often campaigned at the same time, on the same issue, but with different targets, as we will see in Chapter 7. Let us turn to the climate movement and the rise of digitally distributed campaigning.

[66] Han et al. have argued that how movement-based organizations build power *internally* with their members determines their *external power* at influencing targets (Han et al. 2021). In particular, they argue that organizations in the United States which are able to be flexible, committed, independent, and distribute strategy to their members are more likely to be successful.

7
Mobilizing for Climate Action

On 20 and 27 September 2019, over six million students and adults around the world protested for stronger action on climate change. Swedish teenager Greta Thunberg had inspired this movement with her lone school strikes outside the Swedish parliament in 2018. Thunberg and co-leaders of the worldwide movement #FridaysForFuture called for politicians to act with urgency and cut carbon emissions. Thunberg galvanized others to strike from school every Friday and mobilized large crowds for global days of climate action (Wahlström et al. 2019). The impact of the student climate movement is notable. Chancellor Angela Merkel has credited #FridaysForFuture with 'driving an acceleration' of the German government's actions on climate change (Connolly 2019). The student climate strikers have been effective at mobilizing millions around the world because they used distributed mobilizing tactics (Fisher 2019a). Anyone, anywhere, can be part of a global day of climate action simply by registering their event on the #FridaysForFuture's map of actions.[1]

Global days of climate action are not a new idea, although rolling school strikes are. In the lead-up to the 2009 Copenhagen climate summit, 350.org led a global day of action. People were invited to participate to put pressure on their own governments however they saw best. Small chapters of 350.org organized local demonstrations from Ukraine to New Zealand, and urged their national leaders to take action. Cable News Network (CNN) described the 2009 action as 'the most widespread day of political action in our planet's history'.[2] 350.org, an environmentalist group co-founded by university students and by journalist Bill McKibben, was a disruptive newcomer in the environmental movement. Despite its small, mostly volunteer, staff and tiny budget, 350.org was able to organize thousands of demonstrations worldwide, thanks to its use of digitally distributed tactics. 350.org connected activists in small towns and cities around the world through an events map (a predecessor

[1] #FridaysForFuture, 'Map of Actions', https://fridaysforfuture.org/action-map/map/(accessed 7 December 2021).

[2] 350.org, '10 Years', https://350.org/10-years/(accessed 7 December 2021).

Transnational Advocacy in the Digital Era. Nina Hall, Oxford University Press.
 DOI: 10.1093/oso/9780198858744.003.0007

to #FridaysForFuture), which let people register and advertise their planned demonstration.[3] Both #FridaysForFuture and 350.org enabled individuals to join in protests, even if there was no existing 350.org or #FridaysForFuture chapter where they lived. They coordinated participants through a centralized events platform. These campaigns had a common international frame or message, but were targeted at national decision-makers with autonomy for local activists. At the outset, both 350.org and #FridaysForFuture were small teams of non-professional campaigners with few resources, but thanks to the ease of communicating online, they could organize mass mobilizations globally.

Online Progressive Engagement Network (OPEN) organizations helped to develop the digital tools and distributed tactics which many climate activist organizations now use. OPEN organizations coordinated closely with 350.org on their global days of climate action, and more recently have supported the student strikers with training and technology. Older environmental non-governmental organizations (NGOs), such as Greenpeace, have also looked to emulate digitally distributed campaigning, recognizing the power and scale of these mass mobilizations for climate action (Hall et al. 2020; Silberman 2017). Distributed tactics are part of a broader shift in the climate movement in favour of nationally and locally targeted actions, rather than targeting international institutions, such as the United Nations Framework Convention on Climate Change (UNFCCC) (Moor 2020).

This chapter begins by identifying four forms of transnational advocacy campaigns which are often conflated in international relations (IR) advocacy literature. Campaigns that focus on the same issue may occur: (a) at the same time with the same target; (b) at the same time and with a different target; (c) at a different time and with the same target; and (d) at a different time and with a different target. This analytical distinction highlights a form of protest not well recognized by IR scholars: actions which occur at the same time, but with different targets, such as the global climate strikes. Building on these distinctions, it examines the contributions of OPEN organizations to the broader climate movement.

Overall, this chapter illustrates the power of campaigns which target different national actors at the same time. It suggests that distributed campaigning is a key form of protest that has taken off in the past decade. The climate movement has gained power and profile globally thanks to simultaneous, mass

[3] 350.org, 'Get Involved', https://350.org/get-involved/(accessed 7 December 2021).

mobilizations, which local groups of volunteers organize online and face-to-face. It is critical for IR to understand how this digitally distributed protest operates.

Categorizing Transnational Campaigns

Conventionally, IR scholars have focused on transnational advocacy networks which are united around a common cause (Hall 2009; Keck and Sikkink 1998). They have tended to study issue-based campaigns, which focus on the *same target* at the *same time*. Research that fits this model includes studies of the global climate movement (Hadden 2015; Moor 2018); campaigns conducted by human rights networks (Carpenter 2007a and b; Keck and Sikkink 1998); and campaigns against land mines and cluster munitions (Bolton and Nash 2010; Price 1998). However, campaigns which focus on the same target and issue at the same time are not the only way activists can engage in transnational advocacy.

In this chapter, I develop a broader conception of transnational campaigns to capture the ways in which transnational networks of activists collaborate. I focus on transnational campaigns united on the same issue, such as climate change or trade. However, I distinguish whether these campaigns: (a) occur at the *same time*; and/or (b) have the *same target* (i.e. an institution or decision-maker). As Table 7.1 demonstrates, transnational campaigns can then be categorized into four groups, according to whether they are directed at: (a) the same target at the same time; (b) the same target at a different time; (c) a different target at the same time; or (d) a different target at a different time.[4]

This categorization captures the rise of digitally distributed campaigns, which are based on loose connections between individuals who are geographically diffuse and may not associate with any particular civic organization, but are connected through an online platform (Fisher 2019b). Distributed organizing is often defined by 'participatory campaigning that is more bottom-up and relies on technology to mobilise and connect people' (Fisher 2019b: 15).[5] Distributed tactics have become increasingly popular with climate activists (Silberman 2017).

[4] These distinctions were described to me by Ben Brandzel and were outlined in various OPEN documents.

[5] Fisher is citing here a 2016 Netroots Nation panel. Her book describes the US-based resistance movement against President Trump as an example of distributed organizing.

Table 7.1 Types of transnational collaborative campaign

	Same time	Different time
Same target	*A collective campaign* Land mines Cluster munitions Climate movement (Hadden 2015)	*Learning across time* Climate movement (Hadden 2015)
Different target	*Distributed campaigns* US resistance to Trump and mid-term election mobilization (Fisher 2019b)	*Learning across space and time*

OPEN organizations have supported the rise of distributed campaigning in the climate movement. They have sought to connect their own nationally focused campaigns with the broader transnational climate movement, led by 350.org and #FridaysForFuture. Chapters 5 and 6 of this book illustrated how rare it was for these groups to campaign simultaneously on the same issue with the same target. In this chapter, I examine how OPEN organizations use their network to campaign across multiple countries on the same issue, at the same time, but with different targets.

This is important because some scholars believe federate and confederate structures (e.g. Oxfam and Greenpeace) are more effective than network structures at coordinating advocacy across multiple targets, countries, and sectors (Brown et al. 2012). This chapter illustrates how network governance structures, such as OPEN, have coordinated advocacy across multiple targets and countries.[6] Their use of digital technologies facilitates this form of transnational protest. As Newell has noted, 'dispersed coalitions and communication technologies allow many more groups to construct new forms of accountability politics over multiple scales and on a more regular basis' (2008: 137). IR scholars may miss this form of transnational protest if they only focus on protest targeted at international institutions.

In Table 7.2, the first box on the top left captures transnational campaigns that IR literature most typically examines: campaigns at the same time with the same target. Indeed, there have been a few occasions when OPEN organizations have worked together on such a common campaign. In 2019, many European OPEN groups campaigned to ensure a strong progressive turnout at the EU Parliament elections. In 2017, Skiftet, Campact, and MoveOn

[6] This finding contrasts with the assumptions of Brown and colleagues that *network* architectures are most effective for collaborative advocacy with *single* targets (Brown et al. 2012).

Table 7.2 Examples of OPEN's collaborative campaigns

	Same time	Different time
Same target	*A collective campaign* • Great Barrier Reef (2014)* • Trump Business Council (2017) • EU parliament elections (2020)	*There are no OPEN campaigns that I am aware of in this category*
Different target	*Distributed campaigns* • Global Day of Climate Action (e.g. in 2014 and 2019)* • Panama/Paradise papers (2018) • The far right (2016–2020) • Trade campaigns (2014–2020) • Response to the refugee 'crisis' (2015)	*Learning across space and time* • Marriage Equality referendum (Ireland and Australia) • GetUp's campaigns to stop the Adani coal port*

Note: The table is not an exhaustive list of all OPEN campaigns which fit into these categories.
*These campaigns will be analysed further in this chapter.

demanded that members of President Trump's business councils leave the councils, after the President refused to condemn white supremacist violence in Charlottesville. In 2014, GetUp in Australia, Campact in Germany, and 38 Degrees in the UK pushed Deutsche Bank and Barclays Bank to divest from plans to develop a coal-exporting port in the Australian state of Queensland. However, there are relatively few cases where digital advocacy organizations have engaged in collaborative campaigns with exactly the same target, despite the high level of trust and shared values within OPEN. These organizations are member-driven and focus on national targets.

The second box, in the top-right corner, covers campaigns which share the same target, but occur at different times (i.e. at least several months apart). The author is not aware of any such examples. The next category in the bottom left is the most relevant for this study: campaigns which focus on a different target but the same issue, at the same time. Digital advocacy organizations nearly always react to global crises (e.g. refugees, or the COVID-19 pandemic) by framing it within their own national context, and mobilizing their citizens to put pressure on their national governments. OPEN organizations may share the messaging, tactics, and strategies across the network, but are unlikely to run campaigns at the same time, with the same target.

Finally, OPEN groups may campaign in their own national contexts at different times on the same issue. Ireland had a referendum on marriage equality in 2015 and Australia a postal ballot on marriage equality (not officially a referendum) in 2017. In these instances, captured in the bottom right corner of Table 7.2, OPEN organizations may share technology, tactics, and messaging to help their sister organizations run successful campaigns. These are instances of transnational learning and diffusion, where OPEN facilitates digital advocacy organizations to share best practices, and most effective messaging over time and across space.

These four categories provide a framework within which to analyse the patterns of transnational climate campaigns, and how OPEN organizations contributed to the broader climate movement, which I turn to now.

Climate Advocacy

Since at least the 1970s and 1980s, environmental activists, working alongside scientists, have urged states to address climate change (Allan 2017; Asselt 2016: 95; Hadden 2015). Climate activists have engaged in agenda-setting, naming and shaming, providing information, and reviewing government's climate policy and holding them to account (Asselt 2016). For example, the Climate Action Network (CAN) has engaged in naming and shaming governments by presenting a daily 'Fossil of the Day' award at the UNFCCC to a state that is blocking the climate negotiations (Allan and Hadden 2017; Asselt 2016).

Climate activists have influenced national climate policies such as the decision to ratify the Kyoto protocol (Fisher 2004) and to divest from fossil fuels (Cheon and Urpelainnen 2018). NGOs have also had an impact on the UNFCCC negotiations. NGOs influenced negotiations on gender and climate change, and Indigenous groups influenced negotiations on reducing emissions from deforestation and forest degradation (REDD+) (Allan 2018: 564–565). Climate activists also successfully reframed debates on loss and damage as a justice issue, and lobbied alongside vulnerable states for it to be a separate article of the Paris Agreement (Allan and Hadden 2017). NGO advocacy may lead to the closure of coal plants or mines (Cheon and Urpelainnen 2018). However, scholars continue to debate how, when, and why, transnational environmental advocacy has an impact (Blondeel et al. 2019; Murdie and Urpelainen 2015). After all, there are many different ways to understand their influence, including mobilizing people (Cheon and Urpelainnen 2018; Hestres 2015); gaining media coverage (Cheon and Urpelainnen 2018); shaping societal attitudes (Fisher 2019a; Kaplan 2019); changing policy outcomes; or influencing the target (Han et al. 2021).

Targeting the UNFCCC (Same Time, Same Target)

Scholars have charted the growth in numbers of NGOs attending the UNFCCC (Bäckstrand et al. 2017: 562). NGOs come from an increasingly wide range of movements, including women's rights, labour, development, humanitarian, and Indigenous rights (Allan 2018).[7] The UNFCCC is more open to NGOs than many other international negotiations. NGOs can attend the negotiations and host side events (Bäckstrand et al. 2017: 564). The Paris Climate Agreement highlights the role non-state actors can play in review processes, and acknowledges the Non-State Actor Zone for Climate Action (NAZCA), which some argue 'led to a system that institutionalizes hybrid multilateralism' (Bäckstrand et al. 2017: 567). However, not all NGOs choose to engage in the negotiations, or are able to get registered. At COP15, a number of NGOs, including Avaaz and Friends of the Earth, had their accreditation revoked and/or could not attend the negotiations due to changes in the rules of participation (Fisher 2010).

OPEN organizations have rarely, if ever, directly targeted the UNFCCC, although the international climate movement regularly lobbies negotiators at the UNFCCC (Hadden 2015; Moor 2018). Becky Jarvis, who has worked for OPEN for over five years, stated that she has 'never seen OPEN groups be active around the COP', but added that they 'have been strong climate campaigners'.[8] I am not aware of an OPEN organization ever mobilizing its supporters to attend the annual climate negotiations, with the exception of when their country has been the host. For example, Campact in Germany co-organized a demonstration at the 2017 Bonn UNFCCC summit, and Akcja Demokcraja in Poland at the 2018 Katowice summit. Indeed, there is very little discussion in OPEN about negotiation dynamics at the UNFCCC. Rather,

[7] There has been a significant increase in the number of transnational environmental advocacy groups over time: from fewer than ten in 1950 to almost ninety in 2018 (Eilstrup-Sangiovanni 2019: 388).

[8] Online interview with Becky Jarvis, 3 December 2019.

conversations focus on how the network can shift their national governments' positions on climate policy.[9]

At the OPEN summit in February 2018, for example, Akcja Demokracja, GetUp, Campact, and other OPEN organizations brainstormed ideas for an international climate collaboration. They discussed organizing a global delegation of grandparents to attend the UNFCCC in Katowice.[10] However, nothing came of this. This was partly because Akcja was busy with its own climate campaigns targeting the Polish government, and had less time to engage its international allies.[11] There was also some concern that international pressure on the Polish government, especially from Western countries, would backfire and entrench the Polish government's pro-coal position.

OPEN organizations have not engaged directly in insider lobbying at the UNFCCC for several reasons. First, these organizations are issue generalists, not climate specialist NGOs. To gain influence and access to the UNFCCC, NGOs need some climate expertise, which OPEN organizations generally do not have. Asselt suggests that 'as long as non-state actors continue to offer credible and authoritative information, their voices will be heard' (Asselt 2016). Meanwhile, Allan argues that NGOs which 'built their authority on their expertise or their capacity to deliver mitigation results may find more opportunities than those making moral claims' in the climate regime (Allan 2018: 562). Issue-expertise is the source of NGO access, influence, and authority in international organizations, and digital advocacy organizations do not have this expertise (Stroup and Wong 2018; Tallberg et al. 2015).

Second, OPEN organizations have no interest in insider advocacy (lobbying). Their power comes from their ability to mobilize citizens to put pressure on their domestic governments, not from directly lobbying politicians. OPEN groups are also highly networked with each other, and tend to adopt similar tactics (such as online petitions, social media, and demonstrations), but not more radical ones (such as direct action). Other IR scholars have noted that the

[9] In fact, Brandzel noted that after the Paris climate summit: 'the climate struggle returns to many national arenas, where OPEN groups will help lead the fight to implement any positive agreements and fill the inevitable gaps with strong domestic policy. They will build more popular demand to stop the expansion of fossil fuels and support renewable energy.' Ben Brandzel (notes on file with author).

[10] Interview with Weronika Paszewska, co-founder and former executive director of Akcja Demokracja, 10 June 2018. This paragraph also draws on discussions at the OPEN summit, Bangalore, 2018.

[11] Interview with Weronika Paszewska, co-founder and former executive director of Akcja Demokracja, 10 June 2018.

networks between climate advocacy groups shape the radicality of tactics and strategies they employ (Eilstrup-Sangiovanni 2019; Hadden and Jasny 2017).[12]

Third, OPEN groups, like many other climate activists, may have become disillusioned with the UNFCCC process, especially after the failure to reach an agreement in Copenhagen. After the 2009 UNFCCC summit, climate activists questioned whether the negotiations were the most effective location to concentrate their energies (Moor 2020). Not only is it expensive for many organizations to travel to the venue, but many are also more concerned by what their own governments are doing (or not doing) than by the dynamics of international negotiations. Strategically speaking, it makes more sense for NGOs to concentrate their activities on government climate policy in the lead-up to (or after) climate negotiations (Cheon and Urpelainnen 2018; Moravcsik 1997; Putnam 1988). In fact, research has found that the newest climate advocacy groups, #FridaysForFuture and Extinction Rebellion, have predominantly focused their protests at local or national governments, shifting away from 'prior climate mobilizations targeting transnational institutions' (Moor et al. 2020). Although OPEN organizations may not target the UNFCCC, they can still exercise influence on global climate policy.

Global Days of Climate Action (Same Time, Different Target)

OPEN organizations have regularly participated in global days of climate action. Global days of action are often examples of distributed campaigns which involve loosely affiliated networks of individuals who connect through digital platforms, but have their own messaging and tactics (Fisher 2019b). The global climate movement has been immensely successful at coordinating large-scale global distributed actions, thanks to 350.org and #FridaysForFuture. OPEN organizations supported these movements with technology and tactical development.

In fact, soon after OPEN launched in 2013, it began to invest in distributed climate campaigning. In 2013, both GetUp and Leadnow ran national days of climate action targeting their respective governments. Then, at the January 2104 OPEN summit in Germany, OPEN core groups discussed the

[12] Hadden and Jasny find that groups are more likely to adopt protest as a tactic when they are connected directly to an environmental NGO that has already engaged in protests (Hadden and Jasny 2017). Meanwhile, Eilstrup-Sangiovanni takes a population ecology approach and suggests that smaller and newer environmental groups pursue more niche and unconventional tactics, such as climate litigation, while older, 'larger and more resource-rich groups specialise in gaining political access and appealing to mainstream audiences' (Eilstrup-Sangiovanni 2019: 401).

possibility of collaborating on a global day of action in September. During these discussions, they discussed how they could collaborate with global groups such as 350.org, Avaaz, and SumOfUs. They wanted to help create a coordinated global movement which was strongly rooted in national and local distributed organizing.

OPEN expanded its staff to support these initiatives. In 2014, Brandzel hired a young Australian climate activist, Michael Poland, who is a former member of the Australian Youth Climate Coalition (AYCC), to work with OPEN and 350.org on the global day of action. 350.org was planning a large protest in New York alongside distributed protests worldwide to coincide with the UN Secretary General Ban Ki-Moon's climate summit (McKibben 2014). The aim was to put pressure on world leaders during the New York summit, which was seen as an important stepping stone to Paris. OPEN's decision to hire Poland was an investment in the global climate movement.

OPEN wanted to link the climate protest in New York to national mobilizations around the world. The new climate coordinator, Michael Poland, whose salary was financed by both 350.org and OPEN, worked for six months in the lead-up to the September 2014 climate mobilizations. Poland's aim was to bring OPEN organizations 'unprecedented access to the latest international analysis on messaging, targeting, and timing, enabling them to harmonize their domestic plans with the international movement'.[13] Brandzel explained the strategy in December 2013 in OPEN's Climate Action Plan:

> OPEN groups are often submerged in their domestic campaigns and messaging bubbles. So OPEN will serve as a conduit between our member organizations and our international allies (350.org, Greenpeace, Avaaz, CAN, GGCA [Galvanizing the Groundswell of Climate Actions], IPPI etc). We can then help our [OPEN] members calibrate their domestic efforts to provide the maximal possible boost to the international efforts, by synchronising timing, targeting, asks, messaging etc. In 2014 a primary example will be helping to build multi-national support for the September UNSG Climate Summit.[14]

The plan was to build a coordinated, distributed day of climate action across the world.

OPEN groups shared messaging and resources in the lead-up to the global day of action, but targeted their own respective governments. Staff

[13] Ben Brandzel, V. Kann Rasmussen Foundation (VKRF) Youth Leadership application, OPEN-350 proposal (on file with author).

[14] Ben Brandzel, OPEN Climate Action Plan 2014, 14 December 2013 (on file with author).

working at the OPEN secretariat sought to facilitate the exchange of climate campaign plans, resources, and framing between OPEN groups, as well as their international allies. Brandzel's hope was that: 'We can dramatically reduce redundancy and accelerate thinking across the network by ensuring we all learn and improve from each other's experience in real time.'[15] On 21 September 2014, 310,000 people marched through the streets of New York, joined by the UN Secretary General, Ban-Ki Moon (BBC 2014). Alongside this march, there were actions in 2,000 locations in 156 countries, including large marches in Berlin, London, and Melbourne (BBC 2014). It is difficult to determine what proportion of these people were mobilized by OPEN organizations, as there were hundreds of other organizations involved in this global day of action.

OPEN reported that its collaboration with 350.org was a 'huge success', as eight of its organizations directly participated in the global protests.[16] OPEN claimed that some of its member organizations were mobilized thanks to the global OPEN climate coordinator. They highlighted how the 350.org–OPEN partnership meant that they could share customized distributed event pages, email copy, graphics, video content, media statements, field guides, and intelligence on grassroots organizing. Brandzel claimed, in one funding application, that it was the 'first real-time instance of *network facilitated execution enhancement*' [his emphasis].[17] This was the vision that Brandzel had for OPEN: power optimized for domestic influence, yet networked for global scale.

It is hard to assess the impact of the 2014 global climate protests, let alone OPEN's specific contribution to these. A year later, states negotiated the Paris Climate Agreement. For the first time, all members of the UNFCCC agreed to cut their emissions and ensure that global temperature rise would stay below two degrees Celsius (with the aim of limiting the increase to 1.5 degrees Celsius).[18] There were many dynamics which contributed to the success of these negotiations, including: the strong role the French government played in preparing for and chairing the negotiations, and the leadership of UNFCCC Secretary General Christiana Figueres (Walker and Biedenkopf 2020). As I wrote this in 2021, it was too early to say whether states will meet their Paris targets. Yet the protests did ensure that climate change was a high priority for decision-makers around the world.

[15] ibid.

[16] They listed GetUp, MoveOn, LeadNow, 38 Degrees, Enough Is Enough (a new start-up in Nigeria), ActionStation, Uplift, and Jhatkaa.

[17] Ben Brandzel, VKRF Youth Leadership application, OPEN-350 proposal (on file with author).

[18] UNFCCC, 'What is the Paris Agreement?', https://unfccc.int/process-and-meetings/the-paris-agreement/what-is-the-paris-agreement(accessed 7 December 2021).

Global days of action have continued to be a core tactic of the climate movement. OPEN has frequently mobilized its members to take part in globally distributed protests, which have been led by #FridaysForFuture. OPEN groups have rallied their supporters to turn out for the youth climate strikes in March 2019, September 2019, and September 2020. Several OPEN groups offered the youth activists the chance to write to their members directly. De Goede Zaak in the Netherlands developed an events map, where Dutch youth climate strikers could list their demonstration. Subsequently, #FridaysForFuture created its own centralized global events map. MoveOn supported the US-based climate strikers with strategy and educational videos on the Green New Deal (Fisher and Nasrin 2021). ActionStation hosted New Zealand's youth climate strikers' online petition and disseminated its message widely to its membership (Ingoe 2020).

While OPEN organizations were supportive of the #FridaysForFuture movement, they were cautious not to take over with their banners, branding, or spokespersons. OPEN organizations realized that they could undermine the power of the movement if it was seen as orchestrated by politically partisan adult groups. Like others in the climate movement, OPEN groups tried to stay in the background and help build support and organizational structures for the youth movement (Fisher and Nasrin 2021). Campact, for instance, ran a youth climate training camp in summer 2019 to help #FridaysForFuture in Germany to build sustainable organizational structures. As one Campact staffer explained, they are 'super-fast, super young. Most of them are brilliant, but it's a lot of stuff [for #FridaysForFuture] happening at the same time.'[19] Campact sought to give the young activists basic campaigning advice, such as developing ways to count how many people attended their events, so they could release it to the media as soon as possible.

The September 2019 marches were reported to be the largest ever global day of action with around 6 million people taking part across the world on two consecutive Fridays (Taylor et al. 2019). These global marches, in which any one can participate wherever they live, took the existing climate movement by surprise. At an OPEN summit in June 2019, a 350.org global organizer highlighted that 'what kids have tried to do in a week, 350.org have tried to do for a decade. We are a newcomer and among the climate movement we are pretty agile, yet we are amazed and have been bypassed.'[20] Several OPEN activists also reported their initial surprise at how large scale the student protests became.

[19] Luise Neumann-Cosel, campaigns director, Campact, OPEN summit, Langenselbold, June 2019.
[20] Nicolas Haeringer, 350.org, OPEN summit, Langenselbold, June 2019.

Digital advocacy organizations had tried to mobilize people for climate action on the same scale for years. While they were better resourced than the student movement, they were not as effective. A Campact climate campaigner explained that the 2019 school strikes were the biggest climate strikes Germany had ever seen.[21] The strikes changed the public discussion and media attention on the topic: 'everyone was talking about a "climate catastrophe"' which 'none of us had ever thought would happen that quickly'.[22] The German #FridaysForFuture movement likely helped the Green party make significant wins in the 2019 European Union (EU) elections and may have boosted the need for climate action in the 2021 German federal election.

The power of the climate student movement came from it being 'distributed'.[23] As a 350.org campaigner explained, 'it's not just in your capital city, London, Paris. It's in every city, village and every single Friday.'[24] Interestingly, #FridaysForFuture's core strategy relied on face-to-face mobilizing between friends and classmates at school, rather than direct email. A study of the March 2019 European #FridaysForFuture protests found that 54.7 per cent of school students learned about the demonstration through direct social contacts (mostly friends and schoolmates) compared with 45 per cent for adults (Wahlström et al. 2019).[25] Social media was also an important information channel: over 30 per cent of school students and adults learned about the protests through Twitter, Facebook, or Instagram, the latter being particularly important for the younger generation (Wahlström et al. 2019). The result was a 'web of conversation that was very different from 350.org' and digital advocacy organizations which rely principally on email to communicate with members.[26] Face-to-face contact was initially more important than social media for the youth climate movement. However, this changed in 2020, due to the COVID-19 pandemic, when all protests shifted online during the various lockdowns. #FridaysForFuture continued to host school strikes under the hash tag #climatestrikeonline during the pandemic.

[21] Luise Neumann-Cosel, campaigns director, Campact, OPEN summit, Langenselbold, June 2019.
[22] ibid.
[23] Nicolas Haeringer, 350.org, OPEN summit, Langenselbold, June 2019.
[24] ibid.
[25] They also note that 72.4 per cent of people surveyed asked someone else to join the Global Climate Strike (Wahlström et al. 2019: 12).
[26] Nicolas Haeringer, 350.org, OPEN summit, June 2019, Langenselbold, Germany. Many digital advocacy organizations were aware of the limitations of email. A regular theme at summits was how to adapt to new social media platforms (e.g. Instagram) and how to engage people more in face-to-face local organizing, rather than large-scale mobilizing online.

Targeting Deutsche Bank and Barclays (Same Time, Same Target)

Environmental activists have also successfully influenced multinational companies through protest, research, exposés, and orchestrating public outcry (Wapner 1995). NGOs are targeting the corporate sector, consumers, and multilateral banks, due to the increased recognition of the power and authority of corporate actors (Newell 2008). Activists can win important political victories through targeting corporate actors, rather than focusing only on states (Wapner 1995). OPEN organizations have engaged in naming and shaming businesses for their contribution to climate change. Digital advocacy organizations mobilized their members to target businesses which were headquartered in their own country.

Digital advocacy organizations have collaborated and targeted the same business, at the same time. In 2014, GetUp worked with German-based Campact to stop Deutsche Bank from investing in the Abbot Point Port expansion in Queensland, Australia. Expanding the port would have involved dredging the sea bed and dropping three million cubic metres of sediment into the Great Barrier Reef marine park. The port would have become the largest coal export facility in the world, enabling large ships to export coal from the proposed Adani mine in Queensland (Muller 2014). GetUp, along with other Australian environmentalists, was concerned that the expanded Abbot Point Port would ruin parts of the Great Barrier Reef. This campaign was part of a larger movement to stop the Adani-financed Carmichael mine from going ahead (Curran 2020).[27] Adani wanted to build one of the largest thermal coal mines in the world, which was expected to produce around 705 million tonnes of CO_2 per year (Curran 2020). Were it a country, the mine would have ranked in the top ten countries worldwide in terms of greenhouse gas emissions (Ireland and Clausen 2019).[28]

GetUp staff, based in Australia, contacted Campact and asked it to put pressure on Deutsche Bank. Deutsche Bank was one of three international banks that had already helped to finance the Adani group's thirty-year lease on the port. GetUp thought Campact could have more influence over Deutsche Bank than it could, given Deutsche Bank is headquartered in Germany and Campact had over 1 million German members. Campact supported GetUp and ran

[27] Gautam Adani, an Indian billionaire, lodged a request in 2010 to build a large-scale coal mine in Queensland. The original proposal outlined an on-site processing plant and the expansion of railway and port infrastructure to export coal over 200 kilometres from the Galilee Basin through central Queensland to Abbot Point, where it would then be shipped to India and China (Curran 2020).

[28] See also Ward (2015).

an online petition with WWF Germany, urging Deutsche Bank not to invest in Abbot Point. Over 180,000 people signed this petition.[29] GetUp, Campact, Greenpeace, and the Australian Marine Conservation Society, meanwhile, crowd-financed a full-page advertisement in the *Financial Times* with the headline 'Deutsche Bank: Don't Finance the Destruction of Our Reef'. The campaign was also covered in the German newspaper, *Der Spiegel* (Marquart and Kaiser 2014).

Campact and WWF Germany also protested outside the Deutsche Bank annual meeting in Germany in May 2014. At that meeting, a local Queensland businessman, Tony Brown, also presented his case to the board. Brown, a tour boat operator in the Great Barrier Reef who had purchased shares in Deutsche Bank, urged them to not to invest in the project. Brown informed the Board about the potentially devastating impact of the port expansion on the Great Barrier Reef's tourism industry (Muller 2014). Before Brown had even finished his speech, the Bank co-chief executive officer, Jürgen Fitschen, reportedly announced that Deutsche Bank would not finance the development until they received assurance that it would not damage the Reef. As there was currently 'clearly no consensus between the Australian government and UNESCO regarding the impacts of the Abbot Point expansion on the reef', no financial application would be considered (Muller 2014). Brown, Campact, GetUp, the WWF, and other environmental groups claimed this as a victory. However, it is hard to attribute this success to their efforts alone, as the lack of a UNESCO decision appears to have influenced Deutsche Bank's position.[30]

GetUp then worked with 38 Degrees to apply similar pressure to Barclays Bank in the UK. 38 Degrees members sent over 10,000 tweets to the Barclays media team asking for a statement. When they received a short and ambiguous statement,[31] 38 Degrees members sent over 18,000 emails to Barclays demanding that they formally rule out investing in Abbot Point, or any of the railways or mines linked to it (38 Degrees 2014). Barclays announced that they had 'no plans to participate' in financing an expansion. Other NGOs and environmentalists continued to lobby against other banks throughout 2014 and 2015. The US-based NGO Rainforest Action Network, for instance, successfully obtained

[29] Campact, 'Great Barrier Reef', https://www.campact.de/great-barrier-reef/appell/beendet/ (accessed 7 December 2020).

[30] States party to UNESCO subsequently decided not to put the Great Barrier Reef on a danger list. This was criticized by Greenpeace and other NGOs, given the threat of dredging to create a large port in Queensland for the coal mine (BBC 2015).

[31] Barclays, Twitter post, https://twitter.com/barclays/status/479620918931881984 (accessed 7 December 2020).

written commitments from Citigroup, Goldman Sachs, and JPMorgan Chase that they would not back the Abbot Point port (Milman 2014).

The 2014 campaigns to stop international investment into Abbot Point were a partial success, as a number of banks agreed not to finance the port. These campaigns across OPEN are also a good example of transnational collaboration on the same issue, at the same time, and with the same target. Then OPEN executive director, Brandzel, celebrated it as the 'clearest example yet of cross-network collaboration on a specific issue, applying pincer-like pressure from multiple domestic fronts'.[32] It would be wrong to attribute the success solely to GetUp, Campact, and 38 Degrees actions. Their efforts were part of a longstanding campaign in Australia to stop the Adani mine, and many other environmental groups and activists are involved. This example does, however, highlight how quickly these groups can launch petitions and put pressure on businesses.

In January 2020, environmentalists around the world again rallied against the Adani Mine. #FridaysForFuture followed a similar strategy to GetUp, Campact, and 38 Degrees. They put pressure on Siemens, headquartered in Germany, to cancel its contract to provide the railway signalling for the mine. Prominent youth activists, including Greta Thunberg and Luisa Neubauer (one of the most prominent spokespeople of Germany's #FridaysForFuture), mobilized their members online, and were backed by Campact members. However, Siemens announced that it was obliged to fulfil its contract (Readfearn 2020).

In Poland, Akcja Demokracja also reached out to the Polish division of Siemens, after Campact 'invited other organizations to this collaboration'.[33] Akcja Demokracja asked its members to write to the Polish board of Siemens demanding that Siemens Germany withdraw its support for Adani.[34] The Siemens board in Poland even met with Akcja Demokracja and heard its concerns. The Polish campaign was more symbolic, given that the Siemens board in Poland had little influence over the German Siemens' final decision.

Digital advocacy organizations have mobilized their members to put pressure on businesses and banks to undermine fossil fuel production. They have worked together on short, tactical campaigns to name and shame businesses. Their efforts to stop Barclays and Deutsche Bank from financing Abbot Point

[32] Ben Brandzel, email to OPEN, https://us8.campaign-archive.com/?u=753395b9f963c9ea2d6980b7c&id=af6b5691ab (accessed 7 December 2021).

[33] Interview with Weronika Paszewska, co-founder and former executive director of Akcja Demokracja, 10 June 2018.

[34] ibid.

expansion were successful. Digital advocacy organizations' have often mobilized citizens to put pressure on private companies in their headquarter country. The logic is that these businesses are more sensitive to pressure from their fellow citizens than from outsiders. This is the same tactic that was used to break up Donald Trump's business councils, described in the introduction to this book.

National Campaigns for Climate Action (Different Time, Different Target)

Global environmental policymaking is rooted in domestic politics. This is where states develop their positions for international negotiations, and where eventual ratification and implementation of treaties take place (Fisher 2004). Climate activists have long sought to influence global politics domestically (Newell 2008).[35] Typical strategies include urging governments to sign up to international agreements, lobbying to strengthen these agreements' provisions, and monitoring implementation of these agreements (Newell 2008). Scholars should not be 'spellbound by international climate summits', as most protests are local or national (Cheon and Urpelainnen 2018). Domestic mobilization, according to some, has more effect on changing states' climate policies than international mobilizations (Cheon and Urpelainnen 2018).

OPEN organizations subscribe to the view that the nation state is the most critical actor in international climate policy. Their climate campaigns mobilize citizens domestically to put pressure on nationally elected politicians. Most of their campaigns tend to fit in the category of different time and different target, as they respond to national events. MoveOn, for example, mobilized Americans against fracking, the Keystone pipeline, and US oil company ExxonMobil.[36] It worked alongside other traditional US-based environmental NGOs (Sierra Club, Greenpeace, and Friends of the Earth), as well as digital advocacy organizations such as 350.org (Hestres 2015; Newell 2008). Leadnow mobilized Canadians against mining the tar sands in Alberta, have run national days of climate action, and also advocated for a Canadian Green New Deal. At OPEN summits, organizations have frequently shared their campaign tactics, messaging, successes, and failures across their climate campaigns.

[35] Newell suggests that the state 'continues to be the formal, legitimate, and often most democratic vehicle by which national publics in democratic settings express their will within international institutions' (2008: 125).

[36] MoveOn was part the Expose Exxon coalition with over a dozen other US-based environmentalist groups, which mobilized 500,000 people (Newell 2008).

Digital advocacy organizations regularly campaign on climate change because their members are strongly supportive of climate action. 38 Degrees, for instance, polled its members on Facebook about whether it should campaign for an amendment to the 2013 UK Energy Bill. Its members were supportive and so 38 Degrees worked with a broader coalition of NGOs to advocate for decarbonizing the UK's electricity generation by 2030. It asked 38 Degrees members to urge their local MP to #vote4cleanpower and in the final days before the parliamentary vote, 38 Degrees mobilized 2,000 tweets. The amendment was defeated by twenty-three votes, but 38 Degrees may have helped to shift seventeen MPs to support the amendment (Dennis 2019).

Digital advocacy organizations are not issue-specialist climate campaigners, but rather work in coalition with, or in parallel to, other domestic environmental groups. Although GetUp and Campact have in recent years hired staff dedicated to climate campaigning and are powerful players in their respective domestic climate movements. Here I describe some of their climate campaigns in more detail to illustrate how digital advocacy organizations can work in domestic coalitions, and shape political outcomes.

GetUp and the Australian Climate Movement

In 2011, GetUp launched a campaign for a carbon tax in Australia with a coalition of other environmental organizations.[37] The Labour Party, led then by Julia Gillard, was also in favour of stronger climate regulation, and in 2011 passed into law the Clean Energy Act. The Act introduced a cap and trade emissions scheme: during the first three years, the price of carbon would be fixed, before being set by the market. However, the opposition Liberal Party, alongside energy and industrial interest groups, successfully undermined the Act. Then opposition leader Tony Abbott argued that Labour was colluding with wealthy 'left-wing elites' to impose a carbon tax at the 'expense of working people' (Copland 2019). Abbott publicly criticized the campaign for the Act, which had drawn support from wealthy celebrities such as Cate Blanchett (Copland 2019). The Clean Energy Act became a major point of contention between the two main political parties in the 2013 federal election. Abbott won the election and repealed the clean energy legislation in 2014. Since then, Australia's federal government has been led by a Conservative coalition, which is deeply sceptical of regulations to address climate change.

[37] The 'Say Yes Campaign' was a 2011 coalition in support of carbon pricing. The coalition included GetUp and eight other organizations: the Australian Council of Trade Unions (ACTU), The World Wildlife Fund for Nature (WWF), the Climate Institute, Greenpeace, the Australian Youth Climate Coalition (AYCC), the Australian Conservation Foundation (ACF), Environment Victoria (EV), and the Climate Action Network Australia (CANA). See Copland 2019 for details.

Following the 2013 federal election, GetUp continued to campaign on climate change. In 2016, it ran a campaign to save the Australian Renewable Energy Agency (ARENA) after the Abbott government threatened to cut AUS$1.3 billion funding. It mobilized 3,040 members to sign petitions, crowdfund advertisements, and visit their members of parliament (Ireland and Clausen 2019). In the end, the government only cut $500 million, and GetUp claimed that it saved AUS$800 million of government funding.[38]

An ongoing, major focus for GetUp and the broader climate movement in Australia has been stopping the Adani mine. As an active member of the 'Stop Adani' coalition, GetUp has engaged in legal cases, protest events, and mobilizing people online and offline, as well as bank boycott campaigns. Interestingly, it is one of the few GetUp campaigns that has incorporated 'multilevel targets beyond [national] government' (Vromen 2017). The 'Stop Adani' campaign has had some significant victories, in addition to those described earlier. These include preventing the project from gaining public financing to develop a rail network to the coalmine's proposed location (Hasham 2018). Their divestment campaign, which targeted major Australian banks, managed to limit the size of the overall mine (Curran 2020).

However, the 'Stop Adani' campaign is not over. In June 2019, the Queensland government gave Adani the environmental approval to construct the Carmichael mine (Young 2019). On 24 January 2021, workers at the mine first struck coal (Fernyhough 2021). The Adani group operated in favourable political circumstances as the Federal government, led by Prime Minister Scott Morrison, was supportive of expanding coal exports in Australia. Economic considerations may ultimately weigh against the project, given that the price of coal is declining and that there is increased pressure to divest from fossil fuels (Quiggin 2019). GetUp continues to prevent the construction of the mine as part of a broader 'Stop Adani' coalition.

Campact and the German Climate Movement

Campact's founders, Felix Kolb and Christoph Bautz, were strongly engaged in the anti-nuclear movement before starting Campact. They continue to be well connected to Germany's environmental movement, and work closely with other German environmental NGOs.[39] Campact has protested against

[38] GetUp, 'We Saved Arena', https://www.getup.org.au/campaigns/renewable-energy/we-saved-arena/we-saved-arena(accessed 7 December 2021).

[39] Traditional environmental organizations have large memberships in Germany, and have shaped public debate (Gründinger 2017b: 126). Key organizations includes national branches of Greenpeace, WWF, Friends of the Earth Germany (BUND), as well as the Nature Conservation Union (Naturschutzbund, NABU) and the Climate Alliance Group (CAG).

fracking, nuclear energy, and coal power plants in Germany (Speth 2014). It has been part of a broad coalition demanding that Germany adopt an 'Energiewende' ('energy shift') by replacing fossil fuels and nuclear power with renewable energy (Gründinger 2017b).[40] In 2013, for example, Campact co-organized nationwide demonstrations in support of the Energiewende, which involved more than 16,000 people from across Germany. In 2018, Campact ran an online petition targeting Peter Altmaier, the Federal Minister for Economic Affairs and Energy, demanding a shift to renewable energy and a 40 per cent reduction of carbon emissions from 1990 levels.[41]

Campact is a 'major player in public discourse' on environmental issues (Gründinger 2017a). It regularly co-organizes large climate marches and petitions, particularly in the lead-up to the UNFCCC summits. For instance, before the Doha climate summit in 2012, Campact demanded that Germany support an EU-wide emission reduction target of 30 per cent by 2020. When then environment minister, Peter Altmaier took the plane to the Doha climate summit, Campact handed him over 100,000 signatures (Campact 2012).[42] In late 2015, Campact worked in alliance with other environmental groups to mobilize thousands on the streets around Germany in the lead-up to the Paris UNFCCC summit. It also coordinated marches to target the G20 meeting in Hamburg (2017), and the Bonn UNFCCC annual negotiations (2017).

In 2018, Campact mobilized its members to save the Hambacher forest and stop RWE Power planned expansion of a coal mine in Western Germany. Saving the Hambacher forest became a core goal—and symbol—of Germany's climate movement (Graham-Harrison 2019). On 6 October 2018, Campact worked with Friends of the Earth Germany, Greenpeace, and Naturfreunde Deutschland to mobilize over 50,000 people to demonstrate near the forest (Schumacher 2018). Campact's spokesperson and co-founder, Christopher Bautz, spoke at the demonstration alongside representatives from other environmental NGOs.[43] After immense public pressure, the German federal government eventually intervened, declaring that the forest would not be cleared for coal mining but the government did subsidize the energy company RWE Power (*tagesschau.de* 2020).

...

[40] Germany relies significantly on coal and lignite (in 2014, it was 43.8 per cent of gross electricity production) (David 2018: 342).

[41] Campact, https://www.campact.de/ (accessed 7 December 2021).

[42] See also Alamy, https://www.alamy.com/stock-photo-german-environment-minister-peter-altmaier-c-is-presented-a-book-with-52287782.html (accessed 7 December 2021).

[43] 'Stop Koehle', https://www.stop-kohle.de/ablauf-2/ (accessed 7 December 2021).

In summary, Campact and GetUp have been powerful players in their domestic climate movements. Their members and staff strongly support ongoing advocacy on climate change. They have hired dedicated climate campaigners, which is not typical in the OPEN issue-generalist model. More recently, other OPEN groups such as MoveOn, 38 Degrees, or ActionStation, have also run climate campaigns with specialized climate staff. OPEN organizations can run sustained, committed campaigns if their members maintain a high level of support over time. We will see in Chapter 8 what happens when members have a fluctuating interest in an issue.

Conclusion

OPEN organizations have been active contributors to the climate movement from Australia to Germany, Poland to Canada. They have not targeted the UNFCCC negotiations, but are part of a broader shift in climate advocacy towards distributed national and local protests. OPEN organizations have helped coordinate and mobilize supporters for multiple global days of climate action. They have supported the youth climate strikers through financing, training, and mobilizing their own members to take to the streets. The youth-led climate protests have seen millions of people taking to the streets in towns and cities across the world. If scholars are too fixated on advocacy at international summits, such as the UNFCCC, they will miss out on this crucial new and powerful form of protest.

Most OPEN organization's climate campaigns have targeted their own national governments. These digital advocacy organizations have often worked in climate coalitions and influenced domestic climate policy. However, environmental NGOs are better suited to committed, long-term, campaigning and to ensuring that decisions are upheld and pledges implemented. Digital advocacy organizations have also targeted transnational corporations. GetUp, 38 Degrees, and Campact successfully collaborated to stop Barclays Bank and Deutsche Bank investing in Abbot Point port in Australia. While these banks operate transnationally, these examples suggest that businesses may be particularly responsive to pressure from citizens in their company's home country.

Chapter 8 turns to campaigns on refugees, free trade, and Indigenous rights. OPEN organizations faced a dilemma when campaigning on these three issues—should they try to shape their members' preferences, or simply react to them?

8
Staff or Member-Driven?

In 2016, staff at 38 Degrees in the UK surveyed their members on whether they supported Britain remaining in, or leaving, the European Union (EU).[1] Echoing the eventual referendum result, 38 Degrees members were split on Brexit. Although 38 Degrees staff—who are largely urban, young, and highly educated—were committed to remaining in the EU, a significant proportion of their membership was disenchanted with the institution.[2] In the end, 38 Degrees campaigned neither for nor against Brexit, but rather focused on bringing neutral facts to the debate (Hall 2017b).

Why didn't staff override their members and campaign to stay in the EU? 38 Degrees staff were committed to a purely member-driven mode of advocacy. They were worried about losing, or alienating, some members if they chose a strong position on either side of the polarized debate. Digital advocacy organizations derive their power and legitimacy from members, and 38 Degrees did not want to jeopardize its relationship with any members, including Brexiters. 38 Degrees staff saw their role as representing both sides of the Brexit debate. However, some activists in the Online Progressive Engagement Network (OPEN) community were critical of 38 Degrees' decision to remain neutral during the Brexit referendum. OPEN activists saw remaining in the EU as an important progressive cause, and wanted 38 Degrees to mobilize popular support against the Brexiters, who were led by right-wing groups and individuals.[3]

Notably, 38 Degrees is one of the most member-driven organizations within OPEN. It makes campaign decisions based on the results of weekly member surveys, and digital analytics. It most closely follows the member-driven,

[1] They also asked them how important the EU Referendum was compared to other issues, such as the National Health Service (NHS), tax dodging, stopping the Transatlantic Trade and Intellectual Property Agreement (TTIP), protecting the bees, or action on climate change. 38 Degrees survey on the EU referendum in 2016.

[2] The British Labour Party also found itself in a difficult position, torn between leavers and remainers.

[3] Discussions at the OPEN annual summit, Canada, February 2017.

Transnational Advocacy in the Digital Era. Nina Hall, Oxford University Press.
 DOI: 10.1093/oso/9780198858744.003.0008

rapid-response, issue-generalist model laid out in earlier chapters. But could 38 Degrees staff have acted otherwise? Can digital advocacy organizations also shape their members' concerns?

This chapter examines two different logics that digital advocacy organizations may follow. In the *member-driven logic*, organizations respond reactively to members preferences. They use digital tools to quickly aggregate and identify issues that members are concerned about. Their campaigns last as long as their members' interest in a particular issue. In the *staff stewardship logic* staff seek to shape members' concerns. In these cases, staff are driven by particular values and principles. They may choose an issue regardless of initial member support, and stick with it for several years. Over time, they will seek to shape their members' interests, and even shape the membership of the digital advocacy organization to galvanise support.

This first section outlines how these two logics operate within digital advocacy organizations. It then examines variations within OPEN: some groups have followed a member-driven logic, and others a staff stewardship logic. It explores how digital advocacy organizations have campaigned on (a) Indigenous rights; (b) refugee rights; and (c) free trade agreements, as summarized in Table 8.1. This chapter highlights the challenges of mobilizing majority support amongst members of digital advocacy organizations for minority rights. The organizations that sustained influential, impactful campaigns on minority rights followed the staff-stewardship model. Staff in digital advocacy organizations can shape their members' interests over time, as they seek to build a progressive, 'people-powered' movement (Mouffe 2019).[4]

This chapter has broader implications for IR scholarship on norm contestation and the liberal international order. It illustrates the complexity of identifying a progressive position, and building a majority to support it. There

Table 8.1 Case studies of member-driven vs staff-driven campaigns

	Indigenous rights	Refugee campaign	Trade campaign
Member-driven	N/A*	38 Degrees	38 Degrees
Staff-driven	ActionStation	GetUp	Campact

Note: *I am not aware of Indigenous rights campaigns' that have been driven by a member-driven logic.

[4] Mouffe (2019) has called for the construction of a 'left populism', which is not based on particular identity claims (e.g. gender, class, or ethnicity), but rather on a common ideological position. However, she does not look at the role of specific organizations in constructing a left populism.

are new cleavages in politics which override the left–right ideological spectrum. Progressives (and conservatives) have differing views on the benefits of globalization, and whether the state should be the primary actor in world politics (Zürn and Wilde 2016). Cosmopolitans are in favour of more global integration, while communitarians are in favour of strengthening their own nation state.[5] However, there is no progressive consensus on whether free trade agreements are beneficial, or how many refugees a country should take. Voices on both the left and the right are contesting the liberal order, albeit in different ways (Lake et al. 2021).

Member-Driven vs Staff-Driven Logics

Member-Driven

Digital advocacy organizations can be extremely reactive and responsive to their members' preferences. These organizations, unlike most other NGOs or advocacy organizations, can rapidly aggregate their members' preferences through surveys and digital analytics (Karpf 2012). They optimize campaigns to mobilize as many people as possible. This may mean changing the subject line, messaging, or even the colours used in an email. In this mode of campaigning, digital advocacy organizations are quick to start and stop campaigns, and embrace fast failure (Hall 2019a). They construct a progressive movement based on the revealed preferences of their members on any particular day (Karpf 2016). Given the pace of mainstream and social media, and the short attention span of many individuals, this model results in short, surge campaigns on issues which gain popular support. However, if attention wanes on a particular issue, then the campaign is dropped.

In this mode of campaigning, digital advocacy organizations are neither agenda-setters nor intellectual leaders. Rather, they take on issues of high salience, and seek to shift the debate by pulling in crowds at tipping-point moments. They are more likely to 'engage with campaigns when they are winnable' (Vromen 2017). They do not seek to shape their members' preferences but accept their ideas, assumptions, and values, as they are. OPEN organizations focus on maximizing the number of participants in a given

[5] Zürn and Wilde identify two dominant cleavages between: a) statists and globalists, and b) universalists and contextualists, which underpin the differences between cosmopolitanism and communitarianism (Zürn and Wilde 2016). These categories still do not capture all different variations in ideology. Some cosmopolitans are in favour of more open borders for people, but not for capital; and others take the opposite position.

action. They do this by identifying discrete, easy, and attractive calls to action that allow people to act quickly and alone (Han 2014). Their power comes from the quantity of members they can mobilize.

During the five years I participated in OPEN summits, activists frequently discussed the limitations of the member-driven model in its purest form. In January 2016, before Brexit and the election of President Trump, OPEN activists held a long debate on whether digital advocacy organizations were 'winning the battles but not the war'.[6] Activists reflected on how they had secured tangible wins, but overall were not shifting politics in a more progressive direction in their respective countries. They were concerned that a purely member-driven model meant that campaigning decisions were left to the will of the majority, which may become the 'tyranny of the majority'. OPEN organizations run campaigns on issues which easily gain mass support, such as saving the bees; but often find it harder to campaign on issues such as minority rights. Their concern was well placed, given the rise of far-right political parties and movements in many of their national constituencies.

Staff Stewardship

OPEN activists often referred to an alternative approach in which staff played a stronger role in guiding members' actions. They used 'value-led' or 'staff stewardship' to refer to this logic. Rather than react to their members' preferences, staff could shape and transform them. The stewardship model often involved 'organizing' rather than 'transactional mobilizing' (Bond and Exley 2016; Han 2014). This means investing time and energy in developing members' capacities and views (depth of engagement) rather than simply focusing on getting the largest turn-out of members for a particular action (breadth of engagement) (Han 20214).

A staff-stewardship model in its purest form entails elevating core progressive values above the majoritarian concerns of their members. However, digital advocacy organizations still need to keep sufficient member support, otherwise they would lose their power. If they go too far beyond what was accepted by their membership, members would simply unsubscribe from the organization. Hence, many faced a similar dilemma to 38 Degrees over Brexit: were staff willing to act against a significant proportion of their members?

Some digital advocacy organizations responded to this dilemma by trying to build a more progressive list. They could do this by running campaigns with

[6] OPEN annual summit, Australia, 2016.

the explicit focus of attracting new and more progressive members, and/or more ethnically diverse members, which could give them a basis for minority rights campaigns. Staff may also select more radically progressive campaigns to 'weed out' centrist members. For instance, Zazim staff in Israel could choose to run a pro-Palestine campaign rather than a more popular environmental campaign. In doing so, they would encourage more progressive members to sign up, and members that were sceptical of campaigns for Palestinian rights might unsubscribe. By contrast, a purely member-driven model would simply work with the preferences of existing members.

ActionStation in New Zealand went furthest in formalizing the staff-stewardship, value-driven, logic. Under the leadership of Laura O'Connell Rapira, they rewrote the eight-fold path to embed the values that would underpin staff decision-making. They turned it into a twelve-fold path, which listed their commitment to Māori rights and the Treaty of Waitangi, over and above any other concerns. As staff member Eliot Pryor explained:

> we have such a broad umbrella of members now, actually it would be a disservice to our members to just follow what a majority of our members said. Our campaign experience, strategy, vision, it's all of those things together, and the service we offer to our members is [to] bring this all together and show strategic leadership.[7]

ActionStation staff saw their role as not just reacting to their members preferences, but also as shaping them.

OPEN has become increasingly aware of the tension between these two logics and the need to reorient members towards more progressive politics. OPEN's second executive director, Giovanna Negretti, encouraged a shift away from the purely member-driven, reactive mode of campaigning when she started in 2019. She was a strong advocate of minority rights, and had no attachment to the eight-fold path (it was new to her when she started). As part of a broader strategic review of OPEN, she encouraged OPEN groups to reflect on the eight-fold path and to embed value-driven campaigning.[8]

Organizations in the network do not face a binary choice between these two logics, and there is a spectrum of positions. Some OPEN organizations, such as 38 Degrees and Skiftet, adhere more to the member-driven model. Others,

[7] Online interview with Eliot Pryor, ActionStation, 18 March 2021.

[8] Although as executive director, Negretti had no power to force OPEN organizations to adopt a stewardship model. As noted in Chapter 5, OPEN's executive director has more of a facilitative role, helping the network to identify common needs and interests.

such as Campact, GetUp, and ActionStation, tend to be more stewardship-driven. There has also been variation within OPEN organizations over time and across different issues. On some issues, digital advocacy organizations may run a campaign because of their staffs' principled, committed stance on an issue, despite a lack of majority member support. However, they may continue to run reactive, rapid-response, member-driven campaigns alongside a values-based, staff-driven campaign. Hence, these two models can coexist within an organization.

The next section examines ActionStation's prioritization of Māori rights and decolonization, and illustrates how the OPEN model can be successfully adapted for minority rights.

Indigenous Rights

Stewardship Logic: ActionStation and Māori Rights in New Zealand

In 2017, ActionStation staff, under the leadership of Marianne Elliott and Laura O'Connell Rapira, decided to crowdsource a vision for New Zealand. They asked their members what they wanted Aotearoa New Zealand to look like in 2040. They explicitly chose this date because it will mark 200 years since the Treaty of Waitangi was signed between Māori and the British crown.[9] ActionStation staff wanted their members to think beyond everyday politics and towards a future where Māori had greater authority and self-determination within New Zealand, as the Treaty had originally promised (ActionStation 2017).[10] When designing the survey, which was sent to all members, staff explicitly chose to include eleven Māori values and eleven Pakehā (non-Māori) values. Around 5,000 members took the online survey or engaged in 'kai and korero', in-person conversations around the dinner table. The resulting 'people's agenda', *Te Ira Tāngata*, identified key values and vision statements to guide ActionStation's work. Many members chose Māori values, and highlighted that their core vision was to see New Zealand 'Honour Te Tiriti o Waitangi'. While this was a crowdsourced agenda, the questions,

[9] The Treaty of Waitangi acknowledged Māori sovereign authority over New Zealand, *tino rangatiratanga*, and granted to the Crown *kawanatanga* (governance).

[10] ActionStation's work built upon the work of Maona Jackson's 'Matike Mai' report, which called for a constitutional transformation, and specifically to give Māori political authority to run their own affairs. Interview with Laura O'Connell Rapira, 23 July 2021.

choice of values, and compilation of the ultimate vision for 2040 was shaped by ActionStation staff.

Subsequently, ActionStation staff took *Te Ira Tāngata* as a mandate to shift away from the member-driven logic towards a values and staff-stewardship model. They wanted their campaigns to build towards a bold, progressive vision of New Zealand, where Māori had 'rangatiratanga', or sovereignty, over their affairs. ActionStation staff reworked the eight-fold path and embedded the values which would guide their work. These included: being 'progressive'[11] and 'Tiriti honouring'. As they explained, 'We recognise Māori as Tāngata Whenua [people of the land] and Te Tiriti o Waitangi, the Māori version of the Treaty text. If there is any conflict within a campaign between competing values then Te Tiriti will have precedence in giving guidance on our decisions.'[12] This was a strong pledge to protect Indigenous rights over and above members' other concerns, even if these concerns had majority support.

In 2018, Laura O'Connell Rapira, ActionStation's executive director, made the organization a leading advocate for decolonization in New Zealand. She presented the new twelve-fold path to ActionStation's executive board in early 2018. The Board supported the decision to prioritize values-led campaigning with a focus on decolonization.[13] ActionStation staff then changed their internal strategy and metrics to measure organizational success. They set a goal of having 50,000 members take an action for tino tangatiratanga (Māori sovereignty) by the end of 2018. To do this, they sought to diversity their membership and attract more Māori. They reached out to Māori activists who were already running campaigns, and built strong relationships with them. They also changed the structure of the executive board to include both a Māori and Tauiwi (non-Māori) Chair.[14] To my knowledge, no other OPEN group has gone this far in elevating and institutionalizing the importance of Indigenous rights.

ActionStation successfully campaigned for a new national holiday for Matariki, the Māori New Year. It campaigned to protect Māori land at Ihumātao near Auckland airport and for Māori wards in local councils. It also

[11] They specified what progressive meant in the NZ context—it was derived from the 'crowdsourced vision and values in *Te Ira Tāngata*'. ActionStation, 'ActionStation Evolution of the 8-Fold Path' (on file with author).

[12] ActionStation, 'ActionStation Evolution of the 8-Fold Path' (on file with author). See also The Commons, Social Change Library, https://commonslibrary.org/how-actionstation-became-a-values-led-organisation/(accessed 7 December 2021).

[13] Online interview with Laura O'Connell Rapira, 23 July 2021. The Board also agreed that one of the top five organizational priorities was to support 'Pasifika and multicultural communities to speak, advocate and organise around issues of racial justice, and giving Pākehā [white New Zealanders] opportunities to tautoko [support] them'.

[14] Online interview with Laura O'Connell Rapira, 23 July 2021.

advocated for better teaching of Māori history in New Zealand schools, as there was previously very little in the New Zealand curriculum. O'Connell Rapira became a regular columnist in mainstream media and a frequent, powerful speaker at conferences and events.

ActionStation also sought to educate its members about racism towards Māori. In late 2018, ActionStation coached a network of Tauiwi (non-Māori) to fight hate speech and trolling on social media. It trained them to defend the rights of Māori online, challenge racial stereotypes, and educate others about New Zealand's history (ActionStation Aotearoa 2018). In their online interactions, the volunteers were instructed to focus on neutral people rather than trying to convince those who espoused violent comments. This is a good example of what Han would call 'organising' rather than 'mobilising' members (Han 2014).

ActionStation also used surveys to educate its members about racism in New Zealand. In 2018, for instance, ActionStation asked its members a series of true/false factual questions about Māori and the justice system. Questions included: 'True or false: 56 percent of young people in the youth justice system are Māori' (it is false, Maori account for 76 per cent of the youth justice population); 'Why do you think people commit crime?' and 'Do you know anyone who has been to prison?'.[15] Members were also asked to identify which interventions would best prevent and reduce crime from the following list: tougher penalties for people who commit crimes; better mental health services; more police on the streets; better drug, alcohol, and addiction support services; more housing; hard labour for people in prison; better schooling and more connected communities.

ActionStation was already committed to campaigning on discrimination faced by Māori within the criminal justice system, so the results of this survey would not influence its decision whether to campaign on it. Instead, ActionStation used this member survey to: (a) explore the best messaging for its campaign; (b) identify the interventions members were most likely to support; and (c) encourage its members to reflect more deeply on the criminal justice system in New Zealand.[16] ActionStation frequently tried to shape its supporters' preferences rather than simply reacting to their revealed preferences.

[15] O'Connell Rapira (2017) and survey, pp. 73–78, https://www.otago.ac.nz/wellington/otago698784.pdf. Final report, https://actionstation.org.nz/downloads/tow-report.pdf.

[16] ActionStation also regularly asks its members for personal stories which may help in a campaign. For example, in another survey on drug reform and an upcoming referendum on legalizing cannabis, it asked: 'Is there anything else you'd like to tell us? This could be a personal story about cannabis, a thought you had on the campaign to get out the vote, or the referendum (O'Connell Rapira 2017).

ActionStation staff made a long-term commitment to decolonizing Aotearoa New Zealand. No other digital advocacy organizations have been such strong defenders of Indigenous rights. Between September 2018 and August 2019, almost one-third (28.6 per cent) of ActionStation's campaigns related to Māori rights.[17] In contrast, 10 per cent of GetUp's campaigns related to Indigenous rights.[18] ActionStation is also the only OPEN organization to have been led by an Indigenous person, which helped it to build trust with Māori activists.[19] Not all ActionStation's members were supportive of its campaigns on decolonization and Māori rights. Some stopped donating and unsubscribed.[20] Yet ActionStation grew overall as an organization and gained over 150,000 new members, attracted by the organization's newly articulated vision.[21] If ActionStation had continued to follow a member-driven logic, it is highly unlikely it would have sought out new Māori members, built long-term relationships with Māori activists, or prioritized campaigns on decolonization and Māori rights.

Alongside these campaigns, ActionStation still continued to run the OurActionStation petition platform, whereby any member can start their own campaign. There were thus opportunities for purely member-driven campaigns. It also ran other rapid-response campaigns, reacting to members' concerns. In short, it did not abdicate its member-driven, issue-generalist, rapid-response mode of advocacy, but embedded an organizational culture (through goals, metrics, and strategy) to prioritize campaigns for decolonization and Māori rights. Hence, a staff stewardship logic dominated in its campaigns.

Refugee Rights

Member-Driven Logic: 38 Degrees in the UK

In late August 2015, Chancellor Angela Merkel announced that she would open Germany's borders to refugees.[22] Her British counterpart, Prime Minister

[17] See Figures 4.5 and 4.7 in Chapter 4.

[18] GetUp has more recently established a First Nations Justice campaigning group, led by campaigners from Widjabul Wia-bul, Garrwa, Gooreng Gooreng, Wiradjuri, Noongar, Gubbi Gubbi, Kulkalgal, and Yanyuwa nations. GetUp, 'First Nations Justice', https://www.getup.org.au/campaign/first-nations-justice (accessed 7 December 2021).

[19] In 2021 Kassie Hartendorp, who is also Māori, took over the leadership of ActionStation.

[20] The Matariki campaign was 'extraordinarily popular' and over 30,000 people signed within a month. However, the 2018 campaign for Māori wards was not popular with members, and ActionStation received a lot of critical correspondence. Online interview with Laura O'Connell Rapira, 23 July 2021.

[21] Online interview with Laura O'Connell Rapira, 23 July 2021.

[22] This section draws on previously published work (Hall 2017a, 2019a, 2019b).

David Cameron, was adamant that the UK would not do the same. Cameron acknowledged that he was 'deeply moved' by the refugee crisis, but gave no indication of any new UK policies to take in more refugees (Dathan 2015). However, there was an outpouring of public support for refugees in early September, particularly after the death of a young Syrian toddler, Aylan Kurdi. Even the right-wing tabloid *Daily Mail*—not known for its supportive coverage of refugees—ran an unusually sympathetic story, headlined 'The final journey of tragic little boys washed up on a Turkish beach: Mother and sons who died in sea tragedy are taken from morgue after heartbroken father says goodbye to the family he couldn't save' (Stanton et al. 2015). Public pressure mounted on the Prime Minister to welcome more refugees.

Immediately after the Kurdi story had broken, 38 Degrees called a special staff meeting to discuss how it should respond. It decided to launch a rapid campaign to put pressure on Cameron to welcome more refugees. It was driven by a breaking crisis and sense of a sea change in British public opinion towards refugees. It initiated a petition under the slogan 'Refugees Welcome' that stated: 'We don't want Britain to be the kind of country that turns its back as people drown in their desperation to flee places like Syria'.[23] 38 Degrees invited its members to start their own local petitions targeting councils to accept more refugees. A total of 633 local campaigns were launched across the UK, from the Scottish highlands to Southern England. 38 Degrees gathered over 137,000 signatures. 38 Degrees campaigns also led to the formation of local refugee welcome action groups and resulted in thousands of phone calls and more than 78,000 emails sent to members of parliament. Due to this widespread public pressure, Cameron announced on 7 September 2015 that the UK would accept 20,000 Syrian refugees over the next four to five years. This was a dramatic shift in position, although it cannot be attributed solely to the work of 38 Degrees, as there were many other advocacy organizations involved in the refugees welcome campaign.

38 Degrees' reaction to the 2015 refugee 'crisis' exemplifies the strengths of the OPEN model. It could rapidly launch a new campaign because it was constantly on the look-out for breaking-news stories and 'crisistunities'. 38 Degrees mobilized thousands at speed, due to its large and broad membership list, and its use of digital communications. Importantly, it could provide a surge in support for refugees, mobilizing people who were not signed up to refugee-specific organizations, which broadened and bolstered the campaign.

[23] 38 Degrees (2016), 'Refugees Welcome'. https://you.38degrees.org.uk/efforts/refugees-welcome (accessed 27 January 2022).

By 2016, refugee issues were not so high on the public agenda in the UK. Political attention had moved to the upcoming EU referendum, and refugee campaigns were a low priority for many 38 Degrees members. Refugee issues, for instance, rarely made the list of top ten issues in weekly member surveys (Hall 2019a). When I visited 38 Degrees on 27 October 2016, we discussed which campaign emails were most popular with members. 38 Degrees had tested a campaign to help child refugees stuck in Calais, which was front-page news in the UK that week. However, it 'didn't go well full-list' because 38 Degrees members were not interested in supporting the campaign.[24] Meanwhile, a campaign for bees had done well, and, as one staff member noted, 'always did well', with the 38 Degrees membership.[25] This led 38 Degrees to focus on saving the bees rather than refugees. 38 Degrees also did not closely monitor whether, or to what extent, Cameron's pledges to welcome more refugees were implemented. The member-driven logic triggered it to campaign on refugee rights in 2015, but not to sustain these campaigns in 2016.

38 Degrees was not alone. Other OPEN organizations which campaigned on refugee and migrants' rights in 2015 when members' interest was high, did not continue to campaign in 2016 or 2017.[26] The purely member-driven logic is ill suited for long-term campaigns for minority rights, given that campaigns must continue to receive majority support (Hall 2017b).

Stewardship Logic: GetUp in Australia

Although Australia is far away from Europe, it was also touched by the Alan Kurdi moment. Immediately after Kurdi's death, GetUp, along with over twenty Australian refugee advocacy organizations, established the Light the Dark campaign to send a message to the world that 'Australia Says Welcome' to refugees.[27] GetUp and other refugee advocacy organizations called on the

[24] Author's visit to 38 Degrees, 27 October 2016, London.

[25] In that same week, 38 Degrees had a popular member-initiated campaign on the 'bedroom tax'. The bedroom tax or 'under-occupancy charge' was a tax on spare (unused) bedrooms in public housing. In 2016, this tax was extended to pensioners, and resulted in a cut in their housing benefit. A member, Michael Collins, had initiated the campaign because he was concerned for his mother who lived in a council flat with a spare bedroom.

[26] In the academic scholarship I surveyed on refugee advocacy between 2015 and 2019, OPEN groups were rarely mentioned. Rather, scholars highlighted the work of refugee-specific organizations such as Pro-Asyl in Germany (Kleres 2018); Double the Quota in New Zealand (Stephens 2018); and in some countries, such as Poland and Germany, the church (Kleres 2018; Narkowicz 2018).

[27] GetUp! (2015). 'Light the Dark Melbourne' (7 September 2022) https://www.facebook.com/events/treasury-gardens/light-the-dark-melbourne-australia-says-welcome-to-refugees/1064515756893972/ (accessed 27 January 2022)

public to lobby the government to accept more Syrian refugees, and to rally around the hash tags #refugeeswelcome and #LightTheDark. They targeted the then Prime Minister Tony Abbott, who stated on 6 September 2015 that Australia would not increase its overall refugee quota. On Monday 7 September, vigils were held in all of Australia's major cities, and over 10,000 people across Australia attended. Two days later, on 9 September, Abbott declared that Australia would welcome an extra 12,000 Syrian and Iraqi refugees. He likely responded to international pressure, including the UK's changed position, as well as domestic pressure (Hall 2017a).

GetUp, unlike 38 Degrees, was deeply committed to refugee rights. In fact, in 2015, GetUp employed a human rights and refugee rights campaigner, Shen Narayanasamy, and set up a team of campaigners committed to these issues. In its 2015–2016 operating strategy, GetUp committed to a long-term campaign goal of getting all children out of detention facilities managed by Australia.[28] Since then, GetUp's staff have worked consistently on refugee rights and have run a number of different campaigns targeting the Australian offshore detention system (Hall 2017a, 2019b). In 2015, they launched a campaign #No Business in Abuse, which put pressure on international banks and investors to divest from supporting the operators of Manus and Nauru refugee detention centres. In 2016, Narayanasamy even travelled to Europe to meet personally with representatives of European-headquartered banks. Hence, their refugee mobilizations in September 2015 were part of a broader, and longer campaign to change refugee rights in Australia.

Then in February 2016, GetUp ran one of its most successful refugee campaigns: #Letthemstay. The campaign called for 267 asylum seekers to be allowed to stay in Australia, where they were for medical treatment, rather than being returned to offshore detention centres. The detention centres were part of Operation Sovereign Borders, a broad strategy to stop asylum seekers from reaching mainland Australia by fiercely patrolling the northern sea border with Indonesia and forcing boats to turn back. Human rights experts, psychologists, and doctors documented horrific conditions in Nauru and Manus Island detention centres. Many asylum seekers had been abused or committed self-harm (Farrell et al. 2016). GetUp's #Letthemstay campaign resulted from a court case against the Australian government, led by Daniel Webb at the Human Rights Law Centre. When the case looked as if it might fail, Webb approached GetUp because, in his words, 'they're a formidable campaign machine' (Hall 2017a).

[28] GetUp, 'GetUp Operational Plan, 2015–2016', 26. (On file with author)

Narayanasamy worked closely with Webb and built up a close alliance with the Darwin Asylum Seeker Support and Advocacy Network. GetUp's messaging focused on thirty-three babies who would be sent back to offshore detention (Hall 2017a, 2019b). The story made front-page news in the major Australian newspapers, with photos of the babies. GetUp sought to win over the public by highlighting how refugees were much like locals: it featured stories of refugees' jobs, music tastes, and hobbies. GetUp staff worked closely with the broader refugee sector, lobbied politicians, and formed a broad-based movement of churches, medical practitioners, and teachers who called for the government to #LetThemStay.

For several weeks, the campaign headlined news reports, and politicians and many members of civil society voiced their support. Thousands attended protests. The campaign culminated in a dramatic stand-off between guards and doctors at Lady Cilento Children's Hospital in South Brisbane. The doctors refused to release a one-year-old girl named Baby Asha into the hands of the Australian government. They were supported by vocal protestors outside. The government was finally forced to back down and allowed the asylum seekers to stay. However, it was only a partial victory: the government reserved the right to deport the asylum seekers with seventy-two hours' notice and on 26 July 2016 deported a Sudanese man to Christmas Island.

It is unlikely that GetUp would have run the #LetThemStay or the #NoBusinessInAbuse campaigns if it had simply reacted to members' preferences. It would have mobilized people for one-off vigils in September 2015, but its refugee campaigns would not have gone much further. GetUp staff made an organizational commitment to get all asylum-seekers out of detention centres in Nauru and Manus Island. Narayanasamy and her colleagues built partnerships with the refugee advocacy sector, and developed long-term strategies to pursue this goal. Narayanasamy had to work hard to win over a majority of GetUp members. It was difficult to find a frame for GetUp's refugee campaigns which resonated with all of GetUp's members.[29] She had to consistently convince GetUp's members of the importance of refugee campaigns. She also actively sought to broaden GetUp's membership list to include a more diverse group of Australians, who would be more supportive of refugee rights.

In short, 38 Degrees and GetUp followed different logics in their campaigns. 38 Degrees sought to maximize member support at a key tipping-point moment, whereas GetUp worked with the entire refugee sector, tried to shape

[29] OPEN refugee summit, May 2016, Berlin.

its members' views of refugee rights, and had a long-term commitment to assisting refugees, particularly those that Australia had confined to detention.

Other OPEN Groups

Other OPEN groups have also tried to shape their members' views on refugee rights. In 2015, during the height of the refugee 'crisis', #aufstehn in Austria urged local mayors to welcome more refugees.[30] It set up an email tool with the call 'In unserer Gemeinde ist Platz!' ('In our community there is space!') and urged for 'Zimmerstattzäune' ('rooms instead of fences') (Hall 2017a). Although the vast majority of members shared the values #aufstehn put forward when campaigning on refugee issues, 'not all members fully agreed'.[31] #aufstehn received 'a lot of email correspondence' from members who were critical of its campaigns, and it tried to shape these members' views. #aufstehn wrote individual responses to each email and tried to 'convince people who don't agree fully with the importance of the issue' rather than sending an automated response to critical emails.[32]

ActionStation found that many of its members were not supportive of refugee rights when it campaigned to double New Zealand's annual quota. The first email it sent about the campaign 'received a much larger negative response than usual, despite both our teams workshopping it' (Stephens 2018). Murdoch Stephens, who collaborated with ActionStation on this campaign, suggested that there was a 'strand of nationalism among some otherwise progressive people that was awakened by the anti-TPPA [Trans-Pacific Partnership Agreement] focus on sovereignty' (Stephens 2018). Some ActionStation members who had been galvanized by the TPPA campaigns were concerned by both the power of foreign corporations in New Zealand, and an increase in immigrants and refugees. The negative response to their email resulted in ActionStation creating a separate section of its membership list that would not be sent anything to do with refugees. Despite the negative backlash from some members, ActionStation staff remained supportive of running the campaign. The campaign to double the New Zealand quota

30 Interestingly, there were no attempts across the network to develop common refugee campaigns with the same target, at the same time. OPEN groups frequently shared messaging, tactics, and strategies, including at a dedicated summit on refugees in May 2016. However, their refugee campaigns almost always targeted *national* decision-makers and mobilized *domestic* publics.

31 Interview with Maria Mayrhofer, OPEN refugee summit, May 2016. #aufstehn was also somewhat unusual within OPEN, as many of its first campaigns were on refugee rights, so its membership list was more pro-refugee than others.

32 Interview with Maria Mayrhofer, OPEN refugee summit, May 2016.

was ultimately successful; in 2016, the national government increased it from 750 to 1,000 refugees. In 2018, the new Labour government, led by Jacinda Ardern, agreed to an annual quota of 1,500 refugees (Ardern 2018).

ActionStation's then executive director, Marianne Elliott, spoke to MoveOn colleagues in the United States, which reported similar 'reluctance' from some of its members to support asylum seekers (Stephens 2018). During the Trump presidency, MoveOn also became more committed to stewardship in its campaigns for migrant and refugee rights. In 2019, it established a dedicated migrants' rights campaigner, similar to what GetUp had done several years earlier.[33]

These examples illustrate how sustained campaigns for refugee rights relied on staff stewardship and a values driven logic. A majority of members were supportive of welcoming refugees in the immediate aftermath of the death of Alan Kurdi in 2015, but most did not see refugee rights as a long-term priority compared with other progressive issues. The member-driven logic rarely results in long-term campaigns, or follow-up to ensure that governments implement their pledges. Staff-driven campaigns can sustain this pressure over time, even when member support wanes.

Trade Politics: The Transatlantic Trade and Intellectual Property Agreement (TTIP)

In February 2013, President Obama, European Commissioner President, José Manuel Barroso, and European Council President, Herman Van Rompuy, announced that they would launch negotiations towards a Transatlantic Trade and Intellectual Property Agreement (TTIP) (European Commission 2013). In the following years, Campact, 38 Degrees, and a number of other European OPEN groups launched anti-TTIP campaigns, out of concern for the power they gave multinationals. MoveOn did not actively campaign on TTIP. Like most US trade activists, it was more concerned by the Trans-Pacific Partnership Agreement (TPP) (Siles-Brügge and Strange 2020b). Some US activists were even supportive of TTIP because they thought it might increase US regulatory standards, which were less stringent than the those of the European Union (EU) (Young 2017b: 79).

This section compares 38 Degrees' member-driven campaign with Campact's staff-stewardship campaign on TTIP. Here, I focus on their domestic

[33] Interview with MoveOn staffer, 20 June 2019.

campaigns; however, both provided generous financial assistance to new European digital advocacy organizations to advance the anti-TTIP campaign (Kanter 2015). In fact, the anti-TTIP campaigns were an important engine for OPEN's European expansion. New European OPEN organizations were able to attract new members, and funds, through their anti-TTIP campaigns.[34]

Member-Driven Logic: 38 Degrees in the UK

In early 2016, 38 Degrees conducted its regular weekly poll asking members which issues it should prioritize. One of the top issues that members highlighted was a 'campaign to stop secretive international trade deals which mean more privatisation in NHS ...' (Torabi 2014a). In May 2014, 38 Degrees published an explainer on TTIP and asked members whether it should start a campaign. In its communications to members, 38 Degrees highlighted that 'right now, officials in the US and EU are secretly negotiating a hugely influential and dangerous trade deal which would put the profits of big business ahead of our welfare, health and environment'. It emphasized that the investor–state dispute settlement (ISDS) clause in the agreement could allow 'companies to sue governments' (Walker 2014). It ended its post by emphasizing the importance of members' views: 'The 38 Degrees staff team sit down every Monday morning to plan out the week ahead and decide on how we use staff resources. The most important factor when making those decisions is 'what 38 Degrees members think' (Walker 2014). 38 Degrees' staff pick campaigns based on the results of these weekly surveys (Karpf 2016).

Subsequently, 38 Degrees started a campaign against TTIP.[35] 38 Degrees joined other expert anti-TTIP campaigning organizations, including War on Want,[36] Friends of the Earth, the Trade Justice Network, and Global Justice Now. 38 Degrees brought the ability to mobilize thousands of supporters at the municipal and national level to the anti-TTIP campaign (Siles-Brügge and Strange 2020a). In July 2014, it partnered with SumOfUs and mobilized over 25,000 people to send the EU negative feedback on TTIP, causing the EU submissions website to crash (Benthall 2014). In August 2014, it petitioned Vince Cable, then UK Business Secretary, to either oppose or reform TTIP. In its

[34] Meanwhile, ActionStation, Leadnow, and GetUp campaigned against the TPPA.

[35] I don't have access to the results of this survey and assume that members were broadly supportive, given that 38 Degrees has tended to follow the majority view.

[36] War on Want was then led by John Hilary, a long-term campaigner on trade policy issues.

campaign material, it frequently emphasized the 'risk' that TTIP would lead to a privatization of the NHS as part of the liberalization of services under the agreement, a claim made often by anti-TTIP campaigners in the UK (Young 2017b).

38 Degrees also mobilized its members on the streets. On 30 August 2014, it held a Day of Action, which it claimed was 'the biggest number of 38 Degrees members coming together on one day ever' (Torabi 2014b). According to 38 Degrees' records, 9,600 members distributed one million leaflets and 30,000 posters relating to the perils of TTIP. On 27 September, 38 Degrees members attended the UKIP party conference in Doncaster. UKIP had twenty-four members in the European Parliament at the time and 38 Degrees argued that getting UKIP's support was critical: 'whatever you think of UKIP ... they'll eventually vote on TTIP' (Thorogood 2014). 38 Degrees members handed out leaflets urging UKIP to come out strongly against TTIP (Mason 2014).[37] 38 Degrees also mobilized its members to meet and urge their Members of European Parliament (MEPs) not to support TTIP.

Throughout 2015, 38 Degrees members targeted MPs in the Scottish parliament and the European Parliament. For example, in June 2015, 19,000 members co-funded local newspaper advertisements targeting UK MEPs who had not pledged to oppose TTIP. 38 Degrees took part in another TTIP Day of Action on 22 August and mobilized 8,000 members in over 400 locations around the UK to inform people about the dangers of TTIP (Bevington 2014). On 9 and 10 October, members across the UK met with their local MPs to submit anti-TTIP petitions. 38 Degrees' anti-TTIP petitions would ultimately gather over 3.2 million signatures (Benthall 2015).

Then, on 22 April 2016, 38 Degrees targeted US President Barack Obama during his visit to the UK. The organization crowdfunded advertisements in *The Guardian* and *Daily Telegraph* newspapers, and gathered more than 13,000 signatures for a petition urging Obama to stop negotiating TTIP on the basis that it '[would give] corporations more power than people' (Revesz 2016). This is a rare example of 38 Degrees targeting an international decision-maker, but it only did so when Obama was in its home territory (just as Campact had done when Obama visited Hannover in April 2016).

By mid-2016, it appeared unlikely that Obama could get TTIP passed before the US election, due to domestic opposition. The 2016 presidential primaries shifted the trade debate decisively with both Bernie Sanders (a potential

[37] UKIP had already declared that it would work with the Unite union to ensure that TTIP did not jeopardize the NHS.

presidential candidate for the Democrat Party) and Donald Trump (then the leading candidate for the Republican Party) strongly opposing TPP and TTIP (Skonieczny 2019).[38] Obama did not get the TPP through Congress in his last year of office, even though he had fast-tracked it through the Senate in 2015 (Skonieczny 2019).

Meanwhile, the UK political debate shifted to Brexit. 38 Degrees focused almost exclusively on the EU referendum, and subsequently the implications of Brexit. In the lead-up to the June 2016 Brexit referendum, 38 Degrees emailed its members to outline what Brexit could mean for TTIP. In an unusual move by a campaigning organization, it explained that the implications were unclear.

Overall, 38 Degrees closely followed the member-driven logic in its TTIP campaign. It started campaigning when it registered highly in member surveys. It then switched to focus on Brexit, once that became the pressing concern for members and the broader British public. It also made sense in 2016 to drop the anti-TTIP campaign, as it looked increasingly likely that the United States would support it. Notably, 38 Degrees' anti-TTIP campaign was sustained over several years, and hence longer than its campaign for refugee rights. This is likely a reflection of longer-term member preference for anti-free trade campaigns over refugee rights campaigns.

Staff Stewardship: Campact in Germany

Campact invested heavily in the anti-TTIP campaign and it became its major focus for several years.[39] It established a trade team and campaigners focused solely on stopping TTIP and the EU–Canada Comprehensive Economic and Trade Agreement (CETA). Staff identified TTIP as an ideal international treaty to mobilize a large proportion of its membership because it touched on so many issues that Campact members and staff were concerned with, including the environment, food and health standards, the power of corporations,

[38] Both Sanders and Trump argued that the TPP was disastrous and benefitted only the corporate elite, and led to off-shoring of jobs and higher unemployment in the United States (Skonieczny 2018, 2019). Meanwhile, Obama continued to argue that TPP would bring more middle-class jobs to the United States, and counter Chinese dominance in Asia (Skonieczny 2019; Stiglitz 2018).

[39] Campact launched its TTIP campaign website in 2013, claiming that 'the TTIP trade agreement is designed to facilitate corporate profits through fracking, hormone meat, GM food, and lax data protection—and it threatens Europe's democracy. We do not accept this deal.' Campact, 'TTIP', https://www.campact.de/ttip/ (accessed 7 December 2021).

On 18 January 2014, Campact co-organized a 30,000-person demonstration in Berlin under the slogan #WirHabenEsSatt (#WeAreFedUp). In May 2014, prior to the European parliamentary elections, it distributed placards to use at campaign demonstrations, and distributed 6.5 million leaflets to 25,000 supporters, which graded German political parties according to their stance on TTIP (Kanter 2015).

and transparency of government.[40] The anti-TTIP campaign was particularly successful in Germany and Campact played a decisive role in it (Eliasson 2019; Bauer 2016b; Flamant 2015; Gheyle 2020).

Campact's executive directors were strongly embedded in the large anti-trade activist network in Europe. Campact was a member of Seattle to Brussels (S2B), a Brussels-based NGO which coordinated the European anti-TTIP movement (Strange 2015; Gheyle and De Ville 2019; Gheyle 2020).[41] Campact helped to connect the European-wide campaigns with the German campaigns (Gheyle 2020). In November 2013, for example, it co-organized an early meeting of twenty NGOs to mobilize public opinion against TTIP (Gheyle 2020). Working with Attac Germany and other German NGOs, Campact built a coalition of civil society organizations from the environment, farming, food safety, and labour movement sectors. This coalition—'TTIP UnfairHandelbar' ('TTIP Unfair Trade')—included both reformers and rejectionists of a trade agreement (Gheyle 2020). It also exhibited a high degree of professionalization, with several former academics and trade experts working for the 'Stop TTIP' campaign (Eliasson 2019).

Campact tailored its anti-TTIP messages to different segments of its list.[42] Because Campact, like most digital advocacy organizations, keeps a record of what issues members care about and which petitions they sign, it could identify what messaging would work best. Some members received emails about TTIP which warned of the dangers of fracking, while others received emails which highlighted the threat of genetically modified organisms (GMOs). Campact urged its members to sign online petitions and attend massive demonstrations in Germany, which it co-organized.

Its anti-TTIP campaign focused on the threat of ISDS, which it claimed would enhance corporate power to the detriment of the public interest, given that corporations could sue governments (Young 2017b). Campact also highlighted the potential for TTIP to allow chlorinated chicken to be imported and sold in Germany. EU food standards do not permit chickens to be cleaned with

[40] Campact staff had seen the success of the campaign against the Anti-Counterfeiting Trade Agreement (ACTA) to mobilize thousands of people in Germany. Campact staff had not been involved in these mobilizations, but 'deliberately' looked for an international treaty which 'could become the big, new thing, which would upset people'. Focus group discussion with Campact, Felix Kolb, 18 March 2021. He explained that the anti-TTIP campaign was 'a rapid response campaign, which staff strategically choose after missing the ACTA opportunity'.

[41] From 2015 onwards, S2B employed full-time TTIP coordinators to connect EU targeted campaigns with nationally based campaigns (Gheyle and De Ville 2019). They liaised with other organizations, including: Corporate Europe Observatory, Attac Germany, Friends of the Earth Europe, and Greenpeace Europe, to build up a pan-European campaign (Bauer 2015, 20116b; Flamant 2015; Eliasson 2019; Young 2017b: 77).

[42] Focus group discussion with Campact, 18 March 2021.

chlorine, but the same regulations do not exist in the United States (Meredith 2019). However, Campact was clear that its campaign was 'not against America but against the influence of big corporations' (Kanter 2015).

In the summer of 2014, Campact and other members of the 'Stop TTIP' coalition launched a European Citizens' Initiative (ECI) to repeal the EU's negotiating mandate for TTIP and stop CETA (Siles-Brügge 2017; Young 2017b). By October 2015, the ECI had attracted 3.3 million signatures, although the European Commission formally rejected the submission (Euractiv 2015). The ECI was a major focus for Campact and the broader European anti-TTIP campaign (Siles-Brügge 2017). German civil society organizations collected over 1.5 million signatures for the ECI, equivalent to 48 per cent of the overall signatures (Young 2017b). Campact's executive director, Felix Kolb, claimed that it had little overall impact on the negotiations. He explained that as a result of the ECI, 'the issue was debated in the European parliament, where it has been on the agenda anyway'.[43] He also noted that 'it's very hard to impact the European Commission, it's much easier to influence European decision-makers or national governments than the Commission'.[44]

The ECI demonstrated significant public concern across Europe about TTIP and CETA. The European Commission faced particularly strong public criticism about the inclusion of ISDS clauses, which would enable international corporations to sue national governments. In the EU's own public consultations, completed in January 2015, 97 per cent of respondents were against the ISDS (Siles-Brügge 2017). Over the course of 2015, the EU investigated other alternatives to the ISDS and in November 2015 proposed an investment court system (ICS) to the United States (Siles-Brügge 2017). However, some complained that this was a minor change and would therefore not significantly change the power of corporations.

Campact's core strategy was to influence the German government's position on TTIP rather than focusing on European-level decisions. It targeted the Social Democrat Party (SDP), which was in a governing coalition with the Christian Democratic Union (CDU), and seen as easier to shift, given its leftist support base. In October 2015, Campact co-organized one of the largest demonstrations in Berlin since the Iraq war. Between 150,000 (the police's estimate) and 250,000 (Campact's estimate) gathered near the Brandenburg Gate to demonstrate against the TTIP agreement (*Zeit Online* 2015). People were transported to Berlin on 600 specially ordered buses and 5 trains.

[43] Focus group discussion with Campact, Felix Kolb, 18 March 2021.
[44] ibid.

Turnout was well beyond the 50,000–100,000 protestors organizers had expected. Media coverage highlighted the unprecedented number of attendees (*Die Taz* 2015, *Zeit Online* 2015).

Campact members, staff, and leadership attended. Co-executive director and founder, Christoph Bautz, gave a speech at the end of the march alongside representatives of NGOs and left-wing political parties. The demonstration targeted Chancellor Angela Merkel and her governing coalition partner, Sigmar Gabriel, the SDP's leader. Gabriel responded to the demonstration, stating in a full-page newspaper advertisement, that 'there will be no lowering of the standards achieved. The planned agreement is neither good nor bad, Europe has the chance to help shape the rules of globalization itself' (*Zeit Online* 2015).

Campact put pressure on SPD rank-and-file members to stop TTIP and CETA.[45] There was a strong division between the left-wing SPD members, who were concerned that CETA would undermine workers' rights and environmental standards, and the senior leadership, including Sigmar Gabriel, who was pro-CETA and TTIP (Euractiv 2016). Felix Kolb explained that Campact had 'a direct link to rank and file members', and noted that a senior SPD minister even complained that his own party members received Campact newsletters and believed Campact's messaging 'more than their own economics minister, Sigmar Gabriel'.[46] Although there was a major split within the SPD, senior government ministers ultimately decided to support CETA. The German government could then vote for CETA in the European Council.

During the European summer of 2016, there was concerted pressure on heads of state and politicians across Europe to stop TTIP. In September, massive anti-TTIP and anti-CETA protests occurred across Europe (Kay and Evans 2018). In September 2016, Campact and members of the TTIP UnfairHandelbar coalition organized demonstrations, which were attended by over 100,000

[45] In 2016, Campact also began to campaign against the Canadian–EU Trade and Agreement (CETA), which was being negotiated in parallel to the TTIP. Critics perceived CETA as a means for US corporations to gain access to Europe via the back door, as they could easily set up subsidiaries in Canada. There was also widespread concern that if CETA passed, it would be easier for TTIP to get through European parliaments. In March 2016, Campact and the NGO German Federation of the Environment and Nature Conservation (Bund für Umwelt und Naturschutz Deutschland (BUND) mobilized 7,000 people to distribute leaflets outlining each political party's position on TTIP and CETA ahead of state parliament elections in Baden-Württemberg and Rheinland-Pfalz. In their commentary, they noted that 'both the Greens and the SPD replied to us in both federal states that they would not agree to TTIP and CETA if the agreements contain special lawsuits for foreign investors, jeopardize social/ecological standards or impair public services' Campact Blog, (16 March 2016), https://blog.campact.de/2016/03/landtagswahlen-15-millionen-ttip-tuerhaenger-verteilt/ (accessed 7 December 2021).

[46] Focus group discussion with Campact, Felix Kolb, 18 March 2021.

people across seven German states (*Die Zeit* 2016).[47] The German newspaper *Der Spiegel* noted that 'an unprecedented movement of a scope not seen since the Iraq war in Germany has pushed negotiations over the TTIP trans-Atlantic free trade agreement to the brink of collapse. The demonstrations are characterised by a 'level of professionalism not previously seen' (Kay and Evans 2018: 1). Campact and the broader anti-TTIP movement had influence precisely because they could mobilize thousands of people onto the streets.

Donald Trump's election in November 2016 spelled a definitive end to TTIP. However, by October of that year, EU and European national parliaments appeared ready to approve CETA. Campact worked with other NGOs (Foodwatch and OpenDemocracy) to obtain 120,000 signatures for a petition against CETA and filed a complaint on the potential agreement to the German Constitutional Court (BBC 2016). While the court accepted the complaint, it ruled in the government's favour, determining that the EU aspects of CETA could be implemented before national parliaments had voted for it (BBC 2016). Shortly thereafter, on 24 October 2016, the Belgian region of Wallonia announced that it would not support CETA, thereby blocking Belgium's ratification of the agreement.[48] However, the EU addressed Wallonian concerns through a joint interpretative instrument, which was signed alongside the final CETA agreement on 30 October 2016 (European Commission 2016). The EU has since accepted CETA, although at the time of writing CETA had still not been passed by all the national legislatures in Europe.[49]

Campact and other anti-TTIP protestors did not single-handedly stop TTIP or CETA; however, they were successful in mobilizing people against the agreements, and their campaigns significantly influenced public debate. In an interview with the *New York Times*, Peter Sparding, a fellow at the German Marshall Fund in Washington, stated that, 'The protest organizers have set the

[47] However, the demonstrations were reportedly not as large as the organizers had hoped. This may have been because the change in US position meant that people were less concerned about TTIP. In fact, already in August 2016, Sigmar Gabriel had stated that TTIP had 'de facto failed, even though nobody [was] really admitting it' (Stone 2016).

[48] Campact and the other OPEN organizations supported the Wallonians' opposition to CETA, urging them to 'stay strong'. Campact, 'CETA Wallonian Kaempft für uns alle' (22 October), https://blog.campact.de/2016/10/ceta-wallonien-kaempft-fuer-uns-alle/comment-page-26/ (accessed 7 December 2021).

[49] Campact has continued to look for ways to stop CETA's ratification in Germany. In November 2018, it petitioned the Free Voters of Bavaria (Freie Wähler Bayern), who entered a coalition with the Christian Social Union (CSU) in Bavaria's state government to reject CETA. It obtained 100,000 signatures and handed this petition to Hubert Aiwanger, the Free Voters leader, who confirmed that he would also be rejecting CETA. Campact celebrated this as a victory as it meant there was no majority in favour of CETA on the Bundesrat. Bayern holds six votes in the Bundesrat (Federal Council) and thirty-five are needed for CETA to pass. Both the Bundestag (Federal parliament) and the Bundesrat are required to vote in favour of CETA. Campact, 'Erfolg in Bayern'(12 November 2018), https://blog.campact.de/2018/11/erfolg-in-bayern/(accessed 7 December 2021).

tone of the trade debate from the start, and the deal's backers have been playing defense ever since' (Kanter 2015). He elaborated that 'Nearly all German politicians have faced protesters pressuring them to be sceptical about the trade deal and threatening them with a backlash from voters' (Kanter 2015).

Campact has been criticized for oversimplifying the trade debate, and even 'manufacturing discontent' (Bauer 2016a). A 2016 report for the European Centre for International Political Economy, found that Attac Germany and Campact had 'managed to exploit modern online media to determine what citizens think about TTIP and globalization in general' (Bauer 2016a).[50] One OPEN staff member informed me that they often hear that their campaigns are oversimplified, but explained that they 'keep politics for the people'.[51] OPEN organizations argue that they are a member-driven organization, so their campaigns must be understood by as many people as possible. Some MEPs said that the Campact and Attac emails were generically addressed to all MEPs, rather than specifically connecting constituents with their electorate MPs, so did not work. MEP staffers were overwhelmed with emails that were clearly copy-and-paste, so they tended to simply ignore these.[52] However, no other scholarship suggests that that Campact, Attac, or other anti-TTIP campaigns were manipulative, inaccurate, or primarily based on generating money for the organization (Young 2017a; Ville and Siles-Brügge 2017; Gheyle and De Ville 2019).[53]

Campact staff were deeply invested in maintaining their trade campaigns. Between 2013 and 2016, they had broad support for these campaigns from their members. But could they hold members' support to mobilize against other subsequent trade agreements?

[50] Bauer finds that Campact and other anti-TTIP groups dominated over 90 per cent of online media reporting on TTIP in Germany and, as a result, 'biased, negative sentiment queries are the most widely applied TTIP-related queries' (Bauer 2016a: 7). Bauer claims that their anti-TTIP messaging exaggerated the dangers of TTIP, as Germany had the most to gain from TTIP. Bauer's analysis of the anti-TTIP campaign has not been published in peer-reviewed journals, but other scholars have directly cited his concerns (Eliasson 2019). Eliasson, for instance, claims that Campact, 38 Degrees, and Attac are 'campaign companies' and that for their 'business models, TTIP provides an ideal breeding ground to increase brand awareness and funding' (Eliasson 2019; Eliasson and Huet 2018).

[51] Interview with Becky Jarvis, 4 October 2018.

[52] Thanks to Christina Toenshoff for this point.

[53] Scholars who see merit in anti-TTIP campaign are less likely to be critical of Campact (or other NGOs') campaigns; while those who are advocates of the TTIP agreement are more likely to find fault (Eliasson and García-Duran 2017).

The Japanese–European Free Trade Agreement (JEFTA)

In 2017, Campact ran a campaign against the Japanese–European Free Trade Agreement (JEFTA). Although JEFTA had extensive and deep regulatory commitments, most European anti-trade activists did not campaign on it (Young 2017b; Bièvre and Poletti 2020). Activists and the broader public likely had more concern about signing an agreement with the United States—a larger and stronger economy—than with Japan. Campact tested JEFTA campaigns a few times with its members and initially it 'didn't work'.[54] Despite a lack of member support, staff kept trying to mobilize member opposition.

In June 2017, they tried a petition arguing that JEFTA could lead to the privatization of Germany's water services, which would mean that the public would have to pay higher prices for poorer quality water. The petition 'suddenly went quite well' as 'people freaked out' about water privatization, and over 600,000 signed on.[55] One of Campact's trade campaigners explained that:

> we found with JEFTA an issue that relates to everyday life of people. If JEFTA goes through, the water supply could be privatised. This really resonated with people we were writing to. As the Wasserwerker (waterworks) in Berlin were privatised and then the city had to buy them back, and so people can relate [to this issue].[56]

In June 2018, JEFTA was signed by the EU and Japan, but Campact continued to mobilize its members against the agreement.[57] On 29 October that year, ahead of a German vote on JEFTA, Campact members visited German MPs in their regional offices to highlight their concerns about the deal.[58] Campact members, however, did not turn out for anti-JEFTA mobilizations on the same scale as they did for anti-CETA or TTIP demonstrations. JEFTA entered into force in February 2019. Campact's anti-JEFTA campaign demonstrates staff commitment to stopping free trade agreements. However, their influence was limited due to the lack of member support.

[54] Focus group discussion with Campact, 18 March 2021.

[55] ibid.

[56] Interview with Victoria Gulde, Campact trade campaigner, 11 July 2019.

[57] In July 2018, it held a small demonstration at Willy-Brandt Haus in Berlin, the SPD's headquarters. On 15 October 2018, it then obtained legal advice that JEFTA would not guarantee protection of German water from privatization. Campact, 'Jefta Rechtsgutachten', https://blog.campact.de/content/uploads/2018/10/Jefta-Rechtsgutachten__2018-10-22__WEB.pdf(accessed 7 December 2021).

[58] Campact, 'Flickr photos' (29 October), https://www.flickr.com/photos/campact/sets/72157702811298564 (accessed 7 December 2021).

MERCOSUR

In 2019, Campact also campaigned against the EU trade deal with Argentina, Brazil, Uruguay, and Paraguay.[59] It urged the EU Parliament and the governments of EU Member States not to sign the agreement with Jair Bolsonaro, the Brazilian president, given his record as 'a right-wing extremist and militarist'.[60] Campact pointed out that he did not share European values such as 'human dignity, workers' rights, environmental protection'.[61] As the petition was launched, the media reported on the rise of fires and deforestation in the Amazon rainforest and the Bolsanaro government's concomitant lack of concern (BBC 2019). This gave the campaign greater salience to Campact members.

However, there was not strong support amongst Campact members for a campaign on MERCOSUR. According to Campact's trade campaigner, it had 'tested doing something on Mercosur, and EU–Vietnam. Both didn't test very well so [we] decided against it.'[62] This stands in stark contrast with TTIP, where Campact was 'sending off an email every week to our supporters and asking, what is the most important issue Campact should work on? And for a very long time, CETA, TTIP, trade was one of the top issues of our members.'[63]

Campact's trade campaigner emphasized that Campact members, 'although they are generally progressive in their values ... you can't force them to care about something that's 1,000 of kms away', and added that 'if you're a members-based campaign you can only do what people here [in Germany] can relate to'.[64] Other Campact campaigners have emphasized the need to run campaigns that directly link to peoples' lives.[65] Campact did not invest significant staff and financial resources into the anti-MERCOSUR campaign, compared with the TTIP and CETA, given the lack of member interest.[66]

By 2018, trade was no longer a major focus for Campact because member interest in trade campaigns 'vanished at some point'.[67] The decline in member interest for trade campaigns led it to reduce the number of staff dedicated

[59] These Latin American countries are full members of MERCOSUR.

[60] Campact, WeAction Petition, 'Kein handeslabkommmen Mercosur Mit brasiliens Prasident Bolsonaro', https://weact.campact.de/petitions/kein-handelsabkommen-mercosur-mit-brasiliens-prasident-bolsonaro(accessed 7 December 2021).

[61] ibid.

[62] Interview with Victoria Gulde, Campact trade campaigner, 11 July 2019.

[63] Focus group discussion with Campact, 18 March 2021.

[64] Interview with Victoria Gulde, Campact trade campaigner, 11 July 2019.

[65] Focus group discussion with Campact, 18 March 2021.

[66] Although Campact continued to have a dedicated trade campaigner in 2019, she worked around five hours a week on trade agreements, whereas in 2014—2015 its trade campaigner had been full time. Interview with Victoria Gulde, Campact trade campaigner, 11 July 2019.

[67] Focus group discussion with Campact, 18 March 2021.

to trade campaigning, until it was just one person working part-time. Meanwhile, it scaled up its climate campaigning, which garnered more support from members. Campact staff decided it would be difficult to shift members' views, given the broader political landscape after Trump's election.[68] Three factors likely shaped members views: Trump, issue-fatigue, and Wallonia. First, most members were highly critical of Trump, and found themselves in a dilemma because Trump was ultimately responsible for stopping TTIP. Members also felt issue fatigue. They had put so much energy and time into stopping TTIP and CETA, and had seen very little response from the German or EU governments. As Kolb noted, TTIP galvanized 'one of the biggest demonstrations in German history' and 'basically nothing changed'.[69] This was a frustrating experience for many. Kolb also noted that some members were concerned when Wallonia blocked CETA: even if members did not support CETA, they did not think a 'single sub-national unit should be able stop' the EU ratifying a treaty.[70]

Overall, Campact and 38 Degrees followed different logics in their anti-TTIP campaigns. However, in both cases, member support was necessary in order for digital advocacy organizations to have influence. Even in the stewardship model, staff needed to convince members of the importance of a campaign, otherwise it would not take off (Young 2017b). Leaders of unions face similar challenges when mobilizing their members on issues that do not directly affect them. Scholars have found that union leaders who have developed reputations of effectively delivering members' core needs can then 'extract rents' (Ahlquist and Levi 2013).[71] These rents may be political, such as asking members to strike in solidarity with workers in another country. Union leaders need to persuade their members that their collective action could reasonably make a difference and demonstrate that a sufficient proportion of union members share the leaders' 'sentiments about appropriate actions and are willing to act when necessary' (Ahlquist and Levi 2013). Staff in digital advocacy organizations have differing views on whether they can influence their members' views.

[68] As Felix Kolb explained, members 'were confused by the fact that a person they really hated [Trump] has the same position [on TTIP] as themselves'. Focus group discussion with Campact, Felix Kolb, 18 March 2021.

[69] ibid.

[70] ibid.

[71] This theory is developed for unions and other political organizations which are member-based and where members benefit from 'community and social insurance' and the cost of exit from the organization is high because of these benefits (Ahlquist and Levi 2013: 266). Given these scope conditions, it may not easily transfer to digital advocacy organizations, where the cost of exit is low (individuals simply need to unsubscribe from an email list and do not lose any particular community or social insurance).

Conclusion

Progressive, 'people powered' campaigning faces a central tension: what if the majority of members do not want the 'progressive' option? Digital advocacy organizations will not automatically build a 'left populism' by aggregating the preferences of a group of relatively progressive people and following the majority rule. People on the left of the ideological spectrum are split over the benefits and costs of globalization. Members of digital advocacy organizations were divided over whether the UK should remain in the EU or whether their country should welcome more refugees. Furthermore, right-wing populist leaders, such as Trump, have also championed anti-globalization causes, calling for fences to be built along national borders, and free trade agreements to be torn up.

So how do digital advocacy organizations navigate this changing political landscape? How can they contribute to progressive politics, both in their own country and internationally? This chapter has illustrated that there are at least two logics they can follow: member-driven or staff-driven. In the former, staff will quickly shift campaign priorities according to members' interests. This occurred in 38 Degrees' campaigns on refugee rights and, to a lesser extent, in its campaign against TTIP. In the stewardship logic, staff choose to play a crucial role in shaping their members' views over time and try to build a more progressive constituency for their campaigns. This involves significant time and commitment to a particular cause.

The examples in this chapter also suggest that digital advocacy organizations may be most impactful when they mobilize their members over a sustained period of time for a particular cause. ActionStation has contributed to winning a number of important campaigns for Māori rights in New Zealand and helped to shift the terms of the debate. GetUp has mobilized thousands for refugee rights in Australia, in a political climate where both major parties have supported the offshore detention regime. Meanwhile, Campact shaped the German public debate on the risks of TTIP and CETA. In these three cases, each organization worked closely with domestic NGOs and expert advocacy groups (e.g. GetUp and the Human Rights Law Centre or ActionStation and Double the Quota campaign). Digital advocacy organizations complemented expert organizations, and thanks to their large email lists, could broaden these movements.

9
Conclusion

Sitting in the final session of an Online Progressive Engagement Network (OPEN) summit on a cold, grey day in Berlin in November 2017, I was struck by the deep bonds of appreciation and solidarity between OPEN activists. After five intensive days of an overwhelming amount of input and exchange, we were all tired and ready to head home. The facilitator had arranged the chairs in a circle, facing outwards. Over thirty of us sat down, and were asked to close our eyes. Half of the participants were invited to stand in the middle, while the rest remained seated with their eyes closed. The facilitator then asked these participants to put their hand on the shoulder of someone who had made them smile or laugh, then someone they admired or thought had great wisdom. Finally, they were asked to identify someone they thought would change the world. Even with eyes closed, a powerful energy built in the room as people reached out silently to appreciate each other by tapping them on their shoulder. It is this deep trust, respect, and admiration amongst activists that animates the OPEN community. This book brings to life these civic spaces and transnational connections that are less studied by international relations (IR) scholars.

Engaging in ethnographic fieldwork over a five-year period enabled me to take another approach to studying world politics. I looked beyond what happens in capital cities, between government officials, or international institutions. I saw friendships that spanned the globe, conversations which shaped campaigns, and collaborations which led groups to use the same technology. If researchers interested in the impact of digital technologies only look at what people and organizations do online (their digital 'footprints'), they will miss these important interactions.

Using these methods, I discovered that digital advocacy organizations had created a transnational network, OPEN, to diffuse and support a distinct mode of campaigning. MoveOn pioneered this new mode in the United States in 1998. It built up a large list of members by collecting the email addresses of people who signed its e-petitions and then continued to communicate with

Transnational Advocacy in the Digital Era. Nina Hall, Oxford University Press.
© Nina Hall (2022). DOI: 10.1093/oso/9780198858744.003.0009

these members online for a range of progressive causes. MoveOn became a powerful actor in US politics; it was one of the leaders of the anti-Iraq war movement and campaigned for progressive candidates in federal and state elections (Fisher 2019b; Heaney and Rojas 2007; Karpf 2012). Activists from countries as diverse as Poland, New Zealand, South Africa, and Israel were struck by this model and sought to create their own nationally based digital advocacy organizations.

OPEN helped activists to understand the eight-fold path of organizing and launch new digital advocacy organizations. More experienced campaigners provided coaching to newer starts-ups. More established organizations such as Campact and 38 Degrees provided funding to newer initiatives. OPEN ran summits to explain the eight-fold path to newcomers and to induct new organizations into the network. Member organizations exchanged tactics, technology, strategies, and even staff. Activists have crisscrossed the globe from Sweden to New Zealand, sharing their digital campaigning expertise. A Welsh mother working at home has nudged activists in Stockholm and South Africa to start campaigns. Digital technologies have enabled mass mobilizations on the street between people who would otherwise not meet. OPEN organizations have become powerful actors, and in some countries have shaped public debate on domestic and international issues such as climate change, trade, and refugees.

However, these organizations do not fit most conventional IR theories of advocacy, which tend to focus on large non-governmental organizations (NGOs) founded before the internet era. These NGOs wield power and authority, thanks to their issue expertise and long-term commitment to a cause (Stroup and Wong 2018; Tallberg et al. 2015). In most international NGOs, professional staff select and direct campaigns. They draw on their expertise for their cause—whether it be human rights (Human Rights Watch), environment (Greenpeace), or poverty (Oxfam). Staff select campaigns even in the most decentralized, member-based NGOs, such as Amnesty International (Wong 2012). NGOs can access and influence decision-makers because they are recognized for this expertise.

Digital advocacy organizations' power comes from channelling the concerns of a broad, large national membership and mobilizing them rapidly to act at crunch moments. They operate in rapid-response mode: starting, stopping, and switching campaigns frequently. They are multi-issue generalists who have expertise in digital campaigning, but rarely in specific issue areas. They are member-driven. Their members select campaigns and provide the funding and actions to sustain them. Digital advocacy organizations test their campaigns regularly to optimize their messaging and identify the issues most likely to receive member support. Many NGOs use the internet to broadcast their campaigns, but few, if any, use digital analytics to aggregate their members' preferences to identify the issues to campaign on, or the tactics to adopt (Hall et al. 2020; Karpf 2016).

The founders of each OPEN organization chose to establish nationally based organizations because they saw the state as the locus of power. Each organization is member-driven and focused on their national context. They are reactive to national members' concerns rather than to a global agenda.[1] This is why it is rare for these digital advocacy organizations to develop a common collective campaign on the same issue, at the same time, with the same target. IR scholars have noted the importance of national origins in shaping an NGOs' practices and tactics (Stroup 2012). However, IR scholars have largely neglected the influence of members in decision-making in advocacy organizations, and what this means for issue selection and transnational campaigning (Carpenter 2007a and b; Wong 2012).

The book has also challenged IR scholars to reconceptualize the various forms of transnational advocacy and study distributed global campaigns. Transnational advocacy has ceased to be—if it ever was—about simultaneously campaigning on the same issue with the same target (Murphy and Pfaff 2005). Yet, many IR scholars conflate three distinctive elements of transnational advocacy: (a) working with international allies and networks; (b) targeting international institutions; and (c) campaigning on a transnational issue. This is partly because they focus on advocacy at large global summits (Hadden 2015; Keck and Sikkink 1998; Lake et al. 2021).

Activists have mobilized people around the world for global days of climate action using common messages and tactics, but with different targets. Such distributed campaigns often take place far away from international negotiations and are facilitated by the internet. Activists can use social media and email to swiftly coordinate, share images of their protests, and link behind unified messages. In this way, hundreds of small protests, such as the students' climate strikes in September 2019, appear as one large mass movement.[2] The internet

[1] During the COVID-19 pandemic, OPEN organizations rapidly launched new online campaigns focused on the impacts of the pandemic. They followed the pattern we have seen in this book: they focused on domestic targets and worked with domestic allies, and did not campaign collectively at the same time, with the same target on COVID-related issues. However, OPEN activists turned to each other to share ideas, messaging, and tactics. The OPEN executive directors held regular weekly calls, and exchanged ideas (Hall forthcoming).

[2] Groups that are against COVID restrictions have also coordinated large, worldwide rallies on the same day, with the same ask, but targeting national governments. One such day of protest was 20 March

has enabled mass global distributed campaigning to emerge, but these activists still primarily target the state (Keck and Sikkink 1998; Price 2003).

The OPEN organizational model has limitations. Precisely because OPEN groups derive their power from mobilizing their members, they tend to focus on issues that people can directly relate to and are affected by. It is difficult for OPEN organizations to campaign on minority issues (such as refugees or racism) or far-away issues (such as the war in Yemen, or the erosion of democracy in Hong Kong). Following the member-driven form logic, digital advocacy organizations can be ruled by the majority. Mindful of this, some OPEN groups have embraced a staff-stewardship, value-driven logic. Staff have sought to influence their members' views, particularly on minority rights. Some organizations have diversified their membership and staff, and developed partnerships with domestic NGOs who champion indigenous or migrants' rights issues (e.g. GetUp and the Human Rights Law Centre on refugee issues, or ActionStation and Just Speak on criminal justice reform for Māori (i.e. macron on a)). Future scholarship should examine when, why, and how staff in advocacy organizations have transformed their members' views (Ahlquist and Levi 2013).

There are also tensions between different visions for OPEN. Many OPEN activists see the network as a powerful resource for ideas, technology, and resources to 'enhance' their national campaigns. Others hoped that the network would grow and expand into other countries, especially in the Global South, and be harnessed for transnational campaigns. Given limited resources, OPEN members will need to decide whether to prioritize spreading the organizational model into as many countries as possible, helping its current members to improve their national campaigns, or building transnational campaigns for global justice. The network's core mission will shape the way organizations engage with each other and how resources flow within the network.

The next three sections of the conclusion explore the future challenges for digital advocacy organizations and the broader advocacy sector. I then look at the rise of far-right groups online and ask: 'Why have groups on the far right not (yet) replicated the OPEN model?' Finally, I point to the contestation of the liberal global order, fuelled by movements on both the left and right of the political spectrum.

2021, when demonstrations took place in more than forty countries globally. Worldwide Demonstration 'Who is Behind WWD 2021?', https://worldwidedemonstration.com(accessed 7 December 2021).

The Future of Digital Advocacy Organizations

Thus far, there have been no attempts to create OPEN organizations in fully authoritarian contexts. The model depends on decision-makers taking citizens' demands seriously because they are ultimately accountable to them. Future scholarship could examine how digital advocacy organizations have operated in contexts where democratic opposition may be met with severe backlash, if not government repression (Xu 2021). This is particularly important given that some OPEN countries, such as Poland and Hungary, are becoming illiberal democracies, and there is shrinking space for civil society. Scholars could also examine what factors, in addition to regime type, influence whether member-driven digital advocacy organizations will survive and thrive. During my research, activists noted how important internet access and a strong culture of philanthropy is for success. They also noted that in very large countries with ethnic and/or linguistically diverse populations, it can be more difficult to run nationally driven campaigns. We need a better understanding of when and why this model works best.

Digital advocacy organizations are also facing challenging questions about their organizational sustainability. Decision-makers grow tired of the same tactics—online petitions, mass emails—and they tend to lose impact over time (Karpf 2012). More importantly, their members are mostly baby-boomers, who are active on Facebook, email, and Twitter. Yet younger generations are much more likely to use TikTok, Instagram, and YouTube. Over the past five years, I have heard lengthy debates amongst activists about whether the email era was over and how they could adapt to new social media platforms. It is possible that digital advocacy organizations will become irrelevant, and even die out, if they do not adapt to younger generations' digital ways. OPEN organizations should also continue to look for ways to support younger activist groups, without taking them over (Fisher and Nasrin 2021).

In the meantime, most mainstream NGOs are now embracing digital technologies in their campaigns. Future research could examine whether new digital advocacy organizations are transforming and/or displacing traditional NGOs (Hall et al. 2020; Mitchell et al. 2020). Population ecology approaches could be particularly helpful here (Bush and Hadden 2019; Eilstrup-Sangiovanni 2019). Scholars adopting this approach have found a 'stagnation' in the establishment of new international NGOs in the United States and, in parallel, the growth of digitally native campaign groups like MoveOn, Avaaz, and Change.Org (Bush and Hadden 2019). However, we know less about the relationship between digital native organizations and traditional NGOs in countries beyond the United States.

There are bigger ethical questions at stake for any activists who use mainstream social media. Social media companies have a monopoly and, until recently, faced very minimal government regulation for content on their sites. Facebook, for instance, is now the largest advertising company worldwide, with more than 2 billion monthly active users. It systematically collects and monitors its users' activities and sells this data to third parties. Some have called it the world's largest surveillance company (Cadwalladr and Graham-Harrison 2018; Tufekci 2014; Zuboff 2018). Social media has also enabled the dissemination of fake news, the use of customized messages to target particular groups (e.g. dissuading black Americans from voting in the US election), and the unauthorized sharing of personal data with third-parties (e.g. the Cambridge Analytica scandal). Social media provide popular platforms for hate speech and have enabled the far right to spread their messages transnationally (Caiani and Kroell 2015). Some OPEN activists have begun to question whether they should use Facebook at all and several have sought to counter online hate speech and influence government regulation of digital industries.[3]

NGOs, including OPEN organizations, now store large amounts of digital data on individuals, which is at risk of being hacked.[4] If personally identifiable data is leaked in sensitive contexts it may 'spark violence, discrimination, or exclusionary policies. Services can be denied to entire groups and individuals targeted' (Secret Aid Worker 2017). Furthermore, groups may be harmed without individuals ever being identified, 'on the basis of data, on the basis of perceived relationships, or through subtle social dynamics or engineering' (Secret Aid Worker 2017). For these reasons, all advocacy organizations should consider the following questions carefully. What data is collected and why? How is it handled? And who 'owns' this data? One recommendation for the NGO community is 'don't collect it, if you can't protect it'.[5] Activists and scholars should reflect on ethical practices about how to engage in advocacy online.

[3] Campact conducted a study in Hessen in 2018, and found that every third person had experienced hate speech online and that 61 per cent thought the state government was not doing enough. Campact, 'Pilotstudie zu Hass und Hetze im Internet—Täter bleiben meist straffrei' (11 October 2018), https://blog.campact.de/content/uploads/2018/10/Hass_im_Netz_Version_04.10.2018.pdf (accessed 7 December 2021).

[4] Thanks to Stefania Milan for discussions on the ethical practices of digital activism.

[5] Thanks to Lucy Bernholz for this point.

The Rise of Far-Right Transnational Networks

This book has focused on the growth and global spread of *progressive* digital advocacy organizations. Yet while writing this book, the rise of far-right networks has been more prominent. Illiberal transnational movements have been actively promoted by illiberal states, such as Russia (Cooley and Nexon 2020). Illiberal movements have grown in membership and influence in liberal states, including in the UK, the United States, Germany, and Sweden (Cooley and Nexon 2020). A prime example is Steve Bannon's movement: Bannon worked as President Trump's chief strategist and senior counsellor (for just eight months), and after leaving the White House, created a network 'Le Mouvement' to support far-right political politicians in the 2019 European Parliament elections. Political actors on the right have used the internet to connect and form transnational movements (Caiani and Kroell 2015). Far-right groups have been particularly active on platforms such as 8chan and Telegram.[6] Recent research suggests that far-right-wing groups are connected transnationally online but that their campaigns tend to be framed and focused nationally (McSwiney et al. 2021).

Far-right organizations are important for IR scholars to study because they are 'on the offensive against a retreating liberal international civil society' (Cooley and Nexon 2020). Yet, IR has typically focused on external threats, in particular state challengers to the liberal order, such as China or Russia, rather than internal backlash and domestic groups (Lake et al. 2021). Conservative groups in several liberal democracies have sought to replicate the OPEN model, and galvanize far-right movements. However, most of the US copycat organizations have not survived (Right March, Freedom Watch, and the Vanguard) (Karpf 2012). In Australia, the right-wing organization Advance Australia has tried to emulate GetUp's model but it is a top-down, hierarchical organization. It appears to have little interest in devolving power to members yet wants the appearance of being people-powered (this is called 'astro-turfing'). Citizen Go, a global petition platform for conservatives who are concerned about traditional family values, is perhaps the closest to the OPEN model (Whyte 2017).[7]

Future scholarship could examine why the far right has adopted other organizational forms and whether these forms are more effective than those picked

[6] In 2019, 8chan relaunched as 8kun.

[7] Citizen Go is a transnational platform, with country-specific campaigning sites (e.g. its Hungarian site is in Hungarian).

by the left. There are several potential explanations for why the right has eschewed the member-driven, rapid-response, multi-issue model. For one, the far right has done well in elections in recent years and occupies positions of power in many countries around the world. Hence, individuals who might otherwise engage in a far-right advocacy movement are instead involved in far-right political parties and have no incentive to experiment with new organizational forms (Karpf 2016). Another potential explanation is that the far right is better organized on alternative (alt)-media and mainstream social media platforms than the left (Heft et al. 2020). The far right has certainly embraced and benefitted from Facebook, YouTube, and Instagram, which until relatively recently did little to moderate content or de-platform the right (Lowles and Ryan 2021).

There may also be ideological reasons why the right is less likely to adopt a member-driven model. The right tends to be more comfortable using financial power to sway politics. It has fewer qualms about using hierarchical or top-down organizing structures, which are often more effective in digital campaigning than horizontal, 'leaderless' movements (Schradie 2019). In fact, Schradie argues that the right is better at some forms of digital activism precisely because it is not trying to engage people, but rather to direct them (Schradie 2019). Finally, the far right has not formed a network to explicitly diffuse an organizational model, unlike OPEN and Ben Brandzel. Although there may be close personal ties between activists on the right, they may be more likely to exchange messaging, tactics, and finances than support the diffusion of a distinctive organizational model. Future scholarship could explore further the different forms of transnational mobilizations on both the left and the right, and if/how they influence each other (Dennis and Hall 2020).

So, what does all this mean for global politics?

Contestation of the Liberal International Order

IR scholars are now turning their attention to how domestic actors and the public at large are contesting the liberal international order (Farrell and Han 2020; Lake et al. 2021; Simmons and Goemans 2021). A long line of IR scholarship has examined how domestic interest groups can influence foreign policy (Moravcsik 1997; Putnam 1988). However, this earlier liberal scholarship did not 'consider that domestic forces in core states would fundamentally challenge the liberal international order' (Lake et al. 2021). Much IR scholarship, especially in major journals such as *International Organization*, has had a strong liberal bias, and hence did not examine why domestic interest groups, whether on the left or right, have mobilized against globalization.

Yet many people are frustrated that the liberal democratic order was largely created by elites without a democratic debate (Farrell and Han 2020) and they question its neoliberal economic foundations. For some, the rise of international institutions and transnational networks is not a global good, but represents 'defection' from their local needs and identities (Simmons and Goemans 2021). There is a tension between the 'liberal international order' and a 'sovereign territorial order', which underpins political cleavages in many states (Simmons and Goemans 2021). IR needs to examine why certain global issues, such as climate change, migration or trade, create greater public debate and polarization than others, such as biodiversity (Bièvre and Poletti 2020). IR scholars could conduct comparative analysis of the influence of NGOs and transnational advocacy networks across different global regimes, building on the work of NGOs' influence in single regimes (Allan 2021; Hadden 2015; Siles-Brügge and Strange 2020a). This is important because we are simultaneously seeing a more inclusive global system (as more states join international institutions) and a more unequal global system (as powerful states find ways to shore up their power) (Viola 2020).

Civil society actors make 'deliberate strategic choices' about when and how they will shape public opinion, as we saw with OPEN's engagement in trade, refugees, and climate change politics (Bièvre and Poletti 2020). Scholars could look at how political parties, NGOs, advocacy organizations, and social movements use digital technologies to not only communicate to publics, but also to customize and target their messaging and optimize political mobilization (Bjola and Manor 2018; Vries et al. 2021). IR should examine right-wing and left-wing critiques of the liberal international order and ask how the public can be meaningfully engaged in decision-making on international issues. And how can we ensure that a wide range of interests are heard, not only the loudest voice on social media or mainstream news? This is crucial as global, national, and local politics become more intertwined and governments are increasingly concerned by a backlash against global institutions.

...

Digital technology has altered transnational networks (Farrell 2012). It has enabled the emergence, growth, and diffusion of new, powerful forms of advocacy. The internet has also made it easier to engage in transnational advocacy networks and demonstrate international solidarity. Yet, even in an extremely globalized and digitalized world, the digital activists studied here view the state as the locus of power (Germain and Kenny 1998). They are 'rooted cosmopolitans' who care about international issues, but take action nationally (Tarrow 2005).

Many of the most recent, powerful, digitally enabled social movements, such as #FridaysForFuture and #BlackLivesMatter, are also embedded within strong networks of transnational solidarity. However, they have organized themselves in national and local chapters. Regardless of the digital platforms future activists use, most will likely continue to experiment with how to optimize their influence at the domestic versus the transnational level. Groups may look to strike a balance between speaking to national concerns and targeting national leaders, and building broad, global movements with common goals. Digital technology has certainly lowered the cost of coordination, but it has not dramatically changed the calculus of where political power lies.

Appendix

This book combines qualitative and quantitative methods to examine the evolution and the campaigns of a network of digital advocacy organizations. Here, I describe the methods I used to collect the data for this book.

Qualitative Data

Over five years, I conducted more than 100 interviews. In the first phase, I sought to interview most of the founding executive directors of digital advocacy organizations. These semi-structured interviews typically lasted an hour. I asked these individuals to explain how they first heard about the Online Progressive Engagement Network (OPEN) and how and why they became part of the network. In many cases, I conducted follow-up interviews to understand the evolution of each organization during the five years of my study. Alongside this, I interviewed other staff members of each organization, either during field visits, at OPEN summits, or over Zoom. I also interviewed a range of experts and individuals from other non-governmental organizations (NGOs). All of these interviews were transcribed and became the basis for Chapters 3 and 4, and informed the rest of the book.

Alongside these interviews, I attended seven summits of the OPEN community. Each summit typically lasted a week, and all participants stayed in the same hotel, ate meals together, and spent almost every waking moment in each other's company. I often shared a dorm room with other activists. I had instances where individuals shared deeply personal insights into their work and lives. I learned about burn-outs and miscarriages. I met OPEN activists' partners, children, and friends. The boundary between researcher and research subject blurred into friendship. I took part in the final appreciation circle at summits where I felt the enormous gratitude of people participating, and received thanks for my contributions. I engaged not with an instrumental aim of building rapport with my 'subjects' to 'extract data', but as another human curious about how we learn, connect, and grow personally, and within our professional organizations. I also visited the offices of several OPEN organizations to see how they operated on a daily basis. During these visits, I would typically conduct interviews, and, where possible, spend time sitting in the office to understand work patterns.

Throughout this ethnographic work, I was always clear to everyone I spoke with that I was attending as a researcher intending to write a book about the network. I took measures to ensure that people could opt out of interviews with me, or ask me to leave the room during summit sessions.[1] I found that people were genuinely curious to hear about my research and reflect on their own work with an external person, and were eager to see the end results. (I did have to explain that academic work is not produced at the same pace as

[1] I asked people to let me know directly if they did not want me in the room, or to inform the OPEN staff, or facilitators. At one summit the facilitators explicitly said that people could label their sessions 'research free'.

rapid-response campaigning and they would have to wait a few years for the book!). In June 2021, I contacted all the interview participants cited in the book to check their quotes and ask whether they preferred to be anonymous, or cited by name. Most chose to be cited by name.

I also worked with a research assistant, Charlie Lawrie, to compile a list of all the campaign actions OPEN organizations took on refugee rights, free trade agreements, and climate change. We looked at primary data from the organization's websites, social media pages, and NGO websites, and surveyed the relevant academic literature on refugee, trade, and climate advocacy. From this material, we collated timelines of each digital advocacy organization's campaigns and the contribution(s) they made to the broader movement between 2010 and 2020. This data was the basis for the analysis of climate, refugee, and trade campaigns in Chapters 7 and 8. I triangulated this material with interviews of OPEN activists, as well as NGOs and experts on the issue, to understand the contribution of the OPEN network.

Quantitative Data

I collected a dataset to examine broader trends in how digital advocacy organizations campaign. I worked with a former student, Rebecca John, to collect data on digital advocacy organizations finances. This data came from publicly available sources, predominantly from the budgets listed in annual reports. We collected other data on the organizations, such as a list of websites where members' can start their own online petitions (see Table A1).

We then focused on four digital advocacy organizations: 38 Degrees, ActionStation, Campact, and GetUp. These organizations were selected because they are all full members of OPEN, are at least five years old, and represent a range of geographic areas: two are European (UK and Germany), and two are in the Southern Hemisphere (Australia and New Zealand). We collected and coded all their campaign actions over a one-year period (1 September 2018–31 August 2019). We identified a total of 150 campaign actions across the four organizations (21 for ActionStation, 33 for 38 Degrees, 71 for GetUp, and 25 for Campact).

To compile a full list of these four organizations' campaigns, we considered four options: sourcing their campaign actions through their website, through their email correspondence, through social media, or by directly asking the organizations for a full list of their campaigns. We initially tried to create a list of campaigns through their public websites. However, this proved difficult because some of the organizations do not keep their websites up to date with the latest campaign developments, and rarely list dates of when a campaign action (e.g. a petition) begins.[2] Meanwhile, other organizations, such as 38 Degrees, list every campaign they have ever started (14,236 campaigns are listed on their website). Digital advocacy organizations do not see the homepages of their websites as their core means for communicating with members; rather, they rely on email and social media.[3]

We then tried to source their campaigns through email correspondence. We signed up to the mailing lists of all the OPEN organizations and kept a record of the emails they sent and the issues they asked members to campaign on. However, this method was not an accurate reflection of their campaigns because many of the organizations tailor their correspondence; they do not email all campaigns to all members, but instead target campaigns, depending on members' interests. For example, if a member signs up to an environmental

[2] In multiple cases the campaign webpages have expired since we collected this data.

[3] Members and potential supporters are more likely to access campaign webpages via social media or email links. This is why these organizations put less emphasis on the website homepages.

Table A1 Member-initiated campaign websites

Organization	Name	Web address
38 Degrees	Campaigns by You	https://you.38degrees.org.uk/petition/new?source=38homepage
ActionStation	Our ActionStation	https://our.actionstation.org.nz/
aHang	Szabad aHang	https://szabad.ahang.hu/
Akcja Demokracja	Nasza Demokracja	https://naszademokracja.pl/
Amandla.Mobi	Awethu Amandla.Mobi	https://awethu.amandla.mobi/petition/new?source=homepage
Aufstehn	mein #aufstehn	https://mein.aufstehn.at/
Campact	WeAct!	https://weact.campact.de/
Campax	Act Campax	https://act.campax.org/petition/new?source=homepage
Declic	CampaniaMea Declic	https://campaniamea.declic.ro/petition/new?source=header
DeGoedeZaak	DeGoedeZaak	https://actie.degoedezaak.org/petition/new?source=header
GetUp!	communityrun	https://www.communityrun.org/petition/new?source=footer
Leadnow	You.Leadnow	https://you.leadnow.ca/petition/new?source=leadnow
MoveOn	MoveOn	https://sign.moveon.org/petition/start
Skiftet	MittSkifte	https://www.mittskifte.org/
Uplift	MyUplift	https://my.uplift.ie

campaign, the organization is more likely to send that member campaigns focused on the environment rather than, say, human rights. Digital advocacy organizations will also tailor their communications according to where members live, especially when it comes to local campaigns or election campaigning.

I also contacted 38 Degrees, ActionStation, Campact, and GetUp to ask for a full list of their campaigns over a one-year period. I received several lists, but the majority did not have a full list of their campaigns readily available. One organization sent through its monthly email summaries, which it sends out to its members along with a list of milestones. Another organization sent through a list of actions it had taken through Speakout (an internal database) regarding all contact with members. However, this list included training exercises, as well as actual campaigns. I was also concerned about bias in the self-reported lists. Some organizations might only include campaigns which were successful, or in which they invested a significant amount of energy. It was important for me to receive all the campaigns they started, even if they only ran for a very short period of time (e.g. a day or two). In short, the data offered directly from the organizations was not suitable to create lists of campaign actions, but we did use it to triangulate our results.[4]

[4] It is informative that digital advocacy organizations do not keep a clear record of all the campaigns they run (let alone what proportion are successful). It is partly because they run so many campaigns, and also because there is often a mix of member-initiated campaigns and staff-driven ones. It may also be that they have no reporting requirement to list all their campaigns, while other NGOs, which rely on grants, may have. Finally, digital advocacy organizations focus on constantly campaigning and do not dedicate staff to evaluate or keep records of campaigns.

Instead, we relied on social media to compile a list of campaign actions, and examined the entirety of the four organizations' Facebook and Twitter posts between 1 September 2018 and 31 August 2019. Because these organizations promoted their campaigns on social media, this proved to be a more useful method for identifying the campaigns that were launched and when. Our research found that all of these organizations were quite active on Facebook, but less so on Twitter. Their social media posts could also be dated to confirm they were within the time period (this was not the case with website material).

This research focused on campaign actions, therefore we did not include posts which were retweets of news items (e.g. a Guardian article about climate change or refugees), or diffusion of other NGOs' campaigns (e.g. there were many reposts of #FridaysForFuture in 2018 and 2019). We included all the different types of campaign actions, including reports, online petitions, and demonstrations. We also cross-checked these campaigns by examining their websites and/or the list provided by the organization. In two cases, 38 Degrees and GetUp, which had the longest and most complicated lists to code, we consulted other academic experts on these organizations to confirm whether our list corresponded with what they would expect.

For each campaign, we listed the date of the post, the date it was last publicized, where it was posted, the name of the campaign, the URL page, the issue, the target of the campaign, and the type of action (petition, report, demonstration, etc.). It is possible, but unlikely, that organizations would not post a campaign on their social media (Facebook and/or Twitter) pages.[5]

We did not include member-initiated campaigns, unless they were promoted by staff through the organization's social media. This was first because many organizations have separate websites for member-initiated petitions and it would have been difficult to gather all these campaigns, which often numbered in the thousands. Second, we were interested in which campaigns staff invested organizational energy in. For this reason, we also did not include online petitions that were initiated and driven by other NGOs and merely hosted on a digital advocacy website, or retweeted by a digital advocacy organization. We did include campaign actions where the organization was a co-partner in the campaign. This means that our list of campaign actions reflects campaigns where the organization put a certain degree of time and resources.

We analysed whether the campaign had a transnational target (e.g. an international organization, an international business, or an international politician); had a transnational organization that they partnered with (e.g. another NGO which was not nationally based); and whether they targeted a transnational issue. Identifying whether a campaign had a transnational target or partnered with an international NGO was straightforward. However, identifying whether campaigns focused on transnational issues was, in a few cases, difficult.

Some issues were clearly local (e.g. increasing state support for a local library, or funding for victims of sexual violence) and some were clearly international (e.g. campaigns against international trade agreements). There were a large number of campaigns which targeted a transnational issue (e.g. climate change) but were framed in national terms (e.g. stopping the Adani coal mine in Australia, or putting regulations on 'gas guzzling' cars in Germany). Importantly, we coded campaigns as targeting a 'transnational' issue if they addressed a global public good (e.g. climate change) or an issue which traverses international

[5] Thanks to James Dennis for pointing this out.

borders (international trade), even if they focused only on national decision-makers. Many of the campaigns coded as targeting a 'transnational' issue also included a reference to the transnational dimensions in the campaign material (i.e. report, petition, or demonstration announcement). However, it was not imperative for the campaign material to mention a transnational dimension to be included in this category.

Another methodological challenge we faced when compiling this data was how to differentiate between campaigns and campaign actions. There were a few occasions where organizations had taken different actions (e.g. a petition, a report, and/or a demonstration) but these were part of a similar overall campaign. For instance, GetUp had multiple campaigns against the Adani mine and against far-right politicians in the run-up to the 2019 Australian election. For the purposes of this research, we listed campaign actions as separate whenever there was a change in the target or framing of the campaign. We did not include campaign actions as separate entries if they were exact repetitions (i.e. same issue, same target, same ask). For example, if an organization re-posted on Facebook the same petition several times during a week or a month, we would enter this petition just once. However, if an organization released a petition, then a report, and then called for a demonstration, we listed these as separate campaign actions. We ran into some issues with GetUp's campaign actions because it ran a number of campaign actions for which data was no longer available online (the campaign had finished and the websites were no longer active). In these cases, we tried to triangulate with other material such as mainstream media, to identify the campaign target, issue focus, and presence of international allies as best we could.

We also classified the campaign actions into various issue categories, including climate change, environment, trade, health, immigration, migrant and refugee rights, Brexit, and Indigenous rights. These classifications were developed inductively from the data. There is a trade-off between highly precise categories (e.g. banning arms sales to Saudi Arabia) and broader categories (e.g. human rights or the environment[6]). We chose to find common terms across the four organizations wherever possible; however, there were some categories which were specific to each country (e.g. the UK and Brexit; New Zealand and indigenous rights). When campaigns appealed to more than one issue (such as migration and health care), we tended to use both.[7] The results from this analysis are in Chapter 4.

Finally, in February and March 2021, I ran three focus groups where I presented the results of Chapter 6 to staff of OPEN organizations. I ran a session for all OPEN groups, and then two dedicated sessions for 38 Degrees; and another for Campact. I invited feedback on the accuracy of my data, and explanations for the trends highlighted in the graphs. Quotes from these focus groups are cited, with permission, in Chapter 6.

...

My role as a researcher is to hold up an honest mirror, to reflect on the conversations I have taken part in, and to place these conversations within wider debates about the role of NGOs and civil society in transforming global politics. However, one book cannot capture all the nuances of this network. There were hundreds, if not thousands, of conversations in person, over Slack, Zoom, email, and phone that I was not part of. I never attended the Core Group meetings (the main executive body of OPEN), for instance. I have not scrutinized all of their online or offline actions. There are many stones still to be turned over for political communication, social movement, and international relations scholars.

[6] We did separate out climate change from environment, given the number of climate-specific campaigns during the time period we studied.

[7] This follows Vromen (2016), who, in categorizing GetUp's campaigns, has a category which is 'combination of refugees, carbon pollution and mental health'.

References

38 Degrees. (2008). 'Strategic Plan 2008–2011'. London (December) (on file with author).

38 Degrees. (2014). 'Victory: Barclays Won't Invest in Destroying the Great Barrier Reef!' (26 June). https://home.38degrees.org.uk/2014/06/26/barclays-great-barrier-reef-win/ (accessed 7 December 2021).

38 Degrees. (2015). '2015 General Election: The Plan'. https://home.38degrees.org.uk/2015/03/01/election-the-plan/ (accessed 22 January 2022).

Abbott, K. W., Green, J. F., and Keohane, R. O. (2016). 'Organizational Ecology and Institutional Change in Global Governance'. *International Organization*, *70*(2), 247–277.

ActionStation. (2017). 'Te Ira Tāngtata' ('Peoples' Agenda for Aotearoa'). ActionStation. https://drive.google.com/file/d/1vwruHYjgNQmTTmZVlnesjPGuAzFHNn5T/view (accessed 4 December 2021).

ActionStation. (2019). 'Become a Tauiwi Tautoko Volunteer'. *Medium* (2 April). https://medium.com/@actionstation/tauiwi-tautoko-88510ebdb0c6 (accessed 6 December 2021).

ActionStation Aotearoa. (2018). 'Volunteer for the Tauiwi Tautoko Volunteer Project'. *Medium* (8 August). https://actionstation.medium.com/tauiwi-tautoko-88510ebdb0c6 (accessed 7 December 2021).

Ahlquist, J. S., and Levi, M. (2013). *In the Interest of Others*. Princeton, NJ: Princeton University Press.

Al Jazeera. (2016). '"Complete Meltdown of Humanity" in Aleppo'. *Al Jazeera* (14 December). https://www.aljazeera.com/news/2016/12/14/civilians-killed-as-battle-for-aleppo-nears-end (accessed 4 December 2021).

Alinsky, S. D. (1989). *Rules for Radicals: A Practical Primer for Realistic Radicals*. New York: Vintage.

Allan, B. B. (2017). 'Producing the Climate: States, Scientists, and the Constitution of Global Governance Objects'. *International Organization*, *71*(1), 131–162.

Allan, J. I. (2018). 'Seeking Entry: Discursive Hooks and NGOs in Global Climate Politics'. *Global Policy*, *9*(4), 560–569.

Allan, J. I. (2021). *The New Climate Activism*. Toronto: University of Toronto Press.

Allan, J. I., and Hadden, J. (2017). 'Exploring the Framing Power of NGOs in Global Climate Politics'. *Environmental Politics*, *26* (4), 600 – 620.

Amnesty International. (2018). 'We Stand in Solidarity with Civil Society in Hungary' (19 February). https://www.amnesty.org/en/latest/campaigns/2018/02/in-solidarity-with-civil-society-in-hungary/ (accessed 4 December 2021).

Ardern, J. (2018). 'Refugee Quota Increases to 1500 in 2020'. *The Beehive* (19 September). http://www.beehive.govt.nz/release/refugee-quota-increases-1500–2020 (accessed 4 December 2021).

Asselt, H. van. (2016). 'The Role of Non-State Actors in Reviewing Ambition, Implementation, and Compliance under the Paris Agreement'. *Climate Law*, *6*(1–2), 91–108.

Atkinson, J., and Scurrah, M. (2009). *Globalizing Social Justice—the Role of Non-Government Organizations in Bringing about Social Change*. Basingstoke: Palgrave Macmillan.

Australian Associated Press. (2017). 'Australia's Top 20 Power-Brokers' *News.Com* (6 October). http://www.news.com.au/national/breaking-news/australias-top-20-powerbrokers/news-story/1befd0a99d89672707750b56a81c7c14.

Avaaz. (2006). 'Business Plan 2007–2008'. *New York*. (on file with the author)

Bäckstrand, K., Kuyper, J., Linnér, B.-O., and Lövbrand, E. (2017). 'Non-State Actors in Global Climate Governance: From Copenhagen to Paris and Beyond'. *Environmental Politics*, *26*(4), 561–579.

Bauer, M. (2015). 'The Spiral of Silence—How Anti-TTIP Groups Dominate German Online Media and Set the Tone for TTIP Opinion'. European Centre for International Political Economy (January). https://ecipe.org/blog/anti-ttip-german-online-media/ (accessed 4 December 2021).

Bauer, M. (2016a). 'Manufacturing Discontent: The Rise to Power of Anti-TTIP Groups'. European Centre for International Political Economy Occasional Paper.

Bauer, M. (2016b). 'The Political Power of Evoking Fear: The Shining Example of Germany's Anti-TTIP Campaign Movement'. *European View*, *15*(2), 193–212.

BBC. (n.d.). 'The Noble Eightfold Path—Buddhist Beliefs'. *BBC Bitesize*. https://www.bbc.co.uk/bitesize/guides/zf8g4qt/revision/3 (accessed 4 December 2021).

BBC. (2014). 'Climate Change Summit: Global Rallies Demand Action'. *BBC News* (21 September). https://www.bbc.com/news/science-environment-29301969 (accessed 4 December 2021).

BBC. (2015). 'Great Barrier Reef Spared Unesco "In Danger" Listing'. *BBC News* (1 July). https://www.bbc.com/news/world-australia-33350101.

BBC. (2016). 'German Top Court Backs Canada Trade Deal'. *BBC News* (13 October). https://www.bbc.com/news/world-europe-37642261 (accessed 4 December 2021).

BBC. (2019). 'Amazon Fires "Increase 84% in one year"'. *BBC News* (21 August). https://www.bbc.com/news/world-latin-america-49415973 (accessed 4 December 2021).

Belam, M. (2018). 'Don't Post Crisp Packets, Royal Mail Begs Anti-Plastic Protesters'. *The Guardian* (26 September). http://www.theguardian.com/environment/2018/sep/26/dont-post-crisp-packets-royal-mail-begs-packaging-protesters (accessed 4 December 2021).

Bennett, P. W. L., and Segerberg, A. (2012). 'The Logic of Connective Action'. *Information, Communication & Society*, *15*(5), 739–768.

Bennett, P. W. L., and Segerberg, A. (2013). *The Logic of Connective Action: Digital Media and the Personalization of Contentious Politics*. Cambridge: Cambridge University Press.

Benthall, M. (2014). 'TTIP:EU Consultation'. 38 Degrees (10 July). https://home.38degrees.org.uk/2014/07/10/ttip-eu-consultation/ (accessed 7 December 2021).

Benthall, M. (2015). 'TTIP Petition Hand—Ins: October 9th and 10th'. 38 Degrees (12 October). https://home.38degrees.org.uk/2015/10/12/ttip-petition-hand-ins-october-9th-and-10th/ (accessed 7 December 2021).

Berliner, D. (2016). 'Transnational Advocacy and Domestic Law: International NGOs and the Design of Freedom of Information Laws—Arizona State University'. *Review of International Organizations*, *11*(1), 121–144.

Bettles, C. (2017). 'Monsanto Speaks Out to Back Same Sex Marriage'. *Farm Online* (5 September). http://www.farmonline.com.au/story/4903974/monsanto-speaks-out-to-back-same-sex-marriage/ (accessed 4 December 2021).

Bevington, C. (2015). 'Stories from TTIP Action Day'. 38 Degrees (22 August). https://home.38degrees.org.uk/2015/08/22/ttip-day-of-action-3/ (accessed 7 December 2021).

Bièvre, D. D., and Poletti, A. (2017). 'Why the Transatlantic Trade and Investment Partnership Is Not (So) New, and Why It Is Also Not (So) Bad'. *Journal of European Public Policy, 24*(10), 1506–1521.

Bièvre, D. D., and Poletti, A. (2020). 'Towards Explaining Varying Degrees of Politicization of EU Trade Agreement Negotiations'. *Politics and Governance, 8*(1), 243–253.

Bimber, B., Flanagin, A., and Stohl, C. (2012). *Collective Action in Organizations*. Cambridge: Cambridge University Press.

Bjola, C., and Manor, I. (2018). 'Revisiting Putnam's Two-Level Game Theory in the Digital Age: Domestic Digital Diplomacy and the Iran Nuclear Deal'. *Cambridge Review of International Affairs, 31*, 3–32.

Blondeel, M., Colgan, J., and Van de Graaf, T. (2019). 'What Drives Norm Success? Evidence from Anti-Fossil Fuel Campaigns'. *Global Environmental Politics, 19*(4), 63–84.

Bloodgood, E. A., and Clough, E. (2016). 'Transnational Advocacy Networks: A Complex Adaptive Systems Simulation Model of the Boomerang Effect'. *Social Science Computer Review, 35*(3), 319–335. https://doi.org/10.1177/0894439316634077.

Blue & Green Tomorrow. (2013). 'Campaign Group 38 Degrees Faces "Biggest Ever Threat"—from a Parliamentary Bill'. *Blue and Green Tomorrow* (23 August). https://blueandgreentomorrow.com/environment/campaign-group-38-degrees-faces-biggest-ever-threat-from-a-parliamentary-bill/ (accessed 4 December 2021).

Bob, C. (2012). *The Global Right Wing and the Clash of World Politics*. Cambridge: Cambridge University Press.

Bolton, M., and Nash, T. (2010). 'The Role of Middle Power–NGO Coalitions in Global Policy: The Case of the Cluster Munitions Ban'. *Global Policy, 1*(2), 172–184.

Bond, B., and Exley, Z. (2016). *Rules for Revolutionaries*. Vermont: Chelsea Green Publishing.

Bradely, M. (2020). *The International Organization for Migration: Challenges, Commitments, Complexities*. Abingdon: Routledge.

Brandzel, B. 'The 8-Fold Path of New Organizing' (on file with author).

Brandzel, B. (2010). 'Campaigning 2.0' (on file with author).

Brandzel, B. (2019). 'From Moment to Movement: A Guide to Email Writing for Action' (6 April). https://de.slideshare.net/bnwklr/from-moment-to-movement-and-beyond-1256515 (accessed 6 December 2021).

Busby, J. (2010). *Moral Movements and Foreign Policy*. Cambridge: Cambridge University Press.

Bush, S. S., and Hadden, J. (2019). 'Density and Decline in Founding of INGOs in the United States'. *International Studies Quarterly, 63*, 113–1146.

Cadwalladr, C., and Graham-Harrison, E. (2018). 'Facebook Accused of Conducting Mass Surveillance through Its Apps'. *The Guardian* (24 May). http://www.theguardian.com/technology/2018/may/24/facebook-accused-of-conducting-mass-surveillance-through-its-apps (accessed 4 December 2021).

Caiani, M., and Graziani, P. (2018). 'Europeanisation and Social Movements: The Case of the Stop TTIP Campaign'. *European Journal of Political Research, 57*, 1031–1055.

Caiani, M., and Kroell, P. (2015). 'The Transnationalization of the Extreme Right and the Use of the Internet: International Journal of Comparative and Applied Criminal Justice'. *International Journal of Comparative and Applied Criminal Justice, 39*(4), 331–351.

Cali, B. (ed.). (2009). *International Law for International Relations*. Oxford: Oxford University Press.

Campact. (2012). 'Eure Unterschriften fliegen mit zum klimagipfel' (5 December). https://blog.campact.de/2012/12/unsere-unterschriften-fliegen-mit-zum-klimagipfel/ (accessed 7 December 2021).

Cano, R. J. (2010). 'Actuable, una plataforma española para campañas ciudadanas 2.0'. *El País* (22 September). https://elpais.com/tecnologia/2010/09/22/actualidad/1285146062_850215.html (accessed 4 December 2021).

Carpenter, R. C. (2007a). 'Setting the Advocacy Agenda: Theorizing Issue Emergence and Nonemergence in Transnational Advocacy Networks'. *International Studies Quarterly*, *51*(1), 99–120.

Carpenter, R. C. (2007b). 'Studying Issue (Non)-Adoption in Transnational Advocacy Networks'. *International Organization*, *61*(03), 643–667.

Carty, V. (2011). 'Multi-Issue, Internet-Mediated Interest Organizations and Their Implications for US Politics: A Case of MoveOn.org'. *Social Movement Studies*, *10*(3), 265–282.

Castells, M. (2012). *Networks of Outrage and Hope*. Cambridge: Polity Press.

Chadwick, A. (2007). 'Digital Network Repertoires and Organizational Hybridity: Political Communication'. *Political Communications*, *24*(3), 283–301.

Chadwick, A., and Dennis, J. (2016). 'Social Media, Professional Media and Mobilisation in Contemporary Britain: Explaining the Strengths and Weaknesses of the Citizens' Movement 38 Degrees'. *Political Studies*, *65*(1), 42–60.

Chalmers, A., and Shotton, P. A. (2015). 'Changing the Face of Advocacy? Explaining Interest Organizations' Use of Social Media Strategies'. *Political Communication*, *33*(3), 374–391.

Cheon, A., and Urpelainnen, J. (2018). *Activism and the Fossil Fuel Industry*. Abingdon: Routledge.

Civic Space Watch. (2019). 'Germany: ATTAC Ruling Could Affect a Thousand Organisations—Interview with Coalition for Legal Certainty for Political Advocacy' (29 April). http://civicspacewatch.eu/germany-attac-ruling-could-affect-a-thousand-organisations-interview-with-coalition-for-legal-certainty-for-political-advocacy/.

Coggan, M. (2019). 'GetUp Foreign Donation Questioned'. *Probono Australia* (14 January). https://probonoaustralia.com.au/news/2019/01/getup-foreign-donation-questioned/ (accessed 4 December 2021).

Connolly, K. (2019). '"I Feel Fine"': Merkel Dismisses Health Fears after Shaking Bouts'. *The Guardian* (19 July). http://www.theguardian.com/world/2019/jul/19/angela-merkel-dismisses-health-fears-shaking-bouts-donald-trump (accessed 4 December 2021).

Cooley, A., and Nexon, D. (2020). *Exit from Hegemony: The Unraveling of the American Global Order*. Oxford: Oxford University Press.

Copland, S. (2019). 'Anti-Politics and Global Climate Inaction: The Case of the Australian Carbon Tax'. *Critical Sociology*. *46* (5), 623–642.

Crowe, D. (2019). 'Our Approach Is to Remove the Hard Right": GetUp Raises $12 Million in Effort to Oust Conservatives'. (15 April). https://www.smh.com.au/federal-election-2019/our-approach-is-to-remove-the-hard-right-getup-raises-12m-in-effort-to-oust-conservatives-20190414-p51e3c.html (accessed 4 December 2021).

Curran, G. (2020). 'Divestment, Energy Incumbency and the Global Political Economy of Energy Transition: The Case of Adani's Carmichael Mine in Australia'. *Climate Policy*, *20*(8), 949–962.

Dathan, M. (2015). 'Cameron finally breaks silence on refugee crisis—But he still won't take more'. *The Independent*. (3 September) http://www.independent.co.uk/news/uk/politics/aylan-kurdi-david-cameron-says-he-felt-deeply-moved-by-images-of-dead-syrian-boy-but-gives-no-10484641.html

David, M. (2018). 'The Role of Organized Publics in Articulating the Exnovation of Fossil-Fuel Technologies for Intra- and Intergenerational Energy Justice in Energy Transitions'. *Applied Energy*, *228*, 339–350.

Davies, A. (2019). 'Australian Election: Tony Abbott Loses His Warringah Seat to Zali Steggall'. *The Guardian* (8 May). https://www.theguardian.com/global/2019/may/18/australian-election-tony-abbott-loses-his-warringah-seat-to-zali-steggall (accessed 4 December 2021).

Davies, C. (2017). 'Why Suspicion Remains over Polish President's Veto of Contentious Laws'. *The Guardian* (25 July). http://www.theguardian.com/world/2017/jul/25/why-suspicion-remains-over-polish-presidents-veto-of-contentious-laws (accessed 4 December 2021).

Davies, C. (2018). 'Hostile Takeover: How Law and Justice Captured Poland's Courts'. Freedom House. https://freedomhouse.org/report/analytical-brief/2018/hostile-takeover-how-law-and-justice-captured-polands-courts (accessed 4 December 2021).

Davies, D. (2014). '38 Degrees: A Truly "Independent" Campaign Group?' (17 March). https://www.david-davies.org.uk/news/38-degrees-truly-independent-campaign-group (accessed 4 December 2021).

Delegation of the EU to the Central African Republic. (2016). 'Federica Mogherini Discusses Syria in the Margins of OSCE Ministerial Council' (8 December). https://eeas.europa.eu/delegations/central-african-republic/16778/federica-mogherini-discusses-syria-margins-osce-ministerial-council_mk (accessed 6 December 2021).

della Porta, D. (ed.) (2010). *Solidarity Mobilizations in the 'Refugee Crisis': Contentious Moves*. London: Palgrave Macmillan UK.

della Porta, D., and Kriesi, H. (1999). 'Social Movements in a Globalizing World: An Introduction'. In D. della Porta, H. Kriesi, and D. Rucht (eds), *Social Movements in a Globalizing World* (pp. 3–22). London: Palgrave Macmillan UK.

Dellmuth, L. M., and Bloodgood, E. A. (2019). 'Advocacy Group Effects in Global Governance: Populations, Strategies, and Political Opportunity Structures'. *Interest Groups & Advocacy*, *8*(3), 255–269.

Dellmuth, L., and Tallberg, J. (2017). 'Advocacy Strategies in Global Governance: Inside versus Outside Lobbying'. *Political Studies*, *65*(3), 705–723.

Dennis, J. (2019). *Beyond Slacktivism—Political Participation on Social Media*. London: Palgrave McMillan.

Dennis, J. (2020). 'A Party within a Party Posing as a Movement? Momentum as a Movement Faction'. *Journal of Information Technology & Politics*, *17*(2), 97–113.

Dennis, J., and Hall, N. (2020). 'Innovation and Adaptation in Advocacy Organizations throughout the Digital Eras'. *Journal of Information Technology & Politics*, *17*(2), 79–86.

Die Presse. (2016). 'OSZE-Treffen: Wenig Hoffnung in Syrien, keine in der Ukraine' (8 December). https://diepresse.com/home/ausland/aussenpolitik/5131340/OSZE-Treffen-Wenig-Hoffnung-in-Syrien-keine-in-der-Ukraine (accessed 6 December 2021).

Die Taz. (2015). 'Deutschlands größte Demo seit Jahren: Hunderttausende gegen TTIP–taz.de'. *Die Taz* (10 October). https://taz.de/Deutschlands-groesste-Demo-seit-Jahren/!5240720/ (accessed 4 December 2021).

Die Zeit. (2016). 'Handel: Polizei: Wenig Zulauf bei Demos gegen TTIP und Ceta|ZEIT ONLINE'. *Die Zeit Online* (17 September). https://www.zeit.de/news/2016-09/17/handel-polizei-wenig-zulauf-bei-demos-gegen-ttipund-ceta-17140803 (accessed 4 December 2021).

Dominus, S. (2010). 'In Downturn, an Upside: Generosity'. *New York Times* (9 January). https://www.nytimes.com/2010/01/09/nyregion/09bigcity.html (accessed 4 December 2021).

Eavis, P., and Lohr, S. (2020). 'Big Tech's Domination of Business Reaches New Heights'. *New York Times* (19 August). https://www.nytimes.com/2020/08/19/technology/big-tech-business-domination.html (accessed 4 December 2021).

Eilstrup-Sangiovanni, M. (2019). 'Competition and Strategic Differentiation among Transnational Advocacy Groups'. *Journal of Interest Groups and Advocacy*, *8*(3), 376–406.

Eilstrup-Sangiovanni, M., and Bondaroff, T. N. P. (2014). 'From Advocacy to Confrontation: Direct Enforcement by Environmental NGOs'. *International Studies Quarterly*, *58*(2), 348–361.

Eliasson, L. J. (2019). 'Transatlantic Trade Negotiations, Civil Society Campaigns and Public Opinion'. Chapter 27 In D. Dialer and M. Richter (eds). *Lobbying in the EU, Strategies, Dynamics and Trends*. Cham: Springer, 375–288.

Eliasson, L. J., and García-Duran, P. (2017). 'Why TTIP Is an Unprecedented Geopolitical Game-Changer, but Not a Polanyian Moment'. *Journal of European Public Policy*, *24*(10), 1522–1533.

Eliasson, L. J., and Huet, P. G.-D. (2018). 'TTIP Negotiations: Interest Groups, Anti-TTIP Civil Society Campaigns and Public Opinion'. *Journal of Transatlantic Studies*, *16*(2), 101–116.

Ellis-Petersen, H., and Doherty, B. (2020). 'Amnesty to Halt Work in India Due to Government "Witch-Hunt"'. *The Guardian* (29 September). http://www.theguardian.com/world/2020/sep/29/amnesty-to-halt-work-in-india-due-to-government-witch-hunt (accessed 4 December 2021).

Euractiv. (2015). 'Anti-TTIP Petition Signed by 3 Million People'. *EURACTIV.com* (9 November). https://www.euractiv.com/section/agriculture-food/news/anti-ttip-petition-signed-by-3-million-people/ (accessed 7 December 2021).

Euractiv. (2016). 'Germany's Gabriel Gets SPD Green Light to Support CETA'. *EURACTIV.com* (20 September). https://www.euractiv.com/section/trade-society/news/germanys-gabriel-gets-spd-green-light-to-support-ceta/ (accessed 4 December 2021).

European Commission. (2013). 'Statement from United States President Barack Obama, European Council President Herman Van Rompuy and European Commission President José Manuel Barroso' (13 February). https://ec.europa.eu/commission/presscorner/detail/en/MEMO_13_94 (accessed 4 December 2021).

European Commission. (2016). 'EU–Canada Summit: Newly Signed Trade Agreement Sets High Standards for Global Trade' (30 October). https://ec.europa.eu/commission/presscorner/detail/en/IP_16_3581 (accessed 4 December 2021).

Farrell, H. (2012). 'The Consequences of the Internet for Politics'. *Annual Review of Political Science*, *15*(1), 35–52. https://doi.org/10.1146/annurev-polisci-030810-110815.

Farrell, H., and Han, H. (2020). 'Public Governance and Global Politics after COVID-19'. In H. Brands and F. Gavin (eds), *COVID-19 and World Order*. Baltimore, MD: Johns Hopkins University Press, 238–258.

Farrell, P., Evershed, N., & Davidson, H. (2016). 'The Nauru files: Cache of 2,000 leaked reports reveal scale of abuse of children in Australian offshore detention'. *The Guardian*. (10 August) https://www.theguardian.com/australia-news/2016/aug/10/the-nauru-files-2000-leaked-reports-reveal-scale-of-abuse-of-children-in-australian-offshore-detention

Fernyhough, J. (2021). 'Adani Strikes Carmichael Coal, But Does the World Even Want It?' *RenewEconomy* (25 June). https://reneweconomy.com.au/adani-strikes-carmichael-coal-but-does-the-world-even-want-it/ (accessed 4 December 2021).

Finnemore, M., and Sikkink, K. (1998). 'International Norm Dynamics and Political Change'. *International Organization, 52*(4), 887–917.

Fisher, D. R. (2004). *National Governance and the Global Climate Change Regime*. Latham, MD: Rowman & Littlefield.

Fisher, D. R. (2010). 'COP-15 in Copenhagen: How the Merging of Movements Left Civil Society Out in the Cold'. *Global Environmental Politics, 10*(2), 11–17.

Fisher, D. R. (2019a). 'The Broader Importance of #FridaysForFuture'. *Nature Climate Change, 9*(6), 430–431.

Fisher, D. R. (2019b). *American Resistance: From the Women's March to the Blue Wave*. New York: Columbia University Press.

Fisher, D. R., and Nasrin, S. (2021). 'Shifting Coalitions within the Youth Climate Movement in the US'. *Politics and Governance, 9*(2), 112–123.

Flamant, A. (2015). 'TTIP: Lobby or Not Lobby?'. *The Atavist* (7 April). https://albaneflamant.atavist.com/ttiplobbying (accessed 4 December 2021).

Fraussen, B., and Halpin, D. (2017). 'How Do Interest Groups Legitimate Their Policy Advocacy? Reconsidering Linkage and Internal Democracy in Times of Digital Disruption'. *Public Administration, 96*(1), 23–35.

Freelon, D., Marwick, A., and Kreiss, D. (2020). 'False Equivalencies: Online Activism from Left to Right'. *Science, 369*(6508), 1197–1201.

Froio, C., and Ganesh, B. (2019). 'The Transnationalisation of Far Right Discourse on Twitter'. *European Societies, 21*(4), 513–539.

Fung, A., Russon Gilman, H., and Shkabatur, J. (2013). 'Six Models for the Internet + Politics'. *International Studies Review, 15*(1), 30–47.

GetUp. (2017). 'Bring David Hicks Home'. https://www.getup.org.au/campaigns/bring-david-hicks-home (accessed 6 December 2021).

GetUp. (2018). 'GetUp Members Decide 2018 Agenda'. (1 April). https://www.getup.org.au/media/releases/2018/04/getup-members-decide-2018-agenda/ (accessed 4 December 2021).

Gerbaudo, P. (2012). *Tweets on the Streets: Social Media and Contemporary Activism*. London: Pluto Press.

Gerbaudo, P. (2018). *The Digital Party*. London: Pluto Press.

Germain, R. D., and Kenny, M. (1998). 'Engaging Gramsci: International Relations Theory and the New Gramscians'. *Review of International Studies, 24*(1), 3–21.

GetUp. (2017). 'Bring David Hicks Home'. https://www.getup.org.au/campaigns/bring-david-hicks-home (accessed 5 December 2021).

Gheyle, N. (2020). 'Huddle Up! Exploring Domestic Coalition Formation Dynamics in the Differentiated Politicization of TTIP'. *Politics and Governance, 8*(1), 301–311.

Gheyle, N., and De Ville, F. (2019). 'Outside Lobbying and the Politicization of the Transatlantic Trade and Investment Partnership'. In D. Dialer and M. Ricther (eds) *Lobbying in the European Union, Strategies, Dynamics and Trends*. Cham: Springer, 339–354.

Gibson, R. K. (2015). 'Party Change, Social Media and the Rise of 'Citizen-Initiated' Campaigning'. *Party Politics, 21*(2), 183–197.

Gladwell, M. (2010). 'Small Change: Why the Revolution Will Not Be Tweeted'. *The New Yorker* (27 September). http://www.newyorker.com/magazine/2010/10/04/small-change-malcolm-gladwell (accessed 4 December 2021).

Globe Editorial. (2017). 'Close the Loophole for Foreign Money in Canadian Elections'. *Globe and Mail* (24 May). https://www.theglobeandmail.com/opinion/editorials/globe-editorial-close-the-loophole-for-foreign-money-in-canadian-elections/article35107782/ (accessed 4 December 2021).

Goodwin-Gill, G., and McAdam, J. (2018). 'Nothing Surrendered But Much to Be Gained from UN Migration Pact'. *Sydney Morning Herald* (27 November). https://www.smh.com.au/national/nothing-surrendered-but-much-to-be-gained-from-un-migration-pact-20181126-p50if5.html (accessed 4 December 2021).

Gordenker, L., and Weiss, T. G. (1995). 'Pluralising Global Governance: Analytical Approaches and Dimensions'. *Third World Quarterly*, *16*(3), 357–387.

Graeber, D. (2014). *Direct Action* Oakland: AK Press.

Graham-Harrison, E. (2019). 'Greta Thunberg Takes Climate Fight to Germany's Threatened Hambach Forest'. *The Guardian*, Environment (10 August). https://www.theguardian.com/environment/2019/aug/10/greta-thunberg-climate-change-fight-germany-hambach-forest (accessed 4 December 2021).

Graham-Harrison, E., and Cadwalladr, C. (2018). 'Revealed: 50 Million Facebook Profiles Harvested for Cambridge Analytica in Major Data Breach'. *The Guardian* (17 March). http://www.theguardian.com/news/2018/mar/17/cambridge-analytica-facebook-influence-us-election (accessed 4 December 2021).

Green, D. (2016). *How Change Happens*. Oxford: Oxford University Press.

Greenpeace. (2018). 'The Framework: A Summary'. https://www.greenpeace.org/static/planet4-international-stateless/2018/12/22cf06f9-framework-summary.pdf (accessed 4 December 2021).

Gründinger, W. (2017a). 'Actors and Institutions'. In W. Gründinger (ed.), *Drivers of Energy Transition: How Interest Groups Influenced Energy Politics in Germany* (pp. 95–140). Wiesbaden: Springer Fachmedien.

Gründinger, W. (2017b). 'Introduction: What Drives the Energiewende?'. In W. Gründinger (ed.), *Drivers of Energy Transition: How Interest Groups Influenced Energy Politics in Germany* (pp. 11–40). Wiesbaden: Springer Fachmedien.

Gulbrandsen, L. H., and Andresen, S. (2004). 'NGO Influence in the Implementation of the Kyoto Protocol: Compliance, Flexibility Mechanisms, and Sinks'. *Global Environmental Politics*, *4*(4), 54–75.

Haas, E. (1990). *When Knowledge is Power*. Berkeley, CA: University of California Press.

Haas, P. M. (1992). 'Introduction: Epistemic Communities and International Policy Coordination'. *International Organization*, *46*(1), 1–35.

Hadden, J. (2015). *Networks in Contention*. Cambridge: Cambridge University Press.

Hadden, J., and Bush, S. S. (2020). 'What's Different About the Environment? Environmental INGOs in Comparative Perspective'. *Environmental Politics*, *30*(1–2), 202–223.

Hadden, J., and Jasny, L. (2017). 'The Power of Peers: How Transnational Advocacy Networks Shape NGO Strategies on Climate Change'. *British Journal of Political Science*, *49*(2), 637–659.

Hafner-Burton, E. M., Kahler, M., and Montgomery, A. H. (2009). 'Network Analysis for International Relations'. *International Organization*, *63*(3), 559–592.

Hale, T. (2020). 'Transnational Actors and Transnational Governance in Global Environmental Politics'. *Annual Review of Political Science*, *23*(1), 203–220.

Hall, N. (2009). 'East Timorese Women Challenge Domestic Violence'. *Australian Journal of Political Science*, *44*(2), 309–325.

Hall, N. (2016). *Displacement, Development, and Climate Change: International Organizations Moving beyond Their Mandates*. Abingdon: Routledge.

Hall, N. (2017a). 'Innovations in Activism in the Digital Era: Campaigning for Refugee Rights in 2015–2016'. In Helmut K. Anheier (ed) *The Governance Report 2017*,

Democracy, Innovations, Participation, Legitimacy, Indicators (pp. 143–156). Oxford: Oxford University Press.

Hall, N. (2017b). People Power, Populism and the Internet. *Global Policy* (11 July). https://www.globalpolicyjournal.com/blog/11/07/2017/people-power-populism-and-internet (accessed 4 December 2021).

Hall, N. (2018). 'Why Is National Joining the Nationalists?'. *Newsroom* (14 December). https://www.newsroom.co.nz/page/why-is-national-joining-the-nationalists.

Hall, N. (2019a). 'When Do Refugees Matter? The Importance of Issue Salience for Digital Advocacy Organizations'. *Journal of Interest Groups and Advocacy*, *8*(3), 333–355.

Hall, N. (2019b). 'Norm Contestation in the Digital Era: Campaigning for Refugee Rights'. *International Affairs*, *95*(3), 575–595.

Hall, N., and Ireland, P. (2016). 'Transforming Activism: Digital Era Advocacy Organizations'. *Stanford Social Innovation Review (SSIR)* (6 July). http://ssir.org/articles/entry/transforming_activism_digital_era_advocacy_organizations (accessed 4 December 2021).

Hall, N., and Persson, A. (2018). 'Global Climate Adaptation Governance: Why Is It Not Legally Binding?' *European Journal of International Relations*, *24*(3), 540–566.

Hall, N., Schmitz, H. P., and Dedmon, J. M. (2020). 'Transnational Advocacy and NGOs in the Digital Era: New Forms of Networked Power'. *International Studies Quarterly*, *64*(1), 159–167.

Hall, N. (forthcoming). 'Sticking to the State? Transnational Advocacy Networks in the Digital Era', Chapter in C. Bjola and M. Kornprobst, *Digital International Relations*. Cambridge: Cambridge University Press.

Halpin, D. R., Fraussen, B., and Nownes, A. J. (2018). 'The Balancing Act of Establishing a Policy Agenda: Conceptualizing and Measuring Drivers of Issue Prioritization within Interest Groups'. *Governance*, *31*(2), 215–237.

Han, H. (2014). *How Organizations Develop Activists: Civic Associations and Leadership in the 21st Century*. Oxford: Oxford University Press.

Han, H., McKenna, E., and Oyakawa, M. (2021). *Prisms of the People*. Chicago, IL: University of Chicago Press.

Hanegraaff, M., Beyers, J., and Bruycker, I. D. (2016). 'Balancing Inside and Outside Lobbying: The Political Strategies of Lobbyists at Global Diplomatic Conferences'. *European Journal of Political Research*, *55*(3), 568–588.

Hasham, N. (2018). 'Adani Announces Coal Mine Construction Will Begin'. *Sydney Morning Herald* (29 November). https://www.smh.com.au/politics/federal/adani-announces-coal-mine-construction-will-begin-20181129-p50j69.html (accessed 4 December 2021).

Hasham, N. (2019). 'New GetUp Poll Shows Crash in Support for Tony Abbott in Warringah'. *Sydney Morning Herald* (5 May). https://www.smh.com.au/politics/federal/new-getup-poll-shows-crash-in-support-for-tony-abbott-in-warringah-20190504-p51k3q.html (accessed 4 December 2021).

Hayes, C. (2008). 'MoveOn Is Not What You Think It Is'. *AlternNet* (28 July). https://www.alternet.org/2008/07/moveon_is_not_what_you_think_it_is/ (accessed 4 December 2021).

Heaney, M. T., and Rojas, F. (2007). 'Partisans, Nonpartisans, and the Antiwar Movement in the United States'. *American Politics Research*, *35*(4), 431–464.

Heft, A., Mayerhöffer, E., Reinhardt, S., and Knüpfer, C. (2020). 'Beyond Breitbart: Comparing Right-Wing Digital News Infrastructures in Six Western Democracies'. *Policy & Internet*, *12*(1), 20–45.

Heimans, J., and Timms, H. (2018). *New Power: How Power Works in Our Hyperconnected World*. New York: Random House.

Hestres, L. E. (2015). 'Climate Change Advocacy Online: Theories of Change, Target Audiences, and Online Strategy'. *Environmental Politics*, *24*(2), 193–211.

Hopgood, S. (2006). *Keepers of the Flame: Understanding Amnesty International*. Ithaca, NY: Cornell University Press.

Horstink, L. (2017). 'Online Participation and the New Global Democracy: Avaaz, a Case Study'. *Global Society*, *31*(1), 101–124.

Howard, P. N. (2015). *Pax Technica*. New Haven, CT: Yale University Press.

Ingoe, M. (2020). 'A Fight for Our Future'. In T. Doig (ed.), *Living with the Climate Crisis*. Wellington: Bridget Williams Books, 12–20.

Ireland, P., and Clausen, D. (2019). '27—Local Action That Changes the World: Fresh Perspectives on Climate Change Mitigation and Adaptation from Australia'. In T. M. Letcher (ed.), *Managing Global Warming* (pp. 769–782). London: Academic Press.

Johnson, T. (2020). 'Ordinary Patterns in an Extraordinary Crisis: How International Relations Makes Sense of the COVID-19 Pandemic'. *International Organization*, *74*(S1), E148–E168.

Jordan, G., and Maloney, W. A. (1998). 'Manipulating Membership: Supply-Side Influences on Group Size'. *British Journal of Political Science*, *28*(2), 389–409.

Juris, J. S. (2005). 'The New Digital Media and Activist Networking within Anti-Corporate Globalization Movements'. *Annals of the American Academy of Political and Social Science*, *597*, 189–208.

Jurkovich, M. (2020). *Feeding the Hungry*. Ithaca, NY: Cornell University Press.

Kahler, M. (ed.). (2009). *Networked Politics, Agency, Power, and Governance*. Ithaca, NY: Cornell University Press.

Kanter, J. (2015). 'In Germany, Grass-Roots Opposition to a European–U.S. Trade Deal'. *New York Times* (9 June). https://www.nytimes.com/2015/06/10/business/international/transatlantic-trade-deal-pact-europe-eu-us-germany.html (accessed 4 December 2021).

Kaplan, S. (2019). 'The Foot Soldiers of the New Environmental Movement'. *Washington Post* (20 April). https://www.washingtonpost.com/national/energy-environment/the-foot-soldiers-of-the-new-environmental-movement/2020/04/20/6bc98c72-41e4-11ea-aa6a-083d01b3ed18_story.html (accessed 4 December 2021).

Karp, P. (2017a). 'GetUp to Launch Marriage Equality Campaign Tool after Electoral Rolls Close'. *The Guardian* (23 August). http://www.theguardian.com/australia-news/2017/aug/24/getup-to-launch-marriage-equality-campaign-tool-after-electoral-rolls-close (accessed 4 December 2021).

Karp, P. (2017b). 'The Maths of Marriage Equality: How the Yes Campaign Plans to Win 5.5m Votes'. *The Guardian* (29 August). http://www.theguardian.com/australia-news/2017/aug/29/the-maths-of-marriage-equality-inside-the-yes-campaigns-plan-to-win-55m-votes (accessed 4 December 2021).

Karp, P. (2017c). 'Marriage Equality Activists Collect 55,000-Signature Petition for Free Vote'. *The Guardian* (11 September). http://www.theguardian.com/australia-news/2016/sep/12/marriage-equality-activists-collect-55000-signature-petition-for-free-vote (accessed 4 December 2021).

Karpf, D. (2012). *The MoveOn Effect: The Unexpected Transformation of American Political Advocacy*. New York: Oxford University Press.

Karpf, D. (2013). 'Netroots Goes Global'. *The Nation* (16 October). https://www.thenation.com/article/netroots-goes-global/ (accessed 4 December 2021).

Karpf, D. (2016). *Analytic Activism*. New York: Oxford University Press.

Karpf, D. (2020). 'Two Provocations for the Study of Digital Politics in Time'. *Journal of Information Technology & Politics*, *17*(2), 87–96.

Kay, T., and Evans, R. L. (2018). *Trade Battles: Activism and the Politicization of International Trade Policy*. Oxford: Oxford University Press.

Keck, M. E., and Sikkink, K. (1998). *Activists beyond Borders: Advocacy Networks in International Politics*. Ithaca, NY: Cornell University Press.

Khagram, S., V., R., James, & Sikkink, K. (2002). *Restructuring World Politics: Transnational Social Movements, Networks, and Norms*. Minneapolis: University of Minnesota Press.

Kleres, J. (2018). 'Emotions in the Crisis: Mobilising for Refugees in Germany and Sweden'. In D. Della Porta (ed), *Solidarity Mobilizations in the 'Refugee Crisis': Contentious Moves*. London: Palgrave McMillan, 209 – 241.

Kolb, F. (2005). 'The Impact of Transnational Protest on Social Movement Organizations: Mass Media and the Making of ATTAC Germany'. In D. Della Porta and S. Tarrow (eds). *Transnational Protest and Global Activism* (pp. 95–120). Oxford: Rowman & Littlefield.

Krause, V. (2017a). 'Re—Leadnow Society'. Letter to Mr Yves Côté, QC, Commissioner of Canada Elections (24 May). https://fairquestions.typepad.com/files/letter-canada-elections-24may2017-final.pdf (accessed 4 December 2021).

Krause, V. (2017b). 'Who Is Leadnow?' Report submitted to Canada elections (31 May).

Krause, V. (2019). 'Canadian Election 2019: Obama Wasn't the Only American Interfering'. *Financial Post* (22 October). https://financialpost.com/opinion/vivian-krause-obama-wasnt-the-only-american-interfering-in-the-canadian-election (accessed 4 December 2021).

Kreiss, D. (2016). *Prototype Politics, Technology Intensive Campaigning and the Data of Democracy*. New York: Oxford University Press.

Krook, M. L., and True, J. (2010). 'Rethinking the Life Cycles of International Norms: The United Nations and the Global Promotion of Gender Equality'. *European Journal of International Relations*, *18*(1), 103–127.

Lajčák. M. (2019). 'Keynote Lecture'. Tufts University, EPIIC Symposium (8 March).

Lake, D. A., Martin, L. L., and Risse, T. (2021). 'Challenges to the Liberal Order: Reflections on International Organization'. *International Organization*, *75*(2), 225–257.

Lake, D. G., and Wong, W. (2009). 'The Politics of Networks: Interests, Power, and Human Rights Norms'. In M. Kahler (ed.) *Networked Politics: Agency, Power, and Governance*. Ithaca, NY: Cornell University Press, 127–150.

Lavelle, K. C. (2020). *Challenges of Multilateralism*. New Haven, CT: Yale University Press.

Leadnow. (2015). 'Defeating Harper: Reflections on the Vote Together Campaign'. (December). http://www.votetogether.ca/report (accessed 29 January 2022)

Lis, J. (2019). 'Israeli NGO Cancels Plan to Transport Bedouin Voters to Polls on Election Day'. *Haaretz*. https://www.haaretz.com/israel-news/.premium-israeli-ngo-cancels-plan-to-transport-bedouins-to-polls-on-election-day-1.7845806 (accessed 4 December 2021).

Lorde, A. (1984). *Sister Outsider*. London: Penguin Press.

Lowles, N., and Ryan, N. (eds). (2021). *State of Hate 2021, Backlash, Conspiracies and Confrontation*. London: Hope Not Hate Ltd.

McSwiney, J., Vaughan, M., Heft, A., & Hoffmann, M. (2021). Sharing the hate? Memes and transnationality in the far right's digital visual culture. *Information, Communication & Society*, *24*(16), 2502–2521.

Maley, J. (2019). 'Is Tony Abbott Really Being Helped by Advance Australia's Captain GetUp?' *Sydney Morning Herald* (14 April). https://www.smh.com.au/politics/federal/is-captain-getup-a-help-or-a-hindrance-to-tony-abbott-20190412-p51dml.html (4 December 2021).

Maley, J., and Hunter, F. (2019). 'Federal Election 2019: Former PM Tony Abbott Has Lost the Seat of Warringah to Independent Zali Steggall'. *Canberra Times* (18 May). https://www.canberratimes.com.au/story/6131677/former-pm-tony-abbott-has-lost-the-seat-of-warringah/digital-subscription/ (4 December 2021).

Maltby, H. (2017). 'Vote Registration Drive Update'. 38 Degrees (25 May). https://home.38degrees.org.uk/2017/05/25/voter-registration-drive-update/.

Manjoo, F. (2016). 'Tech's 'Frightful 5' Will Dominate Digital Life for Foreseeable Future'. *New York Times* (20 January). https://www.nytimes.com/2016/01/21/technology/techs-frightful-5-will-dominate-digital-life-for-foreseeable-future.html (accessed 4 December 2021).

Margetts, H., John, P., Hale, S., and Yasseri, T. (2015). *Political Turbulence: How Social Media Shape Collective Action*. Princeton, NJ: Princeton University Press.

Marquart, M., and Kaiser, S. (2014). 'Deutsche Bank wegen Kohleprojekt in Australien am Pranger'. *Der Spiegel* (20 May). https://www.spiegel.de/wirtschaft/unternehmen/deutsche-bank-wegen-kohleprojekt-in-australien-am-pranger-a-970477.html (accessed 4 December 2021).

Mason, R. (2014). 'Ukip Vows to Slash Immigration and Cut Taxes in Pitch for Blue-Collar Vote'. *The Guardian* (26 September). https://www.theguardian.com/politics/2014/sep/26/nigel-farage-ukip-conference-tax-cuts (accessed 4 December 2021).

McGhee, A. (2018). 'What is Advance Australia, the New Conservative Lobby Group Taking on Get Up!' *ABC News* (21 November). https://www.abc.net.au/news/2018-11-21/what-is-advance-australia/10520122 (4 December 2021).

McKeon, N. (2017). 'Transforming Global Governance in the Post-2015 Era: Towards an Equitable and Sustainable World'. *Globalizations, 14*(4), 487–503.

McKibben, B. (2014). 'A Call to Arms: An Invitation to Demand Action on Climate Change'. *RollingStone* (21 May). https://www.rollingstone.com/politics/politics-news/a-call-to-arms-an-invitation-to-demand-action-on-climate-change-92885/ (accessed 4 December 2021).

Medie, P. A. (2020). *Global Norms and Local Action: The Campaigns to End Violence against Women in Africa*. Oxford: Oxford University Press.

Mercea, D., and Bastos, M. T. (2016). 'Being a Serial Transnational Activist'. *Journal of Computer-Mediated Communication, 21*(2), 140–155.

Meredith, S. (2019). 'The UK Wants a US Trade Deal—But It's Not So Sure about "Chlorinated Chicken"'. *CNBC* (13 June). https://www.cnbc.com/2019/06/13/chlorinated-chicken-poultry-threat-to-us-uk-trade-deal-post-brexit.html (accessed 4 December 2021).

Merica, D. (2017). 'Trump: "Both Sides" to Blame for Charlottesville'. *CNN* (16 August). https://www.cnn.com/2017/08/15/politics/trump-charlottesville-delay/index.html (accessed 4 December 2021).

Merkel, W. (2017). 'The Limits of Democratic Innovations in Established Democracies'. In H. Anheier (ed) *The Governance Report 2017: Democracy and Innovation*. Oxford: Oxford University Press, 11–126.

Milan, C. (2018). 'Emotions that Mobilise: The Emotional Basis of Pro-Asylum Seeker Activism in Austria'. In D. Della Porta (ed). *Solidarity Mobilizations in the 'Refugee Crisis': Contentious Moves*. London: Palgrave Macmillan, 183–2018.

Milan, S. (2013). *Social Movements and their Technologies*. London: Palgrave McMillan.

Miller, M. (2010). 'Alinsky for the Left: The Politics of Community Organizing'. *Dissent Magazine* (Winter). https://www.dissentmagazine.org/article/alinsky-for-the-left-the-politics-of-community-organizing (accessed 4 December 2021).

Milman, O. (2014). 'US Banks Vow Not to Fund Great Barrier Reef Coal Port, Say Activists'. *The Guardian* (28 October). http://www.theguardian.com/environment/2014/oct/28/us-banks-vow-not-to-fund-great-barrier-reef-coal-port-say-activists (accessed 4 December 2021).

Mishra, P. (2018). 'The Mask It Wears'. *London Review of Books* (21 June), 9–13.

Mitchell, G. E., and Schmitz, H. P. (2014). 'Principled Instrumentalism: A Theory of Transnational NGO Behaviour'. *Review of International Studies*, *40*(3), 487–504.

Mitchell, G. E., Schmitz, H. P., and Vijfeijken, T. B. (2020). *Between Power and Irrelevance: The Future of Transnational NGOs*. New York: Oxford University Press.

Mittelman, M., Kaplan, J., Cao, J., and Colby, L. (2017). 'Behind CEOs' Trump Rift, Frantic Hours of Calls, Calculation'. *Bloomberg* (17 August). https://www.bloombergquint.com/business/behind-ceo-s-trump-rift-48-frantic-hours-of-calls-calculation (accessed 4 December 2021).

MobLab. (2017). 'Our Roots'. *MobLab*. https://mobilisationlab.org/about/our-roots/ (accessed 4 December 2021).

Mogus, J., and Liacas, T. (2016). 'Networked Change: How Progressive Campaigns Are Won in the 21st Century'. NetChange Consulting Report. https://netchange.co/networked-change (accessed 29 Jan 2022)

Moor, J. de. (2018). 'The 'Efficacy Dilemma' of Transnational Climate Activism: The Case of COP21'. *Environmental Politics*, *27*(6), 1079–1100.

Moor, J. de. (2020). 'Alternative Globalities? Climatization Processes and the Climate Movement beyond COPs'. *International Politics*, *58*, 582–599.

Moor, J. de, Vydt, M. D., Uba, K., and Wahlström, M. (2020). 'New Kids on the Block: Taking Stock of the Recent Cycle of Climate Activism'. *Social Movement Studies*, *20*(5), 619–625.

Moravcsik, A. (1997). 'Taking Preferences Seriously: A Liberal Theory of International Politics'. *International Organization*, *51*(04), 513–553. https://doi.org/10.1162/002081897550447.

Mouffe, C. (2019). *For a Left Populism*. London: Verso.

Muller, N. (2014). 'Australian Brings Reef Fight to Deutsche Bank'. Deutsche Welle (28 May). https://www.dw.com/en/australian-brings-reef-fight-to-deutsche-bank/a-17661812 (accessed 4 December 2021).

Murdie, A. (2014). 'The Ties That Bind: A Network Analysis of Human Rights International Nongovernmental Organizations'. *British Journal of Political Science*, *44*(1), 1–27.

Murdie, A., and Urpelainen, J. (2015). 'Why Pick on Us? Environmental INGOs and State Shaming as a Strategic Substitute'. *Political Studies*, *63*(2), 353–372.

Murphy, G., and Pfaff, S. (2005). 'Thinking Locally, Acting Globally? What the Seattle WTO Protests Tell Us about the Global Justice Movement'. *Political Power and Social Theory*, *17*, 151–176.

Murphy, K. (2016). 'Turnbull Government Launches Sweeping Inquiry into Donations'. *The Guardian* (14 September). https://www.theguardian.com/australia-news/2016/sep/15/turnbull-government-launches-sweeping-inquiry-into-donations (accessed 4 December 2021).

Narkowicz, K. (2018). '"Refugees Not Welcome Here": State, Church and Civil Society Responses to the Refugee Crisis in Poland'. *International Journal of Politics, Culture, and Society*, *31*(4), 357–373.

Narlikar, A. (2020). *Poverty Narratives and Power Paradoxes in International Trade Negotiations and Beyond*. Cambridge: Cambridge University Press.

Newell, P. (2008). 'Civil Society, Corporate Accountability and the Politics of Climate Change'. *Global Environmental Politics*, *8*(3), 122–153.

Nonprofit Tech for Good. (2019). 'Global NGO Tech Report 2019'. https://assets_global.website-files.com/5dbeb414117b673d211598f2/5de82e/550d3804cc13ddc75_2019_Tech-report-English.pdf (accessed 4 December 2021).

O'Connell Rapira, L. (2017). 'We Need to Talk about Drugs'. *Medium* (20 July). https://medium.com/@laura.or.rapira/we-need-to-talk-about-drugs-3382983c7e7e (accessed 7 December 2021).

Owen, T. (2015). *Disruptive Power, The Crisis of the State in the Digital Age*. Oxford: Oxford University Press.

Perlstein, R. (2012). 'The Long Con'. *The Baffler* (November). https://thebaffler.com/salvos/the-long-con (accessed 4 December 2021).

Price, M. (2017). *Engagement Organizing: The Old Art and New Science of Winning Campaigns*. Vancouver: UBC Press, On Point Press.

Price, R. (1998). 'Reversing the Gun Sights: Transnational Civil Society Targets Land Mines'. *International Organization*, *52*(3), 613–644.

Price, R. (2003). 'Transnational Civil Society and Advocacy in World Politics'. *World Politics*, *55*(4), 579–606.

Princen, T. (1995). 'Ivory, Conservation, and Environmental Transnational Coalitions—Bringing Transnational Relations Back In'. In T. Risse-Kappen (ed.), *Bringing Transnational Relations Back In* (pp. 227–254). Cambridge: Cambridge University Press.

Putnam, R. (2000). *Bowling Alone: The Collapse and Revival of American Community*. New York: Simon and Schuster.

Putnam, R. D. (1988). 'Diplomacy and Domestic Politics: The Logic of Two-Level Games'. *International Organization*, *42*(3), 427–460.

Quiggin, J. (2019). 'Adani's Carmichael Mine Is Unlikely to Go Ahead, and Most People Know It'. *The Guardian* (3 May). http://www.theguardian.com/commentisfree/2019/may/03/adanis-carmichael-mine-is-unlikely-to-go-ahead-and-most-people-know-it (accessed 4 December 2021).

Rankin, J. (2019). 'EU Court Rules Poland's Lowering of Judges' Retirement Age Is Unlawful'. *The Guardian* (24 June). http://www.theguardian.com/world/2019/jun/24/eu-court-rules-polands-lowering-of-judges-retirement-age-unlawful (accessed 4 December 2021).

Ratner, S. (2011). 'Law Promotion Beyond Law Talk: The Red Cross, Persuasion, and the Laws of War'. *European Journal of International Law*, *22*(2), 459–506.

RBB24. (2018). 'Tausend Menschen Protestieren gegen Migrationspakt'. *RBB24* (3 December).

Readfearn, G. (2020). 'Adani Coalmine: Siemens CEO Has "Empathy" for Environment But Refuses to Quit Contract'. *The Guardian* (13 January). http://www.theguardian.com/business/2020/jan/13/adani-coalmine-siemens-ceo-has-empathy-for-environment-but-will-honour-contract (accessed 4 December 2021).

Revesz, R. (2016). 'TTIP: More Than 130,000 People Urge Barack Obama to Kill Controversial Trade Deal during UK Visit'. *The Independent* (19 April). https://www.independent.co.uk/news/world/americas/ttip-more-than-130000-people-urge-barack-obama-to-kill-controversial-trade-deal-during-uk-visit-a6991286.html (accessed 4 December 2021).

Rogers, R. (2018). 'Otherwise Engaged: Social Media from Vanity Metrics to Critical Analytics'. *International Journal of Communication, 12*, 459–460.

Rother, S., and Steinhilper, E. (2019). 'Tokens or Stakeholders in Global Migration Governance? The Role of Affected Communities and Civil Society in the Global Compacts on Migration and Refugees'. *International Migration, 57*(6), 243–257.

Ruben, J. (2012). 'A Once-in-a-Generation Opportunity, and a Bottom-Up Revolution at MoveOn.org'. *HuffPost* (3 December). https://www.huffpost.com/entry/a-oncein-a-generation-opp_b_2233527 (accessed 4 December 2021).

Rucht, D. (1999). 'The Transnationalization of Social Movements: Trends, Causes, Problems'. In D. Della Porta, H. Kriesi and D. Rucht (eds). *Social Movements in a Globalizing World* (pp. 206–222). London: Palgrave Macmillan.

Rugg, S. (2019). *How Powerful We Are, Behind the Scenes with One of Australia's Leading Activists*. Sydney: Hachette Australia.

SBS News. (2019). 'Activists GetUp Ruled Independent of Parties by Electoral Commission'. *SBS News* (18 February). https://www.sbs.com.au/news/activists-getup-ruled-independent-of-parties-by-electoral-commission (accessed 4 December 2021).

Scholte, J. A. (1999). 'Global Civil Society: Changing the World?'. Centre for the Study of Globalisation and Regionalisation (CSGR) Working Papers Series, N. 31/99, University of Warwick.

Scholte, J. A. (2019). 'Civil Society and Global Governance: Exploring Transscalar Connections'. *Interest Groups & Advocacy, 8*(3), 490–498.

Schradie, J. (2018). 'The Digital Activism Gap: How Class and Costs Shape Online Collective Action'. *Social Problems, 65*(1), 51–74.

Schradie, J. (2019). *The Revolution That Wasn't*. Cambridge, MA: Harvard University Press.

Schumacher, C. (2018). 'Hamburg Für den Hambi'. *BUNDmagazin* (April), 5.

Secret Aid Woker. (2017). 'Secret Aid Worker: We Don't Take Data Protection of Vulnerable People Seriously'. *The Guardian* (13 June). http://www.theguardian.com/global-development-professionals-network/2017/jun/13/secret-aid-worker-we-dont-take-data-protection-of-vulnerable-people-seriously (accessed 4 December 2021).

Setzer, J., and Brynes, R. (2019). 'Global Trends in Climate Change Litigiation: 2019 Snapshot'. LSE, Grantham Research Institute, Columbia Law School, University of Leeds, Centre for Climate Change, Economics and Policy (July). https://www.lse.ac.uk/granthaminstitute/wp-content/uploads/2019/07/GRI_Global-trends-in-climate-change-litigation-2019-snapshot-2.pdf (accessed 4 December 2021).

Sheffield, H. (2018). 'The Platform Decentralising Tools That Help Workers Campaign for Better Rights'. *The Independent* (8 June). https://www.independent.co.uk/news/business/indyventure/trade-union-boohoo-amazon-uber-organise-campaigning-site-decentralising-collective-action-a8378816.html (accessed 4 December 2021).

Shirky, C. (2008). *Here Comes Everybody: The Power of Organizing without Organizations*. London: Allen Lane.

Sikkink, K. (2005). 'Patterns of Dynamic Multilevel Governance'. In *Transnational Protest and Global Activism*. Oxford: Rowman & Littlefield.

Sikkink, K. (2020). *Hidden Face of Rights*. New Haven, CT: Yale University Press.

Silberman, M. (2017). 'Five Years of Building People Power at Greenpeace'. *Mobilisation Lab* (17 February). https://mobilisationlab.org/burning-platform-building-people-power/ (accessed 4 December 2021).

Siles-Brügge, G. (2017). 'Transatlantic Investor Protection as a Threat to Democracy: The Potency and Limits of an Emotive Frame'. *Cambridge Review of International Affairs, 30*(5–6), 464–488.

Siles-Brügge, G., and Strange, M. (2020a). 'Municipal-Level Trade Contestation: Activists and Local Governments, from the Multilevel Agreement on Investment to the Transatlantic Trade and Investment Partnership'. In J. Broschek and P. Goff (eds), *Multilevel Trade Politics: Configurations, Dynamics, Mechanisms* (pp. 324–49). Toronto: University of Toronto Press.

Siles-Brügge, G., and Strange, M. (2020b). 'National Autonomy or Transnational Solidarity? Using Multiple Geographic Frames to Politicize EU Trade Policy'. *Politics and Governance*, *8*(1), 277–289.

Simmons, B. (2013). 'Preface: International Relationships in the Information Age'. *International Studies Review*, *15*, 1–4.

Simmons, B. A. (2014). 'The Future of the Human Rights Movement'. *Ethics & International Affairs; New York*, *28*(2), 183–196.

Simmons, B. A., and Goemans, H. E. (2021). 'Built on Borders: Tensions with the Institution Liberalism (Thought It) Left Behind'. *International Organization*, *75*(2), 387–410.

Skonieczny, A. (2018). Emotions and Political Narratives: Populism, Trump and Trade. *Politics and Governance*, *6*(4), 62–72. https://doi.org/10.17645/pag.v6i4.1574

Skonieczny, A. (2019). 'Populism and Trade: The 2016 US Presidential Election and the Death of the Trans-Pacific Partnership'. In F. Stengel, D. B. MacDonald, and D. Nabers (eds), *Populism and World Politics* (pp. 337–362). Verlag: Springer.

Slaughter, A.-M. (2004). 'Sovereignty and Power in a Networked World Order'. *Stanford Journal of International Law*, *40*, 283–327.

Slaughter, A.-M. (2009). 'America's Edge'. *Foreign Affairs* (January/February). https://www.foreignaffairs.com/articles/united-states/2009-01-01/americas-edge (accessed 4 December 2021).

Slaughter, A.-M. (2016). 'How to Succeed in the Networked World'. *Foreign Affairs* (November/December). https://www.foreignaffairs.com/articles/world/2016-10-04/how-succeed-networked-world (accessed 4 December 2021).

Snow, D. (2010). 'So Loudly They Cannot Be Ignored'. *Sydney Morning Herald* (19 June). https://www.smh.com.au/national/so-loudly-they-cannot-be-ignored-20100618-ymu5.html?skin.text-only (accessed 4 December 2021).

Speth, R. (2014). *Lobbying in Deutschland*. Berlin: Transparency International.

Spiro, P. J. (1995). 'New Global Communities: Nongovernmental Organizations in International Decision Making Institutions'. *The Washington Quarterly*, *18*(1), 45–56.

Sriskandarajah, D. (2017). 'Can INGOs Push Back against Closing Civic Space? Only If They Change Their Approach'. *Oxfam Blogs* (13 October). http://oxfamblogs.org/fp2p/can-ingos-push-back-against-closing-civic-space-only-if-they-change-their-approach/ (accessed 4 December 2021).

Stanton, J., Altin, V., Wells, L., & Sinmaz, E. (2015). 'Father of boys who washed up on a beach had tried to save them' *Mail Online*. (2 September) http://www.dailymail.co.uk/news/article-3219553/Terrible-fate-tiny-boy-symbolises-desperation-thousands-Body-drowned-Syrian-refugee-washed-Turkish-beach-family-tried-reach-Europe.html

Stephens, M. (2018). *Doing Our Bit: The Campaign to Double the Refugee Quota* (1st edn). Wellington: Bridget Williams Books.

Stiglitz, J. (2018). *Globalization and Its Discontents Revisited, Anti-Globalization in the Era of Trump*. New York: W.W. Norton and Company.

Stimmer, A. (2019). 'Beyond Internalization: Alternate Endings of the Norm Life Cycle'. *International Studies Quarterly*, *63*(2), 270–280.

Stone, J. (2016). 'TTIP Negotiations Should Stop, French Government Says'. *The Independent* (30 August). https://www.independent.co.uk/news/uk/politics/ttip-negotiations-should-stop-french-government-says-a7216366.html (accessed 4 December 2021).

Strange, M. (2015). 'Implications of TTIP for Transnational Social Movements and International NGOs'. In J.-F. Morin, T. Novotná, F. Ponjaert, and M. Telò (eds), *The Politics of Transatlantic Trade Negotiations: TTIP in a Globalized World* (pp. 81–92). Abingdon: Routledge.

Stroup, S. S. (2012). *Borders among Activists: International NGOs in the United States, Britain, and France*. Ithaca, NY: Cornell University Press.

Stroup, S. S., and Wong, W. (2018). 'The Agency and Authority of International NGOs'. *Perspectives on Politics, 14*(1), 138–143.

Stroup, S. S., and Wong, W. H. (2017). *The Authority Trap: Strategic Choices of International NGOs*. Ithaca, NY: Cornell University Press.

tagesschau.de. (2020). 'Kohleausstieg: Unternehmen erhalten Milliarden-Entschädigung'. *tagesschau.de* (updated 23 November 2021). https://www.tagesschau.de/wirtschaft/kohleausstieg-bund-laender-einigung-103.html (accessed 4 December 2021).

Sullivan, S. (2013) 'What is a 501(c) 4 anyway?', *The Washington Post*, 13 May https://www.washingtonpost.com/news/the-fix/wp/2013/05/13/what-is-a-501c4-anyway/ (accessed 18 January 2022)

Tallberg, J., Dellmuth, L. M., Agné, H., and Duit, A. (2015). 'NGO Influence in International Organizations: Information, Access and Exchange'. *British Journal of Political Science, 48*(1), 213–238.

Tarrow, S. (2005). *The New Transnational Activism*. Cambridge: Cambridge University Press.

Tarrow, S. (2010). 'Dynamics of Diffusion: Mechanisms, Institutions and Scale Shift'. In R. Kolins Givan and K. M. Roberts (eds), *The Diffusion of Social Movements, Actors, Mechanisms, and Political Effects* (pp. 204–220). Cornell University, Sarah A. Soule. Cambridge: Cambridge University Press.

Tarrow, S., and della Porta, D. (2005). 'Conclusion: "Globalization", Complex Internationalism and Transnational Cotention'. In D. della Porta and S. Tarrow (eds), *Transnational Protest and Global Activism* (pp. 227–246). Oxford: Rowman & Littlefield.

Tarrow, S., and McAdam, D. (2005). 'Scale Shift and Transnational Contention'. In D. della Porta and S. Tarrow (eds), *Transnational Protest and Global Activism* (pp. 121–150). Oxford: Rowman & Littlefield.

Taylor, M., Watts, J., and Bartlett, J. (2019). 'Climate Crisis: 6 Million People Join Latest Wave of Global Protests'. *The Guardian* (27 September). http://www.theguardian.com/environment/2019/sep/27/climate-crisis-6-million-people-join-latest-wave-of-worldwide-protests (accessed 4 December 2021).

Tennant, E., and Wolff, C. (2018). 'Civil Society and the Struggle for a Rights-Based Global Compact'. *Global Social Policy, 18* (3), 343–348.

The Ecologist. (2013). 'Romania Rejects Rosia Montana Gold Mine'. *The Ecologist* (12 December). https://theecologist.org/2013/dec/12/romania-rejects-rosia-montana-gold-mine (accessed 4 December 2021).

The Irish Times. (2019). 'Full-Page Ad in Theresa May's Local Paper Calls on Tory Leader to "Protect the Peace"'. *The Irish Times* (22 March). https://www.irishnews.com/news/brexit/2019/03/22/news/full-page-ad-in-theresa-may-s-local-paper-calls-on-tory-leader-to-protect-the-peace--1579545/ (accessed 6 December 2021).

Thorogood, I. (2014). '38 Degrees Members Leaflet the UKIP Conference on TTIP'. 38 Degrees (28 September). https://home.38degrees.org.uk/2014/09/28/38-degrees-members-leaflet-the-ukip-conference-on-ttip/ (accessed 7 December 2021).

Torabi, A. (2014a). 'Your Decision—27th April'. 38 Degrees (30 April). https://home.38degrees.org.uk/2014/04/30/your-decision-27th-april/ (accessed 7 December 2021).

Torabi, A. (2014b). 'TTIP: Day of Action'. 38 Degrees (2 September). https://home.38degrees.org.uk/2014/09/02/ttip-day-of-action-2/ (accessed 7 December 2021).

Trevisan, F., Bello, B., Vaughan, M., and Vromen, A. (2020). 'Mobilizing Personal Narratives: The Rise of Digital "Story Banking" in U.S. Grassroots Advocacy'. *Journal of Information Technology & Politics*, *17*(2), 146–160.

Tufekci, Z. (2014). 'Engineering the Public: Big Data, Surveillance and Computational Politics'. *First Monday*, *19*(7). https://firstmonday.org/article/view/4901/4097

Tufekci, Z. (2017). *Twitter and Tear Gas*. Oxford: Oxford University Press.

UN News. (2018)). 'General Assembly Officially Adopts Roadmap for Migrants to Improve Safety, Ease Suffering'. *UN News* (19 December). https://news.un.org/en/story/2018/12/1028941 (accessed 4 December 2021).

Vaughan, M. (2019). 'Scale Shift in International Tax Justice: Comparing the UK and Australia from 2008 to 2016'. *Social Movement Studies*, *18*(6), 735–753.

Vaughan, M. (2020). 'Talking about Tax: The Discursive Distance between 38 Degrees and GetUp'. *Journal of Information Technology & Politics*, *17*(2), 114–129.

Viola, L. A. (2020). *The Closure of the International System: How Institutions Create Political Equalities and Hierarchies*. Cambridge: Cambridge University Press.

Ville, F. D., and Siles-Brügge, G. (2017). 'Why TTIP Is a Game-Changer and Its Critics Have a Point'. *Journal of European Public Policy*, *24*(10), 1491–1505.

Vogel, K. P. (2010). 'Right Loves to Hate, Imitate Alinsky'. *POLITICO* (22 March). https://www.politico.com/story/2010/03/right-loves-to-hate-imitate-alinsky-034751 (accessed 4 December 2021).

Vries, C. E. D., Hobolt, S. B., and Walter, S. (2021). 'Politicizing International Cooperation: The Mass Public, Political Entrepreneurs, and Political Opportunity Structures'. *International Organization*, *75*(2), 306–332.

Vromen, A. (2016). 'New-Style Lobbying: How GetUp Channels Australians' Voices into Politics'. *The Conversation* (June). https://theconversation.com/new-style-lobbying-how-getup-channels-australian-voices-into-politics-60625 (accessed 5 December 2021).

Vromen, A. (2017). *Digital Citizenship and Political Engagement, The Challenge from Online Campaigning*. London: Palgrave McMillan.

Wahlström, M., Sommer, M., Kocyba, P., De Vydt, M., De Moor, J., Davies, S., et al. (2019). 'Protest for a Future: Composition, Mobilization and Motives of the Participants in Fridays for Future Climate Protests on 15 March, 2019 in 13 European Cities'. https://protestinstitut.eu/wp-content/uploads/2019/07/20190709_Protest-for-a-future_GCS-Descriptive-Report.pdf (accessed 4 Deember 2021).

Walker, B. (2014). 'Secret EU–US Trade Deal'. 38 Degrees (15 May). https://home.38degrees.org.uk/2014/05/15/secret-eu-us-trade-deal/ (accessed 7 December 2021).

Walker, H., and Biedenkopf, K. (2020). 'Why Do Only Some Chairs Act as Successful Mediators? Trust in Chairs of Global Climate Negotiations'. *International Studies Quarterly*, *64*(2), 440–452.

Wapner, P. (1995). 'Politics beyond the State: Environmental Activism and World Civic Politics'. *World Politics*, *47*(3), 311–340.

Ward, S. (2015). 'Dumping Abbot Point Dredge Spoil on Land Won't Save the Reef', *The Conversation* (16 March). https://theconversation.com/dumping-abbot-point-dredge-spoil-on-land-wont-save-the-reef-38716 (accessed 7 December 2021).

Warkentin, C. (2001). *Reshaping World Politics: NGOs, the Internet, and Global Civil Society*. Oxford: Rowman & Littlefield.

Werksman, J. (2009). '"Taking Note" of the Copenhagen Accord: What It Means'. World Resources Institute (20 December). https://www.wri.org/blog/2009/12/taking-note-copenhagen-accord-what-it-means (accessed 4 December 2021).

Whalley, N. (2016). 'How 38 Degrees Members Helped Stop TTIP'. (31 August). https://home.38degrees.org.uk/2016/08/31/38-degrees-members-helped-stop-ttip/ (accessed 5 December 2021).

White, M. (2010). 'Clicktivism Is Ruining Leftist Activism'. *The Guardian* (12 August). https://www.theguardian.com/commentisfree/2010/aug/12/clicktivism-ruining-leftist-activism (accessed 4 December 2021).

Whyte, L. (2017). '"They Are Coming For Your Children"—the Rise of CitizenGo'. *Open-Democracy* (9 August). https://www.opendemocracy.net/en/5050/the-rise-of-citizengo/ (accessed 4 December 2021).

Wiener, A. (2018). *Contestation and Constitution of Norms in Global International Relations*. Cambridge: Cambridge University Press.

Winck, B. (2020). 'The 5 Most Valuable US Tech Companies Are Now Worth More than $5 Trillion after Alphabet's Record Close'. *Business Insider* (17 January 2020). https://www.businessinsider.com/most-valuable-tech-companies-total-worth-trillions-alphabet-stock-record-2020-1 (accessed 4 December 2021).

Wintour, P. (2017). 'Donal Trump Pulls US Out of UN Global Compact on Migration'. *The Guardian* (3 December). https://www.theguardian.com/world/2017/dec/03/donald-trump-pulls-us-out-of-un-global-compact-on-migration (accessed 6 December 2021).

Wong, W. (2012). *Internal Affairs, How the Structure of NGOs Transforms Human Rights*. Ithaca, NY: Cornell University Press.

Xu, X. (2021). 'To Repress or to Co-Opt? Authoritarian Control in the Age of Digital Surveillance'. *American Journal of Political Science*, *65*(2), 309–325.

Yeo, A. (2011). *Activists, Alliances, and Anti-U.S. Base Protests*. Cambridge: Cambridge University Press.

Young, A. R. (2017a). 'Intergovernmental Policy Makes Transnational Politics? The Unusually Transnational Politics of TTIP'. *Cambridge Review of International Affairs*, *30*(5–6), 527–548.

Young, A. R. (2017b). *The New Politics of Trade: Lessons from TTIP*. Newcastle upon Tyne: Agenda Publishing.

Young, E. (2019). 'The Adani Mine Has Now Got Environmental Approval—So What Next?' *SBS News* (14 June). https://www.sbs.com.au/news/the-adani-mine-has-now-got-environmental-approval-so-what-next (accessed 4 December 2021).

Zachari, R. (2018). 'Helt Felatlig "Granskning" av Skiftet och Amonskollen' (22 August). https://skiftet.org/2018/08/helt-felatlig-granskning-av-skiftet-och-annonskollen (accessed 6 December 2021).

Zeit Online. (2015). 'Freihandelsabkommen: TTIP bringt Rekordzahl von Gegnern auf die Straße'. *Die Zeit* (10 October). https://www.zeit.de/wirtschaft/2015-10/ttip-demonstration-berlin-gabriel-ceta (accessed 4 December 2021).

Zelko, F. (2013). *Make It a Green Peace!: The Rise of a Countercultural Environmentalism*. Oxford: Oxford University Press.

Zhou, N. (2019). 'Captain GetUp: Conservative Group's Satirical Superhero Debuts to Ridicule'. *The Guardian* (9 April). https://www.theguardian.com/australia-news/2019/apr/09/captain-getup-conservative-groups-satirical-superhero-debuts-to-ridicule (accessed 4 December 2021).

Zuboff, S. (2018). *The Age of Surveillance Capitalism*. New York: Public Affairs.

Zürn, M., and Wilde, P. de. (2016). 'Debating Globalization: Cosmopolitanism and Communitarianism as Political Ideologies'. *Journal of Political Ideologies*, *21*(3), 280–301.

Index